*This volume is sponsored by
the Center for Chinese Studies
University of California, Berkeley*

China's Continuous Revolution

China's Continuous Revolution

THE POST-LIBERATION EPOCH
1949-1981

Lowell Dittmer

University of California Press ★ Berkeley Los Angeles London

University of California Press
Berkeley and Los Angeles, California
University of California Press, Ltd.
London, England
© 1987 by
The Regents of the University of California
Printed in the United States of America
1 2 3 4 5 6 7 8 9

Part of chapter 4 appeared previously in somewhat different form in the *American Political Science Review* 71 (March 1977): 67–85. © American Political Science Association.

Library of Congress Cataloging-in-Publication Data

Dittmer, Lowell.
  China's continuous revolution.

  Bibliography: p.
  Includes index.
  1. China—Politics and government—1949–
I. Title.
DS777.75.D57 1987   951.05   86-1330
ISBN 0-520-05656-6 (alk. paper)

To Helen

So the people shouted when the priests blew with the trumpets: and it came to pass, when the people heard the sound of the trumpet, and the people shouted with a great shout, that the wall fell down flat, so that the people went up into the city, every man straight before him, and they took the city.

Joshua 6:20

You can't just force people to believe in these things, right? You can't force people to believe in anything; I spoke about this the day before yesterday. In matters of the mind, you can't force a person to believe; nor can you force a person not to believe.

Mao Zedong
"Concluding Remarks at
the Supreme State Conference"
(March 1, 1957)

Contents

Abbreviations

GENERAL

AFP	Agence France Presse
APC	Agricultural Producers' Cooperative
CAC	Central Advisory Committee
CC	Central Committee
CCRG	Central Cultural Revolution Small Group
CD	Central Document
CPC	Communist Party of China
CPG	Communist People's Government
CPPCC	Chinese People's Political Consultative Conference
CPSU	Communist Party of the Soviet Union
CYL	China Youth League
FYP	Five-Year Plan
GTU	General Trade Union
HAEMP	Hangzhou Automobile Electric Machine Plant
HCMF	Hangzhou Construction Materials Factory
HSF	Hangzhou Silk Factory
KMT	Kuomintang
MAC	Military Affairs Committee
MCC	Military Control Commission
MD	Military District
MR	Military Region
NCNA	New China News Agency
PLA	People's Liberation Army
PRRJC	Provincial Revolutionary Rebel Joint Committee
RC	Revolutionary Committee

PUBLICATIONS

AS	*Asian Survey*
APSR	*American Political Science Review*
BR	*Beijing Review*

CA	*China Aktuell*
CN	*China Notes*
CNA	*China News Analysis*
CNS	*China News Service*
CQ	*China Quarterly*
DX	*Dongxiang*
FBIS	*Foreign Broadcast Information Service*
GM	*Guangming Ribao*
HQ	*Hongqi*
IS	*Issues and Studies*
JFJB	*Jiefangjun Bao*
JPRS	*Joint Publications Research Service*
NYT	*New York Times*
PR	*Peking Review*
QER	*Quarterly Economic Review: China*
QN	*Qishi Niandai*
RR	*Renmin Ribao*
SC	*Studies and Criticism*
SCMP	*Survey of the Chinese Mainland Press*
SPRCP	*Survey of the People's Republic of China Press*
SW	*Selected Works of Mao Tse-tung*
URS	*Union Research Service*
XP	*Xuexi yu Pipan*
ZM	*Zhengming*
ZW	*Zhanwang*

Preface

The idea of a revolution that continues after sovereign power has been seized is not unique, but the Chinese attempt to realize this idea is distinctive from the Bolshevik attempt in a number of respects, and it has had an important and lasting impact on Chinese political development. The Chinese continuing revolution not only "telescoped" historical stages (as Trotsky and Lenin had) but in effect denied the tenets of stage theory and urged a melding of stages (resisting a means/ends division that deferred ends to a future utopia). Emphasizing mobilization from below rather than *Gleichschaltung* from above, it also took a more ambivalent stance toward the material rewards of the revolution, amounting to a Marxist form of inner-worldly asceticism. Continuing revolution always took top priority on the political agenda by leadership consensus, and though this left ample room for disagreement over specific policy implications, it had a perceptible impact on the political atmosphere, at times seeming to make China the "spark" in an international class (or generation) war and generally giving her an international significance exceeding her economic or military capabilities. Even at this writing, the history of continuing revolution enlightens and obscures China's past, spurs and guides her present, haunts her future. Yet if continuing the revolution has been taken seriously as a theoretical innovation, it has not hitherto attracted scholarly attention as a political phenomenon. Perhaps this neglect may be attributed to the trees and forest illusion, or to the reluctance to tackle an issue *in medias res*. But if the owl of Minerva spreads its wings only in the dusk of history, perhaps the time is now ripe to try to understand this epoch-making process.

This task has preoccupied me for much of the past decade. Undoubtedly I bring my share of biases to the topic, but it would probably require psychoanalysis to discover and sort them out: my feelings are mixed. Most of the research was textual, consisting of the analysis of a wide array of documentary sources, gleaned from the contemporary China collections of the libraries of Columbia University, the University of Michigan, the University of Chicago, Stanford University, the University of California, and the Universities Service Center in Hong Kong. In addition, chapters 4 and 6 rely on a series of interviews with recent émigrés from the People's Republic. A sample of convenience consisting of forty-eight émigrés was selected, forty-four of which were interviewed in Hong Kong in 1976–78, the remainder in the United States.[1] Each interview lasted a minimum of six hours (two three-hour sessions), beginning with a set protocol[2] and pursuing interesting answers with follow-up questions; more promising interviews were extended up to a hundred hours. Most were conducted with the help of a hired research assistant and compensation was provided to the informant at the then going rate. Whereas I was unsuccessful in my attempts to replicate the interviews during a three-month sojourn in Beijing in 1982, Anne Thurston succeeded in conducting interviews there with thirty-four informants in 1981–82 on a comparable topic. In view of the fact that she arrived at a more unambiguously damning verdict on the Cultural Revolution than I, it should be noted that her study was limited to "the perspective of those who were its *victims*" (emphasis added).[3] It remains to be determined whether venue systematically biases informant samples or interview findings, now that it is becoming possible to conduct interviews in the PRC as well as Hong Kong.

Responsibility for any errors of fact or judgment that remain I can of course share with no one, but I am deeply indebted to many for their invaluable help. Chalmers Johnson, Hong Yung Lee, and Robert Scalapino read the manuscript in its entirety and offered many useful comments and criticisms. My thinking has benefited from conversations with Doak Barnett, Vic Falkenheim, Avery Goldstein, Harry Harding, Andrew

1. The minimal requirement in my selection was that the informant had lived through the Cultural Revolution. Most of the informants were young Guangdong males who had been among the rank-and-file of the "revolutionary masses" (Red Guards or Revolutionary Rebels) and were then sent down to the countryside, whence they made illegal exits to Hong Kong in 1974–77. But some informants were older, some female, some from other regions of China, some emigrated legally, some had functioned as criticism targets or radical activists. In terms of class background (*jiating chushen*), most were worker/peasant or "free professional" (*shiyuan*), although a sizable minority were of "bad" (i.e., bourgeois, rich peasant, landlord) background. Because this sample "represents" at best the stream of émigrés arriving in Hong Kong at the time, I deliberately abjured any statistical analysis of responses, which might have given a misleading impression of precision and generalizability.
2. A translation of the protocol used in the initial interview encounter is contained in the Appendix.
3. See Anne F. Thurston, "Victims of China's Cultural Revolution: The Invisible Wounds," *Pacific Affairs*, Part I, 57: 4 (Winter 1984–85): 599–621; Part II, 58: 1 (Spring 1985): 5–28. Perceptive and empathetic as she is in her analysis of the plight of victims, Thurston exceeds her data in likening the movement to a disaster that inflicts indiscriminate and universal trauma (see especially Part II, pp. 20–23). The Cultural Revolution was a *political*, not a natural disaster, from which beneficiaries as well as victims emerged.

Janos, Ken Jowitt, Joyce Kallgren, Tang Tsou, Ben Ward, and Chris Wong, inter alia. For editorial support above and beyond the call of duty, I am grateful to Jim Clark, director of the University of California Press. For financial assistance during the years of preliminary research I am indebted to the Social Science Research Council, the Centers for Chinese Studies of the University of Michigan at Ann Arbor and the University of California at Berkeley, the Berkeley Political Science Department, and the Hoover Institution at Stanford. The Universities Service Center in Hong Kong hospitably provided office space and research assistance for the interviews conducted there. Lam Poon-shing and Saulun Yeung provided valuable research assistance, and I thank Don Van Atta, Phyllis Killen, and Susan Stone for editorial help.

Finally, for encouragement and support during a long and sometimes difficult gestation period, I wish to express appreciation to my wife Helen, to whom the work is gratefully dedicated, and to my son Mark.

ONE

The Idea of Continuing
the Revolution

The subject of revolution has elicited a rich and voluminous scholarly literature. Much of that literature has been directed to the *causes* of revolution, under the implicit premise that if these causes could be avoided the probability of revolution might thereby be reduced.[1] The post-Liberation experience of the People's Republic of China, however, brings to focus a different aspect of the revolutionary problematic. The Chinese revolutionaries, being among the few to inherit the fruits of their own upheaval, elevated revolution from an unpleasant but necessary transition to a legitimating ordeal, to be protracted indefinitely.

The desire to continue the revolution after power has been seized is not altogether unique. But in no other revolution in history has this attempt been as protracted, thoroughgoing, and consequential as in the Chinese case. Indeed, our contention is that the attempt to "continue the revolution under the dictatorship of the proletariat" has dominated Chinese politics more than any other single concern in the three decades since the founding of the People's Republic. This is not to say that there were not other important concerns competing for attention—one thinks for example of the drive for international status and autonomy, or national economic reconstruction. Nor is it to say that everyone always agreed upon this ranking of national priorities—there was at least one brief moment when the leadership seemed to have reached a consensus that the revolution had been consummated, and a much longer period during which there was disagreement over how it should be continued. Yet continue it did, following its own implacable logic. Some promoted and made the most of it, some were devoured by it, some accepted it with the ambivalence of the legendary "man who loved dragons."

In view of its centrality, "continuing revolution" would seem to provide the most promising thematic entrée to an understanding of Chinese politics in the post-Liberation era. How was it possible for the revolution to be sustained for so long? Did it succeed, by its own lights?

1. For a timely survey of this literature, see Chalmers Johnson, *Revolutionary Change* (Stanford: Stanford University Press, 1982 revised ed.).

Wherefore did it finally expire—or is the question perhaps premature? In its most recent official pronouncements on this question, the Party leadership has skirted the issue, renouncing the "theory of continuous revolution" but at the same time asserting that the revolution will resume in another guise.[2] Certainly the series of reforms introduced since December 1978 have unleashed momentous socio-economic changes in China—do these betoken reversion to some prerevolutionary "capitalist road," continuation of a revolution that got derailed, or the launching of revolution in a new and quite different form? These are the questions that will concern us in the following study. Perhaps they are not altogether new ones, but this represents the first sustained effort to give them pride of place.[3]

FRAMEWORK OF ANALYSIS

It is appropriate at the outset to define the terms in the argument. The key definition, from which the meanings of all others logically derive,

2. *Resolution on CPC History (1949–1981)* (Beijing: Foreign Languages Press, 1981), pp. 84–85; see also the concluding chapter of this study.
3. A number of excellent articles and one book have appeared that address the question of continuing revolution; these include Stuart Schram, "Mao Tse-tung and the Theory of Permanent Revolution," *China Quarterly* (hereinafter *CQ*), no. 46 (April–June 1971): 221–45; John Bryan Starr, "Conceptual Foundations of Mao Tse-tung's Theory of Continuous Revolution," *Asian Survey* (hereinafter *AS*) 11:6 (June 1971): 610–28; and Graham Young and Dennis Woodward, "From Contradictions among the People to Class Struggle: The Theories of Uninterrupted Revolution and Continuous Revolution," *AS* 18:9 (September 1978): 912–34. It is no detraction to point out that these articles are devoted to the "theory" rather than the actuality of continued revolution, focusing on how Mao reconciled his determination to continue the revolution with classical doctrine. The one book to have appeared under this title—John Starr's *Continuing the Revolution: The Political Thought of Mao* (Princeton: Princeton University Press, 1979)—is actually devoted to a comprehensive treatment of Mao's Thought, also from a "theoretical" point of view.
    The only attempt known to me to deal with continuing revolution as an actual political phenomenon has been made by Richard Loewenthal. See his seminal article, "Development vs. Utopia in Communist Policy," in Chalmers Johnson, ed., *Change in Communist Systems* (Stanford: Stanford University Press, 1970), pp. 33–117; also his sequel, "The Post-Revolutionary Phase in China and Russia," *Studies in Comparative Communism*, 16:3 (Autumn 1983): 191–203. These articles, being relatively brief in compass and at the same time comparative in scope, are unable to do full justice to the peculiarities of the Chinese situation, however, where revolution has been both more protracted and more populist in its dynamics. Also, whereas Loewenthal usefully points to the inherent tension between development and utopia, between "economic man" and "new man" (which allegedly spells the ultimate doom of the latter), it remains unclear from his analysis exactly what sustains the revolutionary animus. Finally, his bivariate analysis omits from consideration the impact of *power*, whether charismatic or bureaucratic (for an approach that juxtaposes power and ideology, see Barrington Moore, *Soviet Politics: The Dilemma of Power* [New York: Harper & Row, 1965]).

is that of revolution itself. Succinctly put, *revolution is the smashing of the structure of political authority.* The "structure of authority" is difficult to indicate empirically, as it consists of a *relationship* between leaders and masses, which may vary depending on regime type. Generally, it may be said to consist of that complex of instruments of violence, bureaucratic hierarchies, institutions of socialization, stratification structures, justificatory arguments, and other political resources whereby a regime ensures that its rules and policies are complied with, that its "order" prevails. Because this structure of authority creates a consensually agreed-upon frame of reference and currency of political exchange, its defense can be (and usually is) rationalized as functional for a political community and not just seen as self-serving for political elites. "Legitimate" politics occurs *within the framework* of this structure.[4] "Revolutionary" politics involves an explicit confrontation between authorities and "rebels," culminating (when successful) in a "breakthrough" for the latter.[5] A breakthrough may involve physical destruction of a regime's security forces, symbolic demonstration of its inability to enforce (or adhere to) its own core values, or some combination of military and symbolic techniques. Through whatever means, a breakthrough results in smashing the old structure and introducing a new one in its place.

Because the above conceptualization of revolution differs in this respect from Marxist and other approaches that place greater emphasis on underlying socio-economic variables (modes of production, class conflict, and so forth), it is worth noting that "politics" will have pride of place. Revolutions are "political" not only in their confrontation with established authority, but in the public character of the challenge they pose. A regime may be afflicted by various "latent contradictions," but until these have been articulated they remain outside the political arena. Thus, although an "industrial revolution" or a "consumer revolution" may precipitate great change, for example, because such phenomena do not explicitly confront political authority, we may ignore them (except insofar as they can be shown to affect such a confrontation). This will be worth bearing in mind when in the concluding chapter we address the prospect of continuing revolution under a reform regime.

Three "functional requisites" follow from this conceptualization of revolution, and we shall argue that all three must be present for revolu-

---

4. The distinction drawn here between "legitimate" and "revolutionary" politics is analogous to Kuhn's well-known distinction between "normal" and "paradigmatic" science. Thomas Kuhn, *The Structure of Scientific Revolutions* (Chicago: University of Chicago Press, 1962).

5. The locus classicus for the concept of "revolutionary breakthrough" is Kenneth Jowitt, *Revolutionary Breakthroughs and National Development* (Berkeley: University of California Press, 1971).

tion to continue. These are charismatic leadership, an illegitimate authority structure, and the constant mobilization of mass support.

Since Max Weber first introduced the concept of "charisma" to social science, it has been defined and redefined, both because of the intrinsic importance of the phenomenon to which it refers and because of the vagueness of the original defintion (e.g., Weber begins by defining the term subjectively, referring to the "supernatural, superhuman, or at least specifically exceptional powers or qualities" of the leader, then shifts to the objective criterion of the followers' *perception* of those qualities for empirical verification).[6] In the redefinition proposed here, charisma is defined by both objective and subjective criteria, but the former are essential, the latter ancillary. The objective criterion of charismatic leadership is the *performance of a salvationary mission*. A "mission" (what the Chinese call a "line") is a set of policies bearing an imputed causal relationship to a desired future political end-state. "Salvationary" implies that the mission has three qualities: it solves the objective crisis in response to which it arises; it is distinctive, ideally sui generis; and it is qualitatively superior to all other missions, "utopian," a touchstone of value. "Performance" consists of (1) the implementation of policies implied by the mission, and (2) the actual efficacy of those policies in bringing about the desired solution. Without a mission to perform, charisma can quickly dissipate from the most mesmerizing personality (as Churchill would discover at the end of World War II).

The subjective dimension of charisma is secondary, consisting of the personal means necessary to perform the end. A charismatic leader should have the *imagination* to conceive a salvationary mission (and the latitude to exercise that imagination), and adequate *symbolic* skills to communicate (i.e., by orating, writing, dramatizing) that mission in a persuasive way. These subjective qualities are not personality-specific,

6. Cf. Max Weber, *On Charisma and Institution Building*, ed. by S. N. Eisenstadt (Chicago: University of Chicago Press, 1968). Following Weber, the most noteworthy contributions to the analysis of the concept of charisma include Edward Shils, two articles in *Center and Periphery: Essays in Macrosociology* (Chicago: University of Chicago Press, 1975), pp. 256–75, 405–21; Joseph Bensman and Michael Givant, "Charisma and Modernity: The Use and Abuse of a Concept," *Social Research* 42, no. 4 (Winter 1975): 570–615; Martin E. Spencer, "What Is Charisma?" *British Journal of Sociology* 24, no. 3 (September 1973): 341–55; Richard J. Bord, "Toward a Social-Psychological Theory of Charismatic Social Influence Processes," *Social Forces* 53, no. 3 (March 1975): 485–97; Arthur Schweitzer, *The Age of Charisma* (Chicago: Nelson Hall, 1984); Joseph Nyomarkay, *Charisma and Factionalism in the Nazi Party* (Minneapolis: University of Minnesota Press, 1967). Representative of those who emphasize the antitraditional, deviant aspects of charismatic ideology is Anthony Piepe, "Charisma and the Sacred: A Reevaluation," *Pacific Sociological Review* 14, no. 2 (April 1971): 147–63. Continuities with traditional culture receive relative emphasis in Ann Ruth Willner's *The Spellbinders: Charismatic Political Leadership* (New Haven: Yale Univeristy Press, 1984).

nor are they necessarily antibureaucratic; a charismatic leadership may be collective and preside over quite elaborate organizational arrangements, so long as (1) a public image of unity and resoluteness is preserved and (2) the organization plays a functional role in performing the salvationary mission.

The second prerequisite for a revolutionary situation is an *illegitimate authority structure*, against which the forces of revolution may array in self-definition. Inasmuch as legitimacy implies popular acceptance of the inherent justice of an incumbent's rule, its loss is indicated by a widespread belief that that rule is no longer just.[7] Such a belief is of course to a considerable degree subjective and contingent upon one's stake in the status quo, but what is being judged is also an objective datum, consisting of the *flawed exercise of power*. Such a flaw is most apt to arise when a political system is subject to demand overload or resource scarcity, which may in turn be precipitated by any number of factors, ranging from pervasive corruption to natural or man-made disaster. Whatever its origin, flawed power exhibits a combination of *apparent strength* and *underlying weakness*. On the one hand, the incumbent is too weak to claim full sovereignty; on the other, the incumbert attempts to belie this weakness by imposing a harshly rigid, suppressive rule that imparts a general sense of constraint. That harshness provides *points d'appui* for a radical critique, while the underlying weakness allows ambit for that critique to be disseminated. In its role as a target of revolutionary criticism, the illegitimate authority structure combines some of the functions of a loyal opposition with those of scapegoating or witchcraft.

The third functional requisite is a *mobilizable mass constituency*. To be "mobilizable," a constituency (or politically significant grouping) must be given adequate reasons to engage in political activities transcending their established routines. These must include prospects for dramatic economic and/or political self-betterment as well as the rhetorical appeals whereby these prospects are rationalized in terms of some broader conception of the public interest. Mass mobilization thus involves an inevitable interaction between the economic system whereby material incentives are produced and the ideological apparatus whereby collective goals are articulated. People do not necessarily revolt simply because they are deprived, either absolutely or relatively, according to this conceptualization; however, some degree of mass deprivation may well facilitate a loss of faith in the legitimacy of the incumbent regime *if* persuasive arguments are presented to link that deprivation to the prevailing structure of authority.

7. See Barrington Moore, *Injustice: The Social Bases of Obedience and Revolt* (White Plains, N. Y.: M. E. Sharpe, 1978).

How may these functions be most efficaciously fulfilled? There are two schools of thought on this question. The dominant school throughout the history of the Chinese Communist revolution has emphasized the quiet but elaborate organizational arrangement of events, in somewhat the way hydraulic engineers arrange for the raising or lowering of water levels (to use one of Liu Shaoqi's favorite metaphors) through a system of locks, rams, and sluices. This will hereafter be termed the "engineering" approach. The revolutionary engineers have held that effective revolutionary tactics are *sequential* (i.e., the revolution must proceed through scheduled stages), *elitist* (i.e., commands emanate from the leadership through a disciplined vertical hierarchy) and *planned* (i.e., there is a priority ranking of necessary tasks, with a functional division of labor for their accomplishment). But also making an occasional appearance has been a minority point of view, which holds that effective revolutionary tactics should be *simultaneous* (i.e., everything happens concurrently, but not because it is organizationally coordinated), *egalitarian* (constituting a relatively "flat" hierarchy, with innovation emanating from the bottom), and *spontaneous* (i.e., there is a functionally indiscriminate division of labor). This vision, redolent of Joshua's conquest of Jericho, will hereafter be dubbed the "storming" approach.

The presence of these contrasting approaches in the history of the Chinese Communist movement has sometimes been attributed to the "struggle between two lines," according to which Liu Shaoqi, Deng Xiaoping, Zhou Enlai, and other managerial types are supposed to have defended the engineering approach whereas Mao Zedong, Chen Boda, Jiang Qing, et al. espoused the storming approach. True enough, it was Mao who wrote the paradigmatic defense of simultaneous, egalitarian, spontaneous peasant uprising at the outset of his career, coining such memorable metaphors as a "spark" setting a "prairie fire" (perhaps originally derived from Lenin's *Iskra*), a "wave," "storm," or "hurricane":

> In a very short time, . . . several million peasants will rise like a mighty storm, like a hurricane, a force so swift and violent that no power, however great, will be able to hold it back. They will smash all the trammels that bind them and rush forward along the road to liberation. They will sweep all the imperialists, warlords, corrupt officials, local tyrants and evil gentry into their graves. Every revolutionary party and every revolutionary comrade will be put to the test, to be accepted or rejected as they decide. There are three alternatives. To march at their head and lead them? To trail behind them gesticulating and criticizing? Or to stand in their way and oppose them?[8]

8. "Report on an Investigation of the Peasant Movement in Hunan" (March 1927), in *Selected Works of Mao Tse-tung* (Beijing: Foreign Languages Press, 1964), vol. 1: 23–24 (hereinafter *SW*).

Mao was also primarily responsible for the "high tide" of collectivization in 1955–56, not to mention the Great Leap Forward and the Cultural Revolution. It is also true, as we shall see in chapter 3, that Mao was the foremost advocate of the micro-equivalent of storming at the level of personal ideological conversion.

Yet Mao was hardly the first to have availed himself of such rhetoric—Li Lisan was a "stormer" well before Mao, and Li Dazhao before him—even the writings of such archetypal "engineers" as Liu Shaoqi are replete with such passages. And if Mao's works are examined in their entirety it seems evident that he laid at least equal emphasis on a decidedly sequential, elite-directed, and well-planned strategy. This emphasis is particularly evident in his essays on the Second Revolutionary Civil War and the protracted War of Resistance against Japan, where his powers of analysis reach their acme. To pick only one example among many (for the bulk of the first three volumes of Mao's *Selected Works* is concerned with such minutiae), note his discriminating instructions on dealing with allies and enemies in "On Policy":

> In the enemy-occupied and Kuomintang areas our policy is, on the one hand, to develop the United Front to the greatest possible extent and, on the other, to have well-selected cadres working underground.... With respect to the anti-Communist die-hards, ours is a revolutionary dual policy of uniting with them, insofar as they are still in favor of resisting Japan, and of isolating them, insofar as they are determined to oppose the Communist Party.... Even among the traitors and pro-Japanese elements there are people with a dual character, towards whom we should likewise employ a revolutionary dual policy. Insofar as they are pro-Japanese, our policy is to struggle against them and isolate them, but insofar as they vacillate, our policy is to draw them nearer to us and win them over.... Our tactics are guided by one and the same principle: to make use of contradictions, win over the many, oppose the few and crush our enemies one by one.[9]

Although Mao did resort with increasing frequency to the storming approach in his later years, his essays are for the most part remote from the impetuous, romantic spirit of a tempest or prairie fire; they are, in fact, intricately organized, contain numerous periodizations, classificatory schemes, and analytical distinctions. They advise attitudes of patience, realism, restraint, prudence, and cool calculation.[10] The resort to storming thus seems to have been a relatively exceptional one, even for Mao. The "two-line struggle" model has an appealing simplicity, but it is

9. "On Policy" (December 25, 1940), in *SW*, vol. 2: 442–43.
10. See Tang Tsou and Morton H. Halperin, "Mao Tse-tung's Revolutionary Strategy and Peking's International Behavior," *American Political Science Review* 59, no. 1 (March 1965): 80–99.

probably misleading to assume that factional cleavages among the leadership may be so neatly and logically accounted for.

For most of the period since the First Civil War (1927–36) the engineering approach was the consensual favorite. From such disasters as the Autumn Harvest, Nanchang, and Canton revolts the Party had learned not to attempt everything at once but to set clear priorities, husband its forces, and proceed in stages. It was from this background that the CPC approached the challenges of building socialism and continuing the revolution after power had been seized.

PROSPECTUS

The sweeping policy reversals of the post-Mao period may be historically comprehended in one of at least three ways. The first would attribute change to an *oscillatory pattern* that has long characterized the Chinese policy process. There are several variants of oscillatory explanation, the most popular of which is the bivariate "two-line struggle" model: policy is under constant contention between "moderate" and "radical" elites, and the policy "line" oscillates according to factional vicissitudes.[11] There are also trivariate,[12] even quadrivariate[13] versions of this model. Common to all is an attempt to reduce the range of policy variation to a limited number of possible alternatives, variation among which is however cyclical and recurrent rather than secular, sometimes following a predicted itinerary, sometimes aleatory. The future is in any case certain, for it has been seen in the past. The second explanation conceives of the post-Mao transformation in terms of the *restoration of a tradition*, con-

11. There are actually two versions of this explanation, one of which focuses on the causal impact of elite factionalism, the other on the internal dynamics of the process of implementation. For good expositions of the former, see Parris H. Chang, *Power and Policy in China* (University Park: Pennsylvania State University Press, 1978, 2d enlarged ed.); also Byungjoon Ahn, *Chinese Politics and the Cultural Revolution: Dynamics of Policy Processes* (Seattle: University of Washington Press, 1976); and Harry Harding, "Maoist Theories of Policy-Making and Organization," in Thomas W. Robinson, ed., *The Cultural Revolution in China* (Berkeley: University of California Press, 1971), pp. 113–65. The best exemplar of the latter is G. William Skinner and Edwin O. Winckler's "Compliance Succession in Rural Communist China: A Cyclical Theory," in Amitai Etzioni, ed., *A Sociological Reader on Complex Organizations* (New York: Holt, Rinehart & Winston, 1969, 2d ed.), pp. 410–38; see also E. O. Winckler, "Policy Oscillation in the People's Republic of China: A Reply," *CQ* no. 68 (December 1976): 734–51.

12. Dorothy Solinger, for example, perceives a cyclical conflict among bureaucrats, who favor increasing state control, marketeers, who give top priority to economic productivity, and radicals, who emphasize class conflict. See her *Chinese Business under Socialism: The Politics of Domestic Commerce, 1949–1980* (Berkeley: University of California Press, 1984).

13. In his discussion of elite attitudes toward the issue of bureaucratization, Harry Harding finds a split among rationalizers, radicals, and proponents of external remedial and internal remedial measures. See his *Organizing China: The Problem of Bureaucracy, 1949–1976* (Stanford: Stanford University Press, 1981).

sisting of established worldviews, policy priorities, organizational predispositions, and cultural patterns, after an unfortunate but temporary radical deviation. That tradition, according to the most widely credited variant of this paradigm, represents a politically disciplined consensus around rapid economic growth and distributive equity, which for a variety of reasons was interrupted by an irrational outburst of radical egalitarianism and ideological inquisition.[14] The minority variant deems the revolutionary tradition to have been so corrupted that its survival was at stake, and thus badly needing revitalization, from which the post-Mao changes are a regrettable relapse.[15] Common to both variants of the restoration scenario (as well as the oscillatory model) is a conception of change within a familiar repertoire. The third explanation, on the other hand, views the post-Mao changes as marking the *end of the epoch of continuing revolution and the dawning of a new era.*

This study, while conceding elements of continuity and cyclical recurrence, is inclined to the third interpretation. The oscillatory patterns of the Maoist era defined themselves against a horizon of continuing revolution, in the context of which *any* tradition was more a forlorn hope than a stable reality. "Continuing the revolution under the dictatorship of the proletariat" retained the revolutionary animus of the pre-Liberation era by sustaining the drive to smash the structure of authority, though that structure had to be continously redefined. The functional requisites of that drive—charismatic leadership, an illegitimate authority structure, and continual mass mobilization—may be viewed as perishable assets. The sequence and manner of their exhaustion (either by successful accomplishment or by a convincing demonstration of unfeasibility) may be expected to have affected the form the revolution took in its successive stages.

Although the chapters follow in approximate chronological sequence, each chapter intends to make specific points in an argument, not simply to provide an historical narrative. To this end, such evidence will be marshaled as seems necessary to corroborate those points being made, and not too much more than that. If some stages in the sequence emerge in relatively lush empirical detail, this is because they have not yet been adequately covered in the literature. Thus the late Cultural Revolution period, which really brought home to all participants the utter folly of

14. Perhaps most persuasively articulated in Frederick C. Teiwes, *Leadership, Legitimacy, and Conflict in China: From a Charismatic Mao to the Politics of Succession* (Armonk, N.Y.: M. E. Sharpe, 1984); the same thesis is implicit in his *Politics and Purges in China: Rectification and the Decline of Party Norms, 1950–1965* (White Plains, N.Y.: M. E. Sharpe, 1979).
15. See Charles Bettelheim and Neil Burton, *China since Mao* (New York: Monthly Review Press, 1978); also Bob Avakian, *The Loss in China and the Revolutionary Legacy of Mao Tsetung* (Chicago: RCP Pub., 1978).

persevering with the "principles laid down," will be analyzed rather exhaustively, whereas the early Cultural Revolution, about which more ink has probably been spilt than any other period of comparable length in modern Chinese history, rates only one chapter.

The first phase of China's continuing revolution marked the heyday of the engineering approach. While the leadership pursued its war against society quite ruthlessly via unpredictable policy lurches, an uneasy consensus was maintained *within the vanguard* on an agenda of centrally planned, hierarchically organized, sequentially paced transformation. The successes achieved during this period not only convinced the leaders of the basic correctness of the policy course they had set but imparted the sense of self-confidence that later allowed them to depart from this course, steering the revolution into new and more hazardous waters. Chapter 2 consists of an analysis of charismatic leadership and mass mobilization during this first phase, relying on a combination of previously published sources and the more recent findings that have emerged in the post-Mao period.

Chapter 3 is concerned with structures of authority during this phase—both the residual structure against which the revolution continued to be directed and the emergent structure being constructed by the CPC. In the course of the remarkable initial successes and concluding failures of this phase, the residual structure began losing credibility as a target, while at the same time the more aversive features of the emergent CPC regime were becoming more visible. The first part of this chapter is concerned with changes in the objective structures, whereas the second investigates critical perception of those changes—particularly the ideas advanced by Mao Zedong, who seems to have devoted considerably more thought to these developments than his colleagues.

Chapter 4 consists of a reexamination of the early phase of the Great Proletarian Cultural Revolution (1966–68). That attempt was to result in the most comprehensive revival of the storming approach since the late 1920s, albeit within a quite new and quite different context. Charismatic leadership became split from the bureaucracy; mass mobilization was pursued more or less spontaneously in response to vague elite cues, using a partially autonomous media network to mobilize an almost fully autonomous factional jumble of "revolutionary masses." The structure of authority against which the revolution was pitted was redefined to amalgamate rhetorically the prerevolutionary authority structure with that group of moderate bureaucrats within the Party who had opposed Mao, thereby conceptualizing a "capitalist road," or "bourgeois reactionary line." Whereas previous accounts of this great upheaval have typically viewed it as a somewhat unconventional purge (which it certainly was), this treatment will attempt to place it in the context of a serious attempt by the dominant ("Maoist") faction of the CPC leadership to "continue the revolution" in the cultural superstructure (which it also was). The purpose is not merely to summarize the rich store of literature on this period but if possible to supplement it with an analysis of its neglected cultural dimension—which, it is argued, *informed* mundane political behavior. The assumption is that amid the disintegration of political structures, ideology came to assume a compensating importance; accordingly, we employ a methodology derived from structural linguistics to analyze the polemical rhetoric, showing how it symbolically reduplicated the authority structures it aimed to destroy.

If 1966–68 was the heyday of storming, the 1968–76 period might be termed "revisionist storming." Without abandoning the basic commitment to permanent mobilization as the only way to preserve revolutionary vitality, the leadership attempted to adapt this approach to the functional imperatives of self-sustaining economic development—albeit with indifferent success. Due to a dearth of relevant scholarly literature, and because developments during this period are so crucial to our understanding of how the prerequisites of revolution were ultimately exhausted, these developments receive scrutiny in no fewer than three chapters. Chapter 5 is concerned with charismatic leadership and the difficulties involved in attempting to arrange for its post-mortem survival. Chapter 6 focuses on the problems of reconciling mass mobilization with both thought reform and economic production. Chapter 7 examines the problems inherent in reconstructing authority at a time when authority structures remained under intense critical scrutiny and periodic public assault. These three chapters are based on a relatively comprehensive collection of primary and secondary sources, supplemented by interviews with former participants.

The final chapter pursues the revolution to its ambiguous denouement, in which it is at once discontinued and reaffirmed. After a brief interregnum during which Hua Guofeng fruitlessly attempted to revive the engineering approach, CPC theorists seem to have arrived at the conclusion that the revolution has in effect burnt out—though there is still considerable ambivalence about this conclusion, arising from the desire to preserve certain revolutionary values and legitimations. If this essay is correct in assigning overriding importance to the effort to continue the revolution during the first three decades after the seizure of power, such ambivalence is understandable. This "postrevolutionary" phase is an extremely formative one in China's political development, during which one paradigm is being abandoned or at least fundamentally reevaluated and various possibilities for a fresh start explored, with unprecedented openness. The People's Republic may long be expected to bear the stigmata of the tumultuous epoch that gave it birth, either by incorporating them (as in the yearning for emancipation and greater personal liberty) or by seeking to repress them (as in the abhorrence of chaos).

TWO

Engineering Revolution

The 1949–58 period was marked by transition from inciting revolution as an objective necessity to pursuing it as an elective option. In the pre-1949 period, charismatic leadership seemed necessitated by the constantly shifting and inherently uncertain nature of the political milieu, which swiftly reduced noncharismatic leadership to factional divisiveness. Mao Zedong and his paladins offered such leadership, formulating a broadly acceptable vision of the future and a shrewdly conceived strategy for its realization. After seizing control of the Party's (then relatively primitive) communication apparatus in the 1942–44 rectification movement (*zhengfeng*), they conveyed this vision to a growing mass constituency. The structure against which the revolution arrayed itself shifted historically from the warlords of the 1920s to the Nationalist government of the early 1930s to the Japanese imperialist army of the late 1930s back to the Kuomintang (KMT) party-state of the 1940s. Each of these regimes embodied two features characteristic of illegitimate authority structures: the arbitrary power of a dictatorship and the weakness of incomplete sovereignty. Mass mobilization was motivated partly by skillful organizational techniques, partly by the redistribution of expropriated landlord or rich peasant property, but perhaps even more effective than these sometimes (as in Jiangxi) counterproductive tactics was the exposure of the indigenous inhabitants to the depredations of an invading army—which in the Japanese case were so severe as to deny them the luxury of political indifference.[1]

Liberation ensconced the revolutionaries in the seat of imperial power in Beijing, vastly enhancing the resources and capabilities available to them but at the same time impelling them to seek equilibration between continued pursuit of their revolutionary calling and fulfillment of the usual functions of governmental authorities. It seems clear in retrospect that stable equilibrium was, however, never achieved, as the regime

---

1. See Chalmers Johnson, *Peasant Nationalism and Communist Revolution* (Stanford: Stanford University Press, 1962).

lunged from one ambitious objective to another. Elite-mass relationships tended to be tense and intrusive, engendering the intra-elite solidarity of "comrades-in-arms." Notwithstanding the nostalgic memories of a "golden age" (*huangjin shidai*) cherished by veterans of the Cultural Revolution in the post-Mao period, there was only a brief hiatus in 1956 when the leadership *flirted with the possibility* of consolidation and stability, allowing themselves to be absorbed into society rather than seeking to transform it, and this possibility was decisively rejected in 1957–58. As we shall see, this rejection, however, split the leadership, prompting the revolution to turn inward and begin consuming its children.

This chapter is concerned with changes in the first two components of the functional triad underpinning continued revolution outlined in the previous chapter, charismatic leadership and mass mobilization. The thrust of the chapter is to show how and why the engineering approach ran aground by the end of the first decade, despite (in part, because of) its achievements. Chapter 3 will then describe the structure against which the revolution defined itself during this period—and, emerging in quiet counterpoint, the structure of the CPC regime.

CHARISMATIC LEADERSHIP

The function of charismatic leadership underwent a sea change in 1949. The violent seizure of power had been completed (though pursuit of assorted enemies would continue), and the "mission" correspondingly shifted from military to political transformation. This transformation was pursued according to the engineering paradigm, with staggered scheduling of task priorities (e.g., formation of elementary before advanced cooperatives, socialization of agriculture before industry), elitist direction (e.g., workers and peasants were enjoined not to overthrow their old masters until a Communist political structure was firmly in place), and increasingly elaborate planning. Yet it was a period of dynamic change and frequent disequilibrium, finally brought to an impasse by its own internal contradictions. Although the early 1950s seemed to demonstrate the compatibility of charismatic leadership and effective bureaucratic administration, by the late 1950s growing friction between the objective and subjective dimensions of charisma became apparent. To see what caused this friction, let us examine each in turn.

The Objective Dimension

The charismatic mission during this period encompassed no less than destruction of the old "world" and construction of a new one—not yet the promised utopia, to be sure, but one moving down that "road." The world to be destroyed included the system of private property, and the "filial" kinship system, both of which underwrote political opposition to Communist rule. The new world to be constructed envisaged a new network of primary-group relationships, comprehensively penetrated by a central political apparatus and integrally linked to a public ownership and planning system.

The Communist leadership had not expected military victory until 1953, or until the end of 1951 at the earliest, and so they were somewhat disconcerted by the unexpectedly swift collapse of the Nationalist regime. The CPC had inherited a crisis: heavy industrial production had fallen to about 30 percent of the previous peak period, and agricultural and consumer goods output had declined to about 70 percent of their previous peaks; hyperinflation had ruined the value of the currency, and economic exchanges were reverting to barter.[2] The immediate priority, Mao made clear in his report to the important Second Plenum of the Seventh Central Committee (CC) (March 1949), was to ensure that the economy did not collapse. Mao declared that the phase of agrarian revolution was at an end for the time being, and that revival of the urban economy should receive top priority.[3]

The Communist recovery program had prompt and rather impressive results: domestic tranquillity was restored, inflation was brought under control by the summer of 1950, a unified national market and generous credit policies led to a brisk revival of the private business sector. Already in 1953 the gross social product was 20 percent higher than in 1933; between 1949 and 1952 national income increased by about 70 percent, and industrial production increased around 150 percent.[4]

When urban industrial workers during this period made demands for higher wages or a voice in management, they were informed that it was in the interest of the working class to cooperate with the bourgeoisie until

2. Mark Selden and Victor Lippit, "The Transition to Socialism in China," in Selden and Lippit, eds., *The Transition to Socialism in China* (Armonk, N.Y.: M. E. Sharpe, 1982), p. 4.
3. Bill Brugger, *China: Liberation and Transformation, 1942–1962* (London: Croom Helm, 1981), p. 54. The most well-known formulation of this decision was that of Liu Shaoqi, who announced in 1950: "Only when the conditions mature for the wide use of mechanical farming, for the organization of collective farms and for the socialist reform of the rural areas can the need for a rich peasant economy cease, and this will take a somewhat lengthy time to achieve." Liu Shaoqi, "Report on Problems Concerning Agrarian Reform," presented to the Second Session of the National Committee of the CPPCC, in *People's China*, July 16, 1950, pp. 28–29. Although Liu's statement was later quoted against him because of its inconsistency with later developments, it seems to have been an expression of an early consensus that later changed in the wake of unexpectedly rapid early successes at land reform.
4. Thus according to Chinese statistics the industrial growth rate averaged about 15 percent between 1952 and 1957. See *Socialist Transformation of the National Economy in China* (Beijing: Foreign Languages Press, 1960), pp. 68–69.

production recovered.[5] Socialization of the means of production was provisionally restricted to the agricultural sector; industry would have to wait its turn on the revolutionary agenda. This prioritization may have been perhaps partly due to a prior commitment to the Red Army's largely peasant constituency, but it also reflected the fact that until industrial production resumed there would be no "pie " to "slice," whereas in the countryside farmland was a fungible resource whose redistribution provided its own incentive. The initial campaign was inaugurated by the Land Reform Law of 1950, which took well over 100 million acres of farmland away from some 4 million landlords and distributed it among 50 million poor and lower-middle peasant cultivators within the first three years.[6]

The "rich peasant economy," despite initial prognostications that it would endure "a somewhat lengthy time," had brief tenure indeed, apparently due to fears that rich peasants might become sufficiently well entrenched to forestall further progress. Nor was this fear entirely unfounded: Chinese villagers, like Soviet kulaks during Lenin's New Economic Policy, showed great enthusiasm for individual farming. The middle subclasses of the peasantry increased rapidly in number and strength, taking over the role once played by landlords and rich peasants. Of the land that changed hands, two-thirds came from landlords and less than one-third from rich peasants; less than two-thirds of that land went to poor peasants, on the other hand, while over a third went to middle peasants. According to a survey conducted in 1952, middle peasants accounted for 62.2 percent of the rural population, compared with 29 percent poor peasants and farmhands, 2.1 percent rich peasants, and 2.5 percent landlords.[7]

5. See Liu Shaoqi, "Zai Huabei zhigong daibiao huiyi shang guanyu gonghui gongzuo wenti de baogao" [A report delivered before the North China Workers' Representative Conference on Problems Concerning Labor Union Work] (May 1949), in *Liu Shaoqi Wenti Ziliao Zhuanji* [A special collection of materials on Liu Shaoqi] (Taipei: Chinese Communist Research Center, 1970), pp. 200–207, and 207–20, respectively. See also the post-rehabilitation report by the Theoretical Research Office of the Propaganda Department of Tianjin Municipal CCP Committee, "Reread Comrade Liu Shaoqi's 'Speeches in Tianjin,'" *Renmin Ribao* (hereinafter *RR*), Beijing, April 21, 1980, p. 5. Xu Dixin later explained that the output value of the plants and enterprises operated by the national bourgeoisie constituted 63.2 percent of the national total, so they had to be protected. "On the Characteristics of the New Democratic Society: Interview with Comrade Xu Dixin," *Xin Shiqi* [New era], no. 8 (August 1981): 2–5.
6. Hugh D. R. Baker, *Chinese Family and Kinship* (New York: Columbia University Press, 1979), p. 184.
7. Xue Muqiao et al., *Zhongguo Guominjingji de Shehuizhuyi Gaizao* [The socialist transformation of China's national economy] (Beijing: People's Press, 1959), p. 61; see also Planning Division of the Agricultural Department of the Central Government, ed., *Liangnian lai de Zhongguo Nongcun Jingji Diaocha Huibian* [A collection of investigations of

Whether such a fragmented agricultural sector could sustain the Stalinist industrialization policy then envisaged seemed, however, quite problematic. Commodity grain had previously been disproportionately produced by rich peasants and landlords, who disposed of larger plots with better equipment and conditions and were hence able to practice commercial agriculture.[8] Land reform, by eliminating economies of scale and creating a small-scale subsistence farm economy, threatened to curtail the continued supply of commodity grain. It was in order to ensure the continued supply of cheap grain that the government in 1953 introduced state monopoly of food purchase, which in turn triggered scattered peasant resistance: in the face of a widening disparity between the price of urban manufactures and farm commodities, peasants sometimes refused to sell.[9] So the government implemented a monopoly in procurement and marketing as well, and in 1955 introduced a new policy of advanced purchase.

All of which underlines the fact that the pressure for collectivization was based on more than a utopian drive for more advanced relations of production. It seemed clear that the best way to forestall consolidation of small-scale family farms, realize the economies of scale of ambitious hydraulic engineering and agricultural mechanization projects, and at the same time ensure an uninterrupted supply of commodity grain was through collectivization.

Thus even while land reform was still in progress in many parts of the country, voluntary Mutual Aid Teams began to be promoted by the issuance of the December 15, 1951, Party Decisions on Mutual Aid and Cooperation.[10] In January 1954 the CC issued a directive to form elementary Agricultural Producers' Cooperatives (APCs), and by the end of the year one hundred twenty thousand of these had been formed. In an important speech in July 1955 Mao successfully resisted efforts by his colleagues to slow the pace and consolidate, and collectivization accelerated; whereas at the time of his speech about 17 million families belonged to APCs, by the end of December 1955, 75 million peasants (63.3 percent

China's rural economy over the past two years] (Beijing: Zhonghua Book Co., 1952), pp. 41–69 ff.

8. Cheng Yang, "Socialism and the Quest for Modernization: The Political Economy of China's Development Strategy" (Ph.D. diss., University of California, Berkeley, 1985), pp. 34–35.

9. The Government Administrative Council of the Central People's Government, "Guanyu shixing liangshi de jihua shougou he jihua gongying de mingling" [Decree on planned procurement and planned supply of food grain], in Nongye Shehuizhuyi Gaizao Wenji [Essays on the socialist transformation of agriculture], vol. 1 (Beijing: Finance & Economy Pub., 1955), pp. 190–93.

10. Charles Cell, Revolution at Work: Mobilization Campaigns in China (New York: Academic Press, 1979), p. 184.

of the total peasant population) had joined.[11] By the end of the following year, nationwide collectivization had been essentially completed.

Socialization of China's relatively small private industrial and commercial sector overlapped chronologically with the collectivization of agriculture (though it came into focus later), and proceeded even more swiftly. Actually, due to the high proportion of the private industrial sector that had been appropriated by prominent officials in the previous government ("bureaucrat capital"), most of Chinese industry could be instantaneously socialized in 1949.[12] Plans for socialization of the remaining private industrial sector were made in the summer and fall of 1955, and in December Mao Zedong, encouraged by the rapid progress of agricultural collectivization, called for 90 percent completion by 1957. In January 1956 another "high tide" appeared, this time for the public–private joint management of all enterprises, and transformation to socialist ownership was essentially completed by the end of 1956.

With that, the socialist transformation of the private economic sector, a process originally slated for completion within fifteen years, had been achieved in only a third of that time. To be sure, the accelerated pace was not achieved without inner-Party controversy, and has subsequently come under criticism by some PRC historians for violating the principle of "voluntariness" and precipitating outright resistance analogous to that which greeted Soviet collectivization, thereby also impairing production.[13] There were also reports of widespread slaughter of private draft

11. Kenneth Walker, "Collectivization in Retrospect: The 'Socialist High Tide' of Autumn 1955–Spring 1956," *CQ*, no. 26 (April–June 1966): 1–43.

12. In an unpublished speech made by Mao Zedong to the Supreme State Conference on January 28, 1958, Mao said, "Beginning from 1949, we have confiscated all bureaucratic capital. The national capital totals more than two billion [silver dollars], the bureaucrat capital should amount to more than twenty billions in all." [Zhou Enlai interrupts: "Including imperialist capital, the total amount is more than twenty billion."] ... "Why can the market be steady and why can the state have control over it? You see, there are ten fingers of which the state has control over eight and a half. This is the socialist state economy. Eight and a half fingers out of ten, that means eighty-five percent. We are talking about industry." According to recently released figures, about 2,700 big industries operated with "bureaucrat capital," and these were confiscated at once and operated successfully by the Communists. Liao Gailong, "Historical Experiences and Our Road of Development: A Report on the History of the CCP" (delivered October 25, 1980, at the National Party School, transcribed from taped record without the speaker's verification). Translated in *Issues and Studies* (hereinafter *IS*), October 1981, part 1, pp. 68–71.

13. The first mention of widespread slaughtering of draft animals as a form of protest in response to unreasonable prices offered for land and farming animals incorporated into the cooperatives came in early 1953, and such reports recurred during collectivization in 1954. See Deng Zihui's address on the basic tasks of rural work at the Second National Congress of the CYL, July 2, 1953, as quoted in *RR*, July 22, 1953; see also Liao Luyan's report on the basic situation of agricultural production in 1954, *Yijiuwuwu nian Nongcun Gongzuo Wenti* [Rural work in 1955] (Beijing: People's Press, 1955), pp. 10–23.

animals and pigs in response to the "socialist upsurge" of 1956, which, together with the deleterious impact on cash crops of cadre discouragement of sideline production, probably contributed to the poor harvest in 1956. The earlier scholarly consensus that Chinese collectivization was achieved with relatively little "violence, resistance and chaos"[14] should perhaps be reassessed in the light of such findings.

Nevertheless, the offsetting political benefits seem undeniable. The landlord class, whose opposition was assumed to be implacable, was politically destroyed, and the possibility of resistance from the middle peasantry effectively preempted. Production did not suffer but made impressive gains. Estimates of the average annual growth of the national product for 1952–57 range from a low of 5.6 percent to an official Communist estimate of 9 percent; even the lower estimates place China high in the international rankings for this period. Industrial production during the 1952–57 period showed an average annual increase of 15 percent, according to official Chinese statistics; agricultural production dropped in 1954 but made a big increase in 1955 amid the "high tide" of collectivization (seeming to vindicate Mao's driving leadership), with an average annual increase of 4 percent for the 1952–57 period.

Socialist transformation, however, entailed more than the socialization of private property. It also involved a reorganization of the structure of primary-group relationships, which centered on the family and kinship networks, and transformation of the structure of local political institutions.

The extended family or lineage system in prerevolutionary China is of political as well as anthropological interest, inasmuch as it has traditionally constituted the seat of local political authority, the imperial political system never having penetrated below the level of the county (*xian*). The clan's legitimating ideology of filial piety, with its inherently conservative and parochial cast, has long made it a target of innovative political leadership, and in fact the Marriage Law of 1950, upon which the Communist reforms are based, replicates many provisions of the Nationalist Civil Code of 1931 (which was not energetically enforced). The Communist Marriage Law set minimum marriage ages (thereby foreclosing child brides), mandated equality of the sexes and freedom of spousal choice, forbade polygamy and infanticide, proscribed elaborate marriage and funeral ceremonies and the exchange of expensive "gifts," and facilitated divorce by mutual consent.[15]

---

14. Thomas P. Bernstein, "Leadership and Mass Mobilization in the Soviet and Chinese Collectivization Campaigns of 1929–30 and 1955–56: A Comparison," *CQ*, July–September 1967, p. 47.

15. Cf. Baker, *Chinese Family*; also Elisabeth Croll, *The Politics of Marriage in Contemporary China* (Cambridge: Cambridge University Press, 1981).

The CPC made a determined approach to implementation, launching a nationwide campaign that began in 1950 and experienced several revivals before finally expiring in late 1953. The initial response to the campaign was a wave of divorces (over five hundred thousand filed for each of the first five years), as previously oppressed wives took advantage of their legal rights; and female suicide, in apparent protest against the refusal of husbands and (male) cadres to comply with the new law. For example, it was reported in 1953 by the National Committee for Thorough Implementation that more than seventy-five thousand deaths or suicides in one year could be attributed to marriage differences, and implementation slackened.[16] Following these early campaigns, judicial construal of the law became more conservative, reducing the incidence of divorce (and suicide) and facilitating emergence of a "new democratic patriarchy."[17]

There has been a tendency among Western scholars to minimize the degree of change in the kinship system, alluding to fairly widespread indicators of "filial" continuity.[18] This, however, does less than justice to the real changes that have been achieved. Most impressive, perhaps, has been the effective elimination of the clan, or extended family, as a political force. Land reform destroyed the economic base of the large-scale lineage organization at one fell stroke by confiscating the trust lands. It was from this land that the clan derived its income, with which it financed education, public works, ancestral ceremonies, community defense, and public relations. At the same time, centralized governmental institutions took over community leadership, education, welfare, entertainment, and of course law and order, thereby rendering the clan functionally superfluous. During land reform there was also a systematic attempt to discredit clan leaders through public criticism. These measures largely demolished the lineage as an effective political entity, though it was to experience a limited revival during the Cultural Revolution as a basis for factional affiliation (particularly in smaller rural communities).

The land revolution also affected the internal structure of the nuclear family. Inasmuch as land was redistributed not to the family as a whole

16. M. J. Meijer, *Marriage Law and Policy in the Chinese People's Republic* (Hong Kong: Hong Kong University Press, 1971), pp. 112–14; also L. Dittmer, "The Chinese Marriage Law of 1950: A Study of Elite Control and Social Change" (M.A. thesis, University of Chicago, 1967), pp. 155–241, 294–99.

17. Judith Stacey, *Patriarchy and Socialist Revolution in China* (Berkeley: University of California Press, 1983), pp. 152 ff.

18. For example: "Today, the family, and women's relationship to it, remains one of the most traditional features of a predominantly rural Chinese society. The outcome of nearly a century of upheaval and revolution, born partly of widespread 'family crisis' among intellectuals and peasants, has done more to restore the traditional role and structure of the family than to fundamentally reform it." Kay Ann Johnson, *Women, the Family, and Peasant Revolution in China* (Chicago: University of Chicago Press, 1983), p. 215.

but to each member on an equal-share basis regardless of age and sex, the initial stage of land reform gave the young and the women an unprecedented sense of importance—in contrast to the traditional system, in which the head of the family had sole right to dispose of the family property. Moreover, the land reform regulations stipulated that each member of the family might take his or her share of the family land out of the family (*fenjia*), for instance in a case of divorce.[19]

The limits of the family revolution were set by the limits of the transformation of property relations and primary-group organization with which it coincided. The incipient thrust of the family revolution was emancipatory and individualistic, and this thrust ultimately conflicted with the collectivist mobilizational orientation of the land revolution, spelling an end to the former well short of the extremely loose family organization characteristic of contemporary American society. If land reform made each family member (theoretically) autarkic, subsequent collectivization deprived the family of land ownership altogether, confining family property to housing, personal possessions, and a leasehold on a small private plot. Communalization in 1958 went still further, eliminating private plots, sometimes even private dining and child-rearing arrangements—though such innovations proved to be temporary in the wake of the Great Leap's failure. At the same time, both restrictions on transfer of residence in the countryside and the permanent allocation of workers to a basic unit following schooling in the cities tended to reinforce the solidarity of the family, whereas the paucity of state-supported child-care and old-age facilities (particularly in the countryside) functionally necessitated emergence of a patrilocal "stem" rather than a nuclear family. Continuing taboos on premarital mingling of the sexes (thought to reinforce the socialist work ethic) enabled various forms of arranged marriage to persist, along with some of the rituals of ancestor worship.[20]

19. Hao Ran describes a representative episode in his land reform novel, *Jin Guang Da Dao* [The bright golden road] (Beijing: People's Literature Publishing Co., 1972), 2 vols. In chapter 52 of vol. 1, the "split" (*fenjia*) of the property of the Gao brothers is described from the perspective of three different groups of villagers.

20. See William L. Parish, "Socialism and the Peasant Family," *Journal of Asian Studies* 34: 3 (May 1975): 613–31. The regime has, however, endeavored to divest such feudal relics of their former content; for example, in 1965 the Qingming festival, the traditional holiday for sweeping out and worshiping at ancestral graves, was renamed the "Memorial Day for Revolutionary Martyrs," thus giving socialist respectability to what was inherited from tradition while at the same time paving the way for change to new forms of grave ritual. In a somewhat more bizarre transformation of traditional ritual, the cult of Mao briefly replaced ancestor worship during the Cultural Revolution. A big portrait of the Chairman was kept over the long altar table where the ancestral tablets had once been kept, with photographs of the family grouped around the portrait. Baker, *Chinese Family*, pp. 196 ff. Time was to prove the substitution provisional.

In sum, revolutionary change did occur in the Chinese family system, particularly during the early period when it was in focus. The clan was abolished, and the new stem family was firmly integrated into the "basic unit" (*danwei*), which became the clan's functional equivalent in the emergent post-Liberation authority structure. The stabilization of that authority structure, to be examined more closely in chapter 3, spelled the end of the family revolution. The leadership did not seem displeased by such a development at the time, indeed the stem family provided a convenient redoubt to which society could retire when more "progressive" (larger-scale) organizational arrangements came to grief. Yet it was inimical to charismatic leadership, and the new family organization would once again be challenged during the Cultural Revolution, as the younger generation was encouraged to renounce the elder.

By the end of 1956 the reorganization of primary group structure and socialization of the "means of production" had been "essentially completed," and with that, the Party's great mission seemed near fulfillment. The leadership consensus at the time was that henceforth, priority could shift to economic production. This shift occurred in 1958, with a simultaneous (and not fully anticipated) shift from an engineering to a storming approach. The results were catastrophic, discrediting the application of storming tactics to economic production and leaving the leadership in search of a new mission. The reasons for both the shift from the engineering to the storming approach and for the calamitous results of the latter arose from changes in the subjective dimension of charismatic leadership, to be examined next.

The Subjective Dimension

Development of the subjective dimension of charismatic leadership in China is paradoxical if viewed from a Weberian perspective. At a time when Mao's charisma—in its classic Weberian sense of an heroic, irrational force—might have been expected to be at its zenith, in the wake of the conquest of national power, it was quite well sublimated within the Party organization. Its antinomian aspect emerged only gradually, in response to tendencies toward organizational rationalization and autonomy, asserting itself in Mao's vigorous, sometimes impetuous and headstrong leadership. But charisma in its classic antibureaucratic sense fully manifested itself only in the wake of cataclysmic *failure*—contrary to what one might have expected from Weber's conception of charisma as the fruit of heroic achievement. The chaotic form it took thereafter was not simply a manifestation of the ineluctable antithesis between heroic and mundane, sacred and profane, but also a case of tactical scapegoating to salvage legitimacy amid terminal disagreement over mission. That Mao should win this showdown is no doubt largely due to his political acumen, but partly also to the role of the heroic leader in traditional Chinese political culture.

The assumption that leadership resides in an extraordinary individual has deep roots in Chinese culture, perhaps even being theological in origin—as in Dong Zhongshu's conceptualization of the cosmic mediating role of the "son of heaven." Belief in an omnipotent and omniscient sage-king—"sage within and king without" (*nei sheng wai wang*)—goes back at least to the Qin unification of China in 221 B.C. The introduction of Marxism in its initial Leninist form represented a modification of this tradition. At the top of the Party vanguard roosted the Politburo, where collegiality obtained; one member might be *primus inter pares*, but each member had certain equal rights (e.g., one vote, the right to be heard in council). The decision to select a personal figurehead to represent this corporate leadership to the public seems to have come in response to the wartime heroization of Stalin and Chiang Kai-shek.[21] The Party seems to have then molded its cult of the (individual) personality to fit existing cultural stereotypes, hoping to facilitate popular compliance. As long as the person playing the role of revolutionary sage-king adhered to the inner-Party rules of consensual decision-making, all (i.e., the entire Party) would benefit from this division of functions.

In the early post-Liberation period, the personification of charismatic leadership and the Party's corporate interests coincided perfectly. Although Mao was the primary beneficiary of the series of successes the Party enjoyed, charismatic infallibility was to a considerable degree "collectivized," and the Party as a whole basked in the glow of revolutionary heroism, all the way down to the local cadres. The problem arose when the bureaucracy began to become institutionalized in pursuit of its own maintenance and enhancement needs on the one hand, and Mao Zedong fell under the spell of his own propaganda and became convinced of his infallibility on the other, leading him to violate the norms of collective leadership in favor of an increasingly unilateral decision-making style.

The Party-state bureaucracy was set up in rather ad hoc fashion in the immediate post-Liberation period but with the passage of time became a vast organizational edifice. The New Democratic State proclaimed in 1949 was a hybrid body consisting of the Communist Party together with a bloc of smaller parties that were supposed to represent the three nonproletarian classes making up the United Front. The Chinese People's Government (CPG) was elected by the Chinese People's Political Consultative Conference (CPPCC), a heterogeneous legislative assembly

21. See Ray Wylie, *The Emergence of Maoism: Mao Tse-tung, Ch'en Po-ta, and the Search for Chinese Theory, 1935–1945* (Stanford: Stanford University Press, 1980), pp. 281–301.

comprising representatives from the various parties, groups, sectors, and interests that had been coopted by the CPC. In 1952, half of the CPG vice-chairmen, half of the vice-premiers in the State Council, the president of the Supreme People's Court, and other officials were still non-Party "democratic personages."[22] A Democratic Construction Association was formed to represent the national bourgeoisie, many of whom received appointments as deputy provincial governors or provincial mayors or served on the Standing Committees of the Political Consultative Conferences at various levels.[23]

The 1949–53 period was one of New Democracy, or People's Democratic Dictatorship, whose mission was to prepare the way for Proletarian Dictatorship during the socialist transition period. As the Party's first experiment with pluralism, brief and superficial though it was, it made an enduring impression. Mao was later to complain that it had allowed bourgeois opposition to socialism to become entrenched, whereas some of the supporters of liberal reform in the early 1980s were to object that New Democracy was "not thoroughgoing" and had been prematurely suspended, with the result that New China failed to come to terms with deeply rooted "feudal" (i.e., autocratic) traditions.[24]

The new government inaugurated in September 1954 to preside over

---

22. Xu Chongde, "A Tentative Discussion of the Change in the Nature of Our Country's Political Power," *Minzhu yu Fazhi* [Democracy and law] (Shanghai), no. 11 (November 25, 1981): 9–12.

23. "On the Characteristics," *Xin Shiqi*, pp. 2–5. (see above, n. 5.)

24. In a discussion of various revisionist influences, Mao remarked to two Albanian visitors in 1967: "One portion is those engaged in democratic revolution. They cooperate during the period of democratic revolution and agree to the overthrow of the national bourgeoisie. They agree to the distribution of land to the peasants but do not agree to the cooperativization movement. Of this group some are our so-called 'old cadres.'" "Conversations with Comrades Hysni Kap and Beqir Balluku" (February 3, 1967), in *Mao Zedong Sixiang Wan Sui* [Long live Mao Zedong Thought] (Hong Kong: n.p., 1969), pp. 663–67. (Hereinafter *Wansui* [1969].) In November 1980 the Chongqing Philosophical Society convened a symposium to discuss the feudal legacy, the proceedings of which appeared in *Guonei Zhexue Dongtai* [Philosophical trends in China], no. 3, 1981. Some of the discussants contended that feudal influence is not merely a "vestige" but actually a kind of "force." The reason has to do with the "two not-thoroughgoings," one being the bourgeois democratic revolution led by Sun Yat-sen and the other the New Democratic Revolution led by the CPC. See *Zhengming* [Contend], no. 49 (September 1, 1981): 86. (Hereinafter *ZM*.) The issue was raised in sharpest form by a young scholar named Jiang Guangxue, who, writing under the pseudonym Ying Xueli and Sun Hui (joint author), wrote an article, "Some Theoretical Problems during the Latter Stage of the Socialist Transformation of Our Nation," which appeared in the Nanjing University *Xuebao*, vol. 4, 1980. Jiang referred to socialist transformation as a "blind mopping-up operation" that had been pursued too rashly, due to the Party's historical "adoration of the spontaneity of the peasant class." The article subsequently came under officially sponsored academic criticism, which elicited a self-criticism from the author.

the socialist transition was an ambiguous one, in essential respects conforming to the classic Leninist mold (a unicameral, single-party state), but retaining certain democratic trappings. The CPPCC for instance continued to function in a "consultative" capacity, providing a fairly anemic claim to multiparty pluralism. The Communist Party monopolized the nominating process for candidates to the National People's Congress (NPC), but delegates were popularly (if indirectly, except at local levels) elected from regional constituencies. The large size, infrequent convention, and brevity of its sessions precluded a very active role in the policy-making process. During the chairmanship of Liu Shaoqi (1954–64), the NPC did at times examine proposals on economic development programs before giving its approval, and at least on one occasion (the Fourth Session of the First NPC, in June 1957), NPC delegates even criticized Mao in relation to the Anti-Rightist movement and the Party's handling of university affairs in Shanghai.[25] Due to such minor but apparently troubling departures from unanimity, the Party increasingly abandoned legislative channels to rule through its own emission of documents. During the Great Leap Forward the NPC fell into desuetude, enacting no new legislation until after the Cultural Revolution.

Aside from its representative and legislative functions, the main task of the bureaucracy was planning and managing economic development. In August 1952, a State Statistical Bureau (*Guojia tongji ju*) was set up under the auspices of the State Council (executive organ of the NPC), followed by the State Planning Commission (*Guojia jihua weiyuanhui*). In 1953 the First Five-Year Plan (FYP), drawn up on the basis of Soviet advice and predicated on extensive fraternal technical and financial assistance, was introduced.[26] Its centerpiece was the importation of 156 complete plants from the USSR, mostly in heavy industry. It called for completion of basic industrialization and collectivization by 1967 (the end of the Third FYP).

The relationship of these burgeoning representative and economic organizations to charismatic leadership was ambiguous. They were creatures of the Party, and the Party retained control over staffing and routine decision-making through such devices as *nomenklatura*, internal Party fractions, and joint appointments. Yet they still displayed a tendency to drift from Party control. The reason for this has to do with the contradiction between their functions as defined in their founding constitutional documents and formal structure and their informal political base.

25. Union Research Institute, *Communist China, 1949–1959* (Hong Kong: Union Research Press, 1960), p. 60. Granted, this episode was exceptional, occurring as it did in the context of the Hundred Flowers movement.
26. Brugger, *China*, pp. 86–94.

According to the former, they should be more or less autonomous and concerned with the implementation of rational-legal bureaucratic rules; according to the latter, they should promote revolutionary charismatic leadership. From the bureaucrat's perspective, this involved a balance between routine performance of one's official role and occasional display of ideological zeal. From the point of view of the Party, it generated an incessant tension between the officials' "forgetting" their charismatic origins (the class struggle, the revolution) and the consequent need for the Party to "remind" them. Forgetting was a direct function of undisturbed office tenure, plus absorption in organizational chores, whether legislative, managerial, or technical-economic. Reminding was done chiefly through rectification movements, whose exemplary purges jeopardized tenure while at the same time affording chances to regenerate charismatic commitment.

By the mid-1950s, this tension between forgetting and reminding, bureaucratic secularization and charismatic revivalism had begun to penetrate the Party leadership itself. This occurred on the one hand due to a process of *reverse cooptation*: those Party leaders sent to manage a bureaucratic organ tended to adopt the organizational interests of that organ as their own, and to represent those interests in Party policy-making councils. On the other hand, Mao Zedong, the Party's personification of charismatic infallibility, began to take advantage of his role for political self-aggrandizement. He took credit for the success of the continuing revolution, and allowed his works to be compiled as the primary embodiment of the Party's collective wisdom. The first heavily edited volume of his *Selected Works* was published in October 1951, the second in March 1952, and volume 3 in February 1953.[27] Beginning with its enshrinement in the Party Constitution of the Seventh Congress, references to Mao's Thought began to appear in the context of tributes to Marxism-Leninism as the Party's official ideology.

Mao seems to have manipulated both public opinion and political levers to eclipse his colleagues, gradually enhancing his power at their expense. Thus in 1953, he asserted his right to final approval over all CC directives: "From now on, all documents and telegrams sent out in the name of the CC can be dispatched only after I have gone over them, otherwise they are invalid. Please take note."[28] The Gao Gang–Rao Shushi incident that marred elite unity in 1954–55 does not seem to have

27. Helmut Martin, *Cult and Canon: The Origins and Development of State Maoism* (Armonk, N.Y.: M. E. Sharpe, 1982), p. 26.
28. Mao Zedong, "Liu Shao-ch'i and Yang Shang-k'un Criticized for Breach of Discipline in Issuing Documents in the Name of the Central Committee without Authorization" (May 19, 1953), in *SW*, vol. 5: 92.

revolved around the position of Mao but that of his immediate subordinates, and according to the most recent revelations, ideological issues do not seem to have been at stake.[29] Yet the political implication of the purge was a further centralization of leadership, warning habitually autonomous provincial leaders by negative example and eliminating the six regional Party bureaus.[30]

A divergence within the leadership first appeared concerning apparently minor issues of timing and pace. Prompted by a poor harvest in 1954 and by serious difficulties in consolidating cooperatives that had been formed without meeting the necessary organizational and material preconditions, Mao in March 1955 proposed a "three-point policy" to "stop" the development of cooperatives in most areas, "contract" the process in areas where APCs had been overdeveloped, and "develop" cooperativization where few cooperatives had been established. Accordingly, the CC Rural Work Department charted a plan to increase the number of elementary APCs to one million (a 50 percent increase) in 1955–56, but to retreat where conditions were not mature. A meeting of Party secretaries from fifteen provinces and municipalities convened in May 1955 to ratify this policy, and Mao made a personal representation to them in which he stressed "developing" over "stopping and contracting," enthusiastically calling for a 100 percent increase. Apparently Deng Zihui and the Rural Work Department insisted on the original plan, and proceeded (with the endorsement of a Politburo meeting convened under Liu Shaoqi) to "contract" about twenty thousand cooperatives back to the stage of Mutual Aid teams.[31] Infuriated by this show of resistance (and by the rumor that two hundred thousand cooperatives had been dismantled), Mao convened a meeting of provincial and munic-

---

29. Deng Xiaoping, "Suggestions on the Drafting of the 'Resolutions on Certain Questions in the History of Our Party since the Founding of the PRC'" (March 1980–June 1981), reprinted in *Hongqi* [Red flag], no. 13 (July 1, 1983): 2–15. (Hereinafter *HQ.*)

30. Kong Zhongwen, "Line Struggles—Eliminating Opposing Factions within the Party: Mao Zedong's 27-year Rule," part 5, *ZM*, no. 73 (November 1983): 71–74.

31. Because of his efforts to resist hasty collectivization and his pioneering advocacy of the responsibility system, Deng Zihui has emerged as something of a hero before his time in recent historical reconstructions. See Editorial Board, "Shenqie huainian Deng Zihui tongzhi" [Deeply cherish comrade Deng Zihui's memory], *Nongcong Gongzuo Tongxun*, no. 5 (May 5, 1981): 7–9; Qiang Yuangan and Lin Bangguang, "Wo guo nongye jitihua de zhuoyue zuzhizhe Deng Zihui" [Our country's outstanding organizer of agricultural collectivization Deng Zihui], *Xinhua Wenzhai*, no. 7 (1981): 187–90; and Dai Qingui and Yu Zhan, "Study Comrade Deng Zihui's Viewpoint on Agricultural Production Responsibility Systems," *RR*, February 23, 1982, as translated in *Foreign Broadcast Information Service* (Hong Kong: U.S. Consulate) (hereinafter *FBIS*), no. 44 (March 5, 1982): K16–K19. As cited in Thomas Bernstein, "Reforming China's Agriculture," unpublished paper presented to the conference "To Reform the Chinese Political Order," Harwichport, Mass., June 18–23, 1984.

ipal Party secretaries at the end of July, where he initiated criticism of "old women with bound feet." [32]

Opposition quickly wilted, and the organization reoriented itself to a more headlong pace. By the end of the year Mao's original target had been effectively advanced from the cooperativization of 50 percent of all agricultural households by the spring of 1956 to 70–80 percent by the end of 1956. Already by the end of 1955, the number of peasant households organized into APCs had jumped from 14 to 60 percent, and, by the end of 1956, to well over 96 percent (of which 87.8 percent were "advanced"). The policy of advancing by stages was therewith abandoned: many households joined advanced APCs in response to an announcement by leading cadres at a meeting of production teams, without having first been organized into Mutual Aid Teams or even elementary APCs. [33]

Mao's successful defiance of elite consensus was accomplished through a shrewd appeal to outside constituencies, in this case Party secretaries of the provinces and municipalities, who in turn represented grass-roots interests. [34] The impact of this bold initiative on production could not be precisely determined until later, but the initial impression was at least not adverse, and, inasmuch as socialization was considered desirable in its own right, Mao's intervention was a provisional triumph. It vindicated his reputation for infallibility and discredited those who disagreed with him, whom he was able to demote or force to make self-criticisms. [35]

32. Yan Ling, "The Necessity, Possibility and Realization of Socialist Transformation of China's Agriculture," *Social Sciences in China* (Beijing) 3, no. 1 (March 1982): 94–123.

33. *RR*, October 11, 1956.

34. According to Vivienne Shue, "It is evident that at the bottom level there had been pressure for a top-level go-ahead to permit the quick, final expropriation of upper-middle and rich peasants they felt they needed to consolidate broad peasant support behind their own political leadership in the villages." *Peasant China in Transition: The Dynamics of Development toward Socialism, 1949–1956* (Berkeley: University of California Press, 1980), pp. 281–92. Although Mao generated political support for his initiative and was hence able to push it through with unexpected swiftness, that it had disruptive consequences is made clear in Selden and Lippit, *The Transition to Socialism*, particularly in the Selden article.

35. Mao arranged to have two long-time supporters, Chen Zhengren and Chen Boda, placed in the Agricultural Department; he also mobilized support from provincial and local officials, who were enthusiastically in favor of his proposal as a solution to their problems of dwindling rural investment and capital seepage. In August he convened an "expanded" Politburo meeting in which a majority supported his decision to accelerate rather than suspend the collectivization campaign, and at the Sixth Plenum of the Seventh CC (October 1955) his opponents were forced to capitulate: self-criticisms were submitted by Premier Zhou Enlai, by Minister of Finance Li Xiannian, Chairman of the State Planning Commission Li Fuchun, Chairman of the State Commission for Large Industries Bo Yibo, and Chen Yi, then mayor of Shanghai. Walker, "Collectivization in Retrospect"; see also Rainer Hoffman, *Kampf zweier Linien: Zur politischen Geschichte der chinesischen Volksrepublik, 1949–1977* (Stuttgart: Ernst Klett Verlag, 1978).

Subsequently there was however an inner-Party backlash against his aggressive leadership, partly in response to developments in the Soviet bloc, partly due to domestic economic difficulties. In February 1956, at the Twentieth Congress of the Communist Party of the Soviet Union (CPSU), Khrushchev suddenly made a public attack against Stalin's personality cult, thereby implicitly jeopardizing all within the bloc (including Mao) who had been guilty of analogous tendencies. At home, whereas agricultural output continued to increase in 1956, the *rate of increase* declined.[36] The overextended expenditure of capital construction resulted in a budget deficit of about 3 billion *yuan*,[37] always a matter of concern to fiscally conservative Chinese financial planners. Beginning around March 13, articles began to appear in *People's Daily* referring to disequilibrium between different production sectors and other difficulties. A public campaign was in fact finally launched against economic adventurism (*jizao maojin*), and although Mao's own words were quoted in support of this retreat and blame placed on overzealous local cadres who had misinterpreted central policy directives, Mao took these criticisms personally and harbored a grudge.[38]

The resurgence of the "engineers" was visible not merely in the nuances of public rhetoric, but in the constitutional restructuring undertaken at the Eighth Party Congress. Not only were references to Mao Zedong Thought deleted from the Party Constitution (at the motion of Peng Dehuai, promptly approved by Liu Shaoqi), but a new position of "honorary chairman," for which there could be only one conceivable candidate, was created. And, in an organizational maneuver that was to be repeated for the gradual removal of Hua Guofeng in 1980, the Secretariat was greatly strengthened, apparently in order to create an alternative leadership nexus. The provision contained in the 1945 Constitution permitting the party chairman to hold the concurrent post of chairman of

36. Yan Ling, "The Necessity," pp. 113 ff.
37. Liao Gailong, "Historical Experiences," part 1, p. 79.
38. On June 19, an article by Deng Tuo (then editor of *RR*) that was particularly harsh in its criticisms of economic adventurism was submitted for approval. The article quoted Mao's words from his preface to *Socialist Upsurge in China's Countryside* that "no one should disregard reality and indulge in flights of fancy, or make plans of action unwarranted by the objective situation, or reach out for the impossible." Mao refused to read the article, scrawling "*bu kanle*" (I'm not going to read any more) in the margin. Liu Shaoqi, however, approved it on behalf of the Politburo, and it was published the following day. See the editorial in *RR*, June 20, 1956. Eighteen months later (at Nanning, in January 1958), in the context of his own blistering criticism of officials in the Finance Ministry, Mao revealed his reasons: "There was an editorial in June 1956 warning against venturesome advance. It looked like it was taking an evenhanded stance, anti-Rightist conservatism on the one hand and anti-venturesome advance on the other. Yet its key point was on the latter.... Why should I read an article that attacks me? *Wansui* (1969), pp. 151–52. See also Roderick MacFarquhar, *Origins of the Cultural Revolution: I. Contradictions among the People, 1956–1957* (London: Oxford University Press, 1974), p. 346, n. 15.

the Secretariat was dropped, and a separate Secretariat was created under a general secretary named Deng Xiaoping. It was the general secretary who was authorized not only to handle the daily work of the CC, but to convene the Central Work Conferences that were regularly held in place of CC Plenums (convened by the Chairman) in the 1962–65 period.[39]

A third way in which Mao's colleagues sought to impose the discipline of collective leadership was to reassert control over elite-mass communications. The organizational rules of the game in inner-Party decision-making hold that in order for intra-elite discussion to be relatively untrammeled it must be confidential, precluding any attempt to mobilize outside constituencies. Thus elite-mass communication must proceed through the established document system, with important statements being emitted from the top only after attaining elite consensus.[40] But, beginning in the mid-1950s, as Mao grew impatient with the bureaucracy and came to resort increasingly to unilateral initiatives, he sought ways to evade the requirements screening his contact with mobilizable constituencies. One of these was to avail himself of the opportunity for ad hoc communications afforded by field trips—as in his 1958 comment to a reporter in Hebei that the commune was "good," which was widely publicized and had a mobilizational impact exceeding even Mao's expectations. An expedient more frequently resorted to, however, was the convention of a central meeting, the proceedings of which could be predetermined through control over the roster of participants and the setting of the agenda, with the expectation that these would then be publicized. Thus Mao's convention of provincial and municipal officials under the auspices of an "expanded" Politburo conference at the end of July 1955, duly publicized in the document stream and eventually (i.e., three months later) in the media, was pivotal in Mao's acceleration of collectivization. But by early 1957 he was also beginning to encounter resistance to such expedients. When nothing appeared in the press following his talk on the handling of contradictions among the people (February 1957) or his March speech to the Party's National Propaganda Conference, Mao complained (in April):

> It is the task of the Party press to represent the political line of the Party. It is wrong to remain silent about the conference on propaganda work. Why has the press not printed a word about it? Why was there no lead article about a high state conference? Why is the political line of the Party kept secret?[41]

39. Hoffman, *Kampf*, pp. 30–45.
40. Michel Oksenberg, "Methods of Communicating within the Chinese Bureaucracy," *CQ*, no. 57 (January–March 1974): 1–39.
41. "Push the Revolution in the Press to the End," joint lead article in *RR*, *HQ*, and *Jiefangjun Bao* (Liberation Army Daily, hereinafter *JFJB*), as translated in *Survey of the Chinese Mainland Press* (hereinafter *SCMP*) (Hong Kong: U.S. Consulate General), no. 4253, p. 23.

Unlike Hua Guofeng, whom Deng and his cohorts would thus maneuver into a politically passive position two decades later, Mao successfully resisted the more limited organizational role his colleagues conceived for him. An inveterate maverick throughout his career,[42] Mao defied the emerging consensus. Anything but chastened by the 1956 campaign against adventurism, he introduced and resourcefully promoted two even more ambitious campaigns: the Hundred Flowers and the Great Leap Forward.

The Hundred Flowers, to be analyzed in greater detail in chapter 3, was not Mao's original initiative—a rapprochement with the Chinese intelligentsia had been pursued for more than a year by Zhou Enlai, Chen Yi, and others—but Mao gave it its name and its distinctive emancipatory thrust, urging the cautious intellectuals to speak out under his personal assurance of complete freedom. This assurance, according to the best recent evidence available, was at least controversial, possibly unilateral, leaving Mao vulnerable to elite criticism when it resulted in intellectual criticisms of the regime well beyond what he had anticipated. The incident also soured Mao's relationship with the intellectuals, who felt understandably betrayed by the anti-rightist mousetrapping that followed the "blooming," while Mao in turn became suspicious of the sincerity of the intellectuals' conversions. Yet it ironically facilitated new radical initiatives in the short run, by eliminating (through purge and intimidation) one likely source of resistance to them.

The decisive watershed in the shift from corporate to personal charisma was the Great Leap Forward. Hitherto the storming approach had been applied to mass criticism movements and to redistributive programs, but never before on such ambitious scale to economic development.[43] Economic development had previously been monopolized by the planning apparatus, a centralized, vertical hierarchy branching out from the various ministries and commissions of the State Council in Beijing to the factories and farms of China. The Great Leap was of course not purely economic in focus—like most campaigns, it was a multifunctional affair. It was in part redistributive, in that it resulted in the formation of communes and the confiscation of private plots. It also had aspects of a rectification campaign, oriented as it was against selfish individualism and in favor of the self-reliant, creative capabilities of the masses. There were utopian elements, such as the widespread belief that the commune was the first step in the imminent realization of communist relations of

42. See John E. Rue, *Mao Tse-tung in Opposition, 1927–1935* (Stanford: Stanford University Press, 1966).
43. True, there was a "mini-leap" to enhance agricultural production in early 1956, but this came more as a concomitant of the successful collectivization drive than as a primary objective. See MacFarquhar, *Origins, 1,* pp. 26–33.

production,[44] or Zhang Chunqiao's article (endorsed in an editorial note by Mao) condemning the "bourgeois wage system" and calling for restoration of the Yan'an free supply system. But its basic, animating rationale was a dramatic acceleration of economic development. It was envisioned that China would suddenly do everything "bigger, better, faster, and more economically," reaching the levels of the advanced industrial countries within fifteen years. And it was the Leap's resounding failure to meet such targets that doomed all of its ancillary objectives.

By dissipating the leadership's accumulated prestige among the masses, the Leap disaster would raise the question of blame. As far as can be determined from the most recent evidence available, there seems to have been a broad leadership consensus in support of the program in its early phases, when its achievements appeared so unprecedented. Chen Yun apparently expressed reservations in 1957 (and was accordingly relieved of his major operational positions), but many normally sober members of the leadership (e.g., Deng Xiaoping, Liu Shaoqi) were also carried away on this wave of enthusiasm. All that having been conceded, Mao was conspicuously in the forefront of the campaign, consistently seizing the initiative and sometimes preempting regular decision-making procedures to present his colleagues with *faits accomplis*. According to Deng Liqun, in a speech to the Chinese Academy of Social Sciences:

> Our mistakes were made by Chairman Mao. . . . One was the People's Commune movement. In many areas, this one supplied and that one supplied, and Chairman Mao was very happy at the beginning. In 1958, not long after the Beidaihe meeting, Xushui in Hebei was the first to advance to communism. It introduced the total supply system. The chairman was indeed very enthusiastic and wanted to find out how Xushui accomplished it. Taking Chen Boda and Zhang Chunqiao with him, he asked the county Party committee secretary to make a report. . . . Chairman Mao added the following passage to the decision on the People's Commune at the Beidaihe meeting: "By introducing the People's Commune, three or four, or five or six years later, the collective ownership system will change to the whole-people's ownership system." . . . He also agreed to setting high quotas and doubling the output.[45]

Another recent commentator had this to say about Mao's increasingly assertive decision-making style:

> After the Nanning Conference in January 1958, Comrade Mao Zedong no longer participated in the meetings of the Politburo. He only listened to

---

44. In the words of one popular jingle, attributed to Kang Sheng: "Communism is paradise/The People's Commune is the bridge" (Gongchanzhuyi shi tiantang/Renmin gongshe shi qiaoliang), quoted in MacFarquhar, *Origins*, 2, p. 129.

45. Quoted in Lu Zhongjian, "On Assessing Mao," *ZM*, no. 35 (September 1, 1980): 24–31.

reports and delivered speeches on necessary occasions. What he said could not be changed. The situation became such that Comrade Mao Zedong alone could criticize the Standing Committee members as he pleased. It seemed that everyone else was wrong, that only he himself adhered to Marxism, and that all the others did not follow the socialist road. His criticisms of others were so severe that he practically put himself over and above the Politburo.[46]

Many of the specific components of the Leap had in fact been bureaucratically generated,[47] but their enthusiastic mass adoption can be traced to Mao's personal endorsement. It was Mao who first proposed the ideal of People's Communes, because they were larger in scale and had a higher degree of public ownership. At the Second Session of the Eighth Party Congress in May 1958, Mao foresaw that China would be able to overtake Russia and realize communism "earlier,"[48] and again in the Beidaihe Resolution (August 1958) he proclaimed that the transition to communism would not be in the distant future. Its achievement would be facilitated by miraculous increases in production (whose feasibility Mao had championed as early as 1955—in his preface to *Socialist Upsurge*, he had also discussed the prospect of doubling or trebling productivity within a short period). In July and August of 1958 the target of doubling the output of steel and grain was formally adopted. And in his speech endorsing this target, Mao indulged in the following reverie:

> Yesterday, I could not get to sleep. I have something to tell you all. In the past, who ever dreamed that a *mu* of farmland could produce ten thousand catties of grain? I never dreamed it. . . . If the situation is allowed to continue, I am afraid that our 1.5 billion *mu* of farmland will be too much. Planting one-third of them is enough; another one-third may be turned into grassland; and let the remaining one-third lie fallow. The whole country will thus become a garden.[49]

Although a certain tension between the bureaucratic predilection for planning and orderly sequence and the charismatic drive for momentum was already apparent in the "high tide" of collectivization, and again in the 1956 "mini-leap," during the Leap the planning and statistical accounting apparatus was utterly decimated. As Mao later admitted, plans were "suddenly abandoned after the Beidaihe meeting."[50] In the Sixty Articles, a system of "dual planning" was introduced (one stipulating a

46. Liao Gailong, "Historical Experiences," part 2, p. 90.
47. David Bachman, "To Leap Forward: Chinese Policy-Making, 1956–1958" (Ph.D. diss., Stanford University, 1983).
48. *Wansui* (1969), p. 204.
49. Liao Gailong, "Historical Experiences," part 2, p. 88.
50. *Wansui* (1969), p. 204. See also Kenneth R. Walker, *Food Grain Procurement and Consumption in China* (Cambridge: Cambridge University Press, 1984), pp. 129–146.

respectably ambitious public quota, the other setting a higher private quota that was actually expected to be met), which resulted in a continuous raising of targets, and a "wind of exaggeration." Mao's scorn for the advice of experts, expressed at the Chengdu meetings (March 1958) and elsewhere, laid the foundation for exclusive reliance on the mass mobilization of unskilled labor.[51] Mao even sought to discredit his more cautious colleagues and consecrate his taste for pell-mell advance in ideological terms. At both the Supreme State Conference in January and at the Chengdu meetings he broached his concept of continuous revolution:

> I advocate continuous revolution. Do not mistake mine for Trotsky's permanent revolution. A revolution has to be struck while the iron is hot, one revolution has to be followed by another, a revolution has to move forward incessantly. The Hunanese have a saying: "The straw sandal has no pattern, its shape evolves as it is being woven." [Our revolution proceeded through] the land reform, and after the land reform there was the mutual-aid team, and then elementary cooperatives, followed by advanced cooperatives. Within seven years things were organized within a cooperative pattern, and the relations of production were transformed. And then we started the rectification campaign, with the technological revolution immediately following.[52]

He also attempted to salvage a starring role for the charismatic leader in leading such a revolution from the damage inflicted by the critique of Stalin's personality cult by distinguishing between "correct" and "incorrect" cults. As he put it at Chengdu on March 10:

> There are two kinds of the cult of the individual. One is correct, such as that of Marx, Engels, Lenin, and the correct side of Stalin. These we ought to revere and continue to revere forever. It would not do not to revere them....Then there is the incorrect kind of cult of the individual in which there is no analysis, simply blind obedience. This is not right. Opposition to the cult of the individual may also have one of two aims: one is opposition to an incorrect cult, and the other is oppostition to reverence for others and a desire for reverence for oneself. The question at issue is not whether or not there should be a cult of the individual, but rather whether or not the individual concerned represents the truth.[53]

The leadership first became aware of problems with the Leap by the fall of 1958, though the gravity of the situation did not fully surface until

51. MacFarquhar, *Origins*, 2, pp. 31, 40.
52. Quoted in Ding Wang, ed. *Mao Zedong Xuanji Buyi* [Supplement to the selected works of Mao Zedong], vol. 3 (Hong Kong: Ming Bao Monthly Pub., 1971), p. 162; also translated in various compendia.
53. Mao, "Talks at the Chengdu Conference" (March 10, 1958), trans. in Stuart Schram, ed., *Mao Tse-tung Talks to the People* (New York: Macmillan, 1975), pp. 99–100.

several months later. As long as he could hold other people accountable for shortcomings, Mao was prepared to make necessary adjustments. At the second Zhengzhou meeting in February-March 1959, Mao harshly criticized the tendency toward egalitarianism and overconcentration commonly found among local cadres. At this time Mao made the startling admission that "while it [viz., the Leap] had a tight grip on production, it ignored livelihood and continued to ignore it until hundreds of thousands of people suffered from malnutrition and people in Beijing had no more than one tael of vegetables each." [54] Yet he still insisted that the basic line was correct—mistakes were in a ratio of one finger to the other nine. While he tried to correct the trend toward egalitarianism and overconcentration, he still felt that most private plots should be incorporated into the commune and that the free supply system and communal mess halls should be continued.[55] When he saw the report of a provincial Party secretary having ordered mess halls dissolved in a particular county, Mao denounced him as a "rightist opportunist." Despite concessions to the need for reform, Mao repeatedly emphasized the need to continue the Leap and strengthen the commune. Mistakes were inevitable but should not give rise to doubts; if there had to be criticisms, these should "follow the order of first affirming the achievements of the Great Leap Forward, affirming the superiority of the People's Commune, and then pointing out the weaknesses and mistakes in their actual workings." [56]

By exposing the full magnitude of the disaster and attributing responsibility to Mao in tactful but unmistakable terms, Defense Minister Peng Dehuai, at a famous series of meetings at Lushan in July and August 1959, reinforced Mao's tendency to identify with the program. In the months following Mao's stinging refutation, radical policies were revived and new ones (such as the urban commune movement) introduced in an otherwise pointless effort to vindicate Mao's position. As Bo Yibo put it, with retrospective insight:

> Unfortunately, during the latter period of the Lushan meeting, Comrade Mao Zedong erroneously criticized Comrade Peng Dehuai and some other comrades and launched a nation-wide struggle against "right opportunism." This

54. *Wansui* (1969), p. 278; also translated in "Mao Tse-tung: Speeches at the Zhengzhou Conference" (February and March 1959), *Chinese Law and Government* 9 (Winter 1976–77): 18.
55. *Wansui* (1969), pp. 288, 284–285.
56. Mao Zedong, "Dui Anhui shengwei shujichu shuji Zhang Kaifan xialing jiesan Wuwei Xian shitang de baogao de piyu" [A critique of the report by Zhang Kaifan, secretary of the provincial Party committee of Anhui province, explaining his order to dismantle mess halls in Wuwei County], in Ding Wang, *Mao Zedong Xuanji Buyi* (1971), vol. 3: 238; also *Wansui* (1969), p. 281

destroyed in a moment all our achievements scored in fighting against leftist mistakes over the past nine months.[57]

Although Peng Dehuai was thus politically destroyed for his effrontery, the underlying validity of his criticisms was to become apparent (although never officially acknowledged) over the next three years, as the Chinese economy plunged into a deep depression. Chinese economists have recently acknowledged the magnitude of the disaster: according to their statistics, industrial and agricultural production increased by an annual average of only 0.6 percent during the period of the Second FYP (1957–62).[58] The impact on Chinese living standards was severe, resulting in millions of deaths by starvation (particularly in Shandong, Henan, and Gansu) and in pervasive malnutrition serious enough to affect population growth rates, as a result of excessive procurement of grain based on exaggerated local reports of increases in yield.[59]

The collapse of the Leap affected the Party's reputation in two ways. First, as already noted, it impaired the prestige of the Party as a whole

57. Bo Yibo, in *HQ*, July 1981, as translated in *FBIS*, July 29, 1981, p. K33.

58. Industrial growth was 3.8 percent while agricultural output declined by 3.9 percent per annum during the second FYP. Industrial output improved by 36.1 percent in 1959 over the previous year, and by 11.2 percent in 1960 over 1959; but in 1961, it declined by 38.2 percent from the 1960 level. Agricultural output increased in 1958 but declined every year thereafter, falling 26.3 percent over the 1959–61 period. Xu Dixin, "Lun wo guo guomin-jingji de biange yu fazhan" [An essay on the transformation and development of our national economy], in Editors of *Jingji Yanjiu*, eds., *Shehuizhuyi Zhengzhi Jingjixue Ruogan Jiben Lilun Wenti* [Some basic theoretical issues of socialist political economy] (Shandong: People's Press, 1980); see also Sun Shangqing et al., "Zai lun shehuizhuyi jingji de jihua yu shichangxing xiangjiehe de jige lilun wenti" [Further discussion of some theoretical issues concerning the combination of planning and market mechanisms in socialist economy], in *Shehuizhuyi Jingji zhong Jihua yu Shichang de Guanxi* [Relations between planning and market mechanisms in socialist economy], vol. 1 (Beijing: Chinese Social Science Press, 1980), pp. 98–99.

59. Gross procurement in 1959–60 reached the remarkable level of 67.49 million tons, which was 32 percent higher than the 1958–59 amount, from an output of 170 million tons, which was 15 percent *below* that of 1958. Net procurement rose from 15.9 percent of output in 1958–59 to 28 percent in 1959–60. Walker, *Food Grain Procurement*, p. 149. The famine is examined in Thomas P. Bernstein, "Stalinism, Famine, and Chinese Peasants: Grain Procurements during the Great Leap Forward," *Theory and Society* 13, no. 3 (May 1984): 339–77. Jürgen Domes, citing *Jingji Guanli* (no. 3, March 1981, p. 3), estimates a loss of over 20 million people between 1959 and 1962. Domes, *The Government and Politics of the PRC: A Time of Transition* (Boulder, Colo: Westview Press, 1985), pp. 38, 274. This loss is reflected in Chinese demographic statistics, according to which the average death rate rose from 11 per thousand in 1957 to 17 per thousand in 1958–61, while the birth rate declined from 34 per thousand in 1957 to 23 per thousand in 1958–61. See Judith Bannister, "Population Policy and Trends in China, 1978–83," *CQ*, no. 100 (December 1984): 717–42.

among the masses, contributing to a demoralization that was to become visible in the corruption described, for example, in the Lianjiang documents of the early 1960s.[60] Second, it damaged Mao's personal reputation for infallibility among the Party elite. Henceforth, Mao's leadership was tolerated or accommodated amid fairly widespread elite skepticism about the wisdom of his policies, a skepticism that extended as high as the CC itself.

Mao was sensitive to this change in elite reception to his initiatives, to which he responded in two ways. First, he acknowledged his own lack of economic competence in a series of inner-Party self-criticisms. Already in his "statement of opinion" of July 14, 1959, written in response to Peng's criticisms, he admitted that "in 1958 and 1959 I should take main responsibility, it is I who am to blame. In the past, the blame was on others. . . . but now I am to blame for I really have taken charge of a great many things." In the same statement, Mao pointed to some of the drawbacks of attempting to apply storm tactics to economic construction:

> Neither coal, iron, nor transportation capacity were correctly calculated. But coal and iron do not stroll through the area by themselves, they must be transported in freight cars. It was precisely this point that I had overlooked. I and Premier Zhou know little of these planning arrangements. I don't want to make excuses, although this is certainly an apology. Until August of last year I applied myself essentially to revolution. For problems of economic, especially industrial, contruction I am really not competent.[61]

And in his speech to the Supreme Conference on National Affairs in September 1958 he conceded that "for eight or nine years we have not actually grasped industry; our emphasis has been placed on revolution." In a talk on February 2, 1959, he said: "Just like children who play with fire, we just feel hurt after touching it because of lack of experience." Mao made another self-criticism on June 12, 1961, that has never been published, although Mao called for its wider distribution in another speech made the following year.[62]

The political upshot of such mea culpas was that Mao in effect withdrew from active participation in economic decision-making, giving rise

60. C. S. Chen, ed., *Rural People's Communes in Lien-chiang*, trans. Charles Price Ridley (Stanford: Hoover Institution Press, 1969). See also Byung-joon Ahn, "Adjustments in the Great Leap Forward and Their Ideological Legacy, 1959–1962," in Chalmers Johnson, ed., *Ideology and Politics in Contemporary China* (Seattle: University of Washington Press, 1973), pp. 257–301.

61. Mao Zedong, "Talk at the Lushan Conference" (July 23, 1959), *Wansui* (1969), p. 302.

62. In order of citation, Mao Zedong, "Summary of a Talk at the Supreme State Conference" (September 1958), *Wansui* (1969), pp. 243–44; "Talk at a Conference of Provincial and Municipal Party Secretaries" (February 2, 1959), *Wansui* (1969), p. 278; and "Talk at an Enlarged Central Work Conference" (January 20, 1962), *Wansui* (1969), pp. 399–423.

to a division of labor within the elite. The division of the Politburo into two "fronts" apparently antedates this occasion, for there are already references to it in the mid-1950s. But now the distinction was more consistently maintained, as Mao retreated to the "second front," leaving operational problems to the "first front" under Liu Shaoqi (who, as ranking Party vice-chairman, was empowered to convene central meetings in Mao's absence) and Deng Xiaoping (who, as general secretary, took charge of day-to-day Party administration). The long-run implication was that any attempt by Mao to recover his own reputation would take ideological rather than operational form. He first took the opportunity to try out his new ideas in the polemic against Yugoslav and Soviet "revisionism"; then in 1964–65 he began to turn that critique against analogous developments in the PRC.

The second aspect of Mao's ambivalent response to his colleagues' less receptive demeanor was one of denial of guilt, and a concomitant tendency to scapegoat those colleagues who seemed to have lost faith in him. From his colleagues' perspective, this was of course unfair; as Deng Xiaoping later put it:

> He always complained with everybody because, he protested, they didn't listen to him or they didn't consult him, they did not keep him informed. Well, it was not true for the others, it was true for me. And I did that because I did not like his patriarchal behavior.... He never wanted to know the ideas of others, no matter how right they might be, he never wanted to hear opinions different from his. He really behaved in an unhealthy, feudal way.[63]

He became acutely sensitive to criticism, retaliating promptly with the application of pejorative ideological "labels" but also keeping score of Aesopian intimations of his fallibility for later, more thorough retribution (the most famous examples being Wu Han's famous play and the "three-family village" newspaper column published in *Beijing Evening News*).

One eventual concomitant of this denial was a reassertion of Mao's infallibility, in a publicity blitz launched with the help of the recently promoted Lin Biao. The vehicle for this revival was the *Quotations of Chairman Mao Zedong*, a small text (designed to fit into a uniform jacket pocket) of quotations extracted from their historical context and arranged thematically. First distributed within the People's Liberation Army (PLA) in 1961, the *Quotations* was printed in a mass edition in May 1964, reprinted in 1965. By the Cultural Revolution, over 700 million copies of the text had been distributed, a number then equal to that of the

---

63. Oriana Fallaci, "Deng: Cleaning Up Mao's 'Feudal Mistakes,'" *Washington Post*, part 1 (August 31, 1980), pp. D1 ff; part 2 (September 1, 1980), pp. A1 ff.

population of China.[64] The campaign to "study" and memorize these excerpts resulted in an extension by analogy of the infallibility principle, as the masses were encouraged to apply Maoist precepts to all walks of life. To judge from the *in camera* statements later leaked and attributed to Mao's colleagues, there was inner-Party resistance, never explicitly bruited, to what was regarded as "vulgarization."

To summarize in terms of charismatic development, a "corporate charismatic" leadership agreed upon a salvationary mission in the immediate post-Liberation period, and successfully performed it during the ensuing decade, relying primarily on engineering tactics. By the end of 1956, the part of the mission on which consensus could be obtained had been "exhausted," with generally favorable results: the economic and family structures had been radically transformed, enemies had been largely destroyed or reeducated (as we shall see in the next chapter), all amid rapid economic growth. That all this had been accomplished was so encouraging that it was perhaps not immediately clear that the exhaustion of a salvationary mission would require a fundamental reorientation if the revolution were to continue. The initial leadership impulse was to retire from the revolution amid plaudits—one reason the bitter harvest of the Hundred Flowers came as such a shock, exposing enclaves of opposition that suggested the revolution was unfinished. Those among the leadership most committed to permanent revolution (and least equipped to "retune" to routine economic management), including Mao and many other symbol specialists, resisted its abandonment. Thus, in the Great Leap Forward, mission was redefined to include economic hypergrowth. Whereas heretofore charisma had remained uneasily corporate in its subjective dimension, the disaster of the Leap marked a shift to personalized charisma, as Mao became semidetached from a bureaucratic staff that he felt had let him down. The shift presaged the polarization between charismatic leadership and bureaucracy that was to culminate in the Cultural Revolution.

A second important consequence is that in the post-Leap redivision of functions, those who assumed responsibility for organizational maintenance tacitly abandoned the mission for the time being, becoming completely absorbed in salvaging the economy. They thereby forfeited responsibility for reformulating the mission to Mao alone, who had meanwhile essentially relinquished operational control of the domestic policy process. This foreboded a tendency toward idealization in the definition of mission. As the Leap lost credibility in the wake of the "three bad years" and no new mission made its debut, there was also a

---

64. Helmut Martin, *Cult and Canon*, p. 26. In toto, about 2 billion copies would ultimately be published.

tendency to shift from a mission-based charisma to one based on a deified personality.

MASS MOBILIZATION

Mass mobilization went through three discernible phases during this period. Each phase coincided with a different combination of mobilizational incentives. The first phase was one of emancipatory rhetoric, accompanied by a mixture of coercive, material, and normative incentives based on the expropriation and redistribution of property. The second phase, the Great Leap Forward, was one of utopian rhetoric and primarily normative incentives (as things turned out) appealing to both material and ideal interests. The third period, that of recovery from the Leap, was one of rectificatory rhetoric and primarily coercive and normative incentives.

The mass constituency upon which the Party based its efforts to maintain revolutionary momentum during the first decade appears to have consisted of those classes who benefited least under the ancien régime and stood most to gain from the revolution: the poor and lower-middle peasants and the industrial working class. Access to this constituency of course improved immensely after elimination of the Kuomintang from the scene, as peasant associations and trade unions were organized on a national scale, specialized publications were inaugurated, and work teams were sent down to assist local Party committees, often still in a rudimentary stage of consolidation, in the mobilization of the masses. Organizational servicing of various social needs coincided with a direct material payoff in the form of a redistribution of property, a political resource that was "free," having been expropriated from the class enemy. In each successive stage in the subsequent socialist transformation this happy coincidence of the class interest of the proletariat in material self-enhancement and the interest of the communist vanguard in the revolution per se was conscientiously maintained. Agrarian reform resulted in a substantial increase in the number of rich peasants, as we have seen, and cooperativization resulted in higher incomes for members than for the peasants outside it.[65] As Vivienne Shue puts it:

> Chinese peasants were not expected to exhibit self-sacrificing altruism in their embrace of socialism. Nor were they expected to shed very quickly their age-old preoccupations and beliefs in favor of ideological attachment to Marxism-

65. The APCs reportedly had a profit ranging from 10 to 20 percent higher than the individual enterprises outside them. See Isabel Crook and David Crook, *The First Years of the Yangyi Commune* (London: Routledge & Kegan Paul, 1966); also see Yan Ling, "The Necessity," pp. 94–123.

Leninism. They were, on the contrary, expected to be willing to cooperate with social and economic change insofar, and only insofar, as they were convinced that change might benefit themselves. Thus ... the policies of socialist transformation, designed at the center to attract the peasantry, were virtually without exception intended to appeal to the perceived self-interest of the majority of the villagers.... The argument that peasants might be moralized and inspired into socialism would simply have been howled down during those years.[66]

The notion that the emancipation of the proletariat implied the emancipation of all mankind was construed to mean that the latter would follow from the former, not vice versa, and it was likewise assumed that the transformation of the social superstructure would inevitably (and more or less automatically) follow transformation of the economic base. The fact that very rapid growth rates were maintained throughout the period of transformation facilitated the encouraging belief that personal self-interest, class interest, and the revolutionary transformation of society were compatible and even mutually reinforcing.

Whereas the most successful mass movements were those designed to promote policies whose implementation produced automatic side-payments for participants, a congeries of campaigns of every sort was launched during these early years, from "aid-Korea oppose-America" to encephalitis control. The self-disciplinary thrust of many of these movements, plus the very profusion of them, tended to abate the enthusiasm of the masses. "Following Liberation, we launched too many movements, one a year without letup," recollects Liao Gailong. "The earlier movements might have been all right. But by that time, the people wanted to live and work happily and peacefully, they did not want commotion any more."[67]

During the Great Leap Forward, the rhetoric shifted from redistributive or rectificatory emphases to a utopian developmentalism that foresaw rapid simultaneous increases in production that would benefit everyone more or less equally. Once again, material and normative incentives were meant to jibe: communes would be formed, large-scale agricultural and industrial projects would be built through pooled efforts, communism was in the offing; production would be so dramatically increased that all could eat well, and possibly gratis.[68] A rise in living standards was originally intended to be deferred, but so astounding were the early reports of production increases, so imminent did the promised utopia appear, that many availed themselves of the opportunities offered by communal mess halls, the free supply system, and so forth to enhance

66. Shue, *Peasant China*, pp. 326–27.
67. Liao Gailong, "Historical Experiences," part 2, p. 90.
68. MacFarquhar, *Origins*, 2, p. 85

their living standards forthwith, to "eat till the belly is tight." In retrospect this may have been prudent, for when the depression struck, the Chinese masses went hungry.

During and after the Leap, Mao made a theoretical innovation in the conceptualization of material incentives that was to prove consequential. During the early phase of the Leap he introduced a "romanticization of backwardness"[69] in a populist paean to the masses' untapped potential: "The outstanding thing about China's 600 million people is that they are 'poor and blank.' . . . On a blank sheet of paper free from any mark, the freshest and most beautiful characters can be written."[70] But this was still placed on a timetable that foresaw the *overcoming* of poverty and ignorance: "Three years of struggle, a thousand years of communist happiness."[71] Later, as the full magnitude of the disaster became evident, Mao moved toward a romanticization of poverty that seemed to discount or even reprove the prospect of its alleviation. Manuscripts he wrote in 1960 contain the following passages:

> Lenin said: "The more backward the country, the more difficult its transition from capitalism to socialism." Now it seems that this way of speaking is incorrect. As a matter of fact, the more backward the economy, the easier, not the more difficult, the transition from capitalism to socialism.[72]

> Hard bitter struggle, expanding reproduction, the future prospects of communism—these are what have to be emphasized, not individual material interest. The goal to lead toward is not "one house, one country house, one automobile, one piano, one television." This is the road of serving the self, not the society.[73]

This critique of consumerism—a new theme in Mao's thinking, which seems to have made its first appearance at Lushan in his defense of the Leap (as recently as the first session of the Eighth Party Congress he had endorsed an increase in material incentives)—was to become increasingly prominent in the next few years. This significant rhetorical shift may be attributed to two factors: the incipient Sino-Soviet dispute, and the disappointing outcome of the Great Leap.

69. The phrase is Maurice Meisner's. See *Marxism, Maoism and Utopianism* (Madison: University of Wisconsin Press, 1982), p. 102.
70. Mao, "Where Do Correct Ideas Come From?" *Selected Readings from the Works of Mao Tse-tung* (Peking: Foreign Languages Press, 1971), pp. 502–4. (Hereinafter *Readings.*)
71. It was at the Nanning Conference that Mao first seized upon the idea of a three-year period of all-out endeavor, which was then widely popularized. MacFarquhar, *Origins, 2,* p. 25; also see Meisner, *Marxism,* p. 190
72. Mao, "Reading Notes on the Soviet Union's 'Political Economy,'" in *Wansui* (1969), pp. 333–34.
73. Mao, *A Critique of Soviet Economics* (New York: Monthly Review Press, 1977), p. 112.

Khrushchev's secret speech had emancipated the Chinese as well as the Russians from the Stalinist model while at the same time undermining the ideological legitimacy of the communist enterprise, and both in Beijing and in Moscow there was a revival of utopian thinking in response to this combined ideological opportunity and crisis. Mao preempted Khrushchev in launching the Great Leap, and Khrushchev responded critically to this upstart's presumption, derogating the Leap as an illegitimate shortcut to a more advanced historical stage by a "pants-less" society lacking the material conditions needed to obviate competition for scarce goods. "If we stated that we were introducing communism at a time when the cup was not yet full, it would not be possible to drink from it according to need."[74] The economic failure of the Leap then added insult to Mao's injury by withholding any foreseeable Chinese realization of these material prerequisites. It must have been galling for Mao to hear his nemesis, Khrushchev, define communism in terms of collectivized affluence (as in the Party Program of the Twenty-Second CPSU Congress, in October 1961), at a time when he had conclusively demonstrated his own incompetence at achieving such grandiose objectives. Thus in the subsequent intra-bloc polemic, rising living standards, or indeed almost any expression of interest in material incentives, became identified with the "capitalist road." Mao seems to have decided that if material prosperity could not be achieved in accord with correct ideological principles, it should be eschewed; materialism was crass and decadent anyhow. As he jeered in his 1965 conversation with André Malraux: "You remember Kosygin at the Twenty-Third Congress: 'Communism means the raising of living standards.' Of course! And swimming is a way of putting on a pair of trunks!"[75]

The implication of this shift to a pejorative conceptualization of material interests was to impute a dichotomous, either/or relationship between poverty and wealth in place of the continuum that had previously obtained: material prosperity in effect became illegitimate. This implication may represent a distortion of Mao's position, which may not have been critical of mass consumerism per se but only of its unequal attainment; yet this is almost certainly how Mao's Thought in its popularized version was construed. In terms of this New Asceticism it became impossible to imagine how virtue and material prosperity could coincide. One may confidently assume that China's broad masses did not suddenly abandon all hope of material self-betterment in the light of Mao's rhetorical shift,

74. *Pravda* and *Izvestia*, October 19, 1961, trans. in *Current Digest of the Soviet Press*, vol. 13, no. 44, p. 9; as quoted in Jerome Gilison, *The Soviet Image of Utopia* (Baltimore: Johns Hopkins University Press, 1975), pp. 6–7.

75. André Malraux, *Anti-Memoirs*, trans. Terence Kilmartin (New York: Holt, Rinehart & Winston, 1968), pp. 369–70.

but the moral opprobrium now attached thereto made it more difficult to arrange for rational distribution of material incentives, and the relationship between "haves" and "have-nots" became characterized by subterfuge, envy, and resentment, protected by attenuated moral justification.

Mass mobilization was revived after the "three bad years" by Mao's 1962 announcement that "During the whole socialist stage there still exist classes and class struggle, and this class struggle is a protracted, complex, sometimes even violent affair." [76] The centerpiece of mobilizational efforts was the Socialist Education movement or "Four Cleans." [77] This may be seen as a preliminary effort in the Chinese countryside to realize the goals of what would subsequently emerge as the Cultural Revolution, working, however, through regular bureaucratic channels. Rectification differed from the campaigns of the 1950s in following an engineering rather than a storming format, consisting of elaborate organization from the top down, including detachment of work teams for visits ranging from a few weeks to over half a year, inspection tours by higher cadres, and staggered long-term scheduling. The attempt seems to have been extremely frustrating for Mao, its chief sponsor, who collaborated first with one set of first-front colleagues, then with another set, resulting in the production of a parade of campaign documents deemed either too harsh, too lenient, or beside the point. The difficult economic straits and the punitive function of the campaign (this time, however, focused on cadres, not on non-Party elites such as bourgeoisie or intellectuals, as in the 1950s) precluded the allocation of material incentives, and normative incentives lacked credibility amid the overall disintegration of morale following the Leap and the frequently shifting campaign objectives.

CONCLUSION

Revolution has been defined as smashing the structure of authority, an action assuming charismatic leadership, mass mobilization, and structural vulnerability. The dynamic elements of this functional triad, charismatic leadership and mass mobilization, correlated fully only during the initial phase of the period in question. The charismatic mission was Herculean but at the same time widely deemed desperately necessary after a prolonged period of national chaos broken only by hopes quickly dashed. The Communist leadership's cumulatively established reputation for in-

76. Mao, "Talk at an Enlarged Central Work Conference" (January 30, 1962), as translated in Stuart Schram, ed., Chairman Mao Talks to the People, p. 168.
77. Richard Baum and Frederick Teiwes, Ssu-ch'ing: The Socialist Education Movement of 1962–66 (Center for Chinese Studies, Research Monograph no. 2, Berkeley, 1968); and Richard Baum, Prelude to Revolution: Mao, the Party, and the Peasant Question, 1962–66 (New York: Columbia University Press, 1975).

fallibility emerged from the wars unbesmirched by any serious blunders. Mass mobilization was inspired by an emancipatory rhetoric that coincided with the redistribution of material benefits, including land for the peasants, jobs and pay for urban workers, offices for (politically reliable) members of the middle class/social elite, and greater personal independence for women and children within the family organization—all of which was justified in terms of the inexorable movement of history toward greater material abundance and social justice.

This overall picture held true only briefly during the early 1950s. Elite consensus began to unravel as soon as the leadership encountered divisive issues in the course of socialization of the means of production, though early divisions seem to have been resolved according to intra-Party norms.[78] Although equivocal results followed some policy decisions, no mortal errors were committed (by the criteria then deemed appropriate), and the Party's core constituency continued to benefit from CPC policies. Notwithstanding the dismaying harvest of the Hundred Flowers, the triumphant progress of the revolution did not really falter until the Great Leap Forward aborted. The Great Leap represented the first attempt following basic conclusion of socialization of the means of production to adopt a new mission for the continuing revolution, that of rapid economic progress. Here the underlying lack of elite consensus combined with the cumulatively amassed personal prestige of Mao Zedong among the masses to short-circuit regular intra-elite and elite-mass communication channels, enabling the Chairman to launch initiatives preempting the approval of collective leadership organs by assembling an ad hoc constituency. This short-circuited policy-making style resulted in a return to storm tactics, abandoning the engineering approach over which Mao felt both he and the masses had lost direction. From the point of view of Mao's colleagues, this was a classic case of power corrupting, giving rise to a Frankenstein's monster they could no longer control. From Mao's perspective, the engineering approach, whose objective necessity in enemy-occupied or "White" areas he had keenly appreciated, brought to the fore in a peacetime context a new type of cadre, whose narrow professional/bureaucratic interests caused one to lose sight of the revolutionary mission.

In the ensuing depression and recovery periods, Mao retreated to the ideological realm in his quest for a new mission for charismatic leadership, whereas most of his colleagues remained on the first "front" trying simply to cope with all the problems of reviving the economy. The staff tacitly abandoned the salvationary mission while attempting to salvage recovery, and although Mao addressed himself to the need for a

78. Frederick Teiwes, *Politics and Purges in China.*

reformulation, most of his energy in fact went into rationalizing its failure and stifling its critics. To the Party vanguard, tenacious public reiteration of the old rhetoric amid various ideologically inconsistent policy adjustments appeared the better part of valor. The infallibility principle was reasserted in exaggerated and simplified terms—if from a defensive position, in the face of ill-disguised ridicule from intellectual quarters—but it was now personalized, as the Party came to absorb the blame for the Leap. The public image of elite consensus was maintained with some difficulty, veiling a growing ideological cleavage that now coincided with an ongoing division of labor.

THREE

Structure
and Its Critique

Revolution, even continuing revolution, is "transitive," implying an object to be overthrown. This object is the structure of authority, which has allegedly forfeited its legitimacy due to some besetting flaw, of which the revolutionary leadership is able to take polemical advantage. While mobilizing the masses against this flawed structure, the revolutionary leadership launches construction of a new structure that will remedy the deficiencies of the old. It soon becomes clear, however, that there is an inherent contradiction between the idea of continuing revolution and any structure at all.

The first part of this chapter examines the evolution of the "bad" and "good" structures of authority during the 1949–66 period. The second half consists of an expostion of the *critique* of the two structures that consecutively arose in response. The overall trend in this period was for the old structure to lose potency as it came under incessant attack, allowing popular faith to be transferred to the new structure introduced in its place. The ironic corollary of this trend was that as the new structure in turn began to lose credibility as a result of the policy errors of the late 1950s, the old structure could no longer function as a plausible scapegoat. Moreover, as the new structure consolidated itself, its own flaws became salient, stimulating mass grievances and raising the problem for the leadership of what their stance should be toward a second revolution, or "counterrevolution." The immediate response, as witnessed in the case of the Hundred Flowers, was repression. At least for Mao, the implications of such a stance were unacceptable, and he undertook a basic rethinking of the project of continuing revolution that was ultimately to result in the launching of the Cultural Revolution.

STRUCTURES

The structure of authority as it existed in China at the time of Liberation was fragmented and inchoate, consisting of a mélange of residual political structures, cultural dispositions, and incompletely reconstructed KMT institutions. The Chinese never really had an effective centralized national state from the Xinhai Revolution in 1911 to the Communist victory in 1949, and society tended to dissolve like a "sheet of loose sand." Whatever coherence remained was imparted by decentralized local authority structures, primarily by the kinship network and by property rights, as suggested in chapter 2. The tenure of the Nationalist regime was too brief and tempestuous for it ever to bring these local structures under its sway, though it did attempt to negotiate mutually beneficial alliances with local elites.

The Residual Structure

The structure of authority against which the revolution had been successfully launched before 1949 was progressively redefined following the flight of the Nationalist regime to Taiwan. The opposition structure was first conceived to include political opponents who posed a credible threat to the new regime, then it was seen more abstractly in terms of a bourgeois-landlord social class, and finally in terms of residual elements of that class (variously defined). The fact that this progressive redefinition of the opposition coincided with successful efforts to incorporate opponents within the community implied that conflict gradually lost its in-group/out-group clarity and became internecine. It also entailed an increasingly intensive search for opponents.

The regime's first priority was to eliminate its "diehard" opponents. A campaign for the Suppression of Counterrevolutionaries (*zhengfan*) was launched in 1950 and, in close connection with agrarian reform, lasted through most of 1951; it resulted in the execution of seven hundred thousand to eight hundred thousand counterrevolutionaries, "not counting those who were imprisoned or put under control," which "should aggregate several millions." The Three-Anti and Five-Anti movements (December 1951–December 1952) also placed the urban bourgeoisie under some constraint, though they were not yet deprived of their property and not usually executed (about five hundred were executed, thirty-four thousand imprisoned, and two thousand committed suicide). A second campaign against counterrevolutionaries, the Sufan (*suqing ancang fangeming*), was set in motion in mid-1955 as a sequel to the campaign to criticize Hu Feng.[1] The chief difference between the Zhengfan and the Sufan campaigns is that the former was conducted in rural areas, small towns, and city slums against those who had served in KMT militia, police, or other "public servants" (*qian gongjiao renyuan*), whereas the

1. Liao Gailong, "Historical Experiences," part 1, pp. 70–73; John Gardner, "The *Wu-fan* Campaign in Shanghai: A Study in the Consolidation of Urban Control," in A. Doak Barnett, ed., *Chinese Communist Politics in Action* (Seattle: University of Washington Press, 1969), pp. 477–593.

latter was mainly directed against non-Communist intellectuals. In the course of Sufan, eighty-one thousand intellectuals were "unmasked and punished," and more than three hundred thousand lost their civil rights because of "political unreliability."[2]

The selection of targets for exemplary criticism in the campaigns involved a more or less elaborate preliminary investigative procedure to ensure that only well-qualified culprits were selected. Political pressures were imposed to intensify the search, particularly during the early phase of the campaigns: beginning in the early 1950s the Party began to set fixed quotas for investigation. By September 1955, 2.2 million people were reported to have been investigated, and one hundred ten thousand "counterrevolutionaries" exposed. In Mao's view about fifty thousand major suspects were still at large, however, and 11 to 12 million people were yet to be investigated when the movement ended.[3] Target selection in response to administrative quotas resulted in a certain ritualization of the process in some cases, as the same targets were trotted out repeatedly at the commencement of the various campaigns and forced to submit self-criticisms.[4]

The "principal social contradiction" during this period was defined as the "contradiction between the working class and the broad masses of the people on the one side and the remnant forces of the big bourgeoisie and the landlord class on the other side."[5] Application of the terminology of class to Chinese social structure entailed rather complex distinctions and subsumptions, which have been competently analyzed elsewhere.[6] Its application accompanied the successive campaigns to socialize the means of production launched in the early 1950s, resulting in the sorting of the Chinese populace (particularly the rural population—in the cities the Party was somewhat less thorough) into more than sixty class designations. This classification, based on a combination of "class status" (based on occupation during the three years prior to 1949) and "family back-

2. *RR*, March 23 and June 18, 1957; as cited in Domes, *Government*, pp. 48, 276.
3. See Mao's speech at the Enlarged Sixth Plenum of the Seventh CC, in *Wansui* (1969), pp. 12–25; an expurgated version may be found in *SW*, vol. 5: 211–35.
4. For example, cf. Lai Ying, *The Thirty-sixth Way: A Personal Account of Imprisonment and Escape from Red China*, trans. Edward Bahr and Sidney Liu (New York: Doubleday, 1969); also the experiences of Liang Heng's parents in Liang and Shapiro, *Son of the Revolution* (New York: Alfred A. Knopf, 1983); and the story of "Old Li" in Richard Bernstein, *From the Center of the Earth: The Search for the Truth about China* (Boston: Little, Brown, 1982), pp. 243–51.
5. At that time, the remnant forces of the KMT on the mainland amounted to more than a million, and the counterrevolutionaries, including Kuomintang spies, and the "historical counterrevolutionaries," totaled several millions. Liao Gailong, "Historical Experiences," part 1, p. 73.
6. See Richard C. Kraus, *Class Conflict in Chinese Socialism* (New York: Columbia University Press, 1981).

ground" (based on the class status of one's parents and grandparents), was usually entered into each person's confidential personnel file (*dang'an*) and kept in the local unit office. As the assumptions underlying this classification became problematic upon "basic completion" of socialization of the means of production at the end of 1956, the files began to take on a life of their own.

The waging of class struggle was systematically linked with political struggle against targets selected to symbolize opposition to specific regime policies. Sometimes a national model would be chosen, and various localities would in turn discover their own exemplars, leading to the exposure of a "Gao Gang of Sichuan," a "Hu Feng of Guangdong," and so forth. This search-and-destroy operation was so effective at inhibiting visible deviation that it operated at a diminishing rate of return, as compliance made it increasingly difficult to locate valid targets. Reclassification of penitent class enemies after a stipulated probationary period (e.g., three years for a rich peasant, five for a landlord) seems to have resulted in a perceptible attrition over time of the target group, colloquially referred to as the "four-category elements" (landlords, rich peasants, counterrevolutionaries, and bad elements).[7]

In the wake of the Great Leap debacle, the regime began to use various mnemonic devices to evoke an opposition no longer physically present. One example is the "recall bitterness meal" (*yi ku fan*), in which a basic unit (production brigade, school class, infantry platoon) would prepare a meal of the humble fare on which they had been forced to subsist before Liberation in order to remind themselves of how much their situation had improved. Richard Madsen describes such tableaux with considerable empathy:

> These recitations of past bitterness would be clothed with solemn gestures to make them profoundly moving events. The sessions would be held at night, with almost all lights in the meeting hall extinguished to evoke the darkness of the past. Peasants who had suffered the most terrible personal degradations would ascend the stage to tell about their past. They would usually weep as they told their stories and sometimes they could not even finish their accounts.

7. The data of the 1953 election indicate that the total number of those who had lost political rights due to bad class status amounted to 8.6 million, or 2.68 percent, of the 320 million total registered voters. The 1956 election data reveal that only 1.8 million citizens—0.6 percent of the registered voters—were denied the right to vote. If this figure is reliable, by 1956 a large number of former "class enemies" had managed to have their hats removed. *Gongren Ribao*, January 19, 1957; *RR*, September 26, 1956, and September 29, 1957; *Zhengfa Yanjiu*, 1957, pp. 6, 27–30; as cited in Richard Kraus, "Class Conflict and the Vocabulary of Social Analysis in China," *CQ*, no. 69 (March 1977): 54–74. See also Hong Yung Lee, "Changing Patterns of Political Participation in China: A Historical Perspective," unpublished paper presented at Workshop on Studies in Policy Implementation in the Post-Mao Era, Columbus, Ohio, June 20–24, 1983.

From the darkness people in the audience would punctuate the speaker's accounts of bitterness with shouted slogans: "Down with the old society! Down with the Kuomintang reactionaries! Down with the landlord class! Long live Chairman Mao!" In the small discussion groups, people would pour out their grief over the bitterness of the past, and express their deep-felt sorrow for their ingratitude to Chairman Mao.... At the end of the training sessions a special meal to remember the bitterness of the past would be held. The meal would consist of the bitter wild herbs which poor peasants often ate in the old days when they could not afford better food. Some of the old people actually wept as they ate the bitter food.[8]

As in the case of the salvationary mission, in its continuing assault upon the structure of feudal-capitalist authority the revolutionary leadership seems to have fallen victim to its own success. The prerevolutionary class structure dwindled upon being deprived of its economic base, and the most courageously forthright dissidents to the Party's policy initiatives (such as Liang Shuming or Hu Feng) were eliminated within the first decade. These developments implied that whereas the leadership had previously been preoccupied with the very real power of this structure of counterrevolution, henceforth they would have to devote increasing attention to shoring up the credibility of its existence. Meanwhile, the structure of *socialist* authority was becoming consolidated, and while it began with a generous endowment of popular legitimacy, this fund was soon depleted not only by the policy errors already alluded to but by its own inherent structural flaws.

Emergent Structure

In the modern Western constitutional democracy or *Rechtsstaat*, the structure of authority is "rational-legal"; that is, the citizenry confers obedience not to charismatic leaders but to a codified set of laws, which may be logically derived from a more general, basic law known as the Constitution. Modern (i.e., post-imperial) China has never had an effectively codified legal code, and in partial consequence the constitutions so hopefully drafted have remained politically spurious—well-intentioned statements of principles without practical effect.

There was some desire to rectify this situation after Liberation. After the CPPCC had been convened, it undertook the development of a nationwide legal system, promulgating the Land Reform Law and Marriage Law and a number of other laws. The first session of the NPC in September 1954 not only approved the PRC Constitution, it also passed regulations governing arrests and detentions and other rules related

<hr />

8. Richard P. Madsen, *Morality and Power in a Chinese Village* (Berkeley: University of California Press, 1984), pp. 135–36.

to the first FYP.[9] In the decade following promulgation of the Constitution more than eleven hundred laws and decrees were enacted to add to those statutes that had provided a loose framework for the administration of justice in the 1949–56 consolidation period.[10]

Although these steps perhaps betokened a sincere commitment to the rule of law, legality was to make less headway in China than in any other state socialist system. The fact that upon assuming power the CPC abolished "all laws, decrees, and judicial systems" previously established is perhaps understandable given its cosmological conception of its mission, but doing so created a legal vacuum. Nor was any general codification of socialist law ever completed, although a number of beginnings were made. As a result, there was no possibility of appeal to various laws, customs, or traditions aginst the policies of the CPC or the will of its local functionaries. Although a number of laws were passed, their vague terminology left ample room for interpretation according to the whim of local Party leaders. Moreover, the regulations establishing the courts stipulated that "Where no [legal] provisions have been made, the policy of the Chinese People's Government shall be adhered to."[11] Thus the People's Courts in practice became responsible for enforcing policies, directives, or regulations more often than laws, and these were commonly marked "provisional," sometimes even "for internal use only" (*neibu*), thereby restricting access to cadres.[12] From 1966 to 1976 the legislative function fell into desuetude (with no laws passed), and directives were issued in the name of a combination of central organs (in fact often simply by Mao himself).

The precise reasons for the stultification of "socialist legality" in China are too complex to detain us here. Continuing the revolution is in any case incompatible with commitment to a set of fixed principles or institutionalized procedures, for the exigencies of the movement are in constant flux. This is not necessarily to say that we are dealing with a regime of lawless terrorism or naked coercion (though these were also at hand). In contrast to the Soviet Union during the Stalin era, the CPC regime relied less on its secret police network than on its manipulation of social organization. Thus the structure of authority in the PRC came to

9. Zhang Youyu, "Revolution and the Legal System: Written in Commemoration of the Sixtieth Anniversary of the Founding of the Chinese Communist Party," *Minzhu yu Fazhi*, no. 7 (July 25, 1981): 5–9.

10. John Gardner, *Chinese Politics and the Succession to Mao* (New York: Holmes & Meier, 1982), pp. 158–59.

11. A. Doak Barnett, *Communist China: The Early Years, 1949–55* (New York: Frederick A. Praeger, 1964), pp. 32, 47, 50–51.

12. Steven Mosher, *Broken Earth: The Rural Chinese* (New York: The Free Press, 1983), pp. 59–67.

consist not of law, not even of an hierarchical apparatus of coercion, but of the compartmentalization of society into *consensually responsive groups*.

First a word about the generation of this consensus, to be followed by a discussion of the structure of the groups. The content of the consensus was defined not by law but by Marxist-Leninist ideology. Yet the precise content of that ideology could not be determined by referring to the canon of sacred texts any more than the correct interpretation of Christianity can be determined by referring to the New Testament. The meaning of the classics remained subject to authoritative construal by the center, and inasmuch as the gates of revelation had not yet closed, from time to time the center could add to the canon by compiling selections from its ongoing stream of ideological commentaries and ideologically relevant policy directives. Thus a "rolling" consensus was generated to follow a sinuously undulating ideological "line" that continually redefined itself via the emission of doctrinal emendations, slogans, and polemics.

It has long been assumed by students of "totalitarianism" that its characteristic emphasis on mobilization entailed a corresponding "atomization" of social structure. In the vivid words of Hannah Arendt:

> The fall of protecting class walls transformed the slumbering majorities behind all parties into one great unorganized, structureless mass of furious individuals who had nothing in common except their vague apprehension that the hopes of party members were doomed, that, consequently, the most respected, articulate and representative members of the community were fools. . . . The chief characteristic of the mass man is not brutality and backwardness, but his isolation and lack of normal social relationships.[13]

Although Arendt was addressing herself not to totalitarian society but to the social breakdown that spawns it, subsequent theorists such as Friedrich and Brzezinski not unnaturally inferred an interest of the new leadership in maintaining such atomization indefinitely: "every human being should, for best effect, have to face the monolith of totalitarian rule as an isolated 'atom.'"[14] This atomization implies an absence of intermediary voluntary associations, kinship networks, or other organized groupings that might impede elite access to a mobilizable mass.[15]

The Chinese experience, however, belies this theoretical prediction. It is true that pre-Liberation China suffered social disintegration, but due

13. Hannah Arendt, *The Origins of Totalitarianism* (New York: Harcourt Brace Jovanovich, 1973 ed.), pp. 308, also 315, 317, 323, *et passim*.
14. Carl J. Friedrich and Zbigniew K. Brzezinski, *Totalitarian Dictatorship and Autocracy* (Cambridge, Mass.: Harvard University Press, 1965), p. 279.
15. William Kornhauser, *The Politics of Mass Society* (New York: The Free Press, 1959), p. 33.

to the underlying strength of the family and kinship network, coherence seems to have been sustained at the primary group level, except perhaps in the coastal cities—not prominent after 1927 in the Communist ecology of success.[16] And in the post-Liberation period, although certain reforms (such as Land Reform or the Marriage Law) had atomizing effects, the regime soon superseded the former and eased enforcement of the latter. After 1956, China began to crystallize into a social structure of much greater rigidity than that characterizing prerevolutionary Chinese society or that characterizing other state socialist societies—greater, indeed, than any society since medieval Europe.[17] In a country that had previously witnessed vast population migrations there emerged a social structure honeycombed with walls—barriers to both vertical and horizontal mobility or communication. These barriers coincided with the boundaries of the "basic unit" (*jiceng danwei*), the basic building block of the social structure. The Chinese aptly refer to these barriers as "frames" (*kuangkuang*).

Why were these frames erected—particularly given the regime's concern with permanent mobilization? The leadership probably saw no contradiction: whereas ideological content might change with the vicissitudes of the historical dialectic, the organizational form could remain fixed. For the basic units were after all not autonomous, but corporately integrated into the centralized administrative network in such a way that they would ensure, not resist, "progressive" change. The leading organization theorists and custodians within the Party (such as Liu Shaoqi) had revolutionary backgrounds in conspiratorial base-building in the White areas, inclining them to emphasize a cellular pattern in which a clear distinction between units was expedient in order to prevent enemy counterintelligence agents from unraveling the entire network upon penetrating one cell. After half a century of social disintegration and national weakness, it also must have seemed appropriate to rebuild a sense of community, not based on the old conservative building blocks of the extended family, but on new ones in which socialist ideals of equality and mutual self-help would be implemented. Such an organizationally enforced solidarity offered the potential for "high levels of social solidarity and cooperation, crime control and social order, as well as a rapid re-

---

16. See Roy Hofheinz, Jr., "The Ecology of Chinese Communist Success: Rural Influence Patterns, 1923–1945," in A. Doak Barnett, ed., *Chinese Communist Politics in Action* (Seattle: University of Washington Press, 1969), pp. 3–78.

17. In the Soviet Union, for example, there is only a rule against migration into the few largest cities (which is not that effectively enforced), not prohibitions affecting the entire urban hierarchy. Martin King Whyte and William L. Parish, *Urban Life in Contemporary China* (Chicago: University of Chicago Press, 1984), p. 21. See also Philip Short, *The Dragon and the Bear* (New York: Hodder and Stoughton, 1982), pp. 20, 75.

molding of the marriage customs, family patterns, fertility behavior, and other social and intellectual habits of the citizenry."[18]

Of what did the unit consist? This varied: the unit might be a geographical district, such as a village or a city street; it could be an institutional, occupational, or other such group within the district—a factory, shop, school, company, government office, hospital, group of carpenters or butchers or writers or artists, even such catch-all assortments as "urban workers," or "agricultural laborers, poor and lower-middle peasants." In any case, every member of society was categorized into a unit. An individual could (and usually did) fall into several different categories—one based on employment, say, one on residence, a third on membership in a mass organization—but only one of these was likely to be "basic," and this was the unit of employment. Each unit was linked to the center through a pyramidal national structure that included a congress and an executive committee at each administrative-geographical level into which China was divided: district, county, special administrative district, special municipality, province, and autonomous region.

The basic unit became the functional substitute for the extended family, the crucial difference being that it was controlled from the center. It assumed the functions of the clan, educating the children, healing the sick, and paying a pension in old age. If a factory worker retired, his son would have first option to take his place. Like the clan, an incest taboo seemed to obtain—people would select mates within the same city or rural county, but not within the same unit. As in a clan, propitious marriages could enhance the unit. Military officers were known to handpick attractive young female recruits with a view to their marriageability, based on the notion of "reflected glory," a practice that resulted in a rather startling florescence of feminine beauty in military ambiance. Otherwise, "mixed" marriages—between peasant and worker, between peasant and educated youth—were so rare that if a college graduate married a peasant it warranted a celebratory notice in the local paper or even in *People's Daily*.

The basic unit controlled the dispensation of employment, welfare, ration tickets, and housing. So intensively did it regulate every facet of the lives of its members that post-Mao reform advocates referred to "unit ownership" (*danwei suoyouzhi*).[19] Workers were assigned to a unit upon completion of their schooling (usually a few days before graduation) under the presumption that they would remain there for life, and if

18. Ibid., p. 26.

19. The theme of "social bondage" (*shehui shufu*) emerges prominently in recent Chinese fiction. See Xu Xuedong's "Transfer" [*Diaodong*], for example, a long short story relating the difficulties of leaving a unit, or Jiang Xuan's "The Corner Forgotten by Love" (also made into a controversial movie).

they were fortunate their wives would be assigned to the same unit. One usually lived in a unit apartment, and in the more modern units, residences were all located in the same compound as the place of employment, making the unit self-contained. When watches and bicycles were in scarce supply one had to obtain permission from unit cadres to buy a bicycle or watch; when child-bearing became regulated for demographic reasons, "consultation" with unit cadres was required to conceive a child.

Whereas it is true that horizontal mobility was not restricted by a general ban on travel or by an internal passport requirement, as in Eastern Europe, a multistranded web of bureaucratic dependency more than made up for this apparent liberality. To obtain permission to travel outside the unit, a member had to ask unit authorities for a few days' leave from work for some concrete reason. If leave was granted, the traveler then had to obtain special ration coupons permitting purchase of rice or bread outside of the province (ration coupons were valid only in the home province). In order to find lodging at one's destination, the traveler must provide a letter of introduction from the home unit. Perhaps in part due to such bureaucratic constraints, the transportation infrastructure remained underdeveloped, with one of the most rudimentary road systems in the world. Permanent relocation from one part of the country was even more difficult, for in contrast to other state socialist systems there was no labor market in China, and assignment to work units was normally irrevocable. In some cases reassignment could be obtained in order to reunite families in which husband and wife were assigned to geographically remote units, but protracted separations were also common, particularly among intellectuals. This became known as the "cowherd and weaving girl" (niulang zhinü) problem, after the mythical separation of lovers who, through divine intervention, could meet once a year by crossing the river of stars over a magical bridge of flying birds. Some seasonal rural-urban migration was permitted to fill industrial labor shortages when they occurred, but the normatively approved direction of population flow was from urban to rural areas, in contrast to the usual pattern in developing countries, and usually contrary to the wishes of the participants.[20]

One of the reasons frequently given for the emphasis on boundaries and unit integrity was the unit's security function. Thus, every block, factory, or compound erected high walls around itself (sometimes with

20. See Ross Munro's series, "The Real China," Toronto Globe and Mail, October 8, 10, 11, 12, and 13, 1977. Also see Gail Henderson, "Danwei: The Chinese Work Unit" (Ph.D. diss., University of Michigan, 1982), since published as Gail Henderson and Myron S. Cohen, The Chinese Hospital: A Socialist Work Unit (New Haven: Yale University Press, 1984); and Yuichi Funabashi, Neibu: One Report on China (Tokyo: Asahi Shimbun, Pub., 1982).

broken glass on top), curfew hours were instituted, armed guards posted, and so forth.[21] Most Chinese carried an assortment of keys for various locks and padlocks; a bicycle, for example, was never left unlocked, even inside a unit. Ground floor windows, whether in city or countryside, usually had iron bars. This emphasis on security was perhaps conducive to unit solidarity, but it also fostered an attitude of indifference toward occurrences outside the unit, including national or international politics. Westerners acquainted with the low Chinese crime statistics found it difficult to reconcile the concern with security with any realistic threat. As a young British professional noted in his diary during a two-year teaching sojourn in Nanjing:

> They genuinely are often quite ignorant about commonplace things in their own society outside their immediate experience. If one asks one's teachers about a fairly routine and mundane point about the administration, one generally gets a collection of different and vague replies. This means that amazing barriers must be surmounted when inter-unit communication is necessary. What would seem to be solvable by a simple phone call elsewhere requires lots of scratching of heads, top-level conferences, and "careful consideration." A more serious offshoot of this is the great wastage involved in the overduplication of jobs, ... Waste in the millions of useless walls around housing estates, offices, everything. Not to keep out intruders, as it often ends up unfinished, but to assert the identity of a unit.[22]

As suggested in this diary entry, the emphasis on unit self-containment informed the handling of information as well: only ideologically "correct" generalities were freely disseminated outside and among units, whereas more specific information was typically treated as "intelligence" and restricted to those authorized to receive it. The resulting information system was shaped like a star rather than a wheel, a vertically organized system lacking in lateral integration. Western travelers were struck by the paucity of plaques or signs to identify government buildings, not because their identity was confidential, but because information just did not circulate laterally. Much of what in the West is publicly available information, regularly shared with citizen and foreigner alike, was classified as restricted material (*neibu*). Telephone books, maps, newspapers, and academic articles or books having no apparent connection with national security were regularly classified *neibu*.[23] Telephone conversations were

21. Ross Munro, October 10, pp. 1, 23.
22. From the China diaries of a young British professional and former member of the Sino-British People's Friendship Association who taught English in Nanjing under the terms of the exchange from January 1975 to February 1977, and graciously permitted me to peruse and to quote from them. (Hereinafter "Diaries.")
23. Peter Van Ness, "Black, White and Grey in China Research," *Far Eastern Economic Review* (hereinafter *FEER*) 123, no. 6 (February 9, 1984): 30–31.

widely suspected to be at least selectively tapped, and there must have been a fairly elaborate recording system in the offices and residences of central leaders, to judge from the copious use of verbatim quotations when they later fell victim to criticism. Public security inspected the mail flowing inside and outside the country with some thoroughness; domestic mail was probably monitored less systematically, though the provision in the 1982 State Constitution restricting such activity to public security forces gives rise to the suspicion that domestic mails must have come under the surveillance of the unit leadership.

But the most pervasive and meaningful form of unit control over information was the file (*dang'an*) system: in a sealed envelope in the personnel section of every unit there was a confidential dossier for every employee, containing not only the normal elements of a biography but any confessions or self-criticisms or political charges made by informers in the past and the Party's summary evaluation of the individual, including a genealogy of the person's class background for the past three generations. The individual had no access to the file; only authorized cadres knew its contents.[24] The reasons for this cult of secrecy can only be surmised, but it is worth bearing in mind that the CPC was born in a threatening milieu in which secrecy was conducive to survival, and that the engineering approach in particular was perfected in enemy-occupied areas.

Naturally, the ambit of the public sector, a realm that in the West mediates between political authority and individual (or family) privacy,[25] was constrained by such considerations. Library borrowing was hedged by numerous discouraging restrictions: a person asking for a particular book must bring a letter certifying his (or her) need for it.[26] At most university libraries, foreign language periodicals, dictionaries, and encyclopedias were kept in reference rooms reserved for teachers and graduate students, access again being contingent upon possessing a certificate proving that one's vocation required it.[27] There was no official prepublication censorship, as in the Soviet Union, but authors (and sometimes editors) were responsible for their publications and liable to purge or public criticism if their selections were deemed politically unsuitable; books might also be withdrawn from circulation at the slightest change in official tastes. Some newspapers (e.g., *China Daily*, *Peking Review*) were designated for

24. Ross Munro, October 10, pp. 2–3; October 8, pp. 1–2.
25. See Jürgen Habermas, *Strukturwandlung der Öffentlichkeit: Untersuchungen zu einer Kategorie der bürgerlichen Gesellschaft* (Neuwied: Hermann Luchterhand Verlag, 1962).
26. Jay Mathews and Linda Mathews, *One Billion: A China Chronicle* (New York: Random House, 1983), p. 291.
27. Fox Butterfield, *China: Alive in the Bitter Sea* (New York: Times Books, Quadrangle Publications, 1982), pp. 360–94.

international circulation, some (e.g., *People' Daily, Red Flag*) for national and international circulation, some (e.g., *People's Liberation Army Daily,* most local newspapers) restricted to national circulation, some (e.g., *Cankao Xiaoxi*) restricted to circulation among officials, some (e.g., *Cankao Ziliao*) restricted to circulation among *high* officials. The distribution of information within the bureaucracy was similarly multitiered, and the power of a given official might be gauged by "political access" to the document stream within the hierarchy[28]—thus one of Zhang Chunqiao's "crimes," for example, would be to give his wife (a lower-ranking cadre) access to higher-level documents.

The "neo-feudal" horizontal segmentation of society by unit frames and the secretion or vertical channeling of information (and free flow of propaganda) gave rise to the impression that there were "two worlds." As every member of a unit learned, there was "a distinction between inner and outer" (*nei wai you bie*), meaning that dirty linen should not be washed in public. Language itself became bifurcated: the heroic public language was used to satisfy ever more probing demands for evidence of thought reform, whereas the private language preserved the traditional norms that keep friendship and kinship ties alive. The two discourses were kept apart as a result of conflicting social demands, but each could be used in its appropriate context.[29] Whereas this disjunction between public and private may to some degree echo traditional patterns of communication and association, the impression of my informants is that under the CPC it became noticeably sharper, more strictly enforced, thereby giving rise to a general evacuation of the public realm.

There were also numerous impediments to *vertical* communication and mobility, encompassing not only the declining prospects for upward promotion as Party recruitment dwindled at the end of the 1950s and higher positions were monopolized by veteran officials on the basis of seniority and retained indefinitely,[30] but the general phenomenon of

28. Oksenberg, "Methods of Communication."

29. Helmut Opletal, "Four Observations on Chinese Mass Media," *The Asian Messenger* 2, no. 3/3, no. 1 (Autumn/Winter 1977): 38–40; also Opletal, *Die Informationspolitik der Volksrepublik China: Von der "Kulturrevolution" bis zum Sturz der "Viererbande" (1965 bis 1976)* (Bochum: Studienverlag Brockmeyer, 1981). The author, an Austrian student, studied at Beijing University and the Beijing Language Institute from 1973 to 1975, returning for further visits in 1976 and 1977. See also Helmut Martin, "Sprachpolitik," in Brunhild Staiger, ed., *China* (Tübingen: Horst Erdmann, 1980), pp. 392–407.

30. Though it sounds rather sweeping to say that the avenues of upward mobility were becoming constricted by the late 1950s, a wide range of evidence may be cited in support of such a generalization. At the highest level, see Franklin Houn, "The Eighth Central Committee of the Chinese Communist Party," *American Political Science Review*, June 1957, pp. 392–404. For two studies of lower-level bureaucratic staffing, one in a rural, the other in an urban context, which confirm a sharp decline of vertical mobility after 1957, see Michel Oksenberg, "Local Leaders in Rural China, 1962–65: Individual Attributes,

"bureaucratism" (*guanliaozhuyi*). This refers to those cadre behavior patterns, whose exact identity and nature has been a matter of periodic discussion and redefinition, which give rise to estrangement between elites and masses. Political estrangement consists partly of an asymmetrical communication flow (you talk, we listen; we talk, you don't listen), partly of *Ressentiment* aroused by cadre privilege (*tequan*). Bureaucratism was regularly dissected but usually attributed to the moral deficiencies of individual officials rather than to the organization itself, illustrating one of the chief differences between Chinese and Western theories of organization. Nevertheless, a number of structural features probably contributed to increasing "bureaucratism" during this period.

In 1956 a cadre rank system was established, consisting of a twenty-six-grade scale.[31] The major divisions fell at grades seven, thirteen, and seventeen: grades eighteen to twenty-six included the vast lower echelons of state employees or "national cadres" (*guojia ganbu*); grades fourteen to seventeen were considered middle-ranking cadres and assigned to positions of leadership at the commune and county levels; while those in grades eight to thirteen were high-ranking cadres (*gaoji ganbu*), usually prefectural or provincial officials or department heads in Beijing. Highest were those ranking grade seven and above—chairman of the CPC, chief of state, chairman of the NPC, premier of the State Council, down to government ministers, CC members, provincial first Party secretaries, and Military Region commanders. Other professions boasted different grade numbers: five for technicians, sixteen for actors, eight for workers in state enterprises, twelve for academics, even four for cooks. An individual's standing in this elaborate hierarchy determined not only monthly pay but how many square feet of housing one might be assigned, whether one traveled by car or bicycle, which schools one's children attended, and whether one had access to foreign films and literature. According to the regulations of the State Council governing transportation, for example, cadres of grade thirteen and above had use of a limousine to commute to

---

Bureaucratic Positions, and Political Recruitment," pp. 155–216; and Yingmao Kau, "The Urban Bureaucratic Elite in Communist China: A Case Study of Wuhan, 1949–65," pp. 216–71, both in A. Doak Barnett, ed., *Chinese Communist Politics in Action* (Seattle: University of Washington Press, 1969). On Party admission, see Roberta Martin, *Party Recruitment in China: Patterns and Prospects* (New York: Columbia University, East Asian Institute Occasional Papers, 1981). Martin finds that after the most rapid growth period in Party history, from 1945 to 1956 (about an 886 percent increase) and another big increase in the 1956–57 period, there was a lull. The period from 1961 to 1969 witnessed an increase of only 3 million (from 17 to 20 million).

31. See Ezra F. Vogel, "From Revolutionary to Semi-Bureaucrat: The 'Regularization' of Cadres," *CQ*, no. 29 (January-March 1967): 36–60; Martin King Whyte, "Bureaucracy and Modernization in China: The Maoist Critique," *American Sociological Review*, no. 38 (1973): 149–63; and Harding, *Organizing China*, pp. 1–32, *et passim*.

their ministries, cadres of grades fourteen to seventeen might travel by car when necessary to conduct state business, whereas cadres in grades eighteen and below received no transportation provisions. High rank gained access to special flights on Trident jetliners housed on the military airfield in Western Beijing, or to the medical expertise and equipment of Beijing Hospital (a resticted facility). Even the availability of telephones and bathtubs was dictated by political position: only department chiefs and agency heads normally rated either a phone or a tub at home—others must use the public telephone and neighborhood bathhouses.[32]

From a macro-sociological perspective, cadre privilege soon became the most salient exception to general egalitarian tendencies in Chinese society. It was not advertised, of course, but the sheer growth of Chinese officialdom made it difficult to conceal. In 1949, the Party could claim only seven hundred twenty thousand qualified cadres, a figure deemed sufficient to cover only about a third of the posts vacant; 3 million cadres were thus recruited between October 1949 and September 1952. Party membership grew from 4,488,000 in 1949 to 17 million by 1961 (only 20 percent of whom had joined before 1949). The bureaucracy was clearly a growth sector of the economy, dwarfing even industry: in Shanghai, where total employment between 1949 and 1957 increased by 1.2 percent per year, and factory workers and staff grew by 5.8 percent annually, health and government workers increased by an annual rate of 16 percent.[33] By 1955, government cadres were consuming 9.6 percent of the national budget, nearly double the figure originally planned (5 percent).[34] Whereas bureaucrats controlled less than 10 percent of China's gross national product before 1949, by 1972 this figure had risen to 30 percent.[35]

The stratified distribution of privileges made it difficult to sustain the myth of "unequal role, equal status." The hierarchical distribution of rank and perquisites, and the use of the dossier system to supplement seniority as a basis for promotion, meant that young cadres were systematically oriented toward ingratiating their superiors rather than to-

32. Mathews and Mathews, *One Billion*, p. 200; Mosher, *Broken Earth*, pp. 59–67. The ranking of cadres also decides the length of their "tails," meaning the number of service personnel and assistants they can have. High-ranking cardes can have drivers, cooks, nurses, doctors, and the right to use vacation resorts provided by the state. If they should be purged and imprisoned, rank will in most cases continue to determine their meal allowance and treatment. Thus Jiang Qing, for example, was said to be eating very well after her arrest and imprisonment. See Bernstein, *Center*, pp. 131–40.

33. Kraus, *Class Conflict*, p. 6.

34. Gordon White, "The Post-revolutionary Chinese State," in Victor Nee and David Mozingo, eds., *State and Society in Contemporary China* (Ithaca, N.Y.: Cornell University Press, 1983), pp. 30–31.

35. Kraus, *Class Conflict*, p. 6.

ward cultivating their subordinates.[36] If they succeeded in doing so, they could look forward to a life of security and gradually increasing income, consumption, power, and status. As official behavior thus became systematically reinforced, cadre motives became suspect even when their conduct was unexceptionable—were they dedicated to service to the people, or to their own careers? The former became a form of public rhetoric that referred to a collective abstraction (the whole people, not you people) or to the future (not now, later). Monopolizing the distribution of workpoints, bonuses, good job assignments, and other postitive incentives, retaining exclusive right "correctly" to interpret higher directives or slogans, cadres could rule rather high-handedly without much fear of retribution as long as they fulfilled the demands of their superiors, and their subordinates had "no exit." Authority, which according to "mass line" conceptions should follow a circular flow, became "transitive." After 1956, the elite-mass distinction thus began to displace "class struggle" as the dominant operational contradiction in Chinese society.

THE CRITIQUE OF STRUCTURE

We have been reviewing two concurrent developments that took place during the first decade of CPC rule: destruction of the remaining vestiges of the pre-Liberation authority structure, and construction of a new, socialist structure. Both were positively evaluated at the time, but they also had their adverse features. The former threatened to eliminate one of the functional requisites of continuing revolution, as well as a convenient scapegoat; the latter introduced the novel possibility to these old revolutionaries of becoming targets of a new revolution. Both of these developments drew to a climax in the brief period from the Eighth Party Congress in 1956 to the wilting of the Hundred Flowers in the spring of 1957, leading Mao to rethink the theory of continuing revolution. What resulted was the theoretical reorientation that would guide him during the last two decades of his life.

Declining Relevance of Class

The Eighth Congress was held, among other things, to celebrate essential completion of socialization of the means of production. This momentous achievement enhanced the prestige of the Party leadership, but at the same time it divested both landlords and bourgeoisie of their economic base and eliminated visible class differences, threatening in the long run

36. Whyte and Parish, *Urban Life*, p. 363.

to deprive the Party of its core constituency. The very reality of classes came into question as several members of the leadership went on record forecasting the imminent extinction of class struggle.[37] The dominant contradiction in the emerging society would be the contradiction between relatively advanced relations of production and underdeveloped forces of production rather than class struggle, and this form of contradiction could be resolved without violent social conflict. To continue to mobilize remnants of cashiered classes against one another on the basis of re-collected injury when the possibility of economic exploitation had been eliminated could only damage the (generally high) productivity of the erstwhile exploiting classes, delay their integration into society, and disrupt economic growth and tranquillity.

We have seen that Mao did not hesitate to censure his colleaques when he differed with them, but at this point he seemed to be in agreement, as borne out in contemporaneous remarks revealed after his death.[38] To be sure, the "basic resolution" of class contradictions did not attenuate his conviction that social conflict was the motor of social progress, but he began to redefine that conflict more optimistically. Thus he shifted increasingly from the focus on classes to the more inclusive concept of "the people" that he had introduced in the United Front doctrines that provided the underpinnings of New Democracy. This supra-class group-ing, aggregated on the basis not of its relationship to the means of production but of its opposition to Japan, was essentially benign; though contradictions still existed, they could be allowed to play themselves out without Party interference.

Ironically, however, whereas the waning of classes was inclining his colleagues to repudiate storm tactics and to commit themselves to the more thorough engineering of national reconstruction, the same pheno-menon disposed Mao to question the continued pertinence of the en-gineering approach. As he put it in his defense of the 1955–56 "high tide":

Sudden change is the most basic law of the universe. . . . We communists hope for the transformation of things in general. The leap forward is different from

37. Thus Liu Shaoqi allegedly remarked that the primary contradiction was not class struggle but "between the advanced socialist system and the backward productive forces," and Deng Xiaoping noted that the old system of class labels "has lost or is losing its original significance." *RR*, September 26, 1956, as cited in Kraus, "Class Conflict."

38. In a letter written to Huang Yanpei on December 4, 1956, Mao stated: "In our country, class contradictions basically have been resolved. (That is to say, they have yet to be completely resolved, and ideological contradictions will continue to exist for a long time to come.)," in "Twenty-three Letters by Comrade Mao Zedong, from the 'Selection of Mao's Letters,'" *RR*, December 25, 1983, pp. 1–4.

the past.... The destruction of balance is a leap forward and is better than balance; imbalance and the causing of trouble are good things.... Balance, quantitative change and unity are temporary and relative, while imbalance, sudden change and disunity are absolute and endless.[39]

While conceding that "the denial of quantitative change can lead to adventurism," Mao differentiated his notion of "wavelike advance" from adventurism by stressing that periods of consolidation were necessary, that "there cannot be a high tide every day."[40] He nonetheless implicitly rejected the idea that social change could be tightly controlled or directed from above. Only through the free interplay of social forces, through the development and resolution of contradictions in society, could continued revolution be successfully promoted. It would be going too far to say that this precluded any active role for the Party in directing the continuing revolution, but Mao was aware that the Party's concern for organizational control made it a reluctant participant in such a process. Thus he exerted all his persuasive skills to try to raise the Party's tolerance of "chaos": "If disorder results it won't be all that great, there will just be a spell of disorder and then things may well move toward order," he said at Chengdu (March 20, 1958). "The appearance of disorder contains within it some favorable elements, we should not fear disorder."[41]

Contradictions among the People

In this open, experimental frame of mind, Mao utilized the Hundred Flowers as an occasion, not necessarily to spur the revolution onward, but to take its temperature. Thus he interceded at the beginning of 1957 in the process of controlled liberalization that had been under way since early 1956 under the aegis of Zhou Enlai, giving a four-hour extemporaneous talk on February 27 at an expanded Supreme State Conference (later to be published in revised form as "On the Correct Handling of Contradictions among the People"). He also convened a Beijing forum on literature, philosophy, and education on February 16 at which he gave another talk; he spoke to the National Conference on Propaganda Work on March 6–10; and he made a tour of Tianjin (March 17), Ji'nan (March 18), Nanjing, Shanghai, and Hangzhou (March 20), giving speeches at each

39. *Wansui* (1969), p. 213.
40. *Mao Zedong Sixiang Wansui* (Hong Kong: n.p., 1967) (hereinafter *Wansui* [1967a]), p. 59.
41. Starr, *Continuing the Revolution*, pp. 306 *et passim*. See also Starr, "Conceptual Foundations," pp. 610–28; Young and Woodward, "Contradictions," pp. 912–34; and Schram, "Mao Tse-tung," pp. 221–45.

stop.[42] His message was that people should discard their previous inhibitions and speak out more freely. Noting the recent occurrence of strikes in China,[43] Mao seems to have wanted to preempt an explosion of the sort that had just transpired in Poland and Hungary by permitting some of the accumulated pressure to dissipate: "If one persists in using methods of terror in solving internal contradictions, it may lead to transformations of these contradictions into antagonistic contradictions as happened in Hungary," he warned, claiming that "certain people" even hoped this would happen, that "thousands of people would demonstrate in the street against the People's Government." With characteristic bravado, he scorned any such possibility: "If a handful of school children can topple our party, government and army by a show of force, we must all be fatheads. Therefore, don't be afraid of great democracy. If there is a disturbance, it will help get the festering sore cured, and that's a good thing."[44] Having dismissed the possibility that any unpleasant surprises would occur, Mao invited regime critics to do their worst:

> In my opinion, whoever wants to make trouble may do so for as long as he pleases, and if one month is not enough, he may go on for two; in short , the matter should not be wound up until he feels he has had enough.... Don't always try to keep a lid on everything. Whenever people utter queer remarks, go on strike or present a petition, you try to beat them back with one blow, always thinking that these things ought not to occur. Why is it then that these things that ought not to occur still do?[45]

If cadres should not repress heterodox "remarks," how then should they respond? Anticipating the advice he would give them at the outset of the Cultural Revolution a decade later, Mao urged them to be tolerant to the point of self-immolation:

> It's certainly not easy for a person to set fire to burn himself. I've heard that around this area there were some people who had second thoughts and didn't set a big fire.... Let those poisonous weeds grow up; let those freaks and monsters come out! Why be afraid of them? At the time we said not to be

42. An original version of the February speech leaked out via the Warsaw Embassy and was published by Sydney Gruson in *New York Times*, June 13, 1957, pp. 1, 8 (hereinafter *NYT*). For a detailed chronology of Mao's activities during this period (and indeed all the top Chinese leaders), see Roderick MacFarquhar, *Origins, 1*, pp. 177–253; see also Li Wupeng in *ZM*, no. 18 (April 1979): 20–31.

43. See T. J. Hughes and D. E. T. Luard, *The Economic Development of Communist China, 1949–1958* (London: Oxford University Press, 1959), pp. 52–56; and Charles Hoffmann, *The Chinese Worker* (Albany: State University of New York Press, 1974), pp. 146–47, for statistics indicating the magnitude of the 1956–57 strikes.

44. Mao, "Talks at a Conference of Secretaries of Provincial, Municipal, and Autonomous Region Party Committees: Talk of January 18" (1957), in *SW*, vol. 5: 358.

45. Mao, "Talks at a Conference of Secretaries ... Talk of January 27," ibid., p. 374.

afraid, but within our Party there were some comrades, like XXX and others, who were loyal and faithful to the Party and the nation, but simply feared there would be chaos everywhere. . . . From now on, in my opinion, there should be a fire within no more than three years, and again within five years.[46]

The primary significance of the Hundred Flowers movement is that for the first time since 1949 there was an attempt to define the structure against which the revolution should be animated in terms of *emergent cleavages* in socialist society rather than as a mnemonic reconstruction of pre-Liberation structures. From the analogy he drew between strikes in China and the Hungarian uprising, and from his images of lifting "lids," testing cadres through "inoculations," "blast furnaces," and the like, we may infer that Mao sensed the vulnerability of the emergent socialist structure, and foresaw that at least parts of it might very well come under popular criticism. He indicated in his writings and conversations at the time, of which we have a quite voluminous record, that he expected "bureaucratism" to come under fire, for example—indeed, he seemed to be inviting such an attack. He had apparently not anticipated that the basic socialist political framework might come under assault,[47] and this perhaps accounts for his willingness so promptly to reverse himself and signal the launching of the Anti-Rightist movement to root out all the "weeds" that had "bloomed."

Yet it is at the same time interesting and characteristic that Mao, in the face of an estimated 90 percent cadre opposition,[48] should attempt to mobilize a dubious and reluctant mass constituency to express apparently spontaneous political opinions. This rather daring opening, which was also to characterize Mao's approach to the Cultural Revolution ten years later, marked a clear departure from the engineering paradigm. Any attempt to conceive of it as a sophisticated political ploy, a trap designed to provide justification for a purge, must yield to Occam's razor: in Mao's position he could have doubtless arranged a purge more parsimoniously

46. Mao, "Zai zui gao guowuhuiyi shang de jieshu hua" [Concluding remarks at a supreme state conference] (March 1, 1957), in *Wansui* (1969), pp. 90–100.
47. E.g., Zhang Bojun proposed again that the CPPCC become the second house of a bicameral parliament and suggested that, as an interim measure, representatives of the NPC, the CPPCC, the CPC, the Bourgeois Democratic Parties, and the mass organizations form a "political design department" to discuss all major policies and programs. For many intellectuals and bourgeois democratic notables, the solution was to eliminate the "absolute leadership of the Party," to allow for a free press "even if it means opposition to the Communist Party," and to permit democratic parties to attempt to control the government through democratic elections—in short, liberal democracy. See Harding, *Organizing China*, pp. 147–48.
48. See Richard Solomon, "One Party and 'One Hundred Schools': Leadership, Lethargy, or Luan?" *Current Scene* 7, nos. 19–20 (October 1, 1969): 25–26.

(as in, say, the Gao-Rao case). It is worth making a brief excursus at this point to try to discover what Mao thought he was doing.

Revolution Migrates to the Superstructure

Mao was at this juncture evolving a new perspective on the dynamics of continuing revolution that would take into account the post-Liberation developments discussed above. From the socialization of the means of production he inferred that if class could no longer be an empirically meaningful criterion for locating the target structure of revolution, he would find one elsewhere, for he was convinced that conflict was eternal and that the revolution must continue. From the Hundred Flowers episode he inferred that repression was not a viable way of dealing with counterrevolutionary forces that challenged the emergent structure of socialist authority; somehow "old revolutionaries" must find a way to join with and encourage such forces, for otherwise they risked betraying the revolution. From the failure of the Great Leap Forward, and from the Peng Dehuai episode in which Peng sought to blame Mao for that failure, he drew more pessimistic conclusions about the future of socialism than he (or his colleagues) had entertained for several years: not only would class struggle continue, there was a real prospect that the class enemy would prevail, with the help of "revisionist" elements within the Party, leading to a reversal of historical evolution backward along the "capitalist road."

The challenge for Mao was to find some basis for this new theory, given that socialization of the means of production was hardly a panacea—both the Soviet Union and Yugoslavia had after all undergone that transformation, only to become teachers by negative example. Here Mao turned to the relations of production and the ideological superstructure, tending to disregard the economic basis of ideas—all the more so after the Great Leap's failure demonstrated his fallibility in the field of economics. Developments in the relations of production and cultural superstructure were *relatively autonomous* and would have to be approached on their own terms without clear guidelines from the economic base. As Mao now saw it, the Russian and Chinese revolutions demonstrated that the transformation of the old relations of production was not contingent upon the existence of fully developed new forces of production. In fact, if one placed the seizure of power, solving the ownership problem and developing the forces of production in this order, then the development of the forces of production always came *after* the change in the relations of production: "You must first change the relations of production in order to make it possible fully to develop the forces of production," Mao wrote in 1960. "This is a universal law."[49] Mao's real concern was persistently

49. *Wansui* (1967a), p. 213.

to push the relations of production toward public ownership, which would in turn promote the forces of production. If "contradictions" arose because bourgeois thinking intervened, it would be necessary to launch class struggles in the superstructure to remove such obstacles.[50]

Thus after the Leap, Mao abandoned the inclusive concept of "people" and reverted to class, calling for "protracted and fierce class struggle." This reversion was occasioned partly by the emergence of what he considered class enemies, partly by Mao's need for class struggle as a political engine to propel further transformations of the relations of production. In view of the fact that classes could no longer be defined on the basis of their relationship to the means of production in the socialist period, a call for class struggle however begged many questions. Should class be determined by current occupational status (*geren chengfen*), by family background (*jiating chushen*), or by political attitudes? China's old and new middle classes preferred the first criterion, which would have exculpated them, but they had little influence. China's political and military bureaucrats preferred the criterion of family background, both because of its administrative convenience and because it sanctioned their elite status unto the third and fourth generations—and they had the clout to prevail throughout much of this period.[51] After 1958, Mao, however, increasingly favored *political attitude* as a criterion of class, which could be defined on the basis of current behavior rather than an objective stigma recorded in some dossier. It was on this basis that Mao once referred to those who obstructed his efforts as a "bureaucratic class."[52]

Which attitude? Obviously, "pro-Mao" was one important factor, lending attitudinal criteria the irremediable subjectivism that would ultimately redound in the factionalism of the Cultural Revolution. But Mao had something more specific in mind. The key attitude to which he turned as a defining criterion of class was *selfishness*. Proletarian virtue,

50. Cheng Yang, "Socialism and the Quest for Modernization," pp. 74 ff.

51. Kraus, *Class Conflict*, pp. 9, 97, *et passim*. See also Stuart Schram, "Classes, Old and New, in Mao Zedong's Thought, 1949–1976," in James L. Watson, ed., *Class and Social Stratification in Post-Revolutionary China* (Cambridge: Cambridge University Press, 1984), pp. 29–56.

52. In 1965 he said: "The bureaucratic class is a class sharply opposed to the working class and the poor and lower-middle peasants. These people have become or are in the process of becoming bourgeois elements sucking the blood of the workers. How can they have proper understanding?" Mao, "Dui Chen Zhengren tongzhi dundian baogao de pishi" [Comments on comrade Chen Zhengren's report on his stay on a spot] (January 29, 1965), in *Mao Zedong Sixiang Wansui* (Hong Kong: n.p., April 1967) (hereinafter *Wansui* [1967b]), p. 31. In his conversation with Malraux the same year, Mao derogated Khrushchev: "I know his theory; you begin by no longer tolerating criticism, then you abandon self-criticism, then you cut yourself off from the masses, and since the Party can draw its revolutionary strength only from them, you tolerate the formation of a new class." André Malraux, *Anti-Memoirs*, pp. 369–70.

according to Mao, was to "destroy the selfish and establish the unselfish." This critique of selfishness, deeply resonant of Chinese cultural tradition, also dovetailed well with popular resentment of some of the emergent socialist contradictions described in the previous subsection. Inequality, privilege, could be clearly derived from selfish motives; less obviously, perhaps, the desire for autonomy of the professional or intellectual, the isolation of the official from the masses, were arguably "selfish." The possible ramifications were countless.

The attitude of selfishness in turn could be traced to the emotion of *fear*. One refused to share, of one's self or one's time or resources, because of a fear of loss. Mao referred to such anxieties in explicitly therapeutic terms as "encumbrances," mental "baggage," and so forth:

> "To get rid of the baggage" means to free our minds of many encumbrances. Many things may become baggage, may become encumbrances, if we cling to them blindly and uncritically.... Thus, a prerequisite for maintaining close links with the masses and making fewer mistakes is to examine one's baggage, to get rid of it and so to emancipate the mind.[53]

Mao's works are replete with testimonials to the crippling effects of fear on the Chinese people. "What should we not fear? We should not fear heaven. We should not fear ghosts. We should not fear dead people. We should not fear the bureaucrats. We should not fear the warlords. We should not fear the capitalists."[54] Nearly half a century later, Mao made another listing of things not to be feared, the so-called "five-fear-nots" (*wu bu pa*): A Communist should fear "neither removal from his post, expulsion from the Party, divorce, imprisonment, nor beheading"— words Wang Hongwen would recall in his speech to the Tenth Party Congress in 1973.[55] In his 1955 "women with bound feet" rebuke, fear was once again at issue: "Too much carping, unwarranted complaints, *boundless anxiety and countless taboos*—all this they take as the right policy in the rural areas."[56]

In a fugitive party in which leadership entailed regularly exhorting people to risk life and limb, coping with fear was not an unfamiliar problem. The standard approach was an allopathic form of therapy in which the patient's anxiety would be assuaged by reassurances of support, minimization of the objective danger, and so forth. This was first

53. Mao, "Get Rid of the Baggage and Start the Machinery" (April 12, 1944), in *Readings*, p. 306.
54. Mao, "Toward a New Golden Age" (July 1919), in Stuart Schram, *The Political Thought of Mao Tse-tung* (New York: Praeger, 1963), pp. 105–6.
55. Statement of 1958, quoted in Yan Jingwen, *Zhou Enlai Pingzhuan* [Critical biography of Zhou Enlai] (Hong Kong: Bowen Shudian, 1974), p. 28.
56. Mao, "On the Cooperative Transformation of Agriculture" (July 31, 1955), in *SW*, vol. 5: 184.

explicitly endorsed in Liu Shaoqi's seminal work, "On the Cultivation of Communist Party Cadres" (usually translated as "How to Be a Good Communist"),[57] and will hence be christened "cultivation therapy"— although strictly speaking, "cultivation" refers to self-disciplinary techniques rather than to interpersonal ministration. Three years following the appearance of Liu's essay, Mao also endorsed this approach:

> So long as a person who has made mistakes does not hide his sickness for fear of treatment or persist in his mistakes until he is beyond cure, so long as he honestly and sincerely wishes to be cured and to mend his ways, we should welcome and cure his sickness so that he can mend his ways and become a good comrade.[58]

Again, in a speech given immediately prior to the launching of the Hundred Flowers, Mao said:

> We must oppose the method of "finishing people off with a single blow." This remolding of the intellectuals, especially the changing of their world outlook, is a process that requires a long period of time. Our comrades must understand that ideological remolding involves a long-term, patient and painstaking work, and they must not attempt to change people's ideology, which has been shaped over decades of life, by giving a few lectures or by holding a few meetings. Persuasion, not compulsion, is the only way to convince them.[59]

Even on those occasions better remembered for his more provocative remarks, Mao reaffirmed his commitment to "cultivation therapy"— witness this passage from his speech to the Tenth Plenum in 1962, better known for his warning of the continued pertinence of class struggle:

> As to how the Party should deal with the problem of revisionism and the problem of a bourgeoisie within itself, I think we should adhere to our traditional policy. No matter what errors a comrade may commit, ... if he should change himself earnestly, we should welcome him and rally with him. ... We permit the commission of errors. Since you have erred, we also allow you to rectify them.[60]

Due perhaps in part to its congruence with deeply rooted cultural patterns, cultivation therapy became the consensually endorsed form of "rectification" and was institutionalized in the form of "criticism and

---

57. Liu Shaoqi, "Lun gongchandangyuan de xiuyang" [On the self-cultivation of Chinese Communist Party members] (Yan'an, July 8, 1939), translated as "How to Be a Good Communist," in *Collected Works of Liu Shao-ch'i* (Hong Kong: Union Research Institute, 1969), vol. 1: 151–219.

58. Mao, "Rectify the Party's Style of Work" (February 1, 1942), in *SW*, vol. 3: 50.

59. Mao, "Speech at the CCP's National Conference on Propaganda Work" (March 19, 1957), in *Readings*, pp. 493–94.

60. Mao, "Speech at the Tenth Plenary Session of the Eighth Central Committee," as translated in *Chinese Law and Government* 1, no. 4 (Winter 1968–69): p. 91.

self-criticism" and "study" (*xuexi*) meetings, which were (and still are) held routinely among members of Party branches, work units, and other "small groups" (*xiaozu*). The intensity of such sessions varied according to the magnitude of the error and the overall political climate. In the most intense, members of the group might be completely isolated from their environment, families, and friends for a matter of months and segregated into study groups dedicated exclusively to the reform of their thought. The more difficult cases might be ostracized and obliged to write repeated self-criticisms before one was accepted.[61] In its more routine form, members of the group disperse and interact in an occupational or residential context between sessions and are permitted to maintain contact with a normal circle of friends and relatives.[62]

Although it is true that Mao endorsed cultivation therapy, in this new context in which the emergent authority structure itself might be fundamentally disoriented, the group consensus upon which cultivation therapy rests could not be relied upon. In the face of hardening socialist "frames," which admittedly were an improvement upon pre-Liberation structural weaknesses and yet still seemed to stultify revolutionary momentum, Mao needed a new and more drastic approach, one that would permit a dramatic breakthrough from conventional inhibitions. To find it, he reached back into his own formative experience, even antedating his admission to the CPC (the Marxist classics, after all, have little to say about the management of emotions). From his youthful confrontations with his father, as he subsequently recollected for Edgar Snow, he learned that if an authority is frontally defied he will usually relent, whereas "when I remained meek and submissive, he only cursed and beat me the more."[63] In Mao's first published article, a discussion of physical culture, he claimed that:

> To wash our feet in ice water makes us acquire courage and dauntlessness, as well as audacity. . . . In order to progress in exercise, one must be savage. If one is savage, one will have great vigor and strong muscles and bones. The method of exercise should be rude, then one can apply oneself seriously and it will be easy to exercise.[64]

More importantly, it would free the patient from a crippling attachment

61. Cf. Robert Jay Lifton, *Thought Reform and the Psychology of Totalism: A Study of "Brainwashing" in China* (New York: W. W. Norton, 1963).
62. Martin King Whyte, *Small Groups and Political Rituals in China* (Berkeley: University of California Press, 1974).
63. Edgar Snow, *Red Star over China* (New York: Grove Press, 1968, rev. and enlarged ed.), p. 168.
64. Mao, "A Study of Physical Education" (April 1917), in Schram, *Political Thought*, pp. 94–102.

to "self" and permit greater dedication to altruistic endeavors. In another autobiographical passage, from his important 1942 speech at the Yan'an Forum on Art and Literature, in which he urged China's intellectuals to dedicate themselves more selflessly to the masses, Mao revealed that he had been able to undergo a conversion only by boldly confronting his own fear of defilement:

> I began life as a student and at school acquired the ways of a student. I then used to feel it undignified to do even a little manual labor, such as carrying my own luggage in the presence of my fellow students, who were incapable of carrying anything, either on their shoulders or in their hands. At that time I felt that intellectuals were the only clean people in the world, while in comparison workers and peasants were dirty. But after I became a revolutionary and lived with workers and with soldiers of the revolutionary army, I gradually came to know them well, and they gradually came to know me well too. It was then, and only then, that I fundamentally changed the bourgeois and petty-bourgeois feelings implanted in me in the bourgeois schools. I came to feel that compared with the workers and peasants, the unremolded intellectuals were not clean and that, in the last analysis, the workers and peasants were the cleanest people and, even though their hands were soiled and their feet smeared with cow dung, they were really cleaner than the bourgeois and petty-bourgeois intellectuals. This is what is meant by a change in feelings, a change from one class to another.[65]

The "change from one class to another" that Mao discusses here had nothing to do with the relations of production. It involved rather a "change in feelings" from the fear of "dirt" (which Mao seemed to associate with workers and peasants) to admiration and respect for those who were "dirty" through direct contact with the object of fear.

Mao had introduced (or revived?—his mother was a devout Buddhist) a therapeutic technique that was not "long-term, patient and painstaking," but abrupt; not gentle, but "rough," even jarring. A classic exposition of what we might call "shock therapy" may be found in his article, "Oppose Stereotyped Party Writing" (February 8, 1942): "The first thing to do in the reasoning process is to give the patient a good shakeup by shouting at him, 'You are ill!' so as to administer a shock and make him break out in a sweat, and then to give him sincere advice on getting treatment."[66] This approach consisted of a deliberately induced exacerbation of the symptoms of illness (i.e., panic) in order to build the patient's resistance. In a pep talk to cadres in which he sought to prepare them to face the aroused masses during the Hundred Flowers, he makes clear that he expected them to undergo a type of trial by ordeal, under-

65. Mao, "Talks at the Yenan Forum on Literature and Art" (May 2, 1942), in *SW*, vol. 3:73.
66. *SW*, vol. 3:56.

lining the homeopathic character of the treatment: "Don't seal these things up, otherwise it would be dangerous. In this respect our approach is different from that of the Soviet Union. Why is vaccination necessary? A virus is artificially introduced into a man's body to wage 'germ warfare' against him in order to bring about immunity."[67] Using a different metaphor to make the same point, he speaks of "tempering" (duanlian):

> Tempering means forging and refining. Forging is shaping by hammering and refining is smelting iron in a blast furnace or making steel in an open-hearth furnace. After steel is made, it needs forging, which nowadays is done with a pneumatic hammer. That hammering is terrific! We human beings need tempering too.[68]

The patient, finding himself (or herself) suddenly confronted by the feared object, would discover that the object was not as terrible as had been imagined, and the ability to cope with the fear would be concomitantly enhanced. In Mao's view, this realization would permit the patient to realize hitherto-untapped potential.

Mao was convinced that confrontation with the feared object could not only transform subjective emotions and induce individuals to commit themselves to the interests of the collective, but could actually counteract the objective power of the feared thing as well. Having previously relied upon intimidation to dominate a cowed subject, the authority will be so taken aback upon being boldly confronted by a suddenly defiant underling that he is apt to panic and resort to extreme measures, or at least will have to reassess the power balance. It is advisable to reinforce this panic or uncertainty and thus throw the oppressor into utter rout, thereby permanently transforming the relationship between feared and fearful. As Mao put it in a famous passage from his "Report on an Investigation of the Peasant Movement in Hunan":

> People swarm into the houses of local tyrants and evil gentry who are against the peasant association, slaughter their pigs and consume their grain. They even loll for a minute or two on [N.B.—the wording of the unexpurgated text is "tread on and roll in"] the ivory-inlaid beds belonging to the young ladies in the household of the local tyrants and evil gentry.... Doing whatever they like and turning everything upside down, they have created a kind of terror in the countryside. This is what some people call "going too far," or "going beyond the proper limits in righting a wrong." ... A revolution is not a dinner party, [etc.] .... To put it bluntly, it is necessary to create terror for a while in every rural area, or otherwise it would be impossible to suppress the authority of the

---

67. Mao, "Talks at a Conference of Secretaries of Provincial, Municipal and Autonomous Region Party Committees" (January 1957), in SW, vol. 5: 369–70.
68. Mao, "Beat Back the Attacks of the Bourgeois Rightists" (July 9, 1957), in SW, vol. 5: 459.

gentry. Proper limits have to be exceeded in order to right a wrong, or else the wrong cannot be righted.[69]

Here, as in no passage Mao wrote apropos of the post-Liberation milieu, the underlying aggression implicit in this type of "shock therapy" clearly emerges. Whatever therapeutic benefits their exemplary suffering or death may have had for the masses, there had never been any pretense that it should benefit the *targets*—quite the contrary. The landlords, local bullies, and diehard elements functioned as scapegoats, teachers by negative example, objects of catharsis for those they had previously oppressed. This was also the case in the campaigns of the early 1950s examined in chapter 2. Not until the Hundred Flowers was mass criticism with the serious intention of reform turned against any of the emergent socialist contradictions reviewed earlier; the results were so shocking for all elites that the experiment was immediately aborted.

Yet in 1966 Mao was to push the experiment much further than he had in 1957. It was not enough to initiate movements in every factory and village, as had been done in the 1950s; Mao had decided to mobilize the masses to expose "our seamy side" from bottom to top and "in an all-round way."[70] Untroubled now by the prospect of popular opposition to his own role after several years' vigorous promotion of a "cult" of his own leadership and worldview, Mao encouraged the masses to overcome their fears of criticism by plunging boldly into the maelstrom. "It was I who started the fire," he conceded at the October 1966 work conference. "I think it is good to give people shocks. I thought about it for many years, and at last I came up with the idea of this shock."[71] Elites and masses had been divided by a barrier of fear, and now they should pierce this barrier and dispel the fear, the masses by attacking the elites whom they had feared, the elites by "turning the character 'fear' (*pa*) into 'daring' (*gan*)" and freely exposing themselves to criticism. To the Red Guards, he wrote several letters praising their revolutionary spirit and authorizing them to "lead yourselves and carry out revolution by your own efforts," and on August 5, he posted "My First Big-Character Poster," urging China's young people by personal example to "bombard the bourgeois headquarters."[72]

69. Mao, "Report on an Investigation of the Peasant Movement in Hunan," in *SW*, 1: 28; as compared with the original text in *Mao Zedong Ji* [Collected works of Mao Zedong] (Hong Kong: Yishan, 1976), vol. 1: 213. "*Tashangqu gun*" is the Chinese phrase for "tread on and roll in."

70. Mao, conversation of February 2, 1967, in *Wansui* (1969), p. 664.

71. Mao, "Speech at a Certain Conference" (July 21, 1966), in *Wansui* (1969), pp. 643–46.

72. Mao's poster and letters of encouragement to Red Guards are translated in Jerome Ch'en, ed., *Mao Papers* (London: Oxford University Press, 1970), pp. 115–17.

As in 1957, the overwhelming majority of the cadres opposed and sometimes even covertly sabotaged this unprecedented movement. They could not as a rule understand how to lead a movement while serving simultaneously as its prime suspects; all their previous experience told them that the targets of movements came to no good end, and the therapeutic slogans urging them, too, to overcome fears and taboos and expose themselves to mass criticism did not always allay their suspicions. "When you are told to kindle a fire to burn yourselves, will you do it?" Mao challenged them on July 21. "After all, you yourselves may be burned." His audience responded gamely:

> We are prepared. If we're not up to it, we will resign our jobs. We live as Communist Party members and will die as Communist Party members. It doesn't do to live a life of sofas and electric fans.[73]

Mene, mene, tekel, upharsin.[74]

CONCLUSION

The unexpectedly swift political and economic destruction of the enemies of the revolution after Liberation left the leadership in a quandary. The immediate impulse was to issue a self-congratulatory declaration to the effect that the revolution had been successfully completed, but it was not long before the leadership began to have second thoughts. Notwithstanding progress in the construction of stable planning and administrative institutions, the Chinese system remained essentially a politics of movement, and the leaders were therefore inclined to apprehend that if the revolutionary tide ebbed a counterrevolutionary tide would soon follow that would leave the socialist beachhead marooned. This possibility was illustrated by the unexpectedly "bourgeois" tenor of the criticisms voiced during the Hundred Flowers, and (for Mao) the treachery of Peng Dehuai's assault, with suspected Soviet collusion, upon a Great Leap Peng had only recently supported (or at least not actively opposed). Still more stable institutions and a demobilized mass would seem the obvious answer, and indeed a majority of the leadership seems to have preferred this alternative. And yet these reconstructed institutions were basically inimical to Mao and those of his colleagues most closely identified with the salvationary mission, constituting a new framework of restrictions against which they instinctively revolted.

Mao's analysis of the emergent opposition structure in socialist society

73. Mao, "Talk to Leaders of the Center" (July 21, 1966), trans. in Stuart Schram, ed., *Chairman Mao Talks to the People*, pp. 253–56.
74. "Numbered, numbered, weighed, divided."—Daniel 5:25. The writing on the wall, interpreted by Daniel to mean that God had weighed Belshazzar and his kingdom, found them wanting, and would destroy them.

was symbolic rather than discursive, elliptical rather than analytic. It is not really necessary to attribute this to Mao's advanced years and the consequent lapse of his intellectual faculties. For Mao to analyze the less appealing aspects of his own regime must have been far more sensitive than to dissect the bourgeois-feudal class structure that existed under Japanese imperialism or KMT dictatorship: the problem of lighting a fire without burning oneself affected the Chairman as well. Ideological precedent stultified his analysis of the dynamics of socialist development, and political considerations inhibited his critique of organizational degeneration. Thus his usual analytical skill was less apparent in his evolving polemic against the "Party persons in authority taking the capitalist road." The various constraints emerging in socialist society to which we alluded above were reduced to "bureaucratism," for example—to the strain between masses and elites. The empirical manifestations of this strain were left so vague that almost any grievance against superior authority could plausibly be attributed to "revisionist" leadership. Though analytically imprecise, this would prove to be a highly effective mobilizational rhetoric, as we shall see in chapter 4.

Inasmuch as the continuing revolution in its cultural phase was to be directed against the excessively disciplined and authoritarian form of organization represented by the Leninist Party-state, the engineering approach preferred by the majority of the cadres (symbolized early in the Cultural Revolution by the issue of "work teams") was really foreclosed from the outset. To be sure, an anarchic cultural revolution against bureaucracy that was protected by an even more stringently disciplined military organization was rather artificial, taking on certain aspects of "queen for a day." But the point of the exercise was pedagogical rather than efficient, with revolution employed as a form of shock therapy. Attachments to prerevolutionary cultural arrangements had become frozen in fear of loss—loss of order, loss of production—and it was hence necessary to shatter fear in order to free its victims for new and more revolutionary commitments. Both participants and their targets would be challenged to overcome their fears by directly confronting the objects of fear. This challenge postulated superhuman forbearance among elites, and imputed great insight and political sophistication to the (not yet fully literate) masses, an ability to make a discrimination between proletarian revolutionary and revisionist leaders that Mao himself had difficulty making, and moreover an ability to do so with little or no organizational guidance. For Communist organizational principles were ideologically suspect and provisionally suspended, only an extremely loose co-ordination among Red Guard participants being achievable through the media and through personal meetings with trusted leaders in the capital or on site.

This iconoclastic approach to mass therapy is not terra incognita to social science. Mao's approach appears superficially similar to what in the psychoanalytic literature has been termed the "counterphobic defense" against latent anxiety. This consists of a deliberate attempt to precipitate the event most dreaded in order to obtain a "flight to reality" from the torments of one's perfervid imagination. Analysts deem the counterphobic defense to be successful in dissipating immediate anxieties and in bolstering self-confidence, but to be critically deficient in providing insight into the source of the fear and therefore unable conclusively to resolve the underlying difficulty.[75] More recent interdisciplinary research views catharsis somewhat more positively, but only under carefully modulated conditions.[76]

Of course psychotherapeutic findings cannot be extrapolated to the Chinese political scene without considerable caution; as they are based upon dialogues with individual patients (in a clinical setting), they cannot easily take group dynamics into account. And although the concept of counterphobic defense provides a plausible account of the therapeutic premises underlying the criticism movement (at least regarding the relationship between repressed emotions and political catharsis), it fails to predict the political consequences—or indeed, to take into account the political motivations—of revolutionary therapy. Some of these will come into focus in the following chapter.

75. Cf. Otto Fenichel, "The Counterphobic Attitude," in his *Collected Papers* (London: Routledge & Kegan Paul, 1955), pp. 163–74.
76. T. J. Scheff, *Catharsis in Healing, Ritual and Drama* (Berkeley: University of California Press, 1979).

FOUR

The Inner Logic of
Cultural Revolution

Chapter 3 followed two parallel developments: on the one hand, the gradual institutionalization of a structure of socialist authority, a structure derived from the organizational principles of the Leninist Party and designed to compensate for the social disintegration and weakness that had afflicted China for much of the previous century and thus more rigid and impermeable than any previous structures since perhaps the Qin dynasty. The institutionalization of a socialist authority structure in turn led to a rift between public and private sectors, the former dominated by a rhetoric of ideological generalities, the latter consisting of isolated subsectors linked by rumor and backstage maneuver in pursuit of particularistic interests.

On the other hand, Mao Zedong and a small, quasi-conspiratorial band of relatively low-ranking assistants proceeded to formulate a comprehensive critique of these emergent "frames," initially in the context of the Sino-Soviet polemic, later in response to frustrations in the implementation of the Socialist Education movement, Beijing opera reform, and other such initiatives. In 1965–66 the struggle was joined, as Mao called upon the "revolutionary masses" to arise and publicly criticize (*pipan*) the "Party persons in authority taking the capitalist road" whom he held responsible for degeneration of the Leninist Party-state into an aversive structure, a repressive "bourgeois dictatorship." The struggle would continue to rage at varying levels of intensity for the next decade, its political implications ramifying well beyond that.

"There are two aspects of socialist transformation," Mao once observed. "One is the transformation of institutions, and the other is the transformation of people."[1] The Cultural Revolution also consisted of two distinct periods, the first of which was characterized by spontaneous mobilization of (subjectively defined) disprivileged strata, lasting from the summer of 1966 through the fall of 1968; the second of which was characterized by elite attempts to sponsor and channel mass mobilization,

1. Mao, "Concluding Remarks," pp. 90–100.

which lasted from late 1968 until the downfall of the Shanghai radicals in October 1976. The period of spontaneous mobilization was focused on the "transformation of people," using institutions as the anvil against which the revolutionary new culture should be forged (with the hammer of ideology). Not until the later period would there be any reasonably systematic attempt at the "transformation of institutions." This chapter is focused on the early period, to be referred to simply as the "Cultural Revolution"; Chapters 5, 6, and 7 will analyze the period of guided mobilization and institutional transformation, to be distinguished as the "late" Cultural Revolution.

All three functional requisites of continued revolution underwent major changes in connection with the Cultural Revolution. First, charismatic leadership became personalized and detached itself from the bureaucratic apparatus; it was no longer actualized through organizational socialization within the cellular network, but directly through the mass media. Second, the pre-Liberation residual structure joined with the socialist emergent structure to function as the target of revolutionary breakthrough. Inasmuch as breakthrough was achieved rather quickly, the organizational hierarchy soon disintegrated (with the exception of the Army, which was assigned to aid the forces of revolution). Thereafter, the only source of coherence was the framework of polemical symbolism within which the Cultural Revolution was fought, which endowed meaning to the experience for its participants. The third requisite, mobilization of the masses, was propelled essentially by the symbolic rewards (plus whatever opportunistic material side-payments could be expropriated) of smashing the cultural superstructure. Socialization of the means of production and the failure of the Leap had precluded redistributive reform or hypergrowth as alternative resource bases for mobilization.

CHARISMATIC LEADERSHIP

As a consequence of Mao's miscalculations in so heavily investing in the Hundred Flowers and Great Leap Forward, his prestige within the Party leadership sank perceptibly, as cadres turned increasingly to the "first front" operational leadership of Liu Shaoqi and Deng Xiaoping for guidance. Mao's leadership initiatives in the domestic policy arena became more episodic, with little sustained follow-through; his statements "tended to be either sweeping and impractical or vague and tentative."[2] Although they always provoked a flurry of response he considered efforts at implementation utterly inadequate. Under these circumstances an adversarial relationship gradually developed between Mao and his orga-

2. Teiwes, *Leadership, Legitimacy and Conflict.*

nizational apparatus. At the same time, however, Mao's prestige among the masses was artificially enhanced during the early 1960s via a publicity blitz, promoted most actively by the People's Liberation Army (PLA). Meanwhile, Mao's assumption of a leading role in foreign policy disputes allowed him to flaunt his ideological preeminence as symbol of the nation-state without economic risk. Paradoxically, then, while the prestige of the Party among the masses declined as a consequence of the "three bad years" following the Leap crash, and Mao's personal prestige within the elite sank for the same reason, his public visibility as an ideological oracle heightened. It was in fact here that the "personality cult" was born, apparently designed to compensate for Mao's slippage among the elite with an enlarged mass constituency. In the absence of any recent heroic achievements this post-Leap revival was however a clear case of synthetic charisma, achieved through the monopolization of public communication and the suppression of dissent. Mao was aware of the fragility of his status, as he indicated in conversation with Snow, and thus welcomed the opportunity to test the depth of spontaneous support by "taking the lid off."

The apparent efficacy of the cult even after organizational constraint was relaxed by the withdrawal of Party work teams in August 1966 may in part be attributed to the simplification, exaggeration, and endless repetition of Maoist slogans. This approach to political socialization may have annoyed other Party leaders, but it probably facilitated assimilation by an incompletely literate and rather naive young audience. Traditional symbolic devices were used with telling effect. Mao appeared in art, stories, and poems as a superhuman figure, different from others and separate from the social environment—as in traditional pictorial art, in which rulers are placed higher or shown in larger scale in order to express status differences. Mao's public appearances were arranged to befit a modern "Son of Heaven": few people were permitted to meet with him; he rarely appeared in public, and when he did the occasion was highly ritualized. He rarely spoke, and when he did his utterances were immediately sacralized. At times his speeches were read for him by an agent.[3]

During the Cultural Revolution itself, the cult was taken to extreme lengths, as Mao and his Thought were ascribed the power to effectuate the achievement of normally impossible feats.[4] Symbolized like Louis XIV by the sun, Mao was built into the polemics as a supernatural force of enlightenment, his splendor being heightened by juxtaposition with the forces of revisionism surrounding and imperiling him. The dossiers of potential opponents were rifled for quotations casting any shadow of

3. Mildred L. E. Wagemann, "The Changing Image of Mao Tse-tung: Leadership Image and Social Structure" (Ph.D. diss., Cornell University, 1974).
4. See George Urban, ed., The "Miracles" of Chairman Mao (Los Angeles: Nash, 1971).

doubt on his infallibility, which were assumed to betoken vicious opposition to his leadership. There is little doubt that Mao fully approved of the cult at the time, the political payoff to him consisting of his ability to mobilize the whole nation (and to intimidate his opponents) by uttering a few words.

Having in effect suspended the formal leadership forums of the Party-state upon adjournment of the Eleventh Plenum of the Eighth CC in August 1966, Mao turned for assistance to an informal personal retinue consisting of his wife, Jiang Qing; her former patron, Kang Sheng; a former secretary, Chen Boda; and a number of junior sub-recruits, most prominent of whom were Zhang Chunqiao and Yao Wenyuan, two municipal officials with backgrounds in the propaganda-culture sector. These "court favorites" lacked an organizational base aside from Mao himself, and this dearth tended to ensure that their interests coincided with those of their patron—only much later, as Mao approached death, did their interests diverge from his because of their wish to survive. They were relative neophytes politically, a fact that facilitated Mao's use of them for unorthodox projects (such as encouraging the masses to attack Party and state) while at the same time ensuring that those projects would be carried out with minimal sensitivity to bureaucratic interests. Such extracurricular trouble-shooting would greatly inhibit their later attempts at integration into the regular hierarchy.[5]

The prevalence of the cult entailed that Mao's language largely superseded normal public discourse. The polemical vocabulary was derived almost entirely from his published writings (including, for the first time, his poetry), particularly as these were anthologized in the "little red book." This reduction of public language to a set of dogmatic clichés apparently transpired under the illusion that actions performed in Maoist language would necessarily conform to Maoist norms, to judge from the outrage expressed against those who "waved the red flag to oppose the red flag." Mao was of course at liberty to add to his public corpus at will, and he did so in the form of a series of "latest instructions." These were immediately relayed to the public through the official media, supplemented by a decentralized network of Red Guard tabloids, whose circulation occasionally surpassed that of official media. Inasmuch as the Party-state apparatus was paralyzed by mass criticism, formal and informal media substituted for the apparatus in coordinating the mass movement, though the decentralized and uncontrollable character of the informal network and the inherent ambiguity of abstract polemics rendered the substitution inadequate.

5. See Lowell Dittmer, "Bases of Power in Chinese Politics: A Theory and an Analysis of the Fall of the 'Gang of Four,'" *World Politics* 31, no. 1 (October 1978): 26–61.

STRUCTURE

By the end of the 1950s the residual structure had become a shadow of its former reality, to be evoked only by the selection of representative criticism targets and other mnemonic devices. What resulted was a period of structural ambiguity, in which a residual structure of dwindling objective significance coexisted with an emergent structure of socialist institutions, and grievances against the latter were systematically redirected against the former. As the residual structure gradually lost plausibility, however, a ritualization of mass criticism occurred. During the Hundred Flowers, a fleeting experiment with spontaneity permitted criticism for the first time to be directed against the emergent structure, provoking a shocked elite backlash. With the Cultural Revolution Mao once again unleashed mass criticism against the emergent structure (more specifically against deviant cadres within it, but these cadres were indicated so vaguely that criticism tended to be indiscriminate), and this time he successfully resisted elite attempts to suppress the movement *in statu nascendi*. By repudiating elite attempts to defend themselves against criticism from their subordinates (and enforcing this interdict with the PLA), the structure of socialist authority was canceled as an active political force—soon it would disintegrate under critical fire as even a passive target. This development left the structure of polemical symbolism to function as the sole source of meaning in the melee.

The polemical symbolism formed its own structure, which metaphorically reproduced the experience of "two worlds" commonly fostered by the institutional segmentation of reality described in chapter 3. In four different dimensions, a set of "binary oppositions"[6] emerged: (1) light/darkness, (2) revealed/concealed, (3) pure/defiled, and (4) active/passive.

1. The metaphor of light was pervasive, symbolized by the color *red*. The orthodox Communist "red/white" color symbolism (as in "white terror," "Red Army") was changed into "red/black" to accord with the light metaphor. Red denoted ideological orthodoxy: "red hearts" (*hong xin*) stood for militance and loyalty; a "red lantern" (*hong deng*) was a source of doctrinal illumination; "red flowers" (*hong hua*) referred to the Red Guards and other objects of praise.[7] Some young rebels even demanded that the "go" signals in traffic lights be changed from green to red! The following message illustrates the frequency of this color's appearance:

6. See Claude Levi-Strauss, *Structural Anthropology* (New York: Basic Books, 1963), chapters 2, 10, 11; also *The Savage Mind* (Chicago: University of Chicago Press, 1966), p. 80.
7. H. C. Chuang, *The Great Proletarian Cultural Revolution: A Terminological Study* (Berkeley: University of California, Center for Chinese Studies, August 1967). I rely heavily on Chuang in this section.

On that day, countless red flags waved in the breeze at Tiananmen Square. Tens of thousands of Red Guards wearing red armbands and carrying red-colored *Quotations of Chairman Mao Zedong* sang with gusto, "Sailing the Seas Depends on the Helmsman." The whole square became a surging ocean of red.[8]

So many people wished to show their love for the Chairman by painting their walls red that there was a shortage of red paint. Jiang Qing finally had to prohibit this "red sea" (*hong haiyang*).

Contrary to red was black—which in traditional Chinese color symbolism has clandestine and sinister connotations, whereas red connotes good luck and prosperity. Thus "bourgeois authorities" were said to use "black language" (*hei hua*), to write "black books" (*hei shu*), post a "black flag" (*hei qi*) and were characterized as a "black gang" (*hei bang*), "black line" (*hei xian*), or "black inn" (*hei dian*).[9] Anthony Grey, a British journalist held prisoner several months by Red Guards, was struck forcibly by the pervasiveness of this color symbolism upon returning to his redecorated apartment:

> Black paint ran down every wall. Every square foot had been daubed with slogans in Chinese and English. . . . Even the sheets of my bed had been daubed with Chinese characters saying "da dao Gelai!"—"Down with Grey!" . . . The bathroom mirror was covered with slogans and there was one other refinement. The bristles of my toothbrush had been carefully painted black with slogan paint. . . . The inside of the bath had been painted black too, putting it out of action.[10]

The primary symbol of light was the "red sun" (*hong taiyang*), identified with Chairman Mao or his Thought. In ritual adherence to the principles of Chinese geomancy (*fengshui*), the exhibition halls of the life of Mao that were constructed throughout the country were invariably built to face east, the source of light, just as the emperors' palaces had earlier been built to face south, the source of warmth.[11] Like the sun, Mao's Thought radiated life: "Sun , rain, and dew nourish the pine trees, Mao Zedong's Thought nourishes [*buyu*] heroes." Thus it was deemed advisable to incorporate it into the body: "Mao Zedong's Thought is the red, red sun in our hearts."[12]

8. *RR*, September 1, 1966, as cited in Chuang, *Cultural Revolution*.
9. *RR*, July 26, p. 4; *Guangming Ribao* (hereinafter *GM*), July 17, 1966, p. 2; *HQ*, no. 9 (1966): 35; all as cited in Chuang, ibid.
10. Anthony Grey, *Hostage in Peking* (London: Michael Joseph, 1970), pp. 104–5.
11. Adrian Hsia, *Die Chinesische Kulturrevolution* (Neuwied: Hermann Luchterhand, 1971), p. 265.
12. *RR* editorial, March 18, 1967, translated in *Joint Publications Research Service* (hereinafter *JPRS*), no. 40525 (April 5, 1967). *JPRS* translations are sometimes questionable; wherever possible I have checked them against the originals.

A secondary symbol of light was fire: "They try everything from struggle to encirclement for attack in their vain attempt to extinguish the flames of the Great Proletarian Cultural Revolution, which are bound to become a prairie fire." "They spread the sparks of revolutionary rebelling." "They light the flames of criticism."[13] Again, only the wicked are assumed to be flammable; fire has an annealing effect on the righteous, "steeling . . . and and maturing them in the furnaces of the great Cultural Revolutionary . . . crucible." Yao Wenyuan was said to have lit the flames of the Cultural Revolution in his November 1965 broadside against Wu Han, and other authorities were warned that they must "not only mobilize the masses and start a fire to burn ourselves, but also take the initiative to appear and carry out self-revolution." Otherwise, "One day, the blazing flames of revolution will burn your monster and devil group all to death." By contrast with the metaphor of fire, the enemy threatens to become a "free-flowing inundation."[14]

The locus of the enemies with reference to the light/dark dimension is, of course, in outer darkness. Yet the most sinister danger is posed by those enemies who seek to emigrate from the world of darkness to the world of light under false pretenses: "The enemy in daylight look like men, in darkness devils. To your face, they speak human language, behind your back the language of devils. They are wolves clad in skins of sheep, man-eating smiling tigers. . . . The enemies without guns are more hidden, cunning, sinister and vicious than the enemies with guns."[15]

2. The second dimension is that of revealed/concealed, public/private. The enemies are "tigers" who must be "lured from their lair"; "snakes" who "crawl underground," hide in "holes," from whence they must be "dragged out"; they "shield" themselves with "masks," or even "fig leaves," which must be "ripped off"; they are "bullets" with "sugar coats," "wolves clad in skins of sheep," and so on.[16] "We have torn aside

13. *Jinggangshan* editorial, no. 5 (December 26, 1966), p. 3; "The Struggle against the Bourgeois Reactionary Line," *Hongqi* (Beijing Aeronautical Institute), no. 3 (December 26, 1966): 3–4; Kuai Dafu, "Destroy the Liu-Deng Bourgeois Reactionary Line and Strive for New Victories," *Hongweibing* [Red guard], no. 15 (December 30, 1966): 2, 4, 17–22. All are Red Guard publications.

14. Wu Bin, "Struggle Firmly against Class Enemies," *Zhongguo Qingnian* [China youth], no. 13 (July 1, 1966), trans. in *JPRS*, no. 39235 (December 22, 1966), pp. 46–48; Commentator, "Cast Away Three Wrong Ways of Thinking," *Tiyu Zhanbao* [Physical education battle news], Shanghai, in *JPRS*, no. 41450, pp. 115–16; "The Flame That Cannot Be Put Out," *Dongfanghong Bao* [East is red news], May 9, 1967, in *JPRS*, no. 42503 (September 7, 1967), pp. 129–35; "Resolutely Smash the Counterattacks of the Bourgeois Reactionary Line," *Hongweibing Bao*, no. 15 (December 15, 1966), pp. 3, 84 (cited in that sequence).

15. *JFJB* editorial, August 23, 1966.

16. At times, a castration threat seemed implicit in the threat to expose; see "Regard Chairman Mao's Works Throughout the PLA," *JFJB* editorial, as translated in *SCMP*, no. 3712 (June 6, 1966), p. 5.

your filthy curtain of counterrevolution and caught you red-handed. We shall strip you of your disguises and expose you in all your ugliness."[17] The archetypal symbol for this imagery is that of an underworld, or Hades, which the Red Guards were also determined to assault: "Overthrow the king of Hell and free all the little devils!"

3. Filth, feces in particular, became one of the more popular metaphors for the enemy. He was "wallowing in the mire," a "pile of dogshit" who must be "criticized until he stinks." "Where the broom does not sweep, the dirt does not vanish of itself." The Cultural Revolution was a cleansing agent: whereas water assumes a counterrevolutionary aspect in relation to fire, here it becomes a revolutionary purgative. "The turbulent stream of the revolutionary mass movement has been washing away the filth left by the old society." "The roaring torrent of the great democratic movement under the command of the Thought of Mao Zedong is flowing on with surging waves under the bright sun, washing the whole of the old world." "The Great Proletarian Cultural Revolution, like a mighty red torrent, is sweeping away the old."[18] Again, the test of the true revolutionary is his willingness to submit to this overwhelming experience, under the assumption that authentic revolutionary ardor is waterproof: "If you are a genuine proletarian revolutionary ... you will surely hail and be inspired by the rise of the hundreds of millions of people, join the masses in making revolution and throw yourselves into the torrent for criticism of the bourgeois reactionary line."[19] The notion of a "test by water" appears again in a *Liberation Army Daily* editorial: "Only by following Chairman Mao's instructions and putting 'daring' and 'doing' above everything else, and courageously plunging into the practice of war—tempering ourselves in the teeth of storms and learning to swim by swimming—can we acquaint ourselves with the laws of war and master them."[20]

4. In deliberate defiance of the traditional Chinese attachment to peace and harmony, the rhetoric of the Cultural Revolution stressed violent action. The rebel forces called themselves (or were called by others) "shock troops" (*chuangjiang*), and "small generals" (*xiaojiang*), chris-

17. "Tear Aside the Bourgeois Mask of 'Liberty, Equality, and Fraternity,'" *RR* editorial, June 4, 1966, in *SCMP*, no. 3714 (June 8, 1966), p. 3.

18. *Hongweibing Bao*, no. 15, p. 3; Wang Li et al., "Dictatorship of the Proletariat and the Great Proletarian Cultural Revolution," *HQ*, no. 15 (December 13, 1966); "A Proposal by 57 Revolutionary Organizations," New China News Agency (NCNA), Beijing, January 29, 1967, in *JPRS*, no. 41202 (May 29, 1967), pp. 23–27; "Hold Fast to the Main Orientation in the Struggle," *HQ*, no. 12 (September 17, 1966), in *JPRS*, no. 29235 (December 22, 1966), pp. 41–44.

19. "Lord She's Love of Dragons," *RR* editorial, December 21, 1966, in *JPRS*, no. 40525.

20. "Study Problems of Strategy in China's Revolutionary War," *JFJB* editorial, trans. in *PR*, January 13, 1967, p. 18. The interest in braving the waves is perhaps also a tribute to Mao's well-known swimming skills.

tened their tabloids "battle news" (*zhanbao*), and referred to their factions in military terms such as "brigade," "regiment," or "garrison headquarters." They described their exploits with cataclysmic metaphors that suggested a desire to feel part of a vast, impersonal, destructive force: "with the fury of a hurricane," "with the force to topple mountains and upturn seas," "with the power of thunder and lightning from the heavens, this has enveloped all China and the world."[21] The enemies, on the other hand, were accused of passive, pacifist tendencies: they tried to "extinguish class struggle," sought rapprochement with American imperialism and Soviet revisionism (*Mei di Su xiu*), espoused "inner-Party peace," a "parliamentary road" to socialism that circumvents violent revolution, and so forth. In public struggle meetings against prominent political figures, these respective roles would be acted out: the target would be forced into an abject, dependent position, forbidden to make extended remarks or to counterquestion, while the surrounding rebel interrogators would assume a questing, aggressive stance.[22]

In denouncing these enemies, rebel polemicists advocated consequential ruthlessness, renouncing what they conceived to be the characteristic Chinese tendency to develop pity for an enemy midway in the attack and then spare him, with the result that he (or she) would revive and counterattack. The contrast between the old and new attitudes toward violence may be illustrated by comparing the Cultural Revolution shibboleths "Beat the dog even when it has fallen into the water" (*da luo shui gou*) and "Once you start beating it, beat it to death" (Lu Xun), and "With power to spare we must pursue the tottering foe"(Mao Zedong)[23]—with Mencius' dictum that if a child fell into a well it was "human nature" to pull it out, even if it happened to be the child of one's worst enemy.[24] Although the vehemence of such expressions was perhaps considered necessary to overcome deeply rooted cultural inhibitions against criticism of authority, once these psychic barriers were breached the distinction between symbolic and physical violence proved impossible to maintain, and the struggle soon began to escalate to truly lethal proportions.[25]

To wit, the dichotomous imagery of the Cultural Revolution portrays

21. "A Proposal by 57 Revolutionary Organizations," January 29, 1967; "Behind-the-Scenes Story of the Yielding of Power in the Seven Ministries of Machine Building," *Fei Ming Di* [Flying whistling arrowhead], February 17, 1967, in *JPRS*, no. 41779 (July 11, 1967), pp. 101–5; *RR* editorial, June 8, 1966, in *Current Background*, no. 392 (October 29, 1969).

22. Cf. "Three Trials of Pickpocket Wang Guangmei," pp. 2–4.

23. Cited in Chuang, *The Little Red Book and Current Chinese Language* (Berkeley: University of California, Center for Chinese Studies, 1968), p. 28.

24. James Legge, trans., *The Chinese Classics, II: The Works of Mencius*, reprint of 1895 ed. (Hong Kong: Hong Kong University Press, 1960), pp. 201–2.

25. Cf. John Gittings, "Inside China," *Ramparts* 10, no. 2 (August 1971): 10–20; see also William Hinton, "Hundred Day War," *Monthly Review*, 24 (July–August 1972).

two worlds: the apparent world is filled with light, purity, and publicity; but this world is suspected of being unreal. Behind "masks" or hidden in "holes," there is a real world of darkness and squalor. This underworld is inhabited by all manner of savage beasts: there are "man-eating" tigers, "noxious vermin," "voracious wolves," "poisonous snakes," and others. As if these metaphors were inadequate to describe the dangers lurking below, the demonology of popular Buddhism is invoked: there are "bull-ghosts and snake-spirits" (niugui sheshen, usually freely translated as "freaks and monsters"), and "demons" who masquerade in "painted skin," speak "ghost language," and practice "black magic."[26]

What divides these two worlds is a forbidding barrier, variously referred to as a "line of demarcation," "shackles," a "fortress," or (most commonly) "frame" (kuangkuang). This barrier is heavily fortified, and must remain so. Between good and evil one must "draw a clear line of demarcation" (huaqing jiexian), and those who "deliberately confuse the line of demarcation between . . . revolutionaries and counterrevolutionaries" are denounced as "two-faced and three-sworded"—that is to say, treacherous.[27] As previously noted, the nuclear family was sometimes rent by this ideological division, which severed husband from wife, parents from children. Yet, paradoxically, it is the wish of the young rebels to shatter this barrier, an act they describe with verbs of violent penetration such as "smash," "crush," "bombard the fortress," and "break the frames." This penetration is said to require courage and to occasion high excitement: "With the tremendous and impetuous force of a raging storm [the rebels] have smashed the shackles imposed on their minds by the exploiting classes for so long."[28]

The motives for penetration appear mixed. On the one hand, the rebels expressed the desire to "destroy all evil winds," "sweep all demons and freaks away," and otherwise annihilate the enemy. They also wished, however, to emancipate the repressed. An article entitled "Don't Be Afraid of Washing Dirty Linen in Public" asserted, for instance, that "fear to discuss our shortcomings and mistakes actually is fear to touch our own souls and dig up the dirty things in our minds."[29] It was felt necessary not only to "dig up dirty things," but thoroughly to assimilate them: "The revolutionary young people must tumble millions of times in the mud of the masses."[30] Emancipation and assimilation of the re-

26. Cited in Chuang, Little Red Book, p. 18.
27. HQ editorial, no. 4 (March 1, 1967), in JPRS, no. 41450, pp. 46–53.
28. "Sweep Away All Freaks and Monsters," RR editorial, June 1, 1966, in SCMP, no. 3712 (June 6, 1966), p. 2.
    For an intimate account of how the concept of a "line of demarcation" might apply within the nuclear family, see Liang and Shapiro, Son of the Revolution, pp. 40–80.
29. GM, March 23, 1967, in JPRS, no. 41450, pp. 53–54.
30. "Learn to Swim While Swimming," RR editorial, August 17, 1966.

pressed was desirable because although this hidden world was a source of danger and pollution, it also harbored an uncanny power, and by unleashing this power the rebels could exploit it to confound their opponents and cleanse the world. The effect was like that of a dam bursting:

> For the sake of our country never changing color, for the sake of the complete liberation of the proletariat , you [viz., Mao] personally lighted the flames of the Great Proletarian Cultural Revolution. ... The billows of the historically unprecedented revolution surge and roll in an irresistible force which sweeps over the old world and which will completely bury imperialism and modern revisionism. The hearts of the revolutionary peoples boil with anger and their spirits are soaring.[31]

To smash the frames was to obliterate the distinction between revealed and concealed and to "drag out" those lurking in darkness into the light. The result was that "ghosts" and "men" intermingled freely without distinguishing earmarks, a situation that was termed "chaos" (*luan*). During the movement's initial stages (i.e., up to the "February adverse current," in 1967), chaos was deliberately fostered, in an apparent attempt to shatter the conventional barriers of shame that supported the emergent socialist authority structure. As Mao told the young rebels: "Do not be afraid to make trouble. The more trouble you make and the longer you make it the better. Confusion and trouble are always noteworthy. It can clear things up ... wherever there are abscesses or infections we must always blow them up."[32] And the rebels responded with enthusiasm: "We want to wield the massive cudgel, express our spirit, invoke our magic influence and turn the old world upside down, smash things into chaos, into smithereens, the more chaos the better!"[33]

Frames are to be smashed, then—but why? Consider once again the structure of polemical symbolism: above is the world of appearance, full of light, purity, public spirit and virtuous action; underground, stealthily concealed, a world of darkness, selfishness, defilement, passive dependency. Dividing the two worlds is a formidable barrier, which seems to arouse intense ambivalence. It is graphically depicted in figure 1.

This symbolic construct corresponds to three dimensions of experience in Chinese social life: moral, psycho-cultural, and stratificational. The moral implications are perhaps most readily apparent: the upper row represents virtue and the lower row represents evil. The barrier dividing

31. *RR*, June 7, 1966, cited in Chuang, *Cultural Revolution.*
32. "Chairman Mao's Important Instructions" (n.d.), trans. in *JPRS*, no. 49826, p. 23. For a penetrating psychoanalytic perspective on "chaos" see Richard Solomon, "Mao's Effort to Reintegrate the Chinese Polity: Problems of Authority and Conflict in the Chinese Social Process," in A. Doak Barnett, ed., *Chinese Communist Politics in Action*, pp. 271–365.
33. Red Guards of Qinghua Middle School (Beijing), "Long Live the Revolutionary Rebel Spirit of the Proletariat" (June 24, 1966), quoted in *HQ*, no. 11 (August 21, 1966), p. 27.

FIGURE I. Polemical Symbol Structure

APPEARANCE	LIGHT	PUBLICITY	PURITY	ACTIVITY
REALITY	DARKNESS	CONCEALMENT	DEFILEMENT	PASSIVITY

the two rows represents moral inhibitions against deviation. China is what anthropologists call a "shame" culture, in which virtue is promoted by assuring group acceptance of a set of norms and by exposing behavior to maximum publicity, so that any deviant is immediately confronted by unanimous censure, just as any act of heroism is greeted by widespread applause.[34] Those human impulses that conflict with official norms must either be repressed or allowed some form of surreptitious or symbolically disguised expression. In such a system, any relaxation of normative controls (as in this case the paralysis of the Party) would allow two distinct "worlds" to become clearly visible where only one had been apparent before, making the intervening barrier subject to challenge. Liberalization would (under these circumstances) threaten moral havoc by subverting conventional controls on immorality, at the same time revealing moral nuances and unwonted pluralism. From the moral point of view the correct response would thus seem to be to reinforce the barrier between the two worlds, decry any attempt to obscure or extenuate this barrier as hypocrisy or subversion, and to drive invaders from the subterranean world back out of sight.

The psycho-cultural dimension of this symbolic construct seems to correspond roughly to the defense mechanism of repression, in which the world of light represents the realm of freedom and rationality and the world of darkness the unconscious realm of repressed and irrational impulses. According to classic psychoanalytic theory, aggressive and sexual impulses are hedged by taboos in most civilized societies and therefore likely to play a prominent role in the unconscious. There is ample evidence that these impulses have been even more stringently regulated in China. In the course of the mass criticism movement, normally illicit sexual impulses were both symbolically and directly expressed.[35] In-group aggression, normally subject to painstaking regi-

34. See Weston LaBarre, "Some Observations on Character Structure in the Orient. II. The Chinese, Part 1," *Psychiatry* 9, no. 3 (August 1946): 215–39.
35. According to Zhou Enlai, sexual promiscuity during the Cultural Revolution accounted for a measurable increase in China's population growth rate. Edgar Snow, *The Long Revolution* (New York: Vintage Books, 1973), p. 45. Vivid eyewitness accounts of such activity may be found in Ken Ling, *The Revenge of Heaven: Journal of a Young Chinese* (New York: G. P. Putnam's Sons, 1972), pp. 14, 31, 30, 119, 121, 146, 250, 332–33; also Liang and Shapiro, *Son of the Revolution*, pp. 126–27. Sexual imagery is also apparent in the

mentation,[36] was unleashed against both Party-government authorities and rival rebel factions.

Prominent though such impulses were, it would be unduly simplistic to "reduce" the elating sensation of freedom described by so many participants solely to the liberation of repressed sexual and aggressive instincts. Within the broad latitude of freedom allowed by the collapse of conventional authority, these young rebels had unprecedented opportunities to exercise initiative, to roam the world, to explore new ideas and pursue their logical implications without official censure, to realize previously untapped potentialities for leadership and self-expression.[37] From a psycho-cultural perspective, then, the Cultural Revolution implied an opportunity to smash taboo barriers and emancipate culturally and psychically repressed vital impulses of all kinds—an opportunity that many Chinese young people found exciting.

The stratificational dimension of the polemical symbolism refers to what Alan Liu calls a "political culture of dualism": the Chinese masses had been taught to cultivate "boundless love" and self-sacrifice for the "people" and "boundless hate" for "enemies of the people."[38] From this

---

language of the polemics: there is a confrontation envisaged between two opposing (and yet strangely attracted) forces, separated by a taboo barrier, the penetration of which is destructive and yet necessary, dangerous and yet thrilling. This seems to be defloration symbolism, as John Weakland has also noted in a quite different (but analogous) context. See his "Chinese Film Images of Invasion and Resistance," *CQ*, no. 47 (July-September 1971): 438–71.

36. A Japanese reporter made these painstaking observations of a Beijing rally in support of North Vietnam in 1965: The buildings in Beijing along Changan Street are equipped with red flags to be hung and lights to be turned on within minutes after they receive an order. Each of the paving stones in the Tiananmen Plaza is numbered, so that students can be given standing orders to form great ideographs and geometrical patterns (e.g., "Fifty students from X Commune stand from A-13 to A-15.") The march routes and dispersion points are all designated in advance (e.g., "When the demonstration is over, the W Commune shall turn at the corner of X, march down Y Street and disperse when they reach the buses waiting at point Z.") When certain paving stones are removed and a blue canvas tent is erected, certain parts of the road become public lavatories that can accommodate about thirty people within ten minutes (the lavatories are directly connected with the sewage system). Since the masses become thirsty from shouting slogans and singing songs, first-aid teams are dispersed throughout the crowd, and stands serving hot water are set up, with a red-colored antiseptic solution used to disinfect the cups. *Yomiuri*, February 25, 1965, trans. in *Daily Summary of the Japanese Press* (Tokyo: U.S. Embassy), March 3, 1965, p. 16.

37. See Gordon Bennett and Ronald Montaperto, *Red Guard: The Political Biography of Dai Hsiao-ai* (Garden City, N.Y.: Doubleday & Co., 1971); as well as Ling, *Revenge*; and Liang and Shapiro, *Son of the Revolution*. For a balanced secondary analysis, see Andrew J. Watson, "A Revolution to Touch Men's Souls: The Family, Interpersonal Relations and Daily Life," in Stuart Schram, ed., *Authority, Participation and Cultural Change in China* (Cambridge: Cambridge University Press, 1973), pp. 291–331.

38. Alan P. L. Liu, *Political Culture and Group Conflict in Communist China* (Santa Barbara, Calif.: Clio Press, 1976), pp. 24–31.

perspective the frames should be smashed and the enemies eradicated, or at least severely punished. The identity of these enemies however remained ambiguous, as residual and emergent criteria for the classification of classes competed with one another in the public arena.[39] If residual criteria were applied, the "spearhead" would be turned downward, targeting representatives of the former propertied classes; if emergent criteria were selected, representatives of the bureaucratic New Class could be targeted. The implication that the class enemy should be destroyed (or at least transformed), in the context of the ambiguous semantics of this term, meant that any heightening of the rhetoric resulted only in an intensification of internecine conflict.

Altogether, then, the polemical symbolism of the Cultural Revolution had at least three dimensions, the third of which contained an unacknowledged contradiction between residual and emergent criteria for defining its referents. It is graphically depicted in figure 2.

FIGURE 2. Semantic Dimensions of the Polemical Symbolism

	Moral	Psycho-Cultural	Stratificational
World of Light	VIRTUE	EMANCIPATION	"THE PEOPLE"
World of Darkness	EVIL	REPRESSION	"THE ENEMY"

Each of these dimensions had different action implications, although paradoxically the "condensation" of divergent meanings in the same polemical symbolism seemed to magnify rather than mitigate its mobilizational efficacy. Both psycho-cultural and stratificational dimensions legitimated smashing the frames of the established authority structure, in the first case for the purpose of emancipation, in the second for repression. Morality, on the other hand, reinforced this barrier, intensifying the excitement attached to its smashing when the authorization of the other two dimensions sufficed to motivate this taboo violation. The empirical referents of each dimension proved to be sufficiently vague to permit tactical flexibility on the part of faction leaders.

MASS MOBILIZATION

Whereas the Cultural Revolution seemed from the perspective of those whom it politicized to represent a merging of the ideal and the real, rhetoric and action, in a revolutionary epiphany, this synthesis was in fact incomplete. It is true that rhetoric played a more integral role in the

39. See Kraus, *Class Conflict*, pp. 143–65 *et passim.*

Cultural Revolution than in previous movements, due to the collapse of the Party-state apparatus that normally orientates mass participation, and to paucity of extrinsic incentives for involvement (such as, say, a plot of land). Nevertheless, not everyone fully entered into the symbol structure, and those who did sometimes smuggled in residual commitments to ulterior objectives—such as political self-aggrandizement, hunger for adventure, or private account-reckoning—to which the "open-textured" character of the symbolism offered ample latitude. Thus the split between particularistic interests and ideological generalities noted above reemerged in chaotic contestation in the public arena—the former in the form of various group and sectoral interests, the latter in the form of certain structurally congruent general tendencies. The interplay between particular interests and structurally congruent tendencies is discernible in the vicissitudes of the mass media.

Group Interests

First of all, the national elites who led the movement, consisting of Mao Zedong and his retinue, were motivated by two objectives, one positive and one negative. The positive objective, which Mao in 1967 gave top priority, was to "transform . . . the cultural superstructure," to "construct a revolutionary world view and eliminate the roots of revisionism."[40] Mao had expressed awareness that such a transformation could not be forced.[41] This awareness underlay his decision in the spring of 1966, in the face of widespread elite misgivings, to remove organizational constraints on the movement, permitting it to develop its own momentum. The masses would be brought to embrace the "correct" by becoming engaged in struggle against the "wrong." "What is correct invariably develops in the course of struggle with what is wrong," as Mao declared in 1957. "The true, the good and the beautiful always exist in comparison with the false, the evil and the ugly, and grow in struggle with the latter."[42] By blaming the "Party persons in authority taking the capitalist road" for previous failure to achieve Maoist norms, the masses would be encouraged to believe that those norms were after all realistic desiderata that could now be achieved with more strenuous efforts. The essence of "proletarian revolutionary" norms in this "two-line struggle" (as argued in the previous chapter) was intrepid selflessness—ideally, martyrdom. And the general criticism themes emanating from the "top" reflexively

40. Mao Zedong, "Zai zui gao guowuhuiyi shang de jieshu hua" [Concluding remarks at the Supreme State Conference] (March 1, 1957), in *Wansui* (1969), pp. 90–100.
41. Ibid.
42. Mao, "On the Correct Handling of Contradictions among the People," in *SW*, vol. 5: 409.

supported these norms, despite specific shifts of polemical emphasis to counter evanescent deviant tendencies that arose in the course of the movement—for example, criticism of "economism," coinciding with a wave of strikes and management buy-offs (higher wages, paid travel to Beijing) in January–February 1967; criticism of a "mountaintop mentality" or "theory of mass spontaneity," coinciding with a Maoist drive against rebel inter-factional conflict in the late summer and fall of 1967; criticism of Liu Shaoqi's Party-building policies, coinciding with the effort to set up Party committees in the fall of 1968.

The negative objective, which Mao in 1967 relegated to subsidiary importance but which in fact tended to assume primacy, was power-political: to purge all "Party persons in authority taking the capitalist road" from their Party and government positions. Mao's evident motive was to eliminate opponents; the motive of his radical retinue, to wash out rivals and improve their own political positions. Throughout the early 1960s Mao's rhetoric contained pointed warnings to those he held accountable for the frustration of his initiatives, whom he would "cap" with ideological "labels" ranging from "bureaucratism" to "revisionism." But the persons being warned were invariably anonymous; thus, it was left unclear to outside observers (and perhaps even to those involved) just who Mao's enemies were. It became clear only in the course of the movement, when through various subtle signals Mao indicated his preferences, whereupon the wheat would be gleaned and the chaff left to the revolutionary masses. At least that was what happened at the highest level; at lower levels the very number of cadres purged implied that purge victims were often decided by the balance of power among rebel factions and local military elites, without clear guidelines from the center.

The relationship between the first and second elite objectives was basically one of functional complementarity. As targets of mass criticism, purged opponents would contribute to the political edification of the masses. The principal purge targets were, of course, Liu Shaoqi and Deng Xiaoping, who came to personify the "bourgeois reactionary line." When the first and second objectives conflicted, the second seemed to take priority. For example, it might have been useful for the purpose of providing an expiatory finale to otherwise unmanageable factional strife to accept the self-criticisms of the principal targets, making way for their reintegration into the moral community along the lines of "criticism and self-criticism" as practiced in the small-group context. This outcome, incompatible as it was with the power-political objectives of the movement, was forgone.

To the masses, the Cultural Revolution was an opportunity for catharsis rather than revolutionary self-transformation, a chance to express demands and grievances normally repressed in the People's Republic.

Mao encouraged catharsis under the assumption that if emotions are pent up they acquire explosive destructive potential. Some of the grievances and demands that found expression were generally shared, such as resentment of "frames." Others were specific to a particular group and tended to reflect their backgrounds and interests.

Students, for instance, manifested an idealistic conception of politics, indignation about its coercive aspect, and a demand for the emancipation of disprivileged strata. In contrast to official publications, which exhibited relative concern with the erosion of "proletarian dictatorship" (by functional experts, intellectual liberalism, the market, and so forth), Red Guard media were most preoccupied with issues of political repression. The same concerns were reflected in their choice of the dates of confrontation between students and authorities as anniversaries or as faction names, as in the "May 16 Group" (*wu yao liu*), a radical faction named after Mao's inaugural manifesto in 1966. The two factions in the Ministry of Machine Industry called themselves "September 16 (*jiu yao liu*) and "September 17" (*jiu yao qi*); Jiangsu's "August 27" (*ba er qi*) faction commemorated the date (in 1966) of the first march on the provincial Party committee by Nanjing University students; and so on. Their anti-authoritarian themes and eagerness to "seize power" reflected the students' sense of status discrepancy between present subordination and future elitehood, together with frustration over growing obstacles to these aspirations.[43] Red Guard criticisms also displayed greater outrage concerning incidents of apparent irreverence toward Mao Zedong and his Thought than did official publications. The emotional cogency of *lèse majesté* to these young rebels (who in Chinese families were still children) may derive from their incomplete separation of politics from a domestic context: Mao appears as the benign father, Liu Shaoqi et al. as unfilial sons, and the young rebel can deny analogous sentiments even while engaging in revolution. Finally, the policy areas selected for special emphasis by student polemicists (viz., education and cultural affairs generally) reflected their academic backgrounds.

Whereas these themes characterized nearly all student groups, there were also a number of issue areas in which their interests diverged. The two primary bases for cleavage were class origin and academic achievement. Those with "five red" (*hong wu lei*) class origins (i.e., children of workers, poor peasants, revolutionary martyrs, cadres, and soldiers) were generally eager to attack "bourgeois intellectual authorities" (i.e.,

---

43. Most manpower studies have made note of the tightening professional job market in China. Cf. John Philip Emerson, "Employment in Mainland China," in Robert Dernberger, ed., *An Economic Profile of Mainland China: Studies Prepared for the Joint Economic Committee of Congress*, vol. 2 (February 1967): 458–59; also Leo Orleans, "Communist China's Education: Politics, Problems, and Prospects," in ibid., p. 515.

teachers and functional experts) but had a vested interest in maintaining the existing class structure that discriminated in their favor politically, and recoiled from any determined assault on the Party or on its successor as a pillar of established authority, the PLA. Students from "five black" (*hei wu lei*) backgrounds (children of counterrevolutionaries, bad elements, rich peasants, landlords, and bourgeoisie) and children of the "intermediate" classes (e.g., teachers, doctors, urban middle-class professionals), on the other hand, had previously been excluded from participation in school Youth League and Party activities, and took advantage of their enfranchisement to articulate a radical critique of the status quo that threw the entire seventeen-year history of Communist rule into critical relief.[44]

Academic achievement tended to crosscut the class cleavage, inasmuch as children from unreliable class origins tended to excel scholastically due to their culturally advantaged family backgrounds and their desire to compensate for political vulnerability. Thus students from "bad" class backgrounds did not necessarily become radical activists, particularly if their academic achievements had given them bright career prospects and a stake in the status quo, in which case discretion might dictate a less active role. Nor did students with "good" (i.e., "red") class backgrounds always join in defense of the establishment, particularly if disprivileged (e.g., poor peasant) backgrounds or low scholastic achievement beclouded their futures. Work-study students (who were both underpaid as part-time workers and undereducated as part-time students) and students who had been "transferred down" (*xiafang*) for work in the countryside were conspicuously prominent among the radicals.[45]

A third basis for potential cleavage among students (and indeed, among all groups) was regionalism. When Red Guards fanned out across the countryside from the urban centers where the movement originated to "spread the sparks of revolution," they often engaged in more "radical" tactics than they permitted themselves in their home towns, and their condescending attitudes toward "backward" native youth provoked a regional xenophobia that local elites often encouraged for their own self-protection.[46] On the other hand, "returned" Red Guards were often the most zealous of all.

In their late response to mobilization, initial support of the local authorities, and anti-intellectual orientation, Chinese workers seemed to

44. See Hong Yung Lee, *The Politics of the Chinese Cultural Revolution: A Case Study* (Berkeley: University of California Press, 1978); see also Stanley Rosen, *Red Guard Factionalism and the Cultural Revolution in Guangzhou (Canton)* (Boulder, Colo.: Westview Press, 1982).

45. See Lee, *Politics*.

46. Ling, *Revenge*, pp. 70–71.

fit the profile Lipset calls "working-class authoritarianism": leftist on economic issues, but rigid and intolerant on social issues.[47] This posture disposed workers to resist initial Red Guard incursions into their factories. As the "power seizure" movement of January 1967 gathered momentum, workers joined in, grasping their chance to bargain for higher wages ("the students wanted power, but the workers wanted money," as a former Red Guard put it).[48] As in the case of students, however, workers were internally divided by conflicts of interest. With their participation in the movement came a tendency to splinter into factions, usually based on trade or income (a tendency condemned in the press as a "guild mentality"). The most conservative "guilds," composed of senior, "model," and unionized workers, lent active support to Party or PLA forces in their conflict with radical student units. The nonunionized contract, piece, rotation, or apprentice workers received low wages and were subject to layoff on a last-hired, first-fired basis; they understandably tended to adopt more radical postures, demanding major changes in the industrial wage scale and administrative hierarchy.[49] Workers from small handicraft industries seemed on the other hand less inclined to join radical factions than did workers in large state factories. Their reluctance can probably be explained by insecurity and/or a greater financial stake in the enterprise (workers in collective enterprises were paid from retained profits, not on salary).

Peasants did not generally become actively engaged in the movement. As victims of the collapse of the Great Leap and beneficiaries of "revisionist" recovery policies of the early 1960s that gave greater latitude to private plots, domestic industries, and the rural market, the peasants seemed generally opposed to radical social programs.[50] So they opposed returning Red Guards who espoused drastic changes, in a few cases threatening (perhaps under "backstage" instigation) to "encircle the cities from the countryside" and quell the radicals. On the outskirts of some large industrial cities, on the other hand, *jacquerie*-type uprisings occurred. These may perhaps be attributed to the salience of urban–rural income disparities in the suburbs, and to the rather large concentrations of rusticated urbanites in these locations, many of whom were quite ready to march back into the cities and demand redress.[51]

47. Seymour Martin Lipset, *Political Man* (Baltimore, Md.: The Johns Hopkins University Press, 1981, expanded ed.), pp. 87–127.
48. Ling, *Revenge*, p. 243.
49. Hong Yung Lee, "The Political Mobilization of the Red Guards and Revolutionary Rebels in the Cultural Revolution" (Ph.D. diss., University of Chicago, 1973).
50. See Anita Chan, Richard Madsen, and Jonathan Unger, *Chen Village: The Recent History of a Peasant Community in Mao's China* (Berkeley: University of California Press, 1984), pp. 96, 170–73.
51. Liu, *Political Culture*, pp. 153–56.

Structurally Congruent Tendencies

If the Cultural Revolution is scrutinized "microscopically," as it were, taking into consideration the interplay of factions within a restricted arena over a limited time span, group interests appear predominant.[52] But if it is looked at "macroscopically," certain general tendencies emerge. Such tendencies were as often as not irrational in terms of the goals dictated by the material interests of the participants, and can more efficiently be accounted for in terms of the implications of the polemical symbol structure. Three such trends were particularly prominent: the tendencies toward *anarchism, polarization,* and an obsession with *exposure.*

Anarchism: Rebel anarchic propensities resulted from the application of the polemical symbol structure to the emergent Chinese stratification system. The symbol structure implied that any form of domination—whether based on economic, status, or political criteria—was illegitimate, any victim of repression justified in rebelling. Whereas for Mao, revolutionary cadres could still be differentiated from "capitalist-roaders" on the basis of empirical information concerning their performance, for the young rebels, lacking such "inside" information, the two classes were defined in more consistently structural terms, according to which those in authority were almost unexceptionally suspected of having "capitalist" propensities. This failure to differentiate not only led to the disqualification of most officials with any experience in running the country (roughly 60–80 percent of incumbent cadres were purged) but made it impossible to establish any authority whatever. If one rebel faction managed to "seize power" it would promptly be assailed by another faction that had been left out of the coalition, which denounced the former in the same language previously used against the established authorities. A seemingly endless series of power seizures ensued.

Mao took note of this development with considerable dismay: "The Shanghai People's Council office submitted a proposal to the Premier of the State Council in which they asked for the elimination of all chiefs," he noted. "This is extreme anarchy; it is most reactionary. Now they do not wish to refer to anyone as chief of such-and-such; they call them orderlies and attendants. . . . Actually, there always have to be chiefs."[53]

Polarization: Most adult authorities had been "toppled" or at least driven into political passivity within the first year of the movement, whereupon the still zealous rebel bands gravitated into conflict with one another. In most conflict arenas, the "free market" of numerous competing conflict groups lasted only a few months, thereafter giving way to

52. See n. 44 above.
53. "Chairman Mao's Speech at His Third Meeting with Zhang Chunqiao and Yao Wenyuan" (February 1967), as trans. in *JPRS,* no. 49826, pp. 44–45.

tendencies toward attrition of intermediate groups and polarization into "two opposing factional organizations" locked into a conflict spiral.[54] For example, in Beijing a conflict between the Geology Institute and the Aeronautics Institute soon subsumed all other local Red Guard organizations and escalated to sustained warfare between what became known as the Earth and Heaven factions; in Guangdong, the struggle became polarized between the East Wind and the Red Flag factions; in Guangxi, between "April 22nd" and "Alliance Command"; in Yunnan, between "August 23rd" and "Yunnan Alliance"; and in Fujian, between the "Revolutionary Rebels" and "August 29th."[55] Such polarization was not consonant with the interests of the groups described above, for pursuit of group interests would logically lead to competition among more than two factions. Polarization also militated against the objectives common to all factions, making it impossible to "unite 95 percent of the people and cadres against 5 percent of the enemy"; in most arenas the two sides were so evenly matched that neither side could destroy the other, with the result that confrontation devolved into extended siege warfare broken by occasional sorties. Mao could not understand this tendency toward polarization, discerning no substantive issues at stake between the two factions: "There is no fundamental clash of interests within the working class," he told representatives of two contending factions. "Why should they be split into two big irreconcilable organizations? I don't understand it; some people are pulling the strings. This is inevitably the result of the manipulation by capitalist-roaders."[56]

This combative impulse and its tendency to escalate derived from the polemics, whose premium on smashing frames required an opposing structure against which a revolutionary breakthrough could be achieved;

54. Editor, "Mass Factionalism in Communist China," *Current Scene*, vol. 6, no. 8 (May 15, 1968).

55. For analyses of the Beijing and Guangdong conflicts see Hong Yung Lee, "The Political Behavior of the Radical Students and Their Social Characteristics in the Cultural Revolution," *CQ*, 63 (September 1975); for a brief summary of Red Guard activities in the other provinces cited see Victor C. Falkenheim, "The Cultural Revolution in Kwangsi, Yunnan and Fukien," *AS*, 9 (August 1969): 580–97. I know of only one exception to this tendency toward bipolarity: in Shenyang (Mukden Province), there were three factions, which coalesced in support of "backstage backers" (*houtai laoban*) Chen Xilian (representing the army), Song Renqiong (representing civilian cadres), and the Navy–Air Force Headquarters (the most consistent source of radical patronage within the establishment).

56. "Chairman Mao's Later Supreme Instructions during His Inspection Tour," *Zhengfa Hongqi* [Politics and law red flag], Guangzhou, combined issues nos. 3–4 (October 17, 1967). Whether "capitalist-roaders" still had any influence at this point is doubtful, but Mao was correct in suspecting that "some people are pulling the strings"—he being perhaps foremost among them. No faction was ever "destroyed" unless its backstage collapsed, with the ultimate outcome to be determined on the basis of negotiations in Beijing.

once the Party-state apparatus had been "toppled," it inspired a search for new opposition that soon brought different rebel factions into conflict with each other. The polarizing tendency derived from the dichotomous syntactic structure of the rhetoric, which in effect denied the possibility of intermediate positions, placing all terms referring to such positions between inverted commas, indicating their nominal or hypocritical character. Within the conceptual framework that the rebels in both factions used to order their arguments (and probably their thinking), it became impossible to draw subtle distinctions; only a zero-sum choice between "bourgeois" and "proletarian" could be made. In a given arena, the conflict inexorably polarized to fit the participants' two-class model of the situation:

> As the two armies face each other, large posters with such slogans as "Provincial Revolutionary Rebel Joint Committee [PRRJC] is very good!" and "Sentence PRRJC to death!" are put up in the streets all of a sudden, and the whole city is resounding with such slogans as "PRRJC is finished!" and "PRRJC is growing up amidst curses!" At this critical juncture every revolutionary comrade, every organization, and the political forces of every faction must clearly indicate his attitude and choose sides. Should the PRRJC really be "Sentenced to death?" This is a question that must be answered unequivocally.[57]

Although the vivid antipodal imagery indeed made this an urgent question, it contained no answer, tending rather to sustain each faction's faith in its own righteousness and its opponent's perfidy. The polemical rhetoric provided a set of conceptual "trenches" confronting each other, so to speak. It did not specify who should occupy which positions (this decision was usually made on the basis of group interests), nor did it contain any instructions about how peace might be negotiated. Although peace was eventually imposed willy-nilly by Beijing, factional loyalties and antipathies were forged that continued to have a subdued effect for many years thereafter, sometimes even surviving the official termination of the Cultural Revolution in July 1977.

Exposure: The "two worlds" structure of symbolism conveyed the general impression of a deep cleft between the world of appearance and the world of reality, that the apparent world contained no reliable indicators of the nature of the real world. This disjunction occasioned a sense of outrage and an ambition to reduce appearances to their underlying naked realities. In short, there was a general suspicion of the conventional, which predicated a correspondence between revealed/concealed and phony/real. The systematically misleading relationship between

57. "Guangdong Rebel Joint Committee Proclamation," *Guangdong Zhan Bao* [Guangdong battle news], February 22, 1967, trans. in *JPRS*, no. 41450, pp. 79–82.

appearance and reality was more subtly indicated by addition of inverted commas or the adjective "*suowei*" (so-called) to the once illustrious title of the target, as in *suowei* scholars (*xuezhe*), specialists (*zhuanjia*), or authorities (*quanwei, dangquan pai*).

The quest for exposure was to be undertaken "resolutely, thoroughly, wholly and completely" (*jianjue chedi ganjing quanbu de*), to quote one of Mao's characteristic contributions to the language,[58] with the ultimate intention of annihilating the sphere of "bourgeois privacy" and realizing the ancient ideal, "all for the public interest, nothing for oneself" (*da gong wu si*). Any indication that an authority was protecting some aspect of the policy process from full public scrutiny aroused suspicion that one was "shielding" the guilty from legitimate criticism.[59] Thus Red Guards and Revolutionary Rebels systematically violated attempts to preserve secrecy by launching raids in search of "black materials," ransacking homes and offices, interviewing interested subordinate officials (or finding allies among them, such as Yao Dengshan in the Foreign Ministry), torturing or otherwise encouraging intimates of the targets to bear witness against them (e.g., Liu Shaoqi's estranged ex-wife and their two children testified voluntarily; his current wife was abducted and "struggled"),[60] and for the first time breaching the Party's hitherto sacrosanct internal file system. "What's so terrific about secrets?" a participant in the notorious raid on the Foreign Ministry files asked rhetorically. "To Hell with them!"[61] Sometimes in the context of such raids rebels would seize the opportunity to destroy their own files—only to plunge into deeper trouble later, for without a dossier one could be suspected of anything.

Once such secret information was discovered, the motto *da gong wu si* dictated that it be made public. This was done either via big-character posters, which could be written anonymously by anyone and soon "covered every available wall and mat," or in rebel tabloids (*xiaobao*), which came to comprise a vast and lively alternative media system. Some tabloids appeared daily, others every third or fourth day; some were printed, some hectographed; some original, others plagiarized; some local, some with national circulations (for several months in 1967, Qinghua University's *Jinggangshan* had a circulation exceeding that of

58. *Mao Zedong Zhuxi Yulu* [Quotations of Chairman Mao Zedong], pp. 98, 143, as quoted in Chuang, *Little Red Book*. See also Alan Liu, *Political Culture*, pp. 153–56.

59. Cf. Neale Hunter, *Shanghai Journal: An Eyewitness Account of the Cultural Revolution* (New York: Praeger, 1969), p. 36: "To them [*viz.*, the Red Guards], Yang Hsi-kuang was saying, 'Hands off the Party leaders! Criticize anyone you like, but the Municipal Committee is sacrosanct.' This was precisely the attitude they were out to destroy."

60. See "Three Trials of Pickpocket Wang Kuang-mei," as trans. in *Current Background*, no. 848 (February 27, 1968), pp. 1–42.

61. Ross Terrill, "The 800,000,000, Part II: China and the World," *The Atlantic* 229 (January 1972), pp. 39–63, at p. 49.

People's Daily).[62] Printed media were augmented by oral communications, which came to comprise a nationwide rumor network. Early in the movement the interdict on inter-city mobility was placed in abeyance in order to facilitate mobilization, and Red Guards set up a network of liaison stations, which functioned like diplomatic missions and were connected by envoys and commercial telegraph facilities. These stations were extremely effective in disseminating news (e.g., in July 1967, Jiang Qing's instruction to "attack with reason and defend with force" was followed within a few hours by Red Guard arms seizures—it was not until a few days later that her instruction was published in the official press). Sensational and irresponsible as it was, this alternative media system was richer in content and often more accurate than the official press.

This almost obsessive rebel interest in exposure seemed, however, to harbor an underlying ambivalence. For although Red Guards denounced authorities for hypocritically concealing their crimes and displaying only their virtues, when an authority actually made a statement revealing reservations about Mao's leadership, however obliquely (as in Deng Tuo's satires of the early 1960s),[63] he would be condemned for "shamelessly" and "audaciously shouting," "fanatically trumpeting," and so forth. Even if one confessed, the confession was invariably rejected as "superficial" and "fraudulent."

The reason for this ambivalence has to do with the fact that secrecy was not *merely* a "cover" used by capitalist-roaders in the Party to protect themselves from public accountability, but a regular dimension of organization—both "revisionist" *and* "revolutionary" leaders communicated through organizational channels, made decisions in closed meetings, and otherwise adhered to the rules of information security. So no one was finally proof against accusations of "coverups." Zhou Enlai came under repeated attack for shielding his vice-premiers, for example, and a purge of acting Chief-of-Staff Yang Chengwu amid allusions to a "black backer" even excited momentary suspicions of Lin Biao. When the May 16th Group was purged in September 1967, Jiang Qing accused its leaders of "collecting black material on every one of us, and it may throw it out in public at any time."[64] As chapter 3 has already indicated, secrecy played a pervasive role in Chinese society as a criterion for organizational

62. T. K. Tong, "Red Guard Newspapers," *Columbia Forum* 12, no. 1 (Spring 1969): 38–41.

63. Trans. in Joachim Glaubitz, *Opposition Gegen Mao: Abendspräche am Yanshan und andere politische Dokumente* (Olten: Walter Verlag, 1969).

64. See *CCP Documents of the Great Proletarian Cultural Revolution* (Hong Kong: Union Research Institute, 1969), pp. 72, 309, and 503 for an indication of the CCRG's shift of position on this pivotal issue.

self-definition and hierarchy. Possession of privileged information helped to define "inside" (*nei*) from "outside" (*wai*), and "top" (*shang*) from "bottom" (*xia*): the unit was thus set off from its environment, Party from non-Party, leaders from masses. It was precisely the multifunctional utility of secrecy—and the invidious element common to these functions—that endowed its critique with such widespread appeal.

The Interplay between Ideology and Political Interest

Noticing the tendency of the movement to fragment into contending interest groups, the central authorities attempted, beginning in the spring of 1967, to impose structure through a concerted media campaign. Thus, on February 23, 1967, *Red Flag* stressed that "the overwhelming majority of cadres at all levels" were "good or comparatively good," and that criticism should henceforth be focused on "China's Khrushchev" (viz., Liu Shaoqi).[65] Beginning April 1, a national criticism campaign was launched against Liu in all official media, with the proclaimed intention of deflecting criticism from secondary targets and thereby mitigating factional strife. This tactic seems to have been temporarily successful in absorbing polemical energies, but as it becames less plausible that Liu posed any real threat to Mao, rebel units tended to ignore Liu, or to adopt him as a symbol for their local opponents, paradoxically leading to an intensification of factionalism by the summer of 1967.

Similarly, a campaign was launched by the center beginning in the fall of 1967 to deactivate the semantic implications of the symbolism.[66] The "frame" that should be "smashed" was in effect psychologized: rebels were told to "dare to rebel against all the things in their minds which do not conform to the Thought of Mao. . . . to let the proletariat seize power in their minds" and "revolutionize the self."[67] Revolution thus reconstrued might relieve besieged authority structures from further storming and power seizures, and salvage penitent cadres: "The fact that a cadre who has made errors can turn from his former adherence to the bourgeois reactionary line, can fight back fiercely against this line and rise up to make rebellion, shows that he has changed his standpoint," a usually leftist official journal editorialized. "This 'going over' is a revolution . . . against the viruses of the bourgeois reactionary line in one's mind."[68] This campaign was however also ineffectual in abating rebel factionalism.

65. "Revolutionary Cadres Must be Treated Correctly," *HQ* editorial, no. 3 (February 23, 1967).
66. *HQ*, no. 15, 1967; "The Great Historical Tide," *RR* editorial, September 22, 1967; Mao Zedong, "Instruction Given during Inspection Tour," *RR*, September 14, 1967.
67. *RR*, February 8, 1967, trans. in *JPRS*, no. 41147.
68. *Wenhui Bao* editorial, February 13, 1967, in *JPRS*, no. 41450.

The inefficacy of such campaigns to coordinate the movement through the media may be attributed to three factors. First, the absence of an organizational command hierarchy with the capacity to interpret media-relayed messages unambiguously and enforce them. The PLA was instructed to enter the vacuum left by the collapse of the Party and fill this role, but the Chen Zaidao incident in Wuhan in the summer of 1967 revealed a cleavage within the PLA between central and regional forces that cast doubt on the hierarchy's reliability. Second, the lack of centralized control over the media network itself. Before 1966, such control made the nation a vast echo chamber, in which a concerted initiative in the pace-making central media promptly reverberated in all provincial and local outlets. The advent of an alternative media network in late 1966 made it more difficult to achieve such mimetic response. Local rebel tabloids typically responded to central thematic initiatives, but they tended to reconstrue them in terms of factional interests, and would then revert to investigative journalism and local polemics. Third, the structure of the rhetoric permitted and even encouraged conflicting interests to be fought out rather than compromised (as demonstrated in the immediately preceding subsection).

CONCLUSIONS

As a form of collective thought reform, the Cultural Revolution is distinguished by its abandonment of highly organized "cultivation" therapy within a small-group context, and its substitution of nondirective "shock" therapy operating within a communications network temporarily freed from authoritative constraints. The focus is on the smashing of symbolic "frames" representing cultural and psychological inhibitions upon the expression of repressed impulses. This symbolic revolutionary breakthrough, by sanctioning the catharsis of previously repressed grievances against targets of criticism, should unleash vital energies and foster the internalization of revolutionary norms. Through such a combination of exhortation and catharsis, "norms and values," on the one hand, become saturated with emotion, while the "gross and basic emotions become ennobled through contact with social values." [69] Without exhortation, catharsis would be illegitimate; but without catharsis, exhortation would become coercive. In previous movements, catharsis was disciplined by the Party apparatus—targets were preselected, and expression of criticism

69. Victor Turner, "Symbols in Ndembu Ritual," in Dorothy Emmet, ed., *Sociological Theory and Philosophical Analysis* (New York: Macmillan, 1970), p. 162; see also Turner's *The Forest of Symbols: Aspects of Ndembu Ritual* (Ithaca, N.Y.: Cornell University Press, 1967), pp. 19–47; and *Dramas, Fields and Metaphors: Symbolic Action in Human Society* (Ithaca, N.Y.: Cornell University Press, 1974), p. 37.

was restricted to official media and cadre-directed small groups—with resulting tendencies toward ritualization.[70] The sudden relaxation of organizational discipline permitted the cathartic function to assume greater prominence than it had in previous movements, giving the Cultural Revolution greater spontaneity and vitality.

The actual impact of the Cultural Revolution on the lives of those involved, so far as this can be determined on the basis of a series of intensive retrospective interviews with a sample of erstwhile participants who emigrated to Hong Kong,[71] coincided to a recognizable extent with therapeutic intentions, though the situation was complicated by various circumstantial factors. Among the most important of these was Lenin's quintessentially political question, "Who-whom?" A former target of criticism was likely to have a quite different perspective than a former participant in mass criticism. And the impact on targets was much more relevant than hitherto, for instead of attacking out-group or marginal scapegoats, the movement turned against the elite, later rehabilitating many of them to high positions. The inability to impose discipline permitted targets to proliferate unmanageably.

The impact of the movement upon targets of mass criticism was profound but essentially negative. Not a single former target felt that there was any correspondence between their errors and the criticisms to which they were subjected, attributing their humiliation rather to bad class background or other "unfair" political considerations. The impact of criticism upon their ideological attitudes ranged from superficially or temporarily successful to counterproductive. As one put it:

> Struggle didn't change my thoughts. It caused me to resist. If they're not right, they can't change my thoughts; if they're right, they don't need to struggle.... The more you're struggled, the more you resist. I would superficially accept, but in my heart, I would hate it. That more than anything else made me decide to leave China. If you completely deny any rightness in someone, he can't accept it.[72]

---

70. See Whyte, *Small Groups and Political Ritual.*
71. The data in this section and in portions of chapter 6 are derived from interviews conducted with forty-eight former residents of the PRC who emigrated sometime between 1974 and 1977. Forty-four of these were conducted in Hong Kong, the remaining four in Berkeley. Please see the preface for a discussion of the interview methodology; a translation of the protocol is contained in the appendix.
72. Informant born in Nanjing in 1934, daughter of a KMT official. She graduated from the Beijing Medical Institute in 1959 and worked in Zhengzhou (Henan Province) from then until 1975, when she legally emigrated to Hong Kong. (Hereinafter informant no. 37.) See also male informant, born 1929 in Guangdong province of free professional family background, state cadre individual status (teacher). College graduate, in literature, of overseas Chinese background, he legally migrated to Hong Kong in March 1976 in order to earn more money (hereinafter informant no. 17). And male informant, born 1928 in Guangdong

The reasons for this often vehement antipathy ranged from the forced or arbitrary character of the professed conversion to the acquisition of new information about the "shadow side" of Chinese politics.[73] It typically resulted in a more cynical, opportunistic attitude toward political involvement: "Now I have changed and become a person who struggles only for my own purposes and does not care about anything else," said one young man, sounding like Tolstoy's Prince Andrei after Austerlitz. "But I still care about China's future."[74] Others, however, denied any change at all or even claimed to have been changed from naive idealism to embittered anticommunism.[75]

On the whole, the impact of the movement upon the political attitudes of the critics and passive onlookers was more consistent with its stated objectives. It is said to have stimulated interest in national affairs and a more active involvement in local politics,[76] aroused revolutionary

---

(Nanhai) of poor peasant family background, worker individual class status (eighth grade technician), migrated illegally in 1974. Interviewed April 25, 1977 (hereinafter informant no. 9). See also Thurston, "Victims of China's Cultural Revolution," Parts I and II, for a penetrating analysis of pathological sequelae in terms of "post-traumatic stress disorder."

73. Informant no. 12. See also male informant, born 1949 in Guangdong, of free professional family background, student individual class status. Sent down to the countryside during the Cultural Revolution, where he was class leader (*banzhang*) of a production brigade, before migrating legally to Hong Kong in May 1975. Interviewed May 3, 1977 (hereinafter informant no. 23).

74. Male informant, born in Nanjing in 1946 of free professional family background, student class status, was a member of the CYL, became a Red Guard and was then "sent down" to the countryside, where he became a Mao Zedong Thought study class leader in the brigade. Migrated illegally to Hong Kong in 1973 (hereinafter informant no. 38). Also second interview with male informant, born in Zhongshan, Guangdong, in 1946 of free employee family background, student class status. He was a fourth grade worker in a Guangdong machine repair factory. Interview conducted July 23–24, 1977 (hereinafter informant no. 29). Also see female informant, born 1950 in Guangdong, of free employee family background, student individual class status. She was sent down to the countryside during the 1968 demobilization, where she functioned as a kindergarten teacher, before migrating illegally to Hong Kong in 1973. Interviewed May 13, 1977 (hereinafter informant no. 20).

75. Male informant, born 1944 in Shanghai, of free professional family background, student individual class status, worked as thirteenth grade technical cadre in a Shenyang factory. Migrated illegally to Hong Kong in 1974. Interviewed May 18, 1977 (hereinafter informant no. 31). See Connie Squires Meany's collection of interviews with a number of industrial workers conducted in Hong Kong in 1980, which she generously made available to me (hereinafter Squires collection). Also informants no. 38, 29 (second interview), and 20.

76. Male informant, born 1944 in Guangdong, of overseas Chinese (Indonesian) family background, student individual class status, he was a rank eighteen government cadre in Hebei and chief of surgery at the People's Medical Institute (*renmin yiyuan*) in Yutian *xian*, before migrating legally to Hong Kong in 1973. Interviewed April 21, 1977 (hereinafter informant no. 4).

ideals,[77] and provided timely warning against the deviations of which the targets stood accused.[78] "The Cultural Revolution was a revolution to touch people's souls," averred a former cadre. "Previous movements were only partial, they weren't as expansive and penetrating."[79] The exemplary punishment meted out to criticism targets had its impact, as did the rhetoric adjuring greater self-sacrifice, and the eye-opening participation in a movement that smashed conventional frames and permitted the exploration of a wide range of new experiences.[80] True, a perverse identification with underdogs was still sometimes confessed, betraying the influence of Mencius rather than Mao, but this seemed to be a minority response and prudence kept it well concealed (until Hong Kong).[81]

As far as expectations about the system and political behavior within it are concerned, the impact of the movement was more nearly uniform. This is one of the more surprising findings from this survey of former participants. For both cadres and masses, both ex-targets and former rebels or bystanders, the ideological message of the movement seems to

77. "The Cultural Revolution was a revolution to touch men's souls. Previous movements were only partial, they were not as expansive and penetrating. But the Cultural Revolution was a comprehensive, very penetrating revolution. Many families were split into two factions, thus illustrating how thoroughly the movement penetrated." Informant no. 32.

"The Cultural Revolution was a very impressive mass campaign because the masses wanted revolution and the purpose of revolution was to change the way of life. Otherwise, what was revolution for? The existence of individualism had to be recognized. People gave up things in their endeavors. But what were their endeavors for? There must be some things worthy of their endeavors, otherwise who would want to take the chance?" Informant no. 35.

78. "During the mass criticism I changed my thoughts because I thought, 'Oh, what that person did was wrong!' Without struggle, economic progress would be better. But some people would oppose the Party, and the Party would lose its moral authority." Informant no. 37.

79. Informant no. 32.

80. As one former "rightist" put it, "The Great Proletarian Cultural Revolution penetrated to every corner. Every person was touched by it. Before, people had been narrow-minded, but following the Cultural Revolution, everyone began to have a sense of responsibility." Informant no. 15.

81. One former worker, CYL member, and Red Guard seemed willing to forgive all targets (although he had not personally been targeted): "Frankly speaking, the fact that these four elements could live in society instead of being confined to labor reform camps was proof that they had not committed serious mistakes. The fact that they had lost a lot of freedom deserved our sympathy. The so-called traitors and secret agents were just the same. There were just some historical problems that had nothing to do with their current behavior." Male informant, born 1944 in Guangdong, lower-middle peasant family background and individual class status, received primary education up to third grade. Became a workpoint recorder for his commune in rural Guangdong before illegally migrating to Hong Kong in late 1975. Interviewed July 8, 1977. (Hereinafter informant no. 11.)

have been well understood and broadly accepted as politically "correct" for the system as a whole, regardless of their personal attitude toward that message. Thus it was generally credited that revisionism was indeed implicit in the pre-1966 developmental pattern, entailing bureaucratism and increasing stratification between mental and manual workers, countryside and city. It was likewise believed that an exclusive (or at least excessive) focus on economic growth and enhanced material welfare resulted in selfish individualism detrimental to revolutionary ideals. Respondents generally accepted the equation of revisionism with Liu Shaoqi and Deng Xiaoping. They also conceded the inherent superiority of the Maoist revolutionary norm (viz., fearless self-sacrifice) *in principle*— though this did not necessarily entail any personal commitment to follow it. And there was clear recognition that post-Mao China had turned from that norm back to revisionism, though there was no great sense of indignation about this reversal. As one informant put it, in a rather extreme formulation: "Liu Shaoqi stood for the capitalist class line. The capitalist class is concerned with money, and the masses needed money. Thus in practice the masses agreed with Liu Shaoqi's line. This feeling intensified after the Cultural Revolution."[82]

All this is to say that the Maoist justification for the Cultural Revolution claimed wide credence. "Struggle" was necessary if the revisionist "frames" were to be broken, and is historically inexorable in any case.[83]

82. Male informant, free professional family background, student individual class status, worked as a village high school teacher on Hainan Island before legally migrating to Hong Kong in October 1974 for reunion with overseas Chinese relatives. Interviewed May 26, 1977. (Hereinafter informant no. 21.) Even more favorably: "My opinion of Liu Shaoqi changed after the Cultural Revolution. He worked for people's welfare. Life was relatively good under Liu and there were improvements in livelihood." Male informant, born 1945 in Guangxi province of capitalist class background, nonetheless became CYL member, later a primary school teacher (hence a state cadre). Legally migrated to Hong Kong in 1975. Interviewed July 10–11, 1976. (Hereinafter informant no. 26.)

More typical: "Without the Cultural Revolution, Liu Shaoqi would practice capitalism, which would harm the interests of the majority of the people. People might feel capitalism was not so bad for a period of time. But to develop capitalism further would divide workers from peasants and cause polarization between cities and villages. Liu Shaoqi had to be overthrown, although a very big price had to be paid for his downfall." Male informant, born 1944 in Shanghai, of free professional family background, student individual class status, worked as thirteenth grade technical cadre in a factory in Shenyang. Migrated illegally to Hong Kong in 1974. Interviewed May 18, 1977. (Hereinafter informant no. 31.)

It is noteworthy that although their attitudes differed, all three informants shared an "economist" *cognition* of Liu.

83. "Without struggles, contradictions cannot be resolved. With a large territory, a large population, and complicated problems, it is impossible to have no struggles." Male informant, born 1934 in Singapore, of overseas Chinese class background, worked as an architect (hence as a tenth grade central state cadre) until his legal departure in April 1975. (Hereinafter informant no. 36.)

"If you want progress, you have to have struggle."[84] There are different forms of struggle (class struggle, factional struggle, line struggle, antagonistic and nonantagonistic contradictions), but these analytical distinctions were little understood and less regarded. All struggle derived from the inevitable but intolerable emergence of differences of political opinion, and would tend to intensify until those who erred were either rectified or destroyed.[85] "The so-called class struggle is just a title; even trivial things in a campaign might be escalated to this title."[86] The Truth was unique and exclusive. "In order to unify [tuanjie], it is also necessary to unify thinking," as one informant put it. "Therefore, all those who have made mistakes must be struggled."[87] These convictions were professed notwithstanding a *preponderant personal aversion* to struggle—few ventured to generalize from subjective preference to objective necessity.

In sum, despite the material and psychological toll it took, the impact of the early spontaneous mobilization phase of the Cultural Revolution on culture was to persuade the Chinese people to accept Mao's overall vision of history. This vision included his rationale for the Cultural Revolution and the whole notion of a "two-line struggle" that was implicit in the Manichaean imagery of the polemics. To this degree, the transformative impact of the Cultural Revolution was indeed profound. The language of cultural radicalism became generalized to the public sector so that everyone who participated in that sector moved within its categories. To be sure, group interests—whether based on old patterns such as kinship or on new ones such as occupational association—did not perish because the language used to express them became taboo. They reasserted themselves, giving rise to considerable semantic confusion (as well as sporadic internecine violence) as a bidding war arose between interests determined to appropriate ideologically legitimate self-justifications. But the belief in the abstract verities professed in the polemics seems to have survived, at least until the death of Mao Zedong and the arrest of his most ardent supporters allowed the language itself to be reconsidered.

84. Informant no. 17.
85. Informants no. 9, 15, 23, and 32. See also female informant, born in Hangzhou in 1956, of landlord family background, student class status, legally migrated to Hong Kong in February 1976 (hereinafter informant no. 34). And male informant, born 1956 in Guangdong, free professional family background, student individual class status, sent down to a production and construction military camp (*Shengchan jianshe bingtuan*) in the Changjiang countryside. Migrated illegally in November 1976 to get out of the countryside. Interviewed May 6, 1977 (hereinafter informant no. 16).
86. Informants no. 34 and 16.
87. Informant no. 9.

FIVE

Charismatic Succession?

Due to the pivotal importance of the period in the ultimate fate of the Chinese Revolution, this and the two following chapters are devoted to the attempt to consolidate and continue the Cultural Revolution between 1968 and 1976. By 1968 there was overall agreement that the Cultural Revolution could not be permitted to continue in the chaotic form it had assumed; however, it is easy to lose sight of the fact that the mood about what had been achieved was still quite optimistic. Charismatic leadership seemed to have been revitalized, such that a few words from Mao seemed capable of eliciting immediate national compliance. The masses had been mobilized, and in a more penetrating, less ritualized manner than in any previous movement since land reform. Finally, the frames had been smashed: not merely the frames of the residual structure, but the frames of the emergent socialist regime—creating the opportunity for a new, fully legitimate structure to be built. True, the Cultural Revolution had been more specific about what should be destroyed than about what should be constructed in its place, but the obverse implications of the critique of the "capitalist road" seemed to offer broad guidelines for a socialist new world.

The reasons this new world failed to materialize had to do with critical failures in each of the three functional requisites of continuing revolution alluded to at the outset of this study. The so-called "late" Cultural Revolution period is so crucial because it was at this time, and not during the highly disturbing but superficially successful period of spontaneous uprisings, that these failures occurred. This chapter will analyze charismatic leadership and its disintegration over the issue of how to consolidate and perpetuate itself. Chapter 6 examines the attempt to continue mass mobilization as an end in itself, in the face of difficulties in finding a rational linkage to economic production on the one hand, and problems in correlating cultural transformation with political struggle on the other. Chapter 7 is concerned with the fragmentation of the emergent political structure in the context of succession conflict and the other systemic malfunctions noted.

According to the conventionally accepted conception of charisma, succession is tautologically impossible, for charisma is defined as a uniquely personal quality that defies transmission. The definition proposed here emphasizes in contrast the performance of a salvationary mission, and there seems to be no a priori reason why the successor to a charismatic leader should not also be able to conceive and perform such a mission (e.g., cf. Nehru's succession to Gandhi). If charismatic succession fails, as it certainly did in the case of Mao Zedong, it fails for empirical rather than definitional reasons, and therefore empirical research is called for to explain that failure.

The following account focuses, then, on mission, and on the struggle to recover it on the one hand and to bequeath it on the other. This struggle not only pitted potential successors against one another, but elicited a conflict of interest between incumbents and would-be successors. The struggle went through three phases. In the first phase, explicit pre-mortem succession arrangements were made in order to eliminate rivalry and facilitate a smooth transition, but these arrangements were hampered by continuing inter-successor friction and finally derailed by an incumbent-successor (Mao vs. Lin) disagreement over the very nature of charismatic leadership. In the second phase, specific pre-mortem succession arrangements were suspended in favor of a vague commitment to "collective" succession, but Zhou Enlai in fact quickly emerged as implicit heir apparent, and a divergence emerged between Mao and Zhou over the definition of mission. Mao's position seems to have been damaged by the indecisive factionalism that greeted the campaign to study "proletarian dictatorship," however, and he withdrew to a much less active (indeed, partially disabled) role. At about the same time, Zhou Enlai withdrew to the hospital with what was to prove terminal stomach cancer. In the wake of Mao's retirement and Zhou's fatal illness, a new set of potential successors emerged and began to compete actively to "grasp" the "line" (i.e., preemptively define the mission) that would legitimate their accession and delegitimate rivals. From his position as ultimate arbiter of the mission, Mao feebly roused himself to forestall its preemption, adopting a balance-of-power strategy and shifting repeatedly from one potential successor to another. The end result was that not only was charismatic succession frustrated, but the prestige of the leadership as a whole suffered grievously from the damage done to its image of resolute unity and decision-making infallibility.

THE COLLAPSE OF PRE-MORTEM SUCCESSION ARRANGEMENTS

The end of the early Cultural Revolution brought a transition from ideological struggle to relatively naked power struggle. This is partly because principled ideological opponents had been eliminated in the purge. But probably an even more important factor was the sharp curtailment of central power that resulted from the movement. To begin with, the central Party-state apparatus was decimated by mass criticism and sweeping purges. As for the regional apparatus, Mao had in the course of the movement convinced its leaders that he would not hesitate to throw them to the wolves without any semblance of due process. Thus, they had no recourse but to learn to fend for themselves if they wished to survive—and many did so with considerable skill, becoming "self-reliant" in the process. The "revolutionary masses," a vocally supportive but rambunctious melee, had been silenced by their demobilization. The resulting "power shortage" intensified the scramble for power—as in a market, as supply declined, demand increased. The catastrophically abortive Lin Biao succession should be placed in this context. This analysis of the incident will begin with a brief review of its itinerary, then proceed to an examination of underlying inter-successor and successor-incumbent conflicts.

Rescission of Successorship and Polarization

The ostensible reason for Mao to disown the pre-mortem arrangements he had made on behalf of Lin Biao was a dispute over the state chairmanship that Liu Shaoqi had vacated—an essentially ceremonial position that seems to have acquired disproportionate symbolic significance in the uncertain political milieu. Mao's own position was not immediately at risk: Lin apparently anticipated a postsuccession challenge from Zhou Enlai, and sought leverage against him from the nominally superior position of chief of state. He suggested that Mao himself assume the position, expecting him to decline and offer it to Lin. As expected, Mao rejected the post, first offering it not to Lin but to Zhou at a February 1970 meeting of the Politburo Standing Committee; the latter, however, declined, fearing that Mao planned to replace him as premier with Zhang Chunqiao.[1] In March, upon issuing directives on revision of the State Constitution, Mao first indicated his preference that the position be abolished. Yet Lin once again proposed to Mao that the position be filled in July, when a committee for revision of the Constitution was established under Mao and Lin; once again Mao rejected the idea. "If there is no chief of state, where can we put Vice-Chairman Lin?" wondered Lin's wife, Ye Qun.[2] To Lin, Mao's veto was a clear signal that he had fallen from grace—how far, he could only speculate, but the precedents were not encouraging—and he began to seek recourse to desperate expedients.

On the first day of the Second Plenum of the Ninth CC (August 23–September 6, 1970, at Lushan), Chen Boda proposed to the twenty-

1. Reuters (London), February 9, 1970; in *FBIS*, February 9, 1970, p. B7.
2. Han Suyin, *My House Has Two Doors* (New York: G. P. Putnam's Sons, 1980), pp. 505 ff.

five assembled delegates that the agenda be tabled and there be discussion of a new State Constitution that would include the post of State Chairman, nominating Mao to fill this post. Chen's motion was supported by the eight military leaders of Lin's faction, but the military region commanders sustained Mao in his objections to the idea. After two and a half days of debate, a majority of the Plenum rejected the proposal and approved disciplinary sanctions against Chen. On September 15 Mao issued a "letter to the whole Party" calling for a rectification campaign to "raise the ability to distinguish true and false Marxism" (*tigao bianbie zhenjia Makesizhuyi de nengli*)—that is, to criticize "false Marxist" Chen Boda.[3] Lin declined Mao's invitation to join in the criticism of Chen. In December 1970, at an enlarged Politburo meeting convened at Beidaihe (the "North China Conference"), Lin and his supporters were criticized but a majority still declined to take a strong position against Chen; finally, in April 1971 (at the "Meeting of the Ninety-nine"), the "eight big generals" were obliged to submit self-criticisms for their support of Chen's proposal, thereby driving a wedge between Lin and his most powerful military backers. In January 1971, Mao had the Thirty-eighth Army transferred from Beijing and moved to "let some air in" to the CC's Military Affairs Commission (formerly dominated by Lin) by appointing his own supporters. Early in 1971 a campaign was launched admonishing military cadres to overcome arrogance, conceit, harshness, and other nonproletarian behavior.[4]

As Mao's moves against Lin monopolized public communications channels and official meeting forums, any attempt by Lin to resist was driven underground. In February–March 1971 he apparently authorized his son Lin Liguo to prepare a plan for a violent coup d'état. Although the "Outline of 571 Project" later revealed was alleged to have been such a plot, it was actually only notes taken on a random talk, containing abundant evidence of resentment but no operational plans. It seems safe to assume that foul play must have been afoot to precipitate the breakneck flight that culminated in the September 13, 1971, incineration of Lin Biao, his wife, and several aides—though Zhou Enlai asserted in the immediate aftermath of the incident that Lin had not even dared to implement his scheme, inasmuch as only a "handful of people" were

3. The joint editorial for the new year (1971) stressed the need to study Marxism-Leninism to uncover "phony Marxists," and a drive was launched against "5/16" (the May 16th group), whose "backstage boss" was now said to be Chen Boda. Leo Goodstadt, "China: Calendar of the Conspiracy," *FEER* 74, no. 48 (November 27, 1971), pp. 20–25; see also *China Topics* (Hong Kong), May 19, 1969, YB527. The movements against Chen climaxed in a long series of articles anonymously criticizing him that appeared in *RR*, *HQ*, and *GM* between March and July 1971.

4. Ying-mao Kau, ed., *The Lin Piao Affair* (White Plains, N.Y.: International Arts & Sciences Press, 1975), pp. xix–lxxvii.

willing to help him out.[5] Much more detailed charges (but no new evidence) of plans to assassinate Mao and his supporters (including Zhang Chunqiao and Yao Wenyuan) were presented at the public trial a decade later, and an even more elaborate (but never consummated) plan was subsequently alleged by an anonymous but seemingly well-informed defector.[6] The precise details of the confrontation thus remain elusive, but all accounts concur on its essentials: there was friction between Mao and Lin arising from Mao's decision to rescind his pre-mortem succession arrangements, leading to conspiratorial activity on both sides that culminated in Lin's death.

Inter-successor Conflict

Having received an unprecedentedly explicit endorsement as Mao's sole designated successor (it was written into the Party Constitution at the Ninth Congress), Lin committed the tactical blunder of alienating other major power-holders and attempting to staff the apparatus exclusively with his "own" people. Thus he found himself in a politically isolated position when his patron deserted him. To be sure, it would have been difficult to propitiate those who had previously figured in the succession lineup and stood to gain if Lin's heir apparency were disclaimed, but Lin might have attempted to co-opt them by promoting their efforts in functionally spcialized areas not politically threatening to him, or by offering tacit quid pro quos in his successor regime, and he made no apparent effort to do so.

Zhou Enlai was to Lin's right ideologically, but as a power pragmatist par excellence he would surely have been open to a cooperative working relationship. But Lin seemed to regard Zhou as a threat, and he not only balked at relinquishing control over Zhou's administrative organization but interfered in Zhou's field of special competence, foreign policy. Lin also inhibited reconstruction of the governmental apparatus by delaying, or failing to expedite, the rehabilitation of cadres. Zhou turned to Mao, who issued an injunction (in his speech to the Ninth Congress) to "liberate them without delay," but results were not forthcoming, leading Mao to complain of the situation in December 1969.[7] Mao was in high

5. *NYT*, October 7, 1972, p. 12.

6. Yao Mingle, *The Conspiracy and Death of Lin Biao* (New York: Alfred A. Knopf, 1983). Although interesting and not implausible, the mysterious circumstances of its publication make it impossible to corroborate this version.

7. When Mao saw Snow in December 1970, he made three points: One was an invitation to Nixon to visit China, one was the decision to scale down the cult of personality, the third was the decision to purge Chen Boda. Chen's name was not mentioned, but Mao observed that he was dissatisfied with the results of the Cultural Revolution, that he had been told a lot of "lies" about it. Chen Boda had been chairman of the CCRG. Snow, *Long Revolution*, p. 174; see also Huo Huisheng, "Chen Boda kuatai yu Mao pai mingyun" [Chen Boda's fall and the

dudgeon (somewhat delayed) about the chaos precipitated by the Cultural Revolution, as he indicated in conversations at the time, and seemed willing to strike any compromise necessary to facilitate rapid economic recovery; he may well have been concerned lest the Cultural Revolution become the sort of economic albatross the Great Leap had been—a catastrophe which, he must have recalled, had placed him on the political defensive for nearly a decade. Zhou's restorationist policies seemed a better bet economically than Lin's low-tech agrarian industrialization; forced to choose, Mao chose the more experienced if conventional Zhou, and the two joined forces at the Second Plenum in an attack against radicalism.

In foreign policy, the available evidence suggests that Lin sought to consolidate his own position by provoking a confrontation with the Soviet Union along the Ussuri.[8] The first border clash was appropriately timed (a month before the Ninth Congress), and was according to available evidence initiated by Chinese troops; the resulting crisis seemed ideally conceived to foster the sort of "garrison state" mentality most compatible with Lin's preferred style of military radicalism. He used it to justify the imposition of martial law on the exposed northern cities (in the rigors of which Liu Shaoqi expired), and to mobilize the masses to dig air raid tunnels, accumulate grain reserves, and otherwise support the PLA. Yet the escalation of tension along the border was a double-edged sword. While enhancing the functional indispensability of the PLA, it bolstered the argument for withdrawing troops from participation in civilian political organizations so they could return to their units and devote themselves to military training and preparation. It also jeopardized the radical international stance of equidistance between the two superpowers, so exacerbating tension with the one that it became expedient to turn to the other for supplementary deterrence—"Two against one is better than one against two," as Mao later quipped in explaining his opening to the United States. Rapprochement with the West was, however, less compatible with Lin's bureaucratic interests than any conceivable alternative,

---

fate of the Mao faction], *Zhanwang* (hereinafter *ZW*) (Hong Kong), no. 233 (October 16, 1971): pp. 15–19. Richard Nethercut, "Lin Piao and the Cultural Revolution," University of Hong Kong, Centre of Asian Studies Working Paper, May 1970.

8. This is my own interpretation. Plausible alternative scenarios are explored by Thomas M. Gottlieb, *Chinese Foreign Policy Factionalism and the Origins of the Strategic Triangle* (Santa Monica, Calif.: RAND Corp., R-1902-NA, November 1977); Kenneth G. Lieberthal, *Sino-Soviet Conflict in the 1970s: Its Evolution and Implications for the Strategic Triangle* (Santa Monica: RAND Corp., R-2342-NA, July 1978); and Thomas W. Robinson, "The Sino-Soviet Border Dispute: Background, Development, and the March 1969 Clashes," *American Political Science Review* (hereinafter *APSR*), 66, no. 4 (December 1972), pp. 1175–1202; and Harold C. Hinton, *The Bear at the Gate: Chinese Policymaking under Soviet Pressure* (Stanford: The Hoover Institution Press, 1971).

as it tended to favor the modern urban industrial sector and shore up the moderate forces of archrival Zhou Enlai.[9]

Lin's position was ideologically compatible with that of the radicals, and indeed at the outset he seemed to have established a useful alliance with Jiang Qing. At a time when Jiang was still persona non grata in Beijing cultural circles, Lin convened a "Forum on Literature and Art in the Armed Forces" in Shanghai under her patronage, and wrote a letter instructing that "from now on, the army's documents concerning literature and art should be sent to her." But further cooperation was complicated by the clash between grassroots radicals and regional military forces that erupted in Wuhan in the summer of 1967. This split the radicals into groups, military and cultural. A brief discursus on the background of this cleavage may be useful.

Jiang Qing provided the nucleus for what became known as the "cultural radicals" (*wenge pai*) by assembling a group of relatively young radical literati to help in her reform of Beijing opera after her 1965 hegira to Shanghai, led by Yao Wenyuan and Zhang Chunqiao. Jiang also had a good connection with Kang Sheng, dating back to their common province of origin and to Kang's sponsorship of her Party membership and support of her marriage to Mao (under somewhat awkward circumstances). A second component of the group, however, revolved around Chen Boda, whose entrée was facilitated not by Jiang but by Mao, whom Chen had long served as secretary, editor, and ghost writer. Chen had also worked with Lin Biao, as the main compiler of the quotations from Mao's *Selected Works* to which Lin wrote an introduction before publishing in analect form.[10] Chen brought in train a group of Beijing literati with whom he had developed contacts as editor of *Red Flag* and deputy head of the Academy of Science, including Wang Li (from the *Red Flag* staff), Mu Xin and Qi Benyu (of the *Guangming Daily* editorial staff), and Guan Feng, Lin Jie, Lin Bishi, and Wu Zhuanji (all researchers in the Department of Philosophy and Social Sciences, Academy of Science). In May 1966, when Peng Zhen's "Cultural Revolution Group" was disbanded, this rather disparate array of radicals was brought together under the

9. Evidence that the PLA disagreed with the idea that the United States was no longer as great a danger to China as the Soviet Union may be found in Huang Yongsheng's speech of July 31, 1971. Improved relations with the United States might lead to a reduced military budget, particularly in the areas of ICBM and advanced aircraft development. Lin, "Speech on Mao's Works" (1966), as quoted in Thomas Robinson, *A Political-Military Biography of Lin Piao, Part II. 1950–1971* (Santa Monica, Calif.: RAND Corp., 1971), p. 324. Lin Biao, "Informal Address at Politburo Meeting" (May 18, 1966), as trans. in Martin Ebon, ed., *Lin Biao: The Life and Writings of China's New Ruler* (New York: Stein & Day, 1970), pp. 253–67.
10. Claude Julien, "The Lin Biao 'Mystery': Part I. From Promotion to Decline," *Le Monde*, December 28, 1971, pp. 1, 3; translated in FBIS, January 4, 1972, pp. B1–B5.

chairmanship of Chen Boda and Vice-chairmanship of Jiang Qing (with Zhou Enlai as "adviser") as the "Central Cultural Revolution Small Group" (CCRG). Nominally an ad hoc committee operating under the auspices of the CC, the CCRG's actual power rivaled that of the Politburo during much of the period of spontaneous mobilization.

When radical Red Guards came into conflict with more conservative local military forces in July–August 1967, the CCRG was blamed for having encouraged the young rebels to arm "for self-defense." At this point Jiang Qing scapegoated the Beijing branch of the CCRG. Wang Li, Lin Jie, and Guan Feng were purged one after another in the fall of 1967; Qi Benyu followed in January 1968, a move that forced *Red Flag* to suspend publication for three months. This clean sweep of Chen Boda's protégés cannot have endeared Jiang to Chen. As the only member of the Politburo Standing Committee without an organizational base, Chen was left in a high but stranded position, and he apparently began to combine forces with military radical Lin Biao. It soon became clear that Lin had ambitions of his own, for which he could use a capable symbol specialist. Official documents have revealed that it was Chen who prepared the first draft of Lin's ill-fated report to the Ninth Party Congress.[11] Having chosen sides, Chen fell from Mao's grace, as the latter escalated his criticisms of the PLA in November 1969 (Chen made no public speeches or statements after October).

After 1967 Lin seems to have had little use for Jiang Qing and the Shanghai subgroup of the CCRG, whose political interests could be disentangled neither from the Chairman on whose patronage they depended nor from the local antimilitary radicals whose support they still cultivated. Jiang Qing's star reached its zenith in the spring of 1967, when cultural and military radicals were still in coalition. She made frequent (and apparently effective) appearances before Red Guard rallies, and, in May, *Red Flag* published two of her speeches. After the Wuhan incident in August 1967 she promptly went into eclipse. Only six of the original seventeen CCRG members survived the autumn of 1967, and the vacancies were never restaffed. Following the rustication of Red Guards in the fall of 1968, Lin Biao reportedly obtained Mao's permission to have Jiang curtail her political activities, and her public appearances diminished accordingly. Jiang Qing and her protégés remained notably silent at the Ninth Party Congress, and Lin Biao, in a lengthy review of the Cultural Revolution, attributed even the revolutionary model operas (*yangbanxi*) to the "revolutionary masses" without so much as mentioning her name. In August, Lin proceeded to have the operas revised

---

11. Jacques Guillermaz, *The Chinese Communist Party in Power, 1949–1976* (Boulder, Colo.: Westview Press; 1976), pp. 461–68.

"under the direction of the Party CC," again without her involvement; this revision highlighted the role of the Red Army. The CCRG was apparently disbanded at the Ninth Congress, receiving no further mention in print until December 1970. At this point Jiang Qing and her Shanghai protégés reemerged to present a series of soirees to visiting delegations on behalf of the Foreign Ministry[12]—suggesting that her support was now being solicited by Zhou Enlai in the emerging confrontation with Lin. That the cultural radicals supported Mao and Zhou in this struggle is made clear in the 571 documents, which provided for their assassination.

Successor-Incumbent Conflict

Lin had ineptly handled his relations with other major political actors, but he might have weathered this storm had his relationship with the Chairman stood him in good stead. Thus Mao's change of heart was absolutely crucial to Lin's fall. Lin Biao was neither the first nor the last successor Mao would ever designate, but he would prove to be Mao's last chance to pass the scepter to a fellow radical with the requisite "power base" to govern effectively.[13] In view of the damage to the radical cause and to his own charisma that Mao's second self-reversal would incur, the reasons therefor are worth thoroughly exploring.

One possibility that has been suggested is that Lin simply lacked the personal prerequisites for charismatic leadership. True, Lin was not prepossessing in appearance: slight, short, balding (hence the perennial cap), frail, afraid of sun, valetudinarian, a poor public speaker, he failed to impress the Red Guards to whom he appeared at rallies. He would

12. The rump CCRG presented evening parties featuring revolutionary Beijing opera performances to delegations from the Communist parties of Albania, North Vietnam, Australia, Burma, Indonesia, and France. But they were held not under the auspices of the CCRG, but on behalf of the Ministry of Culture of the State Council. *Dagong Bao* (Hong Kong), December 24, 1969, p. 1. In an apparent effort to regularize cultural activities, the State Council formed a "Cultural Group" in August 1971, chaired by veteran cadre Wu De (a CC member, vice-chairman of the Beijing RC and second secretary of the Beijing Party Committee) but including a number of lesser cultural radicals. The membership included Liu Xianquan (CC member, chairman of the Qinghai RC, and first secretary of the Qinghai Party Committee), Shi Shazhua (alternate CC member and deputy director of NCNA), Wang Mantian (vice-chairman of the Tianjin RC and secretary of the Tianjin Party committee), Yu Huiyong (a composer of revolutionary Beijing opera), Di Fucai (member of a government department, of the Beijing RC, and of the Chinese People's Association for Friendship with Foreign Countries), Huang Houmin (a leading journalist), Wu Yinxian (vice-chairman of the China Photographic Society and vice-president of the Beijing Cinema College), Hao Liang (a singer in revolutionary Beijing opera), and Liu Qingtang (a male ballet dancer). Although Jiang Qing, Zhang Chunqiao, and Yao Wenyuan often accompanied the group, none were listed as members. Ibid., p. 265.
13. Dittmer, "Bases of Power," pp. 26–61.

proceed jerkily and uncertainly through a prepared text, his voice hoarse, lacking both resonance and an air of conviction. Possibly because he was aware of these personal limitations, before he emerged as a major figure in the early 1960s he led one of the most reclusive lives of any major Chinese politician. In speeches before a military audience, on the other hand, he is said to have spoken forcibly and directly.[14] His revolutionary escutcheon was immaculate, his military contributions earning him a reputation as "the greatest tactical genius the communist armies had produced."[15] Moreover, his usurpation of the heir apparency from a well-established successor designate demonstrated no mean political prowess.

More important than Lin's unimpressive personal demeanor (in what is after all a nonelectoral system) is the fact that he was able to conceive and briefly to execute a salvationary mission. Within a brief tenure he was able to introduce his own distinctive political structure and style of mass mobilization (to be more amply described in chapters 6 and 7). These conformed to Lin's military radical vision, with its strong emphasis on discipline, self-sacrifice, and unconditional obedience—egalitarian with respect to status and material incentives, but hierarchical with respect to power. For Lin all but worshiped power, as he made clear in many writings and statements. In perhaps his most famous speech, delivered in the dawning of the Cultural Revolution, he emphasized its violent underpinnings: "Struggle is life—if you don't struggle against them, they will struggle against you. . . . if you don't kill them they will kill you." Thus "once they have political power, the . . . working people will have everything. Once they lose it, they will lose everything. Production is undoubtedly the base; however, it relies upon the change, consolidation, and development resulting from the seizure of political power." In another stark passage from the same speech, he tried to place his thoughts in some sort of theoretical context:

> Among the areas of the superstructure—ideas, religion, arts, law, and political power, the last is the very center. What is political power? Sun Yat-sen thought it was the management of the affairs of the masses. But he did not understand that political power is an instrument by which one class oppresses the other. . . . Of course, suppression is not the only function of political power . . . [but] suppression is the most essential.[16]

14. Nethercut, "Lin Piao."

15. MacFarquhar, *Origins*, 2, p. 244; see also Lee Ngok, "Lin Piao's Military Tactics as Seen in the 115th division," University of Hong Kong: Centre of Asian Studies Working Paper, April 22, 1970; and Robinson, *Biography*; and Liu Yunsun, "The Current and Past of Lin Biao," *Zhonggong Yanjiu* [Chinese communist studies] (Taipei), vol. 1, no. 1 (January 31, 1967): 61–77.

16. Lin Biao, "Informal Address," pp. 253–67.

According to Lin's conception of charismatic leadership, power flowed ineluctably from the brilliance of the epoch-making hero-leader. He made his first flattering estimate of Mao's "genius" (*tiancai*) as early as September 1962, in his speech to the Tenth Plenum of the Eighth CC. Four years later he repeated it: "Chairman Mao's sayings, works, and revolutionary practice have shown that he is a great proletarian genius. . . . He is unparalleled in the present world. Marx and Engels were geniuses of the nineteenth century; Lenin and Comrade Mao Zedong are the geniuses of the twentieth century."[17] And, in words that Mao was to recall with bitter irony a few years hence (mocking, however, only the second clause in the sentence, never the first), Lin said that "Every sentence of Chairman Mao's works is a Truth, one single sentence of his surpasses ten thousand of ours." Throughout the 1960s, one may search Lin's public record in vain for any indication that his attitude ever deviated from awestricken sycophancy. "I . . . ask the Chairman for instructions and do everything according to his orders," he related to his colleagues in his speech to the Eleventh Plenum of the Eighth CC (upon his elevation to second rank in the Party hierarchy). "I do not interfere with him on major matters nor do I trouble him on minor matters. Sometimes I cannot avoid making mistakes and cannot follow the Chairman's thoughts." Because even he could not always "follow" Mao's thoughts, Lin told the masses, "we must carry out not only those instructions we understand, but also those we fail to understand for the moment, and must try to understand them in the course of carrying them out."[18] Difficulties in understanding could be circumnavigated by simply memorizing isolated quotations, even entire sections, from his writings, and carrying them out to the letter.[19] Lin's own exemplary ascent to glory was publicly referred to not as an instance of merit vindicated, but of fealty rewarded: "we should take Vice Chairman Lin Biao as our shining example in always remaining boundlessly loyal to Chairman Mao, to his Thought, and to his proletarian revolutionary line."[20]

Lin made a concerted attempt to induce the broad masses to share his reverence for Mao Zedong and his Thought, and thereby implicitly also to adopt his conception of leadership. That conception may have emphasized elite-mass equality and reciprocal communication in theory, but in practice it fostered a vast status and power differential. Leaders should command and followers should obey—unconditionally, immediately, respectfully. Obviously, messages could not be expected to percolate up from the masses, but would echo the thoughts of the "genius" at the

---

17. Ibid., p. 265.
18. NCNA, Beijing, January 23, 1968.
19. Lin Biao, "Speech on Mao's Works" (1966), as quoted in Robinson, *Biography*, p. 324.
20. NCNA, January 23, 1968.

helm; because these thoughts were probably too complex for simple people to comprehend, they were reduced to simplified formulas and often reiterated. This emphasis on rote learning and mimesis of heroic models gave to military radicalism a certain ritualistic quality. There were "morning prayers, evening penitences, rallies falling-in, reporting for and quitting work and making duty shifts, buying and selling things, writing letters, making phone calls, even taking meals"—all of which were surrounded by icons of the Chairman, signifying loyalty.[21] One observer well versed in Western religious traditions perceived the emergence of certain "liturgical forms" designed to reaffirm commitment to a "salvation history." Thus geographical sites associated with the Chairman became shrines from whence visitors would sometimes take a bit of earth or bottle of water as mementos.

It has been reported that the railway station in Tianjin has been converted to a Mao Zedong's Thought lecture hall. All other pictures were removed, all advertisements; a huge statue of Mao and more than one hundred portraits of him were set up, along with three hundred posters and quotations. School children begin their day by wishing Mao a long life and bowing to his portrait.[22]

Even if we assume for the moment that Lin's professions of loyalty were absolutely sincere, the question arises: can two charismatic leaders coexist? Can there be two suns in the sky? At first Mao seemed to bask in the warm glow of Lin's praise for him, and he publicly embraced his new "closest comrade-in-arms" as he had never embraced another. He joked and laughed with Lin during their joint appearances on Tiananmen, glancing benevolently and paternally over Lin's shoulder at the text as he struggled through a speech.[23] The two seemed inseparable. In fact, Lin made it a point never to appear in public except in Mao's company (about

21. Li Yizhe, "Guanyu shehuizhuyi de minzhu yu fazhi" [Concerning socialist democracy and law], *Ming Bao Yuekan* [Ming Bao monthly], Hong Kong, November 27, 1975, pp. 11–20.
22. R. L. Whitehead, "Liturgical Developments in China's Revolutionary Religion," *China Notes* (East Asian Department, National Council of Churches, New York) 7, no. 3 (Summer 1969). A young Red Guard writes of a close encounter with the Chairman in similar terms: "He was gone. All that remained of him was the touch of his hand on the hand of a few who had been lucky enough to get close to him.... Those Chairman Mao had touched now became the focus of our fervor. Everyone surged toward them with out-stretched arms in hopes of transferring the sacred touch to their own hands. If you couldn't get close enough for that, then shaking the hand of one who had shaken hands with Our Great Saving Star would have to do. And so it went, down the line, until sometimes hand-shakes were removed as much as one hundred times from the original one, spreading outward in a vast circle like waves in a lake when a meteor crashes into its center." Liang and Shapiro, *Son of the Revolution*, p. 123.
23. Nethercut, "Lin Piao."

forty times altogether between the first mass Red Guard rally in August 1966 and the Ninth Party Congress in April 1969), and he was always photographed together with Mao, each time standing a deferential step behind. He also retreated together with Mao for two months or more on half a dozen occasions in the course of the Cultural Revolution. Though Mao later was to claim he found Lin's professions of esteem overweening, during the entire 1962–70 period when the cult of personality had its heyday Mao made no visible attempt to resist it, in fact lending public support to such mass tributes as the Tiananmen parades or the proliferation of Mao Zedong Thought study classes (organized in response to Mao's May 7, 1966, letter to Lin Biao urging the latter to "turn the whole country into a great school of Mao Zedong Thought"). In a 1965 conversation with Edgar Snow, Mao frankly defended the cult in terms of political expedience.[24] The only indication to the contrary, a letter allegedly written to Mao's wife in June 1966, was not revealed until after Lin's death and there is reason to question its authenticity.[25]

Sometime during the period from the Ninth Congress to its Second Plenum, Mao reconsidered. This was not merely a question of radical economic policies or even the chief of state position; Lin's entire conception of charismatic leadership he began to find objectionable. In a later conversation with Snow (December 1970) he first publicly indicated that the cult had gone too far and that he wanted it modulated.[26] In 1971 a campaign was accordingly launched to study the Marxist-Leninist classics, thereby also shifting the emphasis in the rehabilitation of cadres from rote fanaticism to some demonstration of intellectual mastery—with which trained Party cadres may be assumed to have been more comfortable.[27] The "theory of genius" (tiancailun) was publicly denounced.

Mao changed his mind about his own cult partly because he sensed that Lin was splitting charisma into two components: a symbolic component, which was the recipient of worshipful awe, and an operational

24. Jean Vincent, Agence France Presse (hereinafter AFP), Paris, February 11, 1968. Reviewing the meeting of the Shanghai RC in early 1968 at which the experience of the past year was analyzed, Mao said that the organization of the study classes was a good thing; many problems could be settled thereby. Classes to study Mao's thoughts were thus promptly opened everywhere. See NCNA, February 8, 10, 17, 1968; NCNA, Beijing, February 25, 1968. Many of these "study classes" were in fact informally established courts and jails.
25. The letter, dated June 8, 1966, was first revealed in late 1972. It refers to incidents that demonstrate that it could not have been written before the third week of July, 1966 (in particular, references are made to Mao receiving foreign visitors, which are easy to check). The document probably dates from 1969 or even later. Cheng Huang, "China: Purloined Letter," 78, no. 49 (December 2, 1972): 10–11.
26. Snow, Long Revolution, pp. 167–77.
27. Ding Wang, Wang Hongwen Zhang Chunqiao Pingzhuan [Biography of Wang Hongwen and Zhang Chunqiao] (Hong Kong: Ming Bao, 1977), pp. 5–6.

component, which defined the mission. This split represents the purely power-oriented aspect of the conflict, and there is no question that Mao was acutely sensitive to it. In the summer of 1969 the formula designating military leadership began to appear: "The PLA, founded by Chairman Mao and directly led by Vice-Chairman Lin." But why can the founder of the army not also be the leader, Mao wondered, so the formula was revised to read: "The PLA, founded and led by Chairman Mao and directly led by Vice-Chairman Lin," and finally (in the draft State Constitution approved by the Second Plenum of the Ninth Congress), Mao was designated "supreme commander of the whole nation and the whole army" with Lin as "deputy supreme commander" of same.[28] Lin was obviously trying to create a role for himself as Mao's most loyal follower and authoritative exegete, also allowing himself to be ranked among the "three assistants" of geniuses—Engels for Marx, Stalin for Lenin, Lin Biao for Mao—two of whom, it should be noted, duly succeeded their illustrious forebears.

Considerations of power may have been primary, but policy was also involved. In other words, the fact that Mao was unwilling to share his charisma should not obscure the fact that the two men's conceptions of the role of leadership did in fact diverge. The personality cult served a quite different function as a rhetorical justification for emancipation of the "revolutionary masses" from repressive bureaucratic authorities than it did as the dogma of a lock-step military dictatorship. Mao's writings and recorded *obiter dicta* are too replete with antiauthoritarian, even iconoclastic themes (true, his actions are more mixed) for us to doubt that Lin's conception of power must have been anathema to this erstwhile anarchist.[29]

Consequences

The impact of the Lin Biao episode (*jiu yi san shijian*, or September 13 incident, as the Chinese call it) upon charismatic leadership was devastating, not only in the obvious sense that the exaggerated efficacy attributed to Mao's leadership resisted moderation (a "moderately infallible" leader?), but in the doubt cast on Mao's judgment by the rejection (and death) of a second hand-picked successor. It is difficult today to conceive of the shock this misadventure provoked when it was first disclosed to study groups at the end of November 1971. A former soldier recalled:

28. *China Notes* (hereinafter *CN*) (Hong Kong), no. 380 (October 8, 1970); *China News Analysis* (hereinafter *CNA*) (Hong Kong), no. 777 (October 10, 1969).
29. See Franklin W. Houn, "Rejection of Blind Obedience as a Traditional Chinese and Maoist Concept," *Asian Thought and Society* 7, no. 19 (1982): 18–31; and vol. 7, no. 21: 264–79, especially pp. 270–73.

We received an order at night to assemble at the ceremonial hall. I had never seen the soldier before who read us the central documents. The meeting was closely guarded. Wherever we went we were watched, even in the restrooms. When I heard the central document I was shocked so much that my heart seemed to leap out, and I could not believe my ears. The meeting lasted for three days. We were not allowed to exchange opinions among ourselves. We were not allowed to leak the contents of the meeting. I dared not tell even my wife.[30]

One might suppose the waning of charisma to have been at least counter-balanced by some closure of the vast elite-mass hiatus—and so it was. But because this waning resulted from an infraction of Maoist norms, it was taken to imply not that the masses were the true geniuses, but that they were also justified in *their* violation of those norms. As a former cadre put it:

At the beginning, I think people were very suspicious. Later it had a profound impact, to think that such a person of high position could become counterrevolutionary. It convinced people that Party people were no better than ordinary people. . . . The relations between the PLA and the masses got worse and worse after this, but this had nothing to do with Lin Biao.[31]

MAO AND ZHOU

After the disastrous outcome of Mao's second attempt to set pre-mortem succession arrangements, he seems to have decided to post-pone the issue until after his death. Finding no single candidate worthy to replace him, he opted for collective succession. A more cynical inter-pretation would be that he learned from the Lin Biao episode to trust no one, and was hence quick to check any grouping that began to acquire too much power—in other words, that he was actually opting for *no* succession.

In any case, the post-mortem succession option would prove unsat-isfactory for two reasons. First, there was no established procedure for

30. Male informant, born 1946 in Guangdong, of worker family background, student class status (junior high school graduate), participated in a Red Guard faction during the Cultural Revolution, legally emigrated to Hong Kong in December 1976. Interviewed June 7, 1977 (hereinafter informant no. 14).

31. Male informant, born 1932 in Guangdong (Taishan), of poor peasant and revolutionary martyr family background, soldier individual class status (having "joined the revolution" when he was thirteen years old). He joined the Party when he was seventeen and was a deputy leader of the CYL, a position equivalent to that of an eighteenth grade cadre. Left China illegally in 1973 because he was afraid he might be prosecuted for committing manslaughter in the course of the Cultural Revolution. Interviewed May 30, 1977 (hereinafter informant no. 19).

post-mortem selection—such a procedure would have necessarily curtailed Mao's input—making postponement so uncertain that all eligible candidates preferred at best to preempt favorable succession arrangements or at worst to forestall such preemption by other candidates. This situation led to recurrent elite infighting, broken by brief periods of tenuous balance. Second, Mao himself (for whatever reason) was vacillatory in his touting of candidates, sometimes seeming to favor one successor, only to reconsider later. The result was continual lurching from one policy line *qua* succession vehicle to another and back again.

Mao went through a period of withdrawal after Lin's death, retiring from active politics amid rumors of serious illness.[32] As in the twilight of the Great Leap Forward, he detached himself from domestic politics while playing a more active role in the international arena (e.g., China's admission to the United Nations, the Nixon visit). Between his August–September 1971 tour of the provinces (in order to muster support for his anticipated confrontation with Lin) and the Tenth Party Congress (in September 1973), he made no public speeches and appeared only once before the Chinese people, remaining publicly accessible only to distinguished visitors.[33] He had allowed himself an unprecedented public intimacy with Lin, and he may have been embarrassed about his complicity in Lin's ill-fated and short-lived rise to eminence, loath to join in public criticism of one so closely linked to a cause to which he was still committed, simply depressed about Lin's death, or all three. In any case, he made no public statement condemning Lin, and not until the Tenth Congress, two years after Lin's death, would Mao even lend his presence to Lin's repudiation.[34]

In contrast to his previous (1960–65) "retirement," there has never been any question that Mao's withdrawal was voluntary. As Mao himself

32. According to a Hong Kong report, in 1972, Mao was stricken with Parkinson's Disease, which caused him a great deal of pain and inhibited his muscular control and speech patterns, though not his intelligence. Thereafter he began to receive foreign visitors in his own library, rather than in the Great Hall of the People or elsewhere. Chen Zhihui, "Mao Zedong de jiating beiju" [Mao Zedong's family tragedy], *ZM*, no. 18 (April 1979): 44–47.

33. Although he made no public appearances, in 1974 he received twenty-three foreign visitors and up to the end of October 1975 he had received fifteen. *CNA*, no. 1019 (November 7, 1975).

34. The so-called three basic principles ("Practice Marxism, not revisionism; unite, don't split; be open and aboveboard, don't intrigue and conspire") quoted three and a half months after Lin's death in reference to Lin, seem to have been first cited in a joint editorial published a month earlier, where they were, however, treated separately and placed in a different sequence. "Zongjie jingyan jiaqiang dang de lingdao" [Sum up experience in strengthening Party leadership], *RR*, *JFJB*, *HQ*, December 1, 1971. In this citation the "three principles" derived respectively from (1) July 1, 1970; (2) "all along" stressed by Mao, at the Seventh Party Congress for example; and (3) 1964. On only the first of these occasions is it remotely possible that the original referent of the phrase was Lin Biao.

put it in a talk to "liberated" cadres above ministerial level in the fall of 1974:

[S]ince then there has been more work, even several ministers can't take care of it, and they always come to me and the premier. So frequently did they request directions from me that I told the premier I was through with it. (Zhou Enlai interrupts: "Whenever I retreat they come to me no more.") In this way they have been doing things by themselves and the accomplishments are great and the works are good."[35]

And in view of the fact that the post-Lin purge of the Politburo left the Standing Committee with only one active member besides Mao himself,[36] there is equally little question that Mao was in effect abdicating in favor of Zhou Enlai. In the words of a subsequent Party historian: "Following Lin Biao's death in Ondor Han, Comrade Zhou Enlai, supported by Comrade Mao Zedong, took charge of the work of the Party Central Committee. . . . At the beginning, Comrade Mao Zedong allowed him to do so."[37] The cultural radicals had split with Lin in advance of his alleged coup attempt, and were now willing to unite with Zhou in a post-crisis joining of ranks. And, inasmuch as they had been almost completely eclipsed by the Lin Biao regime, and the subsequent campaign against Lin tended to have a spillover effect tainting all radicals, Zhou was in turn gracious enough to lend them his sponsorship, giving Jiang Qing frequent occasions to appear for diplomatic functions and apparently taking a benign, avuncular interest in Wang Hongwen upon his debut. Although Jiang Qing's appearances increased, the nature of these appearances indicate that she was for the time being limiting herself to her role as cultural impresario and not yet claiming political omnicompetence.[38] Now terminally ill, Kang Sheng made a more limited comeback from the Lin Biao imbroglio, replacing Chen Boda as Mao's "expert on theory" (group leader of the Central Theory Small Group) as well as assistant editor of

35. "Mao's Talk to 'Liberated Cadres' and 'Wuhan Cadres'" (Fall 1974), as translated in *IS* 11, no. 2 (February 1975): 91–93.
36. Viz., Zhou Enlai. Of the twenty-five full and alternate Politburo members elected at the Ninth Party Congress, only twelve continued to make regular public appearances after September 1971. Julien, "'Mystery.'"
37. Liao Gailong, "Historical Experiences," part 2, p. 98.
38. After August 1971, Jiang began appearing on special cultural occasions, and in certain "special activities in connection with foreign delegations" (hitherto the exclusive domain of State Council members) in company with Zhou or Li Xiannian. Beginning in the fall of 1972, she also began appearing alone, or in the company of her own protégés, Zhang or Yao (as for the exhibition by a Japanese ballet troupe on November 6). At the Tenth Congress, she started appearing at revolutionary Beijing opera performances in the company of highest state visitors. Wolfgang Bartke, "Die politische Profilierung von Chiang Ching," *China Aktuell* (Hamburg, Institut für Asienkunde), February 1975, pp. 44–46 (hereinafter *CA*).

the committee in charge of the *Selected Works of Mao Zedong*. He also maintained his links with Jiang Qing, authorizing the Central Party School's literary study group to participate in radical criticism campaigns.[39]

Zhou Enlai, whose visible political activities easily eclipsed those of any other central leader on the scene during this period, emerged as de facto heir apparent and acting chairman. He assumed this role in a far more skillful manner than had Lin Biao, consistently protesting that succession was "collective," attempting to co-opt Jiang Qing and Wang Hongwen, agreeing to a formula that allotted many more CC seats to "mass representatives" than ever before, never evincing the insecurity that had driven Lin to try to arrogate power.

Yet he did take advantage of the momentary power vacuum to try to superimpose his own mission. In the eighteen months following the death of Lin he attempted to resuscitate the engineering approach to continuing revolution, which conceived a positive relationship between economic growth and prosperity and the realization of socialism, sequential and well-organized advance under hierarchical leadership, and so forth. In industry, radical criticisms of "unreasonable rules and regulations" gave way to greater emphasis on cost control procedures and accounting,[40] individual management of enterprises was again endorsed (as of early 1972), and material incentives made their reappearance under the rubric of "reasonable rewards." In January 1973, provincial and local commerce departments were told that they could vary prices according to product quality, and supply and demand. In agriculture, CC Document (*zhongfa*) no. 82 (issued December 1971) established the basis for the so-called New Agricultural Policy, which guaranteed private plots and payment according to work. The model Dazhai brigade was reconstrued to exemplify simply working hard to improve irrigation and the general condition of the fields, not to refer specifically to the more politicized and egalitarian Dazhai workpoint system.[41] Communes and production brigades could no longer recruit from the production team without its explicit consent. Prices paid for industrial crops were raised in order to provide the material base for light industry, and the prices for agricultural inputs were lowered.[42] The masses were instructed to distinguish between "grasping revolution for the sake of production" and the reaction-

39. Ruan Shanqing, "What Role Did Kang Sheng Play in the Great Cultural Revolution?" *Dongxiang* [Trends] (Hong Kong), no. 18 (March 16, 1980): 25–28 (hereinafter *DX*).

40. Economist Intelligence Unit (Hong Kong), *Quarterly Economic Review: China*, no. 3 (July 20, 1971), and no. 4 (October 14, 1971). (Hereinafter *QER*.)

41. *China Topics*, YB 594 (August 1974).

42. Editor, "The PRC Economy in 1973," *Current Scene* (Hong Kong) 12, no. 3 (March 1974): 1–12.

ary theory of "production first," between economic accounting for the sake of revolution and "profits in command," and other such subtle distinctions. Taking advantage of the thaw in relations with the West (including the visit of Richard Nixon in February 1972) that followed Lin's fall, the PRC purchased large quantities of grain abroad, and in 1973 authorized whole plant imports on a scale greatly exceeding that of the early 1960s.

The radicals were soon discomfited by the thrust of such policies, no less by the "Criticize Revisionism" campaign Zhou used to discredit radical opposition to them. As Mao's nephew and leftist protégé Mao Yuanxin put it in a speech to a Propaganda Work Conference in Liaoning:

> Why are there some people who are so interested in the criticism of Lin Biao's ultra-leftist line? I always feel there is a sense of vengeful counterattack. In other words, there has been a small-scale restoration since the criticism of Lin Biao's ultra-leftist line last year. . . . If they continue to carry out this criticism, the next targets to be criticized will be . . . the Great Cultural Revolution and the New Things that have emerged since the Great Cultural Revolution.[43]

Mao obviously shared their concern, but was somewhat inhibited in his response by an appreciation of Zhou's political utility and by the knowledge (by 1973) that Zhou was stricken with cancer and could place no realistic claim on succession in any case. In view of the damage the Lin Biao misadventure had done to his reputation, he also had to show some concern for his own credibility. Thus he authorized an allegorical criticism campaign against the "Duke of Zhou" (Confucius), but did not permit it to proceed to its logical outcome in Zhou's public exposure and purge, as had the campaigns of 1966–68, apparently intending it rather to serve as a warning (earlier allegations that the Four launched the campaign without his authorization have since been discounted).[44]

Mao also took a number of other steps during this period, many of them from behind the scenes, to shore up the radical cause. To wit: First, he elevated the young radical Wang Hongwen from a humble position in Shanghai to vice-chairmanship of the Party, apparently intending to

43. "*Liaoning Daily* on Sworn Follower, Lin Biao Issue," in *FBIS*, April 26, 1978, p. L8.
44. According to Liao Gailong ("Historical Experiences," part 1, p. 98): "Later, he [Mao] became vexed because he [Zhou] restored the correct original line. Thus, Comrade Mao Zedong criticized the resurgence of 'Right' deviationism. Later, he further initiated a struggle to criticize Lin Biao and Confucius, to oppose Comrade Zhou Enlai." A former high cadre (*gaoji ganbu*) interviewed in Hong Kong related that when Jiang Qing complained to Mao in 1972 that Zhou was rehabilitating unreconstructed capitalist-roaders and restoring "revisionist" programs and asked permission to criticize him, Mao demurred, explaining that to criticize Zhou would throw the nation into chaos. Why not criticize Confucius, he suggested.

groom him as his successor. In the preparatory meetings prior to the Tenth Congress he disregarded objections and called upon senior colleagues "to elect boldly young people to responsible work posts, to be vice-chairmen of provincial Party committees and the Party's Central Committee; for instance, Wang Hongwen." In his enthusiasm for Wang, who is said to have reminded him of the young and idealistic Mao Zedong, he reportedly even took him into his private residence to live.[45]

Second, he introduced many of the more radical themes in the "Anti-Lin Biao and Confucius" campaign. Thus the quotation that prompted the revival of mass mobilization in the summer of 1973, "Going against the tide is a Marxist-Leninist principle," first appeared in a *People's Daily* commentary that Mao apparently ghostwrote.[46] It was Mao who first noticed Zhang Tiesheng's famous letter in *Liaoning Daily* (where Mao Yuanxin had published it) protesting the inequity of university entrance exams for sent-down youth, and by having it published in *People's Daily* he forestalled the reintroduction of college entrance exams, also setting in motion the movement against "taking the back door" (*zou houmen*).[47] (This movement won the applause of the masses but annoyed cadres, eventually inducing Mao to retract his support.) Finally, Mao supported launching the radical Shanghai journal *Study and Criticism*, initially allowing his calligraphy to be used in the masthead, and there is also evidence that he made occasional pseudonymous contributions.[48]

The Campaign to Criticize Lin Biao and Confucius (*pi-Lin pi-Kong*)

45. Takashi Ito, "Politics and the People," Kyodo (Tokyo), August 15, 1977; trans. in *FBIS*, August 19, 1977.

46. *China News Service* (hereinafter *CNS*), no. 485 (September 20, 1973); Yan Jingwen, "Beijing quanli douzheng jinru xin gaochao" [Beijing's power struggle advances to a new high tide], *ZW*, no. 283 (November 16, 1973): 6–9. The quotation first appeared in a signed commentary in *RR* on August 16, 1973, p. 3, under the name Yang Bu—possibly a pseudonym, since no leading official in Beijing is known by that name. This call for rebellion against the "current" was issued only two days before the seventh anniversary of the Red Guard movement.

47. Xu Zhuanfu, "'Pi Lin zhengfeng' jitui 'fan chaoliu'" ['Anti-Lin movement' fends off 'against the current'], *Zhanwang* [Prospect] (Hong Kong) no. 284 (December 12, 1973: 5–8. (Hereinafter *ZW*.) Although the Zhang Tiesheng incident was publicized in *Liaoning Ribao* on July 19, *RR* did not publish it until August 10, and if Mao had not personally requested it, it might never have been published. As in the June–July 1966 situation, the campaign seems to have been stalemated prior to Mao's intercession.

48. *Xuexi yu Pipan* published an editorial under the pseudonym Fang Hai in every issue. In the December 16, 1973, issue, for example, Fang Hai wrote a passage without quotation marks on the ideological reform of the intellectuals. Two weeks later, the New Year's Day message of the pacemaking "two papers and one magazine" (*liang bao yi kan—Renmin Ribao, Jiefangjun Bao*, and *Hongqi*) attributed an identical passage to Mao. This suggests either that "Fang Hai" was Mao's penname, or at least that Fang's writings had Mao's blessing. *CNS*, no. 504 (February 14, 1974).

however proved not only difficult to implement but had little evident deterrent effect on Zhou's rightward drift. Zhou Enlai retired to the hospital on the evening of May 9, 1974 (where he continued to receive frequent visitors), having installed Deng Xiaoping as acting premier and heir apparent. This was a clear public signal of Zhou's retirement from successorship, and the relationship between Mao and Zhou henceforth assumed the character of a contest among incumbents to designate the successor. Zhou seems to have gone about setting the stage for his succession far more deliberately than Mao. He stepped up the rehabilitation of veteran cadres and proceeded to make appointments to complete the staffing of his administrative hierarchy in the fall of 1974, expecting to ratify these formally at the forthcoming Fourth NPC. Meanwhile, the struggle to define the mission continued, and potential successors played an increasingly active role in this, perceiving in the mission a vehicle through which they might rise to charismatic leadership.

The climactic confrontation between the flagging incumbents, each still championing his own respective vision of the salvationary mission, erupted in the first half of 1975. Zhou emerged from his hospital to chair the Fourth NPC, where skeletal plans were presented for a massive modernization project that would see the nation through to the twenty-first century. Perhaps beginning to lose his tactical finesse at this point, Zhou failed to co-opt the radicals into this project, in fact all but freezing them out. Mao launched an almost immediate alternative in the Campaign to Study Proletarian Dictatorship, whose evident purpose was to offer a theoretically definitive elucidation of the distinction between the "proletarian revolutionary line" and the "bourgeois reactionary line" or "capitalist road" that he perceived to be still coexisting within the same leadership, making it feasible to attack the latter without collateral damage to the former. Yet the distinction he and his radical colleagues were attempting to draw failed theoretically (e.g., see the inconsistency between Yao Wenyuan's emphasis on ideological leadership and Zhang Chunqiao's focus on the different economic bases of the two lines) as well as practically, giving rise to another round of internecine factionalism. The radicals proved unequal to the task of pacifying the situation, leaving the field, perforce, to the moderates.

THE PASSAGE OF POWER

The final period was one of increasingly complex and intense struggle: its complexity is due to the fact that it involved continuing conflict among incumbents to designate their successors, inter-successor conflict to discredit rivals and retain favor, and finally conflict between incumbents and successors as Mao sought in effect to pursue a "null-succession" option and keep all would-be successors at bay. Its intensity was due to the fact that Mao was obviously at death's door. Underlying these frantic political conflicts and to some extent a consequence of them was a waning of charisma, as Mao Zedong finally abandoned the attempt to define a salvationary mission, and as Zhou's rival attempt to do so withered in the face of radical polemics.

Inter-incumbent Conflict

Following Mao's implicit repudiation of his Four Modernizations program in the drive against bourgeois right, Zhou seems to have withdrawn from the political scene; he had retired to the hospital as early as May 1974, but in view of the fact that he continued to entertain visitors and to pursue such elaborate political projects as restaffing his State Council and arranging for the NPC, the radicals considered this something of a tactical ruse.[49] Now, however, he seems to have lapsed into political inactivity, leaving his affairs in the hands of the blunt and energetic Deng Xiaoping, whose positions as first vice-premier and acting premier gave him strong claim to Zhou's mantle.

Zhou's selection of Deng as his successor, however, also tended to bias the selection of Mao's successor in Deng's favor. The reason is that inasmuch as Zhou was senior vice-chairman of the Party as well as premier, whoever succeeded him would also be favorably situated to succeed Mao himself. The choice was limited to the three surviving vice-chairmen: Ye Jianying, Wang Hongwen, and Deng Xiaoping. But Ye was too old to come under serious consideration, and Wang had fallen from favor due to his handling of the Hangzhou incident (to be explicated in chapter 6). Thus Deng Xiaoping, as first vice-premier and sole eligible vice-chairman, stood on the threshold of total power. And just before his death on January 8, according to rumors reaching Hong Kong, Zhou left a "last will" endorsing Deng.

Zhou's plans were, however, undone by the timing and sequence of the retirements of strategic members of the older generation. At Zhou's behest, Deng delivered the eulogy at the premier's memorial service on January 15 on behalf of the CC, the State Council, and the PLA, and the text was published in all newspapers throughout the country and read repeatedly over all national and provincial broadcasting stations on January 15 and 16; a television recording of the latter half of the speech was also released for nationwide distribution on January 16.[50] Mean-

49. "Although Premier Zhou is seriously ill, he is 'busy' finding people to talk with," Wang Hongwen allegedly complained to Mao. "Those who often visited the Premier's residence include comrades such as Deng Xiaoping, Ye Jianying and Li Xiannian." Central Document (CD) no. 24 (1976), as translated in IS 13, no. 9 (September 1977): 80–110.

50. N.B.: Deng made no reference in this speech to "stability and unity" (anding tuanjie), or even to "stability"—terms for which he had come under attack by the radicals. But he also omitted reference to the campaign against the Rightist reversal of verdicts that the radicals were promoting.

while, the Politburo promptly deadlocked over Zhou's succession. That his own death should have preceded Mao's was obviously inopportune, as it gave Mao the chance to override Zhou's succession arrangements (it seems not to have occurred to Zhou to retire before his own death). With Zhou, Kang Sheng, and Dong Biwu now dead, both Zhu De and Liu Bocheng mortally ill, and six of the remaining members absent because their main work lay in the provinces, the radicals were able, with Mao's concurrence, to block Deng's selection. Roughly half the votes went to Deng and the other half to Zhang Chunqiao, second vice-premier and the radical choice. Hua Guofeng, a dark horse with relatively little experience at the national level, emerged as the compromise candidate.

On February 7 it was announced that Hua had been appointed acting premier and CC vice-chairman. When Deng was purged of "all offices inside and outside the Party" on April 7 in the wake of the Tiananmen Incident, Hua was appointed premier and first vice-chairman of the Party, placing him next in line to Mao. In view of later developments Hua is assumed also to have been groomed by Zhou, as a contingency selection. It is also true, however, that the radicals made no overtures to the new heir apparent, as they would have done had Mao made his wishes clear; on the contrary, they attempted to implicate him as a "capitulationist."

Inter-successor Conflict

The potential successors, having after all a greater stake in succession than the incumbents, were inclined to preempt the process without quarter or scruple. As Mao and Zhou faded from the scene they began to seize the initiative, constructing factional networks (to be described in greater detail in chapter 7) to defend their respective positions. Considerations of balance were no longer evident in the staffing decisions for the Fourth NPC, and in the ensuing period the escalation in conflict could be gauged not only by increasing mutual exclusion,[51] but by the fact that the two potential successor organizations no longer respected each other's spheres of functional specialization: the radicals attacked moderate management of the economy, and the moderates attacked radical management of the propaganda and culture organs.[52]

Successor-Incumbent Conflict

Whereas Zhou's presence was no longer apparent after the summer of 1975, Mao continued to operate from behind the scenes. He tended,

---

51. "They have already labelled us the 'Shanghai Gang,'" complained Zhang Chunqiao. "In a certain reception for foreign guests, they intentionally arrange us in a group. At that time I told the premier my opinion of it." Reported by Xu Jingxian on November 29, 1976, and quoted in CD no. 37, trans. in IS 15, no. 2 (February 1979), pp. 94–111.
52. See CD no. 24, pp. 79–112; CD no. 37 (1977), pp. 94–111.

however, to abandon ambitious ideological innovations and adopt reflexive, balance-of-power tactics, shifting support unpredictably from one side to the other. He faulted the radicals for factionalism (a number of his criticisms have subsequently been published by the moderates),[53] apparently blamed them (fairly or unfairly) for the failure of the Campaign to Study Proletarian Dictatorship, and sided with Deng in his critique of their administration of culture.[54] He sharply reprimanded Jiang Qing for her attempt to turn the *Water Margin* campaign (to be described in chapter 6) to political account.

By the fall of 1975, as a result of the radicals' own tactical blunders as well as Mao's disenchantment, cultural radicalism had reached its nadir. Throughout the summer the media were bereft of the themes repeated everywhere in the spring: the "new-born things," the Xiaojinzhuang model, the revolutionary operas. Rehabilitation of purged veterans (e.g., Yang Chengwu, Luo Ruiqing) reached a "high tide" in July–September 1975. The moderate offensive against the radicals seemed to have been successful on all fronts. Then, suddenly, their fortunes turned. The radicals themselves attributed their salvation to the Chairman's providential intervention: on December 30 *People's Daily* published a letter from a group of graduating Qinghua University students, claiming that the "big debate over the revolution" that followed the "rightist wind for the reversal of verdicts" in July, August, and September had been launched by a "series of great instructions that came directly from Mao at the key moment."[55]

In fact it is hard to account for such a reversal except by the Chairman's personal intercession. What brought this change of heart? One reason is that certain signals aroused all his old suspicions that the moderates were in fact "anti-Mao" (one of the few words Mao bothered to learn in English), and that the radical "new things" upon which he had after all staked his reputation would not survive a moderate succession. The first such signal came in the form of a request approved by Deng and Education Minister Zhou Rongxin from Qinghua University President (and Party Committee Vice-Chairman) Liu Bing in August for the dismissal of Chi Qun and Xie Jingyi. These two were of a somewhat different origin from the Shanghai group: Chi was an officer in the 8341 elite guard assigned to Mao, and Xie the daughter of Xie Fuzhi, Mao's chief of secret police (following Kang Sheng's retirement). Mao thus considered Liu Bing's letter an ill-concealed attempt to attack Mao himself, and he wrote a letter back in which he placed the incident in the context of the struggle

---

53. Jiang Qing's letter to Mao of November 19, 1974, as quoted in CD no. 24, complains that she has been "neglected and given almost no work."

54. Mao allegedly expressed his approval in talks with Deng in early July, and in a written statement on July 14, as quoted in CD no. 37.

55. *CNS*, no. 596 (December 31, 1975).

between the two classes and the two roads. Mao's letter was promptly published by the grateful radicals, setting off criticism of the impending education "rectification" promised by Deng and Zhou Rongxin.[56]

Another such signal was contained in an address by Deng Xiaoping to a State banquet for National Day on October 1, in which he quoted the Chairman as saying: "The entire people must continue to follow the important instructions of Mao Zedong: to study the theory of the dictatorship of the proletariat, to struggle against revisionism, and to take care to promote stability and unity and to further national economic development."[57] Although Deng did not identify the original citation, on the same day that the speech was published another lead article in *People's Daily* also attributed the three commands to Mao.[58] Fruitless attempts to track down this "three-point directive" suggest, however, that Deng was exercising liberal poetic license.[59] On January 1, having apparently only recently become cognizant of the matter, Mao sharply repudiated Deng's directive: "What? Stability and unity does not mean giving up class struggle! Class struggle is the key link, upon which everything else depends."[60] Both of these incidents indicated to Mao that, as he presciently noted of Deng later that winter, "he said he would never reverse the verdict. It cannot be counted on."[61]

A second possible reason for Mao's fateful change of heart is more personal, having to do with the Chairman's deteriorating health. There is ample testimony that the Chairman retained full command of his mental faculties until the end, but continual pain and physical disability (for example, he could no longer read) prevented him from attending formal meetings and made him increasingly dependent upon those close to him.[62] As of 1973, Mao's wife seemed to have lost this proximity as a result of personal incompatibility, taking up residence in the official guest

56. See Wang Xizhe's remarks in *Qishi Niandai*, no. 2 (February 1981): 20–23.
57. *RR*, October 1, 1975, p. 2.
58. Ibid.
59. The directive was not attributed to Mao in provincial broadcasts or articles, and none of the articles later quoting it printed it in the customary boldface type. It was not included in the Mao quotations on National Day and has never been printed in Mao-quotation form before or since. *CNS*, no. 597 (January 7, 1976).
60. Mao's repudiation is prominently quoted in the New Year's joint editorial of *RR*, *HQ*, *JFJB* (January 1, 1976).
61. *RR*, March 28, 1976.
62. According to a member of the Schmidt delegation, which met with Mao in December 1975, "Mao cannot rise from his chair with his own strength. He moves his arms with difficulty, he cannot fully close his mouth, his voice is broken, and the articulation of every word creates considerable difficulty for him. . . . There is however consensus that the illness of the 82-year-old Chairman says nothing negative about his mental [*geistliche*] abilities. Mao Zedong follows what goes on around him with alertness." Rudiger Machetzki, in *CA*, December 1975, pp. 767–770.

house. Zhou retained direct access to Mao until he was personally incapacitated in the fall of 1975. For a while Mao was close to Wang Hongwen, but when Wang fell from favor in May 1975 he retreated to Shanghai. Then in the fall of 1975 Jiang Qing regained access by recalling Mao Yuanxin from Liaoning to serve as secretary of her personal office. Mao Yuanxin, a nephew who had been raised in Mao Zedong's household after his father was killed by the warlord Sheng Shicai, had managed to stay in Mao's good graces. At this point he seems to have reinforced his uncle's radical impulses, perhaps by subtly nuancing the information he related about the outside world. As the Chairman's health further declined, Jiang Qing also regained access to him.

Yet the Chairman remained ambivalent to the end. Having rescued the radicals from political oblivion, he watched as they tried to press their advantage, scrambling to a position of dominance second only to Hua and Mao in the new Politburo (upon Deng's "retirement" in February)—and then dropped them from favor. When Hua and Jiang presented Mao with alternative scenarios for the campaign against Deng, Mao opted for Hua's more moderate plan. Deng's errors represented a "contradiction among the people," and neither Deng nor those who had supported his 1975 modernization plans should be purged. Jiang made speeches on February 23 and March 2 advocating a harder line, but to no avail.[63] Mao is said to have asked Ye to persuade Deng to submit another self-criticism, but even after lengthy discussion the latter refused, saying he had always tried to act according to the center and Chairman Mao; the errors he had committed in the past he had long since given up (*jiaodaiguo*), so he was not thinking of writing another self-criticism.[64] When at the end of March the radicals arranged to hold an expanded meeting of the Politburo to criticize Deng, inviting their supporters at Qinghua and Beijing universities, Deng remained silent and seemingly indifferent throughout the meeting. Upon its conclusion his only response to the criticisms was "My ears are deaf, I could not hear well" (*ting bu qingchu*).[65] Deng had apparently arrived at the shrewd tactical estimate that he was sure to outlive Mao and prevail over the hated radicals in the long run in any case, so there was no need to stoop to another self-criticism.

Although the radicals eventually succeeded in bringing Deng down by holding him responsible for the Tiananmen Incident, they could not plausibly claim to have regained Mao's favor for the succession. Hua's competing claim is stronger, but clouded by the attendant circumstances:

63. "In China there is an international capitalist agent named Deng Xiaoping," Jiang claimed in one of her speeches. "It might be correct to call him a traitor. Nevertheless, our Chairman has been protecting him." CD no. 24.
64. Zhang Changxi, in *ZW*, no. 338 (March 1, 1976): 4.
65. Zhou Xun et al., *Deng Xiaoping* (Hong Kong: Guangjiaojing Pub., 1979).

Hua was reporting to Mao *on the progress of the anti-Deng campaign* on April 30, whereupon the Chairman, his speech impeded, responded with a written directive containing these three instructions: (1) take your time, don't be anxious; (2) act according to past principles; and (3) with you in charge, I am at ease. "If you have any questions, ask Jiang Qing," he added (according to Jiang Qing, in a later interpolation). According to the best evidence so far available, Mao explicitly designated no successor.

Lost Mission

Upon the collapse of the "bourgeois right" campaign, Mao seems to have given up attempts at theoretical clarification of the revolutionary mission, resigning this task to future generations, and his terminal statements on this question even suggest pessimism about the capability of his successors to rise to the occasion. On December 31, Mao met with the Nixon delegation, revealing in an interview with Nixon's daughter Julie a despair over the political proclivities of China's youth reminiscent of his mood on the eve of the Cultural Revolution. "Young people are soft. They have to be reminded of the need for struggle," he told her.

> Mao had rated the chance of permanent success of his revolution less than fifty percent. The Chairman told us, there will be struggle in the Party, there will be struggle between classes, nothing is certain except struggle. . . . it is quite possible the struggle will last for two or three hundred years.[66]

His last public instructions appeared in an article by the editorial departments of *People's Daily*, *Red Flag*, and *Liberation Army Daily* on May 16, which quoted him attacking "high officials" and calling upon the masses to rise up against them. On June 1 he convoked a group of Politburo colleagues (viz., Hua Guofeng, Wang Hongwen, Ye Jianying, Zhang Chunqiao, Yao Wenyuan, Li Xiannian, and Chen Yonggui) for what were to prove his last (apocryphal) recorded remarks. In these he gave voice to feelings of persecution and doom, characterizing himself as "the target of everyone, an isolated poor old man standing alone." While foreseeing the possibility that "in China a restoration of the bourgeoisie would occur everywhere," this would only be a temporary setback, and "in a few decades, centuries, at the latest a few ten thousand years, the red banners will again wave everywhere."[67]

After a series of natural disasters of the type that traditionally augur dynastic changes in China, Mao passed away on September 9, 1976, at

66. Julie Nixon Eisenhower, in *Ladies' Home Journal*, January 1976, as quoted in *The Hong Kong Standard*, December 27, 1976, p. 9.
67. Quoted in *CA*, November 1976, p. 581.

12:11 A.M., at the age of eighty-two.[68] Although in retrospect his charisma would seem to have so ebbed that he could neither transfer it to a chosen successor nor protect his own reputation from posthumous abuse, this was by no means clear at the time. The evidence at hand was ambiguous. On the one hand, he seemed ultimately triumphant: his "latest instructions" could override constitutional law, his *obiter dicta* were tantamount to Central Documents. The inordinate significance attached to two "forgery" episodes in the last year of Mao's life—the first of which resulted in the dismissal of Deng Xiaoping, the second (a quibble over whether Mao had told Hua to follow "past" principles or "principles laid down") in the arrest of the Gang of Four—demonstrated the authoritative character ascribed to his every word. On the other hand, compliance sometimes seemed ritualistic, an impatient charade masking self-interested behavior.

Succession arrangements remained unclear for about a month, during which both sides engaged in negotiation and backstage scheming. The underlying basis of cleavage was obviously the issue of succession, and the lack of a solution suggested a deadlock. Apparently Jiang sought the position of Party Chairman for herself, with Hua relinquishing his premiership to Zhang Chunqiao (rumors and wall posters had predicted such appointments some three weeks after Mao's death).[69] As of Mao's death Jiang probably counted on the support of Chen Yonggui and Ji Dengkui, plus the four charter members of the "Gang." Of the ten remaining Politburo members, the moderates could probably rely on another six (Ye Jianying, Xu Shiyou, Liu Bocheng, Chen Xilian, Li Xiannian, and Wei Guoqing), leaving four "swing" votes (viz., Hua Guofeng, Li Desheng, Wang Dongxing, and Wu De). It is not clear that a vote was actually taken prior to October 6 but it is reasonable to suppose so, nominating Hua as the most plausible candidate for chairman even before the traditional forty-day period of mourning had elapsed as a way of winning over the undecideds and forcing the Four to their reserves. Chen Yonggui and Ji Dengkui had served under Hua as vice-premiers for the preceding six months, hence their ideological loyalties to the Four were placed under organizational cross-pressure. Hua's nomination flushed out the opposition of the Four (Jiang called him "incompetent"), who

68. In 1976 the PRC was hit by seven earthquakes, affecting Hebei, Yunnan, Sichuan, and Gansu provinces and the major cities of Beijing and Tianjin. The worst of these occurred in Tangshan on July 28. It measured 8.2 on the Richter scale and reportedly claimed 655,337 lives and injured another 800,000, making it China's worst since 1556. *SCMP*, January 5 and 6, 1976.
69. Leo Goodstadt, *China's Watergate: Political and Economic Conflicts, 1969–1977* (New Delhi: Vikas Pub., 1979), pp. 4–12.

proposed Vice-Chairman Wang Hongwen as an alternative. They succeeded in blocking Hua on the first ballot, but after a heated disucussion he was elected during a second meeting. Having placed the Four under close (reportedly including electronic) surveillance (Hua had functioned concurrently as Minister of Public Security since January 1975), the moderates were now in a position to move swiftly at the slightest sign of "illegal" activity in resistance to the majority decision, which was not long in emerging.

How elaborate or effective such conspiratorial activities were is hard to gauge.[70] Though there is little credible evidence of a radical plot to launch a coup and seize power on a national scale, there was some effort to organize local resistance in Shanghai—all of which came to naught upon the announcement of the arrest of the Four on October 6.[71] On the morning of October 7, a meeting of the Politburo was held at which leaders of the moderate faction read reports on the arrest, and the Politburo unanimously supported Hua's decision and elected him chairman of the CC. On October 8, the new Politburo announced its first two decisions: to establish a memorial hall in Beijing to house the corpse of Mao Zedong (in violation of Mao's personal wishes), and to publish volume 5 of Mao's *Selected Works* (Hua accepted chairmanship of both the building committee and the editorial board). The Politburo report announcing the arrest was meanwhile secretly circulated nationwide to middle and high ranking cadres.[72]

The political repercussions of the arrest seem to have been quite widespread, belying Hua's claim that the issue had been drawn "without firing a single shot or shedding a drop of blood." Serious disturbances erupted in Fujian, necessitating the presence of PLA troops to maintain order; chaos was also reported in such provinces as Jiangxi, Hubei, and Hebei. Although Fujian is the only province in which the PLA was ordered to intervene, radio broadcasts spoke of "civil war" in Sichuan, and "beating, smashing, and looting" were reported from northern Shandong in the November 1976–May 1977 period, southern Jiangxi,

70. Jiang Qing apparently contacted Mao Yuanxin, political commissar of the Shenyang MR, to request support from his division in Beijing (the reason being that the "8341 troop" was said to be preparing to help the reactionaries stage a coup), but Yuanxin needed the approval of Li Desheng, commander of the MR, to give the troops marching orders, and Li in turn consulted with Vice Chief of Staff Yang Chengwu in Beijing, who informed Hua and other high functionaries of Mao Yuanxin's request. This report is impossible to corroborate. Certainly continuation of the campaign to criticize Deng would have provided the radicals with ample opportunity to embarrass and perhaps even purge members of the moderate group.

71. See Ronald Suleski, "Changing the Guard in Shanghai," *AS* 17, no. 9 (September 1977): 886–98.

72. *Ming Bao* (Hong Kong), October 28, 1976, p. 1.

Guizhou, and Baoding (a railroad center 110 miles southwest of Beijing). In fact, newscasts and commentaries reported damage in twenty-one of the twenty-nine administrative units in the country.[73] There was little indication, however, whether such unrest was recent or whether the reports referred to chronic troubles, and it was also unclear to what extent disorder could be attributed to organized resistance by loyal followers of the Four and to what extent to crimes of opportunity during a transitional lapse of central authority.

CONCLUSION

Charismatic leadership in Chinese political culture is associated with a religiously derived conception of infallibility difficult to approximate in any case, but the Cultural Revolution raised popular expectations of an immaculate sun-god that it proved impossible to sustain. There was also a contradiction between seeking to preserve the charisma of the incumbent and making effective provision to transfer charisma to a successor. One of the tactics Mao used to try to avoid incurring blame for errors without altogether giving up the boldly experimental approach he required to redefine his mission was to retreat to the "backstage" while engaging emissaries to act on his behalf (and accept blame if the experiment failed). Nevertheless, the Chairman's responsibility for the steep rise and fall of Lin Biao proved inescapable, and his failure to purge the radicals he had so frequently chastised was unaccountable unless one assumes some complicity. The myth of infallibility was also incompatible with the snakelike oscillations of the Party line during the late Cultural Revolution period, which owed as much to Mao's own ambivalence as to changing objective circumstances. Paradoxically, a man who loved to ignore balance and forge blindly and one-sidedly ahead proved during his last years to be such an accomplished weaver and bobber that the charismatic mission he had hoped to instill was almost completely obscured.

The attempt to translate charisma into a set of impersonal doctrines that could be transmitted from one leadership to another also proved unfeasible. There are at least two reasons for the failure to codify charisma: first, fear of expropriation of the code to serve the power-political interests of those intrinsically hostile to Mao or his Thought; second, uncertainty about the policy content of the code, requiring continual tactical readjustment in light of political and economic exigencies. Thus the exact content of the code could never crystalize. Nor did the code serve the maintenance and enhancement needs of China's dominant political or-

---

73. *SCMP*, January 1, 1977, p. 4; November 29, 1976, p. 4; January 1, 1977, p. 1; October 17, 1976, p. 3; Domes, *Government*, p. 140.

ganizations, who might otherwise have had an interest in its perpetuation—quite the contrary!

All of which is to explain how the transmission of charisma was complicated by the problems—both inherent and idiosyncratic—of the donor. But there were also problems on the side of the potential recipients. Generally speaking, for a would-be successor to demonstrate the self-assurance, imagination, and communicative skills that constitute the subjective dimension of charisma would be to risk coming into conflict with the incumbent leadership. Thus any aspirant to charismatic succession would probably tend to mask such qualities. Even after taking such discretion into account, however, it is difficult to find candidates on the scene who demonstrated much potential.

Lin Biao, diminutive, sickly, and unprepossessing as he appeared, at least had a brilliant military record of which something might have been made, and his decision to launch a preemptive coup against Mao showed audacity in conception if not in execution. He did have a power base that was deep if not particularly broad, and some of his writings (particularly his essay on people's war) exhibit theoretical imagination and an innovative capability. But he continued to allow his thinking to be so dominated by militaristic attitudes that he seemed incapable of operating within the more fluid and compromising milieu of civilian politics. Lin's charisma implicitly assumed the impassioned motivation generated by revolution or war; in a peacetime context, he proved incapable of mobilizing the masses—only of regimenting them. The civilian populace for its part seemed relieved to be delivered from his Draconian regime.

The cultural radicals were "court favorites" without broad or deep power bases or any outstanding achievements to speak of. Their spectacular political ascent could be attributed almost entirely to Mao's personal power. Liege to a jealous lord who customarily bade them undertake tasks apt to estrange them from everyone else, they found it impossible to broaden their base. Even had circumstances been more auspicious, the Four lacked the political qualities to claim charismatic leadership. Wang held promise but was inexperienced, overshadowed by Zhang and paralyzed by the rigors of Cultural Revolution politics. Yao was solely a wordsmith, a "pen" (*bi*). Zhang, in addition to possessing what was probably the keenest theoretical intellect of all potential successors, had considerable political skill, as he demonstrated during the Cultural Revolution in Shanghai. At his trial, he demonstrated at least the courage of dignified silence. But he never ventured to emerge from the shadow of Jiang Qing to strike out on his own; his consistent willingness to subordinate himself to her showed poor political judgment. As for Jiang, she was a resourceful innovator in the artistic realm, contributing to the politicization of drama and to the melodramatization of politics. She had the courage of her convictions and an indomitable will, but she was a fanatic, inclined to appeal only to true believers. Apparently unversed in theory, shrill and splenetic, Jiang fit all the Chinese negative female stereotypes too well to overcome deeply ingrained prejudice against women in politics.

Among the available contenders, only Zhou Enlai was at all qualified to fill the subjective criteria for charismatic leadership. A politician of great charm and acumen, he conceived in the end a visionary program capable of appealing to the interests of China's officialdom. But never did he venture to create his own political language, preferring to manipulate the words of others—even his culminating "Four Modernizations" he owed to Mao. And not once did Zhou dare to assert himself beyond the bounds of prudence for what he believed in. It is a sad commentary that this great nemesis of the Gang of Four also chaired the committee that brought trumped-up charges against Liu Shaoqi.

An informative controversy has arisen within the comparative communist literature concerning the character of the succession crisis, to which the events related in this chapter might profitably be related. At issue is whether the succession crisis magnifies or mitigates the leadership's capacity for policy innovation. Rush has contended that such a crisis tends to freeze the innovative capacity of the system, for such decisions beg the unresolved question of who is to decide them.[74] Bunce argues on the contrary that such crises stimulate political innovation, as fledgling successors endeavor to consolidate their regime with policies calculated to appeal to a new constituency.[75] The relevance to the above discussion is obvious: without an innovative mission, charismatic succession is impossible.

The Chinese experience suggests that one crucial and hitherto neglected factor concerns the phase in the development of the succession crisis at which conflict breaks out. Both Rush and Bunce are basically oriented to a post-mortem succession scenario. But the Chinese case suggests that a "succession crisis" in Rush's sense of a paralysis of will is apt to begin well before death of the incumbent. During the pre-mortem phase, there are conflicts of interest not only between potential successors, but between incumbents and their designated successors. Both Liu Shaoqi and Lin Biao made anticipatory bids to define an innovative mission, which excited Mao's suspicions of betrayal, and he rescinded his choice. Mao's subsequent refusal to select a successor fostered a stable balance of power between heirs apparent, in which no one was in a strong

74. Myron Rush, *Political Succession in the USSR* (New York: Columbia University Press, 1965); and *How Communist States Change Their Rulers* (Ithaca, N.Y.: Cornell University Press, 1974).
75. Valerie Bunce, *Do New Leaders Make a Difference? Executive Succession and Public Policy under Capitalism and Socialism* (Princeton: Princeton University Press, 1981).

enough position to approve and implement imaginative new policies. Instead of elite pluralism, an *immobilisme* was generated characteristic of coalition cabinets in multiparty parliamentary systems.

The period most hospitable to policy innovation seems to be immediately after a winner emerges from a post-mortem showdown. During this period, the emergent successor must attract a bureaucratic constituency and assemble a mass base, if one is to survive. To do this, policies must be introduced promising (and hopefully delivering) a dramatic improvement in popular fortunes. This is so even if that winner proves to be only transitional, as in the case of Hua Guofeng (or, in comparative communist terms, Malenkov, Nagy, or Dubček). Only after a successor has fully consolidated control over the administrative apparatus and cultivated a base is it possible to dispense with policy innovation and rely more heavily on the coercion of dissent.

SIX

Permanent Mobilization

A "revised storming" approach was adopted toward mass mobilization during the late Cultural Revolution. This represented a continuation of the storming approach insofar as mobilization was still considered a valued end in itself and not just a means to redistribute property, to boost economic production, or to pursue other ends. Only through continuous mobilization, it was felt, could a revolutionary transformation of the cultural superstructure be achieved. It ("revised" storming) differed primarily in its fluctuating but generally enhanced concern for organizational integrity, and in its clearer recognition of the sensitivity of the relationship between mobilization and economic production. Yet both of these shifts came reluctantly and somewhat half-heartedly, succeeding neither in stabilizing a favorable economic climate nor in sustaining revolutionary enthusiasm among the broad masses. The purpose of this chapter is to analyze the reasons for this failure.

The chapter is divided into two parts. The first deals with the political economy of mobilization: the causal relationship between mobilization and production. The second examines the impact of mobilization upon cultural transformation, its main objective. As the deepening factional cleavage became articulated with a functional division between economic and ideological bureaucracies, the political economy and the moral economy of mobilization grew incommensurable.

POLITICAL ECONOMY

Throughout the post-Liberation epoch, the relationship between mobilization and economics has had two aspects: as a dependent variable ("effect"), mobilization presumes the provision of material incentives sufficient (in combination with normative incentives) to motivate the masses to participate—which in turn assumes an adequate level of economic production. As an independent variable ("cause"), mobilization has been aimed at stimulating more intense, zealous efforts at increasing production. These two aspects of mobilization are interdependent in the sense that without an increase in production it becomes uneconomic to provide the masses with increased material incentives, and without mobilization it becomes more difficult to increase production. Political considerations may temporarily override this interdependency: it is possible to mobilize the masses with enhanced material incentives in the absence of increased production through deficit financing, for example, or to increase production without enhanced material incentives by more heavily emphasizing normative or coercive incentives. But over the long term, such alternatives are not economically cost-efficient and hence are unlikely to be sustained.

Let us first focus on mobilization as a dependent variable. During roughly its first decade, the regime maintained a positive correlation between mass participation and enhanced material incentives. The base from which these improvements were measured had been artificially lowered for many sectors of the population by years of protracted warfare, economic instability, and cumulative deterioration of public goods (e.g., the transportation and communication infrastructure, irrigation and waterworks, forestry). By seizing uncontested national sovereignty for the first time since 1911 and vigorously launching a series of political and economic reforms, the regime was able to arrest these tendencies. Economic recovery and growth ensued, providing an expanding "pie" from which workers and peasants could receive larger shares. Many of the movements launched during this period were redistributive in nature, resulting in the transfer of fungible assets (such as land) from the former ruling classes to the working classes.

With the completion of the socialization of the means of production at the end of 1956, the cheapest source of material incentives to allocate among mass participants had been exhausted. Redistributive movements were not yet abandoned—the Great Leap resulted in the redistribution of property through the merging of cooperatives into People's Communes, for example, and there were periodic experiments with different workpoint allocation systems or shifts of responsibility for collective property from one administrative level to another—but because of the alienation of control over property from masses to cadres, none of these redistributions resulted in perceived enhancement of material incentives, and some of them resulted in perceived deprivations.

Nor did increases in production, which, with the exception of the Great Leap, were generally strong—sometimes excellent in the industrial sector, less impressive but still positive after discounting population growth in the agricultural sector—result in an enhancement of material incentives for the working classes. After 1963 there was a remarkable period of nominal wage stability (and de facto attrition) in the modern urban sector that was to last until 1977. The only significant wage hike, in 1971–72, applied only to people who had been on the bottom two rungs of the wage ladder for extended periods. Agricultural incentives are more difficult to measure in view of the incommensurability of work-points in various regions and various other problems peculiar to this sector, but the best available estimates indicate a similar stagnation of living standards.

The Cultural Revolution represents a continuation of this trend toward stable or even slightly declining material incentives accompanied by extremely high rates of capital investment, steadily increasing economic growth, and declining rates of productivity. Normative incentives were no longer reinforced by material incentives, but rather used to rationalize their absence. Thus the themes of selflessness and altruistic sacrifice for the collective ran like a red thread through the entire Cultural Revolution decade, justifying continued struggle (labor) in the absence of any particular material benefit therefor. Benefits would be accumulated not in heaven but by future generations on earth, from the enhanced productivity that cumulative collective investment would facilitate.

Although increased production should therefore in principle *not* be correlated with *material* incentives, there was certainly a prospect of linking *normatively* motivated mobilization to increases in production. The most concerted effort along these lines seems to have been made during Lin Biao's tenure. The need for economic recovery and resumed growth in the late–Cultural Revolution period was not the liability for Lin that it was to prove for the cultural radicals, for his emphasis on austerity, discipline, and collective morale, and his reassertion of a tight, militaristic organizational framework, could readily be put to constructive account. In fact, the Cultural Revolution gave the first major new impetus to the construction of locally financed, "small-scale" factories in the rural areas since the Great Leap.[1] The emphasis was on "small and comprehensive" units (capable of turning out all kinds of industrial products, both heavy and light), using indigenous methods and native equipment. Direction of small industrial and agricultural enterprises was given to the commune, that of middle enterprises to the *xian*, that of the large operations to the province; the intermediary echelons—the commune and the administrative region—functioned to verify the actions of those directly subordinate to them. Before the Cultural Revolution, only a few provinces could turn out equipment for small nitrogenous fertilizer plants in complete sets, but afterward a large number of provinces could do so, with the result that by 1968 the productive capacity of such plants

1. For planning and statistical purposes, these are factories that "employ sixteen or fewer people and use mechanical power, or 31 or fewer and do not use mechanical power." Independent power plants are "small-scale if their generating capacity is less than fifteen kilowatts, regardless of the number of employees." *CN*, no. 325 (August 21, 1969).

constituted more than a third of the country's total capacity for nitrogenous fertilizer production, increasing to 40 percent in 1970 and 60 percent in 1971.[2] By 1970 more than twenty provinces, municipalities, and autonomous regions had set up manual tractor plants, small machine industries and various types of plants for the manufacture of farming implements and spare parts. About 90 percent of the counties throughout the country (96 percent by 1971) were said to have their own "factories" for the repair of farming implements and machines; small iron and steel plants, small coal mines and pits, small cement plants (which by 1971 turned out more than 40 percent of national cement production), small hydroelectric power stations, and small chemical works also mushroomed across the country. There were vast labor-intensive projects to construct waterworks, drainage, and irrigation (as in the Huai-Hai Valley); or to extend the infrastructure of communication and transportation (as in the construction of roads and bridges). The large oil fields began operating at Dagang off the Hebei coast, and at Shengli off the Gulf of Bohai. Self-sufficiency was emphasized, with Dazhai and Daqing serving as models of development without state support.[3]

A major radical initiative was also launched in the agricultural sector under the apparent auspices of Lin Biao and Chen Boda. Partly to counter spontaneous capitalist tendencies that had cropped up in the countryside during the lapse of central control, partly for ideological reasons, there was a tendency to encourage the shift of the unit of accounting from the production team to the brigade or commune, to discourage material incentives in favor of some accounting of political attitudes, and to put pressure on private plots.[4] Thus the size of communes seems to have increased significantly in the late 1960s (the total number of communes being reduced from some seventy-five thousand to fifty-four thousand). In Shanghai municipality, the stronghold of the cultural radicals (who probably collaborated with Lin on this issue), 34.2 percent of the total collective assets on the communes were held at the commune level and only 15.1 percent at the brigade level.[5]

2. *CN*, no. 325 (August 21, 1969).

3. Marianne Bastid and Jean-Luc Domenach, "De la Revolution culturelle à la critique de Confucius: L'evolution de la politique interieure chinoise, 1969–1974," in Claude Aubert et al., eds., *Regards froids sur la Chine* (Paris: Seuil, 1976), pp. 126–72.

4. *CNA*, no. 712 (June 14, 1968); *Union Research Service* (hereinafter *URS*) 57, no. 14 (November 18, 1969): 174; 58, no. 23 (March 20, 1970): 323; 59, no. 5 (April 17, 1970): 58. See also Jürgen Domes, *China after the Cultural Revolution: Politics between Two Party Congresses*, trans. Annette Berg and David Goodman (Berkeley: University of California Press, 1975), pp. 611–77; and David Zweig, "Agrarian Radicalism in China, 1968–1978: The Search for a Social Base (Ph.D. diss., University of Michigan, 1983).

5. Bill Brugger, "Rural Policy," in Brugger, ed., *China since the "Gang of Four"* (London: Croom Helm, 1980), pp. 135–73.

The radical program for ideologically motivated labor-intensive investment encountered difficulties when Lin Biao's star went into eclipse in mid-1970. The peasants manifested passive resistance to such policies as centralized administration within the commune or the reduction of private plots.[6] In industry, radical investment priorities came under reconsideration in mid-1970, as China began preparations for its Fourth FYP (to be launched in 1971). Under cover of the 1970–71 critique of "ultraleftism," Zhou and his supporters reemphasized central economic priorities, including the need to adhere to central planning, observe cost-accounting procedures, and introduce comprehensive rationality ("one chessboard") to what otherwise threatened to become a "cellularized" patchwork of self-sufficient economic units. The proliferation of investment in small-scale plants utilizing indigenous technology lacked overall coordination, ignored economies of scale and comparative advantage, and tended to divert investment funds from the capital-intensive modern sector in the cities, where little new capital construction had occurred since 1966. The new emphasis on the large-scale urban industrial sector thus coincided with a wave of imports, including "turnkey" plants for the production of chemical fertilizers, synthetic textiles, and petrochemicals.[7] This shift of emphasis presupposed a more rapid rehabilitation of cadres, who in effect monopolized the requisite technical and managerial competence.[8] Needless to say, the rehabilitation of cadres also enhanced the political position of Zhou Enlai.

Despite this setback, radical industrialization strategy survived the fall of Lin Biao, under the putative patronage of Mao and the Gang of Four. Any reemphasis of the modern urban industrial sector necessitated the introduction of new equipment and technology, which implied an opening to the West (in view of the Sino-Soviet vendetta), making China hostage to international market vicissitudes, possible bourgeois cultural spillover, and loss of "self-reliance"—industrial imports would continue, but sporadically, amid controversy. Thus a rift opened between

6. Leo Goodstadt, "Purifying Profit," FEER 73, no. 38 (September 18, 1971): 7–8; Henry S. Bradsher, "China: The Radical Offensive," AS 13, no. 11 (November 1973): 989–1001.
7. Colina MacDougall, "Walking the Rustic Tightrope," FEER, vol. 67, no. 10 (March 5, 1970): 46–49; and MacDougall, "Another Backyard Boom," FEER, vol. 67, no. 12 (March 19, 1970): 27–28; Goodstadt, "China," pp. 20–25; Kojima Reiitsu, "Accumulation, Technology, and China's Economic Development," in Mark Selden and Victor Lippit, eds., The Transition to Socialism in China (Armonk, N. Y.: M. E. Sharpe, 1982), pp. 238–66.
8. Liberated cadres comprised 84 percent of all factory cadres in Bengbu, Anhui; 27 of 36 in three production brigades in a Shandong commune; over 90 percent at the Hua'nan Colliery; 21 of the 28 cadres at the Changsha Meat Processing Factory; 95 percent of the scientific and technical cadres at the Changjiang Metallurgical Works; and 100 percent of the cadres in the Hangzhou Electrochemical Works. CN, no. 315 (June 12, 1969); see also CN, no. 311 (May 8, 1969).

the "two legs" of Chinese industry, with the small-scale indigenous sector continuing to grow rapidly, large-scale heavy industry languishing, or lurching ahead between strikes and critical assaults. Steel had an average annual growth rate of only 2.8 percent between 1970 and 1976, coal 6.2 percent; by contrast, chemical fertilizer grew 12.2 percent, electric power 10.3 percent, crude oil production (led by the radical Daqing brigade) 19.7 percent.[9] Although the resulting sectoral imbalance would lead to the import surge of 1977–78, the small-scale rural industrial sector survived the fall of the radicals intact, thanks to local political backing and an inadequate transportation infrastructure.

After the fall of Lin Biao, the campaigns of the Cultural Revolution decade became engrossed in cultural issues, generally avoiding new initiatives in the eonomic sector. An important exception was the campaign against "bourgeois rights" in the spring of 1975. Launched less than three weeks after the Fourth NPC, which it was obviously designed to upstage, it resulted in the publication of Mao's first "latest instruction" and in the first signed theoretical articles by high-ranking cadres (namely, Zhang Chunqiao and Yao Wenyuan) since the late 1960s. The argument was that the central question that had precipitated the Cultural Revolution in the first place—was China moving toward socialism or back toward capitalism?—had yet to be resolved. The basic reason for backsliding tendencies, it was now stated more clearly than ever before, was not residual formations from prerevolutionary society but *emergent* revisionist tendencies, or "new bourgeois elements." Class was no longer defined solely in terms of ownership relations; Mao followed Lenin in contending that the relations of production included two other factors— mutual relations among people and the pattern of distribution—any combination of which might affect class status. Inasmuch as "bourgeois rights" (*faquan*) continued to exist in socialist society, proletarian dictatorship was still necessary in order to restrict them. And what were bourgeois rights? On February 22, *People's Daily* published three pages of quotations from Marx, Engels, and Lenin, introduced by a joint editorial note from *People's Daily* and *Red Flag*, to clarify this issue. The note pointed out, again quoting Mao, that "in our country today there is a commodity system [*shangpin zhidu*], the wage system is unequal, there is an eight-grade wage system, and so on." Zhang Chunqiao's April 1 article went on to identify the peasants and other collectively organized workers as "small producers" (in connection with which Mao had said, quoting Lenin, that small production engenders capitalism continuously).

As the first radical attempt since the 1960s to set forth positive alternative economic proposals, the campaign generated considerable interest,

9. See Leslie Evans, *China after Mao* (New York: Monad Press, 1978), table 4, p. 61.

for both its general thrust and certain provisions were dissonant with the program of the Fourth NPC, which it nominally affirmed. The new State Constitution guaranteed the three-grade ownership system, "individual labor of nonagricultural individual laborers within limits permitted by law and under the unified direction of the street organizations in the towns and cities, and of production teams in the villages." Article Nine stated that "the state protects the citizens' right to ownership of their income from work, their savings, their houses, and their means of livelihood." The draft plans (though not the Constitution) reportedly also included provision for a general wage increase.[10] Thus the Constitution and other NPC documents explicitly provided for "bourgeois rights," whereas the statements of Mao and his ideological comrades-in-arms indicated that they were seeds of capitalism. The critique of bourgeois rights regarded any wage increase to be potentially indicative of "special privilege," and not only successfully advocated a rescission of the contemplated wage increases but gave rise to short-lived attempts (in February) to abrogate all bonuses (which had been sanctioned for workers on the bottom two rungs of the wage ladder in late 1971) and introduce "Saturday voluntary labor." A move was afoot to consider a basic reform of the eight-grade wage system hitherto standard in all state enterprises.[11] Some of the campaign polemics suggested Maoist reservations about agricultural incentive systems as well, and scattered prohibition of peasants' sideline production or confiscation of private plots was reported.[12]

Considerable controversy arose, amid voluntary initiatives to actualize radical economic injunctions prematurely and popular resistance to these initiatives. No explicit change in official policies encouraging radical activism was announced by either central or provincial authorities, leaving activists in limbo about what reforms were implied by the radical critique.[13] The effect was to give everyone a sense of bad faith about current economic practices without requiring anyone to rectify them.

10. A CD inviting proposals for a revision of wages and work grades was reportedly circulated among Party and government cadres at the end of February 1975.

11. Reform of the wage system would have entailed raising the first grade and lowering the eighth, but doing so reportedly foundered on the opposition of Deng Xiaoping, who opposed lowering the top grade until a higher economic level could be attained. The attempt to encourage voluntary overtime also drew little support. Only Henan province is known to have launched a movement in March for factory workers to carry out voluntary labor for limited periods on workdays; the movement seems to have been short-lived. References from Shanghai and Beijing factories and Liaoning coal mines, among others, betokened an effort to revive it in November 1975.

12. CNS, no. 599 (January 21, 1976). See also Zweig, "Agrarian Radicalism," which shows how leftist intervention in the villages varied with time and location and in impact.

13. As an RR editorial noted, "As to systems which involve economic policies, [we must] seriously carry out investigation and study, and take a cautious attitude." "Grasp Theoretical Study, Promote Industrial Production," RR, March 11, 1975.

Shanxi Radio thus reported that a production brigade in Baoji County was a progressive unit, but that

> in the course of study some comrades had a muddled understanding of the question of the relationship between the transformation of small production and reliance on the poor and lower-middle peasants. They separated transformation of small production from reliance on poor and lower-middle peasants and set the former against the latter. They held that the poor and lower-middle peasants had been relied on in the previous political movements but that this time was different and it was necessary to transform small production.[14]

Inasmuch as the campaign was apparently intended only to prepare the way for communist ideals without yet adjuring the masses to adopt them, it gave rise to considerable confusion. Guangdong Radio reported two types of "wavering": one type is "only seeing the inevitability of the existence of bourgeois rights in the current stage without seeing that they must be restricted, even expanding them." The other is "only seeing that the mentality of bourgeois rights must be destroyed without seeing that it is essential resolutely to implement the Party's policies in the current stage, and arbitrarily changing the Party's rural policies."[15] The ultimate impact of this theoretically ambitious campaign was merely to forestall moderate wage increases, thereby further detaching the radicals from any realistic relationship to current economic difficulties.

What was the impact of mobilization as an independent variable, or "cause"? Largely due to radical influence, not only was mobilization no longer employed to stimulate production, but the latter came to be regarded with a distinctly jaundiced eye; the ultimate result was a negative trade-off between production and mobilization. The radicals affirmed the proposition that revolution necessarily contributed to production, but having asserted it in the abstract they demonstrated little evident concern with establishing its truth in practice; in fact, they displayed a consistent suspicion of those who paid too much attention to production, regarding such people as potential dupes of "economism."

The chief reason for this fateful disengagement of mobilization from production has to do with the structural fragmentation to be discussed in the following chapter, in the course of which the mobilizational apparatus fell under the sway of the radical faction and the apparatus of economic planning and management came under exclusive moderate control. Once factional responsibility for these two different functional sectors had been established, the objectives and inherent logic of the contest between them

---

14. Shanxi Radio, August 18, 1975; see also Radio Sichuan, September 3, 1975, first published in *RR* on August 28.
15. Guangdong Radio, September 4, 1975.

became clear. To the extent that the economy prospered, the moderate claim to functional indispensability would be enhanced, for they alone could claim competence to manage the economy. But it did not necessarily follow that any decline in economic production redounded to the advantage of the radicals. There are actually two variables, the economic conjuncture and the degree of radical interference in economic production, whose interaction is graphically depicted in figure 3.

FIGURE 3. Economic Correlates of Mobilization

Economic conjuncture

		Expansion	*Recession*
Radical economic activism	*High*	I MODERATE GAINS, RADICAL TOLERATION	2 RADICAL LOSSES
	Low	3 MODERATE GAINS	4 RADICAL GAINS, MODERATE LOSSES

The moderates stand to gain most during periods of expansion, as in contingency 3, although radical activism (contingency 1) might then also be more easily tolerated. Contingency 2, high radical activism during economic recession, is apt to trigger a classic scapegoating reaction. Only if radicals remain quiescent during a period of recession are they then favorably positioned to mount an effective attack on the moderates without risk of becoming scapegoats.

The Lin Biao period, from 1968 to 1971, fits most easily into contingency 1. This was a period of simultaneous economic expansion and radical activism, in the course of which the moderates gradually recovered control over the economy. The period of the antiradical Criticism of Lin Biao campaign, in 1972–73, on the other hand, fits contingency 4. Zhou Enlai and his State Council now had uncontested sway over the economy, while the radicals remained relatively quiescent. But growth during 1972 failed to match targets over a wide area and was well below the gain recorded the previous year.[16] Part of the reason for the slowdown was adverse weather conditions, which damaged commune

---

16. Growth in the combined gross value of industrial and agricultural production probably did not exceed 5 percent, though precise figures are unavailable. This gain is only half the figure officially claimed for the previous year and probably smaller than at any time since 1967. The year 1972 saw an actual fall in the output of food grains and a number of other agricultural products. *QER*, no. 2 (March 13, 1973).

enterprises and forced a shift of resources from industry to agriculture; the more fiscally prudent attitude toward small-scale industry may have also had a short-term contractive effect, as many smaller and less productive units were shut down in an effort to improve efficiency.

Thus by the end of 1972 the economy may have become something of a millstone around the necks of the moderates, perhaps contributing to Mao's decision to unleash the radicals in the spring of 1973. Fortunately, the economy simultaneously made an impressive recovery (the estimated gross value of industrial output rose from 9 percent in 1972 to 11 percent in 1973). This recovery implied a shift from moderate scapegoating (contingency 4, from January to September 1973) back to moderate gains and radical toleration (contingency 1, from October to December 1973). Economic expansion could tolerate radical mobilization only up to a certain point, however, before it began to be adversely affected. In the first four months of 1974 the radicals made the economy a major issue, criticizing management for neglecting ideology in pursuit of economic objectives (particularly the distribution of material rewards of various types). This shift was apparently authorized by the Chairman himself. On May 5, Mao said: "I see nothing wrong with posting big-character posters in the streets even if the foreigners want to read them, and certainly not if the Chinese want to read them. If the masses get angry, let them give vent to their anger, and if things get too bad we can clean them up later."[17]

In mid-May, the CC accordingly issued Central Document (CD) no. 18, which permitted posters to be displayed publicly and stripped cadres of their immunity from being criticized by name. There is not much evidence that this directive had much impact in the villages; in the cities, however, a flood of grievances resulted, protesting against arbitrary arrests, police brutality, and widespread torture of prisoners, along with corruption among officials, an inadequate health service, poor safety conditions in factories, and inadequate compensation for victims of work-related accidents. Local and provincial officials came under attack, particularly still-incumbent military politicians.[18] Many workers and peasants began traveling to Beijing to post their posters on the wall opposite the

17. Quoted in Wang En, "Yijiuqisi nian zhonggong zhengju yanbian tedian" [Characteristics of Chinese Communist political developments in 1974], ZW, no. 311 (January 16, 1975): 9–11.
18. Regional targets included MR commanders Li Desheng in Shenyang, Zeng Siyu in Ji'nan, Han Xianchu in Lanzhou, and Ding Sheng in Nanjing. Among those at the provincial level and above who were attacked by name were thirty-five military cadres, seven MR commanders, six MD commanders, and nine first secretaries of provincial Party committees and concurrent RC chairmen. Hua Guofeng was sharply criticized (twenty posters appeared in Beijing on June 16) for his record in Hunan by writers who were so well-informed that they must have come from that province.

door of the municipal Party committee on Wangfujing Street, in hopes of bringing national attention to their plight. Violence was reported in Guangzhou and elsewhere between rival groups of armed youth and the urban militia. The poster campaign in Beijing reached its acme on June 28 with more than fifty new posters, most of them aimed at local cadres' abuse of power and suppression of the mass movement.[19]

In apparent response to radical mobilizational disruption, industrial production declined precipitously.[20] By the summer of 1974 the agricultural outlook was also bleak.[21] No connection between these two developments was publicly admitted, for a balance was still being maintained between the two factions at the central level; nevertheless, it seems clear from the shift in campaign tactics in the summer of 1974 that such a connection was recognized. Jiang Qing is said to have objected to the notion that "the people regard food as the first requisite, so when revolution and production are in conflict the grasp of revolution should be somewhat slackened, and in calamities where agricultural production cannot catch up revolutionary movement should be postponed"[22]—but she apparently complied nonetheless.

By early 1975, as radical mobilizational activity subsided, the economic situation simultaneously deteriorated, once again favorably positioning the radicals for a mobilizational offensive (contingency 4). By 1975 it was no longer plausible to blame a recession on destruction wrought during the Criticism of Lin Biao and Confucius, and the rad-

19. Senior members of the Beijing municipal RC (Jia Ding, Yang Shaoshan, Chen Shuhuai) came under fire for stifling mass enthusiasm and turning the RC into a "dead body"—all but one of the twenty-four mass representatives appointed to that body in 1967 had been edged out as "extremists," it was pointed out, and no full committee meeting had been held in four years. Wang En, "Dazibao shengji shuoming le shemma?" [What does the promotion of big-character posters indicate?], ZW, no. 299 (July 16, 1974): 9–11.

20. The campaign adversely affected production in at least two ways. The rallies, meetings, forums, and study courses must have exacted millions of work hours, even had all participants limited their involvement to formally sanctioned activities. But factional conflict also diverted workers from their jobs and led them either to participate or to stay home in order to avoid getting involved. See for example the report in RR, October 11, 1974, as cited in CNS, no. 546 (December 4, 1974).

21. According to newspaper reports, China's 1973 winter wheat crop was damaged by rains, and production dropped appreciably. At the same time, the large Soviet grain purchase precipitated the sharpest rise in food prices in twenty-two years, amounting to an increase of more than 20 percent by the end of the year (and nearly doubling world prices for wheat and soybeans). The following year saw a further drop in grain production. All of which meant that China had to incur greater costs to compensate for her own shortfall. See Dittmer, "The World Food Problem: A Political Analysis," in Gerald and Lou Ann Garvey, eds., International Resource Flows (Lexington, Mass.: D. C. Heath, 1977), pp. 21–36.

22. "Jiang Qing's Letter to the Delegates Attending the CCP CC All-China Conference on Professional Work in Agriculture" (July 1975), trans. in IS 11, no. 10 (October 1975): 86–87.

icals successfully characterized it as the fiscal hangover of a massive (moderate) buying spree. China's economic position in the early 1970s had made a cogent case for an increase in foreign trade, from the perspective of the moderates, while the opening to the United States (and attendant lifting of the blockade) now made it for the first time politically feasible. Total trade had been no higher in 1970 than in 1959, while GNP had almost doubled. The abandoned Soviet projects were now coming on stream, so China had the capacity to absorb new industrial projects. Certain industries had either developed bottlenecks, or had the potential for rapid growth if an injection of advanced technology were available.[23] Thus the moderates sharply increased total trade in the early 1970s, particularly imports. Between 1970 and 1975 the growth in trade was 27.26 percent in money terms, about 9 percent in real terms. By late 1974, China had absorbed $2 billion (U.S.) in foreign machinery and technology (including more than thirty complete plants) in less than two years, and more than three thousand foreign technicians and advisers were present in China.

But in the fall of 1973 oil price increases triggered a worldwide "stagflation" that increased the prices of China's imports while reducing demand for her exports. Beijing ran a deficit of some $566 million in 1973, increasing to $1.27 billion the following year, despite a decline in the purchase of large-scale capital goods.[24] This was China's largest trade deficit since 1949; in every year from 1954 to 1974 China had held a favorable trade balance with the rest of the world. According to some estimates, China's foreign exchange reserves were reduced from around $400 million in 1972 to virtually nothing in 1975.[25] Moreover, despite the relative stability achieved in 1972–73, the growth rates realized in the immediate wake of the Cultural Revolution could not be sustained, and the rate of increase in productivity had slowed markedly by 1975. But economically appropriate measures to raise productivity (e.g., capital investment in modern urban plants) threatened to widen the gap between worker and peasant salaries, between city and countryside.[26] By early 1975 these developments had culminated in a combination of elite disenchantment and recrimination over moderate economic policies and mass discontent over wage freezes.

In their campaign to study the dictatorship of the proletariat and criticize "bourgeois rights," the radicals were able to exploit these dis-

23. QER, quarterly report no. 1 (March 6, 1975); and no. 3 (August 19, 1975).
24. Christopher Howe, China's Economy: A Basic Guide (New York: Basic Books, 1978), pp. 135–38.
25. John F. Copper, "The Rise and Fall of Teng Hsiao-p'ing," Asian Affairs 4, no. 3 (January/February 1977): 184–96.
26. Bonavia, FEER 95, no. 4 (January 28, 1977): 8–9.

contents to a limited extent. Partly due to radical criticisms, Sino-American trade was curtailed in 1975 by 50 percent, and the trade deficit was reduced by 35 percent. The radicals were ideologically inhibited from dealing rationally with wage inequities, however, and liable to intimidate the moderates from doing so as well. Their pursuit of mobilization in the context of discontent over wages ironically allowed wage grievances to become conflated with radical polemics, causing mobilization in certain industrial areas to degenerate into strikes and factional violence. Thus the railroads suffered a decline in total activity during the first quarter of 1975, and in the second quarter industrial output also declined. Contingency 4 underwent a permutation to contingency 2, and the radicals (with obvious reluctance) temporarily curtailed their mobilizational efforts in the early summer of 1975.

Hitherto the central policy process had remained responsive to negative feedback even though the ideological split overlapped with a division of responsibilities between economic and mobilizational functional realms; now, as the senior leaders who had previously arbitrated the allocation of blame faded from the scene and the succession struggle intensified, this responsiveness was lost. Thus, in the final year, mobilizational activities against the "Three Poisonous Weeds" (i.e., Four Modernizations) were pursued relentlessly despite the fact that the radicals as well as the moderates had lost control of mobilizational activities. Thus economic disruption was exacerbated at a time when it could be least easily afforded in view of the Hebei earthquake and an overall economic slump. Again mobilization became a cover for strikes, slowdowns, factional violence, and similar tactics, as every attempt to increase production came under suspicion as a possible manifestation of the "theory of productive forces."[27] The Chinese estimated a shortfall of 40 percent for plan quotas in 1976 (roughly corroborated by Western sources), for an annual GNP growth rate ranging from a mere 3 to 3.5 percent (with agricultural growth remaining below 2 percent, industrial growth estimated between 4 and 5 percent).[28] Although China's trade balance continued to improve, in fact accumulating a record $1.2 billion surplus in 1976, the domestic budget deficit amounted to about $5 billion (also a record).

Radical mobilizational efforts had neither enhanced economic production nor had they contributed to capital accumulation, as might have been more consistent with the radical ideological position. In the absence of any clearly stipulated positive economic objectives and with a persistent tendency to focus criticism on those responsible for the economy,

27. *CA*, December 1976, pp. 671–88.
28. M. D. Fletcher, "Industrial Relations in China: The New Line," *Pacific Affairs* 52, no. 1 (Spring 1979): 78–95; *QER*, no. 1 (March 31, 1977).

mobilization ultimately tended to degenerate into vandalism. Although mobilization would continue through the summer of 1976, this did not betoken support for radical economic policies so much as an opportunistic venting of economic grievances.

CULTURAL TRANSFORMATION

Participation in mass mobilization was intended to contribute to what Mao called the "transformation of people."[29] Three dimensions of such a transformation may be analytically distinguished: cognitive, attitudinal, and behavioral. The cognitive dimension refers to beliefs about how the world is constituted; the attitudinal dimension to relatively enduring predispositions and to the norms and values on which these are premised; the behavioral dimension to everyday practices. Post hoc interviews revealed considerable change in each dimension, though not necessarily in the direction intended by the leadership.

Cognitive Change

The cognitive impact of three different stages of mobilization will be examined separately: the (early) Cultural Revolution, the Criticism of Lin Biao and Confucius, and the late-Cultural Revolution movements (namely, "bourgeois rights," *Water Margin*, Criticism of Deng).

The thematic impact of the Cultural Revolution, as noted in the conclusion to chapter 4, was to persuade participants that revisionism was implicit in the nation's developmental pattern as it had hitherto proceeded and that "struggle" was necessary if this course were to be altered. Revisionism was clearly understood to mean bureaucratic authoritarianism and increasing stratification between mental and manual workers and between town and countryside, and a focus on economic growth, raising living standards, and material welfare at the expense of revolutionary values. Our informants generally accepted the truth of these themes, as well as the personal equation of revisionism with Liu Shaoqi, Deng Xiaoping, and the other "capitalist-roaders" (though as cadre rehabilitation accelerated in the course of the late Cultural Revolution, blame became increasingly circumscribed to Liu). But radical attempts in the late Cultural Revolution period to augment and elaborate upon these themes appear to have been much less successful.

The Criticism of Lin Biao and Confucius campaign seems to have failed either to establish an equation between Lin Biao and Confucius or to convince people of the depravity of the latter. The attempt to establish an equation between Lin Biao and Confucius may have been obfuscated

29. Mao, "Concluding Remarks," pp. 90–100.

by the concurrent Aesopian attempt by the radicals to establish an equation between Confucius and Zhou Enlai, but in any case neither equation was widely accepted. Lin Biao was a more unequivocally negative reference point than the historically remote Confucius, even (if memory served these informants correctly) before news of his coup plot became public. Lin was "very stupid" (*da bendan, da caobao*), and there was "no comparison" (*mei fa bi de*) with the learned sage of yore.[30] In the case of Zhou Enlai, on the other hand, the analogy was vitiated by the positive regard in which the Premier was still held (except by admirers of Confucius).[31]

Attempts to denigrate the reputation of Confucius seem also to have failed, oddly enough in view of the fact that such criticism has been a facet of cultural modernity in China since the May Fourth movement.[32] Whereas all informants understood the values and principles that Confucius represented, these were not held in disesteem. For the young he was no more than an object of mild curiosity. For the older generation he continued to exact deference or at most qualified reproof.[33] Whether this reservoir of goodwill for the sage represents some underlying continuity of values or simply cultural nationalism could not be determined.

The Campaign to Study the Dictatorship of the Proletariat (or Criticism of Bourgeois Rights), the Criticism of *Water Margin*, and other campaigns during what was to prove the radicals' swan song were least successful of all in penetrating the masses' cognitions, to judge from our informants' responses. The basic thrust of these campaigns represented

30. Representative of the former is the former cadre who revealed that although he wrote a big-character poster during the Criticism of Lin Biao and Confucius, he criticized only Lin Biao but not Confucius, "because I greatly respect Confucius." Informant no. 17. Representative of the more qualified position is the former central cadre who said: "His teachings were bad, too authoritarian. Worst of all is the doctrine of the li [*lijiao*]. But his respect for learning is good." Informant no. 37.

31. "Lin Biao has always been bad," contended a former Red Guard. "He was a fascist. He used only a suppressive method to change people's thinking." Informant no. 25.

32. See Kam Louie, *Critiques of Confucius in Contemporary China* (Hong Kong: Chinese University of Hong Kong Press, 1980); Tien-wei Wu, *Lin Biao and the Gang of Four: Counter-Confucianism in Historical and Intellectual Perspective* (Carbondale: Southern Illinois University Press, 1983); and, of course, Joseph Levenson, *Confucian China and Its Modern Fate: A Trilogy* (Berkeley: University of California Press, 1968 ed.).

33. "I only know that Confucius was a great sage [*da shengren*] and a great educator who made a very great contribution to Chinese civilization," said a former kindergarten teacher. "This impression can never be changed." Informant no. 20. See also male informant, born 1944 in Guangdong, of lower-middle peasant family background, student individual class status, former CYL cadre, deputy secretary of the CYL general branch, and a member of the Standing Committee of the local RC during the Cultural Revolution. He worked in the headquarters of an enterprise engaged in construction of a hydroelectric power station. Emigrated to Hong Kong illegally because of "political problems" in 1972. Interviewed June 6, 1977 (hereinafter informant no. 13).

continuity with early Cultural Revolution themes, emphasizing egalitarianism and self-sacrifice (in the case of bourgeois rights) and fidelity to
revolutionary values (in the *Water Margin* and Anti-Rightist Reversal of
Just Verdicts campaigns), but the campaigns were more subtly argued,
perhaps presupposing greater popular familiarity with Marxist texts and
Chinese literature than proved warranted. In any case, a majority of these
informants had no correct conception of bourgeois rights, which they
diversely misconstrued as "the power of convention," "selfishness,"
"dictatorship," "class differentiation," and whatnot.[34] The confusion
that greeted the campaign to study *Water Margin* is perhaps understandable in view of the fact that Jiang Qing herself may have misconstrued
Mao's intentions, but in any case most of our informants were baffled by
Mao's sudden repudiation of the popular hero Song Jiang and did not
know who he was supposed to represent on the contemporary political
scene.[35]

Attitudinal Change

Two of the most distinctive aspects of the Cultural Revolution as a form
of mass attitudinal change (besides its emphasis on "struggle," that is,

34. "Bourgeois rights are non-democratic, dictatorship.... They don't allow others to
oppose them, don't allow them to go against the current. I think Mao himself was the
biggest example of bourgeois rights—anyone who opposed him was knocked down!"
Informant no. 15. "Bourgeois rights are formed by the habit of power [*xiguan quanli*]. The
structure of society produces man's need for power, wealth and status, extending even to the
realm of abstract thinking and concepts." Male informant, born 1956 in Guangdong, free
professional family background, student individual class status, sent down to a production
and construction military camp (*shengchan jianshe bingtuan*) in the Changjiang countryside.
Migrated illegally to Hong Kong in November 1976 to get out of the countryside. Interviewed May 6, 1977. (Hereinafter informant no. 16.)
   As far as the critique of selfishness underpinning the bourgeois rights campaign is
concerned, considerable skepticism or even recalcitrance was evident. Several opined that
this vice was "intrinsic" (*benxing*): "Even small children understand how to eat well, dress
well." Informant no. 37. "Only lazy people want equality," said a former Red Guard and
sent-down youth. Informant no. 8. Although some warned against stratification, most were
keenly interested in higher living standards. One interviewee manifested the contradictions
with considerable sensitivity: "Although the Communist Party demands equality among
the people, bourgeois rights are a product of objective reality. On the one hand, they are
residues left over from before the Liberation. On the other hand, they are also needed by
society nowadays. The objective reality of today's social organization is that, between the
leaders and the led, there are differences in wages, differences in cultural levels, and a rather
weak material foundation.... This, caused by objective reality and history, cannot be
eliminated at the present stage. This is the fairness of unfairness because both society and
masses need leaders." Informant no. 17.
35. "All along I had thought Song Jiang was a righteous person, a heroic figure. I was
confused when Song Jiang was criticized. I do not know whom Song Jiang was supposed to
represent. I think he symbolized some kind of thought [*mou yi zhong sixiang*].... People
were indifferent to it." Informant no. 38.

already alluded to earlier) were its glorification of manual labor as a transformative experience, and its idealization of closer relations between elites and masses. Change was achieved with respect to each of these aspects, but the degree and direction of change depended on the experience of participants, the most decisive criterion being whether the participant conceived himself/herself to have been a victim or beneficiary of the change at issue.

In terms of traditional Chinese conceptions of vertical mobility, manual labor represented an absence (or loss) of status, but from the Maoist (indeed, from the Marxist) perspective labor is the source of human value. Thus if elites (or their children) who had risen "above" manual labor were obliged once again to perform it, their haughty attitudes toward the working classes would be transformed. Although manual labor on a rather substantial part-time basis was introduced in all educational and administrative institutions, two categories of citizens were subjected to a more concentrated regimen: *déclassé* officials and radical youth.

The former were installed in "May 7 cadre schools," originally intended to facilitate greater contact with the working classes as well as to acquaint cadres with the concrete problems of production; however, cadres were soon insulated from the indigenous population, due to friction between cadres and peasants. Although "some cadres were very frightened," according to a former cadre, "afraid of hard work on the one hand and of the masses on the other," the situation was alleviated through subvention to such an extent that such schools were usually not economically self-sufficient. Recollections were not particularly bitter, sometimes even wistful:

> I stayed in a May 7 cadre school for half a year, planting fruit trees and growing vegetables. The work there was easy and the living conditions were good. All the people there had made mistakes and they therefore tended to look down on one another. With good appetites, ample sleep, and fresh air, a lot of people gained weight after they came to the cadre school. Living happily together, many did not even want to return to their own work units.[36]

One former inmate, who at times evokes Solzhenitsyn's Denisovich in her tributes to the solidarity induced by shared suffering, emerged with a new attitude toward manual labor that would have gratified Mao Zedong (cf. chapter 2):

> The distaste one has for mud—with its usual mixture of phlegm, mucus, urine and faeces—vanished once we had taken off our shoes and socks and started walking around in the warm and yielding ooze. It was slippery and wet, but it

36. Ibid.

did not seem at all "dirty." ... The thought suddenly struck me: Is this what they mean about "changing your attitude" toward physical labor?[37]

Whereas redemption through labor was quietly deemphasized in cadre rehabilitation after the fall of Lin Biao, it remained an important "career option" for China's urban youth throughout the Cultural Revolution decade; the most authoritative estimate places the number of participants in the "up to the mountains and down to the countryside" (*shangshan xiaxiang*) campaign at 12 million, or about 10 percent of China's urban population.[38] The transition was far more drastic for urban youth than for cadres, both because of the more sheltered previous experience of these youth and because of the harsher quality of the objective experience. Although production brigades received a certain subsidy to defray absorption costs, these youth were expected to become self-supporting settlers in this new subculture for the rest of their lives—this was to be no mere rite of passage in an urban career plan. A few no doubt succeeded in renouncing old aspirations and adapting to this new life style (unfortunately thereby eliminating themselves from this sample)—their success evoked an ambivalent combination of admiration and contempt from their confreres.[39] But others found a way, albeit with some cognitive strain, to adapt recidivistic ambitions to their new environment. Two representative tales, the first a "success," the second a failure, may be recounted by way of illustration:

The daughter of a well-to-do Beijing Party cadre and enterprise director (*changzhang*), having been active in the China Youth League (CYL), joined the Red Guards during the Cultural Revolution and volunteered to go down to the countryside upon their demobilization in response to Mao's call for educated youth to do so. Although her father attempted to dissuade her, she opted for a remote and austere rural commune in Heilongjiang. After her second year there, she decided however it was "just too tough" for her, so she returned home, crying to her mother that she could endure no more. Her mother urged her to remain in Beijing illegally and they would support her, but her father felt that as a cadre this would place him in an awkward position. After a year's medical leave, she returned to her commune, but her objectives had changed. She strove to

37. Yang Jiang, *A Cadre School Life: Six Chapters*, trans. Geremie Barme (Hong Kong: Joint Publishing Co., 1982), p. 33; also see p. 36.
38. Thomas P. Bernstein, *Up to the Mountains and Down to the Villages: The Transfer of Youth from Urban to Rural China* (New Haven, Conn.: Yale University Press, 1977), p. 2.
39. "We all admired her on the one hand, but privately said she was foolish on the other." Informant no. 15. On this general question, see Thomas P. Bernstein, "Communication and Value Change in the Chinese Program of Sending Urban Youths to the Countryside," in Godwin Chu and Francis L. K. Hsu, eds., *Moving a Mountain: Cultural Change in China* (Honolulu: University Press of Hawaii, 1979), pp. 341–63.

join the Party, which was easy because of her background, and the second time members of the production team were chosen to be sent to the university she was selected: she was intelligent, exhibited a good attitude (*biaoxian*), and had good cadre relations. She chose to study foreign languages, in order to minimize the chances of being sent back to the countryside, choosing Swedish because it was more distinctive (short supply, high demand) than English. She now cut herself off from political activities and did nothing but study. But when the first students were selected for a cultural exchange with Sweden, she was passed over because of her deficient political performance. So during her final two years in college, she became politically activist: she lived on campus, helped other students wash their clothes and clean the rooms in the morning (to develop better mass relations), and cultivated relations with the workers' propaganda team (which had responsibility for *gongzuo fenpei*—allocation of work assignments) by procuring expensive cigarettes for them through the "back door" and inviting them to her home to celebrate Spring Festival (Chinese New Year). When mass movements arose, she kept three objectives in view: (1) demonstrate activism, (2) avoid insulting cadres, and (3) avoid becoming a target. To realize these objectives, she kept her mouth shut during the opening stages of the campaign, expressing herself only when it became clear which direction the movement was taking and then writing a poster that merely synthesized officially acceptable views. She wrote well, and her posters were always lauded, though closer scrutiny would reveal that they contained nothing original. If the movement "became bad" (like the May 16th clique), she would quickly publish a self-criticism before others had begun to criticize her. As a result of her efforts, upon graduation she was assigned to work for the New China News Agency (NCNA), universally regarded by her peers as an excellent placement.[40]

Comrade Xie (pseudonym) was the only son in a family of free professionals, and his parents had implanted in him a desire for an intellectual career. He did well in both studies and in student activities in high school and nourished a hope to be admitted to Qinghua University upon graduation. He had just received notification of his acceptance into the CYL, a significant breakthrough, on the eve of the Cultural Revolution. During the Red Guard movement he faced a dilemma when both parents came under attack for revisionist tendencies. He resolved it by "drawing a clear line of demarcation" and inviting Red Guards to come to his house and rebel against his mother. Throughout the movement he endeavored,

40. Female informant, born 1956 in Hangzhou, of landlord family background, student class status, graduated high school before the beginning of the Cultural Revolution. Left Beijing legally (overseas Chinese family connections) in February 1976 (hereinafter informant no. 3).

in this compensatory manner, to be very "red," becoming a member of the radical Red Flag faction in Guangzhou. When his faction was suppressed at the end of 1968 and he was sent to the countryside, he was greatly dismayed and nonplussed. But he soon discovered opportunities to realize his old ambitions even within this austere new environment. He worked hard, cultivated cadre relations, becoming the production team's Mao Zedong's Thought adviser, rising to chief brigade adviser (*zong fudaoyuan*). He also worked very hard, wearing only a pair of shorts so as to become brown in the sun (symbolizing his transformation). He was thus one of the few sent-down youth to receive large quantities of money and food at the end of the year when profits were distributed. By way of cultivating mass relations he lived in a peasant household and developed good relations with the entire family, learning to speak fluent Hakka and sparking a romance with the family's eldest daughter. (At the same time, however, he maintained correspondence with his original intended, who had been sent down to a camp on Hainan Island.) These efforts finally bore fruit in 1973, when the Party branch selected him to go to college. But his plans were dashed by "one careless mistake":

> I wrote to my girl friend on Hainan Island that I would be going to college. I also revealed in my letter that my hard work in the past five years and everything concerning my transformation was only for the purpose of getting out of the village to go to college. I don't know how but the peasant's daughter got the letter and read it before it was mailed. . . . She said that I had cheated her and was a rascal [*liumang*]. I tried to get the letter back; the most damaging things I wrote in the letter had to do with my pretense at thought reform—all the love-talk was of minor importance. But . . . I was unable to get back my letter. What was more frightening, they took the letter to the Party branch! That was the end, everything about me was finished! Five years of hard work had all been wasted!

After vainly attempting to coordinate a joint escape with his girl friend on Hainan Island, Xie struck out on his own for Hong Kong. "I began as a true revolutionary but ended up as a phony," he concluded sardonically. "Such was the transformation of my thought."[41]

These experiences, representative of any number that might be cited, illustrate the tenacity of individualistic ambition and seriously discredit any claim to the transformative potency of manual labor. Perhaps one reason for its inefficacy was the available counterexample of those who were still able to move upward by adapting to the changing skill market, making fools of those who had humbled themselves through labor. Appa-

41. Male informant, free professional family background, student class status, migrated to Hong Kong illegally in August 1974. Born 1948 in Guangdong, refused to reveal more. Interviewed July 13, 1977 (hereinafter informant no. 7).

rently "ambitionists" who specialized in the manipulation of symbols were able to go far, as indicated by such popular sayings as "Liars can move up in the world" (*shuo jiahua de ren neng shangqu*), and "Those who sing a high-pitched melody can climb" (*diaozi gao de ren neng shangqu*).[42] These hapless youth remained resentfully aware that radical elites who verbally endorsed the value of manual labor were able to avoid it. Aside from that, manual labor was in fact very "tough" (*ku*), boring, perhaps inherently difficult to love.[43] For whatever reasons, *none* of these youthful informants transformed their dread of physical labor by participating in it, and most came to abhor it all the more, though some gleaned sympathy for the peasants trapped in such fates.[44] The contrast with the milder reaction of sent-down cadres deserves further consideration—perhaps their more thorough indoctrination inured them to hardship—perhaps also, their limited sojourn, and subsidized living standard, was less traumatizing.

With regard to relations between masses and elites, the mobilizational experience of the Cultural Revolution brought into view an ideal with which the masses had perhaps had little empirical experience but yearned for, nonetheless: "The purpose of the Cultural Revolution was to introduce democracy."[45] This did not necessarily conjure up images of an electoral apparatus, multiparty legislature, or civil rights, but participants did hope for greater political equality between elites and masses and more freedom of expression.[46] The early Cultural Revolution, as an explosive breakthrough from a high degree of constraint to unaccustomed freedom, seemed suddenly to actualize these repressed desires. "It was almost as if a frog jumped out of a well and saw the ocean—it almost drowned!"[47] The big-character poster provided the means to penetrate and expose previously unapproachable elites under cover of anonymity; for many, the appearance of the first poster in their unit remained a memorable occasion.[48] After the Red Guards had shown the way, "the masses were not as afraid of the leaders as they had been before,"[49] and in fact "the leaders became afraid of the masses."[50] Previously the attitude of the masses toward cadres (particularly Party cadres) had been "respect and avoidance" (*jing er yuan zhi*), "daring to get angry, not daring to voice it" (*gan nu bu gan yan*), fearing cadre retaliation. Though retaliation admittedly remained a risk, "masses became more daring in expressing

42. Informant no. 7. Also male informant, born 1947 in Guangdong, of free professional family background, student individual class status, sent down to state farm during the Cultural Revolution after graduation from high school. Emigrated illegally in July 1974 to Hong Kong. Interviewed April 26, 1977 (hereinafter informant no. 22).
43. Informant no. 3.   44. Informant no. 25.   45. Informant no. 36.
46. Informants no. 9, 38.   47. Informant no. 15.   48. Informant no. 8.
49. Informant no. 37.   50. Ibid.

their opinions to the cadres,"[51] and "Because of the Cultural Revolution, many leaders dared not retaliate against the masses."[52] Cadres in fact often became quite ingratiating. In the words of a former medical technician in Zhengzhou:

> Before the Cultural Revolution I didn't know who was the unit [Party] Secretary, didn't know who were the cadres. They didn't talk to us, didn't know our names, lived in separate residences [gao gan lou, or high cadre apartments]. ... After the Cultural Revolution, they moved and lived in the same apartment building with us. They were closer to the masses. Their children played with ours, they walked around in the yard, talked with us, and if we had some problem, we could talk with them. They didn't necessarily solve your problems, but you could talk with them.[53]

Activists, too, who had previously functioned as clandestine informants, felt vulnerable in this role after the critique of Liu Shaoqi's work teams (and especially of his wife's "Taoyuan Experience" during the "Four Cleans"), and became "more concerned with mass relations because they were afraid they might get struggled."[54]

Despite a consensus among these informants that mass mobilization had resulted in greater political equality and more reciprocal elite-mass communication, this outcome was not deemed an unmixed blessing. Three complaints appeared most frequently: first, this was democracy without law, and the work norms and regulations that had previously obtained fell into desuetude.[55] In this connection, cadre corruption, meaning specifically the informal allocation of favors (e.g., housing), became rife.[56] Second, cadres often tended to backslide into old patterns of arrogance and authoritarianism. "Many cadres really changed. But many changed back ... It was a question of time."[57] Third, democracy did not necessarily result in the elevation of merit. The new leaders might be more accessible but they were incompetent "good old boys" (lao hao ren), whose concern for mass feedback impaired their leadership.[58]

The tragic paradox was that greater political equality, in the context of an overwhelming emphasis on ideological conformity (yiyuanhua), ultimately resulted not in expanded freedom of expression but in its sharp

---

51. Ibid.   52. Informants no. 23, 36.   53. Informant no. 37.
54. Informant no. 31. Also: "During meetings, they expressed their opinions [fayan] more, wrote more big-character posters; during mass criticism, they made more criticisms.... Before, they were appointed by the leadership. Afterward, they were elected by the masses, had to receive a simple majority." Informant no. 37.
55. After being rehabilitated, "veteran cadres tended not to make decisions with the speed and assurance they had in the past, because they were afraid and tried to protect themselves from criticism." Informant no. 35.
56. Informant no. 22.   57. Informants no. 22, 31, 36.
58. Informant no. 35.

curtailment: "The Cultural Revolution had been expected to bring greater freedom but its actual consequences were just the contrary."[59] Politics was "in command," but people tried to avoid discussing politics unless they were with close friends, relatives, or members of the same faction. The reason was that what could be said publicly was so limited that one might only repeat the same clichés. When informants were asked to reconcile reports of constrictive conformity with other reports (often from the same informant) of improved elite-mass contact and greater responsiveness to grievances, it was explained that the masses in effect practiced ideological self-censorship before voicing their suggestions to cadres.[60]

> After the Cultural Revolution, I obviously talked about politics more than before. I talked with all kinds of different peole. I talked in different political terms to people with different political viewpoints. I would not discuss my true feelings. What I talked about was all lies.[61]

The rhetorical emphasis on rebellion and struggle in the context of pervasive ideological conformity led to some ironic consequences, such as "Holding high the red flag to oppose the red flag," or "The fleeing thief shouting 'Catch the thief!'" In fact very few of these informants thought that "going against the current" was praiseworthy, and even they knew it was not prudent. There was no legal distinction between "against the current" (*fan chaoliu*) and "counterrevolutionary" (*fandong*), some pointed out.[62] None of the official models of such behavior were held in much esteem (particularly not Zhang Tiesheng). More valid exemplars were sometimes cited, such as Li Yizhe in Guangzhou or Li Chunsheng in Beijing, who were generally viewed as valiant but quixotic figures.[63]

Behavioral Change

The attempt to transform everyday practice to conform to ideological precept had its most telling impact on routine meeting behavior and on workaday participation in the economy. In both realms, the impact was to promote more exacting conformity to prescribed routines, combined with progressive detachment of affect and covert resort to evasive maneuvers.

Chinese peasants have long complained that whereas the Nationalists imposed too many taxes (*shui*), the Communists held too many meetings (*hui*), but during the Cultural Revolution decade meetings were convened with redoubled intensity. "Study" (*xuexi*) meetings were held

59. Informants no. 21, 37.   60. Informants no. 16, 31.   61. Informant no. 22.
62. Informants no. 16, 32, 34.   63. Informants no. 4, 22.

twice as frequently as before, usually meeting at least two afternoons a week. Previously the texts studied were more intellectually challenging, at least for cadres and intellectuals, consisting for example of studies of the history of the Soviet Communist Party or Marxist political economy, but now they usually consisted of selections from Mao's *Selected Works* or the latest editorials from the "two papers and one journal" (*liang bao yi kan*—*People's Daily, Red Flag, Liberation Army Daily*). After 1971, they consisted of more central documents (*zhongyang wenjian*). Sometimes the reports were of great interest, such as the report following the first Sino-Soviet border clash, or Lin Biao's unsuccessful escape attempt, but usually the texts failed to hold the interest of the participants, who did not bother to hide their indifference (particularly if they were of good class background).

> During the meeting, a lot of people would do other things—write letters, read novels, knit, chat—sometimes the talking was so loud you couldn't hear the report, and the leader would say, "Don't talk so loud!" People would fall asleep, and he would say, "Wake up, you!" Some people didn't even attend. Sometimes they took roll to control for this, but that was only temporarily effective.[64]

During a movement, the normal meeting schedule was greatly intensified (*jinzhang*). For the Criticism of Deng Xiaoping in 1976, workers in a technical agricultural machinery plant on Hainan met seven nights a week, in meetings lasting until 11 P.M.[65] During the campaign to criticize Lin Biao and Confucius, political study was held six days a week, with all of Tuesday, Thursday, and Saturday devoted to study. Thus workers lost their weekends, while management sacrificed half the work week to political activities. A new campaign would be signaled by the release of a packet of central documents and by publication of an editorial in the "two papers and one journal"; the provincial Party committees would then issue provincial documents to be dispatched to every locality, triggering a proliferation of local documents. Then rectification would commence. Big-character posters would appear—spontaneously during the early Cultural Revolution, usually composed by a writing committee (in careful adherence to central documents and editorials) thereafter. A campaign had its own dynamic, and the early phase was most dangerous, particularly for participants with bad class backgrounds or "historical problems," because of the need to identify criticism targets. If a self-

---

64. Informant no. 37. See also Claudie Broyelle et al., *China: A Second Look*, trans. Sarah Matthews (Atlantic Highlands, N.J.: Humanities Press, 1980), p. 111, which is an account based on several years' residence in China during the Cultural Revolution decade.

65. The intensity of the meeting schedule varied somewhat depending on the enthusiasm of the local cadres in charge, so the Hainan plant's schedule may have been exceptional.

criticism was submitted at this stage of the movement it stood less chance of being accepted than if submitted at the end. The terminal stages of a movement were marked by an emphasis on "unity," which might "put a mask on things for awhile." [66]

Generally speaking, the campaigns of the Cultural Revolution decade fostered acute critical sensitivity to the failings of cadres and intellectuals and enhanced the power of the workers. Management was in effect deprived of the use of mobilization as a negative sanction as well as of any control over positive sanctions (due to the wage freeze and the "iron rice bowl"). The result was a precipitous decline in the morale of both management and labor and a corresponding increase in strikes (*bagong*), slowdowns (*daigong*), absenteeism (*kuanggong*), and general "softness, laziness, disunity" (*ruan, lan, san*).[67] The most disruptive of these forms of labor indiscipline was the strike—which was also most severely sanctioned, hence least frequently encountered. Strikes did, however, affect industrial production in the second quarters of 1974, 1975, and 1976, creating particularly damaging bottlenecks in the transportation and heavy industrial sectors.

Perhaps most notorious was the series of strikes that hit the central industrial city of Hangzhou, beginning in 1972 and reaching a violent climax in late 1974 and 1975, when factional conflict resulted in fatalities, industry ground to a halt, and there were serious shortages. Official postmortems explain the Hangzhou strikes in terms of a conspiracy theory, assigning blame to one Weng Senhe, vice-chairman of the Zhejiang Trade Union Federation, former Revolutionary Rebel (also however sometimes described as a "plump, gray-haired cadre"), and radical "agent" for Wang Hongwen.[68] But available eyewitness testimony suggests a rather different interpretation. If some of the strike leaders were former rebels, it should not be forgotten that there were "loyalist" as well as "radical" rebel factions; it seems unlikely that any "radical" rebels could have survived the military purges of the early 1970s with their leadership positions intact. The initiators of the strike were workers whose worldview may have more closely approximated that of Deng Xiaoping than that of the Gang of Four—they wanted bonuses and higher wages, which were taboo from the Maoist perspective.

The 1974 incident began in the spring, when workers at the Hangzhou Automobile Electric Machine Plant (HAEMP) requested resumption of the payment of "subsidiary wages" (*fuzhu gongzi*—equivalent to a bonus). But the factory Party committee rejected the request, even when it received the support of the municipal industrial bureau. When workers

66. Informant no. 34.
67. Squires collection.
68. *Ming Bao*, January 3, 1977, p. 1; *Hong Kong Standard*, April 12, 1977, p. 16; etc.

at the Hangzhou Silk Factory (HSF) and the Hangzhou Construction Materials Factory (HCMF) heard of the HAEMP request they made similar demands, as did workers in the city and provincial coal mines. At this point one Zhu Wufu, one of the local faction leaders during the Cultural Revolution and now a member of the HCMF's Revolutionary Committee (RC), became engaged on behalf of the petitioning workers, and also recruited other members of his network. The strike began in the HCMF and spread to the HAEMP and the HSF and beyond, until at least half the city's industries had shut down. After Liu Di, minister of light industry, failed to resolve the dispute, Wang Hongwen himself came to Hangzhou. Contrary to what one might have expected had Wang conspired to foment the strike, Wang adopted a very hard line, putting strikers in jail.[69] The workers split between those who supported the strike and those who opposed it, reflecting Cultural Revolution cleavages, and Wang's "simple and ruthless methods" only polarized the situation and caused the strike to spread further, and include some nonindustrial production, administrative, and educational units.

As a result of Wang's failure, Deng Xiaoping was sent to resolve the problem. He took a more moderate stance toward worker wage demands—no doubt partly because he could sincerely sympathize with them:

> Once Deng Xiaoping arrived in Hangzhou, he stationed the PLA in the factories to protect the buildings and machines. He also assigned soldiers to take over the work posts directly, relying on the minority of the workers who had not joined the strikes to learn the techniques for running the machines and continue production. Deng Xiaoping also read some of Zhou Enlai's directives to the effect that the central government would investigate and discuss the workers' practical demands, and those with real difficulties would be resolved as soon as possible. He also pointed out that wage problems were the same all over the country and that it was impossible to solve the wage problems of Hangzhou's workers first—the whole country's wage problems had to be resolved, but they had to be resolved step by step.[70]

Deng's more tolerant attitude toward practical demands allowed him to adopt a discriminating and pragmatic negotiating posture beyond the range of the radical Wang. In accord with the principle "leniency to those who are honest, harsh treatment to those who refuse" (*tanbai congkuan, kangju congyan*), he succeeded in luring most of the workers back to work while subjecting the "ringleaders" (such as Zhu) to labor reform.[71]

69. Informant came to Hong Kong from Hangzhou in August 1976, and declined to divulge much information about himself, though he insisted he was actively involved as a member of the Hangzhou work force. Interviewed May 24, 1977 (hereinafter informant no. 40).
70. Ibid.   71. Ibid.

Far more common than strikes were various forms of slowdown (*toulan*), which impaired production without anyone's publicly taking responsibility for doing so. "There have been continual slowdown strikes since 1968," reported a former member of a local RC Standing Committee.[72] Just how much organization was behind such movements is problematic, because it remained invisible. Least organized was *tuigong* (absenteeism)—people would stay home because they were dissatisfied with their pay, or bored, or because they saw other people doing so (and getting away with it). Somewhat more openly organized was the *daigong* (slowdown), which consisted of stopping production in a plant while allowing workers to work on their private projects, drink tea, or sleep.[73]

The slowdown or strike was sometimes related to factionalism, insofar as if one faction was in power the other would refuse to work.[74] But factionalism if anything was even more pervasive than labor indiscipline, ranking among the most significant stigmata of the Cultural Revolution era on everyday life. In 1966–68 factionalism took the form of openly constituted fighting bands (*zhandui*), into which much of society was mobilized into active or passive support. In 1969–71, punishment was meted out to identifiable *zhandui*, and in the 1971–76 period factions usually operated more clandestinely. Their core membership nevertheless harkened to the cleavages formed during the period of spontaneous mobilization, and members retained their ideological identity during subsequent movements. Estimates of the rate of factional participation varied considerably, but the consensus seems to be that there was a gradual decline and only a minority remained actively engaged. Each faction was likely to have representation on the unit RC, later perhaps even on the Party committee, and the unit activists (*jiji fenzi*) were also likely to be split into factions; therefore, "to really be a good person was impossible."[75] In some units conservatives held a majority, in others radicals; conservatives had the upper hand in most units following reconstruction of the Party, but particularly in those units in which intellectuals were strongly represented (schools—even PLA schools—hospitals, some government organs, many Beijing and Shanghai factories), radicals retained a preponderant influence.

The strongest motive for individual factional involvement seems to have been to acquire "greater power within the unit."[76] If a person was "not too good" factionally speaking, others would not work for him. One could talk heart-to-heart only with other faction members. In some villages factional cleavages coincided with traditional rivalries between

72. Informant no. 13.   73. Informant no. 37.   74. Informant no. 13.
75. Informant no. 35.   76. Informant no. 38.

family-name lineages, reviving clan feuds.[77] Middle-aged workers and cadres—those with vested interests in the status quo—tended to join conservative factions, whereas younger workers, young intellectuals, "black elements," and ambitious cadres inclined to join radical factions. The faction leadership would attempt to recruit members from the political majority to decide issues of interest to them, and this middle majority was more ideologically flexible than the factional core (e.g., "I joined whichever faction had the largest organization").[78]

The chief disadvantage of factionalism was of course that it tended to exacerbate intramural conflict. Factions might fight about anything—in one case there was even conflict in the formation of a factory soccer team, the best player in the plant having been excluded because he belonged to a weaker faction.[79] Any policy the center failed to define precisely or left to subordinate organs to determine locally became an arena of factional conflict: the distribution of housing could occasion factional conflict, for example, or the recruitment of youth to be sent down to the countryside. If there were conflicting signals from the center indicating elite controversy, as in the spring of 1975 over wage policy, there was factional conflict anticipating and lobbying for desirable changes. By the same token, "what decided victory or defeat in factional struggles was central policy."[80] Once central policy was set, the majority quickly fell into line, with the membership of the losing faction lapsing into temporary passivity.

Another informal escape mechanism used to cope with the everyday difficulties posed by permanent mobilization was "taking the back door" (*zou houmen*). People took the back door because the demand for certain goods and services exceeded the supply, which might be artificially restricted, or rationed. Under these circumstances, those "gatekeepers" who controlled the supply of specific goods or services (e.g., truck drivers, doctors, carpenters, blacksmiths, salespersons, and most importantly

---

77. Male informant, born 1940 in Guangdong of lower-middle peasant family background, lower-middle peasant class status. Had been a member of the CYL, received education up to grade four in primary school before becoming a peasant, also a class leader (*banzhang*) in the militia. Illegally emigrated to Hong Kong in April 1977. Interviewed August 1–2, 1977 (hereinafter informant no. 10).

78. Male informant, born 1946 in Guangdong, of worker family background, student class status (junior high school graduate), participated in a Red Guard faction during the Cultural Revolution, legally emigrated to Hong Kong in December 1976. Interviewed June 7, 1977 (hereinafter informant no. 14).

79. Informant no. 37.

80. A legal émigré from Guangdong (Xinhui), male, born 1948 of worker family background. Had been a CYL member, a Red Guard, and a junior high school graduate, before becoming a second grade worker in a small automobile repair and assembly factory in Guangzhou. Interviewed July 3, 1977 (hereinafter informant no. 24).

cadres—particularly personnel cadres) could use their discretionary power to allocate gifts and curry favor. All informants without exception had used the back door, and most considered it legitimate or at least necessary under the circumstances, though most tacitly agreed with the Gang of Four in deeming cadre privilege unjustified in view of the structural advantages of high position.[81] Though back door transactions were certainly not unheard of before 1966, the Cultural Revolution had caused them to proliferate far beyond the original elite network, informants agreed, due primarily to the disintegration of formal institutions.[82]

In sum, the late Cultural Revolution seemed to reveal the shadow side of the explosive emancipation its advocates glimpsed during the initial period. The cathartic breakthrough did not usher in the utopia but at best brought a fleeting sense of euphoria that soon gave way to an incessant, compulsive pounding, as campaign followed campaign in accelerating tempo. The cognitive insight into the necessary priority of the public interest was not denied, but merely gave way to boredom in the absence of available alternatives; later attempts to specify and elaborate this insight into a comprehensive philosophy eluded most of its audience. Behaviorally, participants conformed by exhibiting the types of action prescribed in the appropriate contexts, albeit with progressive detachment of affect and a rising coincidence of deviant extracurricular behavior. In their attitudes, participants often expressed vehement antipathy to values and norms they numbly affirmed at a cognitive level. The constant undulations of the polemical dialectic entailed that only those "targets" survived who were capable of utterly flexible opportunism. By the end of ten years of cultural transformation, the utopian vision revealed in the initial breakthrough had been almost completely obscured by tactical considerations.

CONCLUSION

The attempt to link mass mobilization to economic growth on the one hand and to thought reform on the other failed, seriously crippling efforts to continue the revolution. In our analysis of this failure, we have focused

81. Male informant, born 1941 in Guangdong of bourgeois family background, student class status (university graduate). He was a sixth grade technician (and thus a state cadre) in a farm machine factory. Interviewed July 5, 1977 (hereinafter informant no. 1). Also male informant, born 1945 in Guangxi of capitalist family background, nevertheless became CYL member, later a primary school teacher (and hence a state cadre). Legally emigrated to Hong Kong in 1975. Interviewed July 10–11, 1975 (hereinafter informant no. 26). See also B. Michael Frolic, *Mao's China: Sixteen Portraits of Life in Revolutionary China* (Cambridge, Mass.: Harvard University Press, 1980), p. 130.
82. Informants no. 15, 35, 37.

first on economic factors, then on psycho-cultural transformation. The same sequence will be followed in these concluding remarks.

Why did mobilization fail to stimulate economic production? First of all, the conceptualization of mobilization as a *dependent variable* ("effect") of economic factors was forsworn in principle, under the pretense that the masses would be motivated purely by altruistic ideals. This approach was a hallmark of all radicals during the Cultural Revolution, with the distinction that Lin Biao placed somewhat more compensatory emphasis on coercion, the cultural radicals on ideological saturation. This has not always been the case. As we noted in chapter 2, material incentives were once effectively used (in conjunction with normative appeals) to mobilize the masses. But the redistribution of the means of production had exhausted the main source of relatively inexpensive material incentives. The use of normative incentives as a form of credit for deferred material satisfaction suffered a credibility gap after the Great Leap Forward, in the course of which Mao discovered that material incentives pandered to base and selfish motives anyhow. Henceforth, though certain implicit benefits (e.g., designation as "activist," Party membership) remained available, mobilization increasingly detached itself from explicit material incentives. Mobilization became economically autonomous, a politics of gratuitous self-dramatization.

Second, neither did a clear understanding of the role of mobilization as an *independent variable* ("cause") emerge, though the interdependence of production and revolution was affirmed in the abstract. There was no correlation whatever between mobilization and material benefits, as wage levels remained frozen notwithstanding all mobilizational vicissitudes. With the exception of small-scale rural industry, which continued to grow rapidly through the 1970s under radical ideological sanction but isolated from urban movements, mobilization and production proved to be inversely correlated. The model heroes (e.g., Zhang Tiesheng) and model units (e.g., Xiaojinzhuang) of the 1970s did not even advertise any correlation between mobilization and productivity, but the value of mobilization for its own sake. The reason for the decoupling of mobilization and production has partly to do with the factional split, of course, but underlying it was an old, unresolved contradiction between two different approaches to continuing revolution: the economy had fallen sway to the "engineers," who ran it as a Stalinist "revolution from above," with five-year plans, a centralized ministerial bureaucracy, and rigid adherence to authoritarian discipline; the apparatus of propaganda and culture had so completely assimilated the values of "storming," on the other hand, that mobilization spontaneously assumed an anti-bureaucratic, anarchic orientation.

The reasons for the failure of mobilization to induce lasting and wholehearted psycho-cultural transformation are somewhat more complex. Two explanations may be discounted or at least qualified at the outset. It is true, as noted above, that mobilization became detached from material incentives, that its "lessons" hence received no systematic "positive reinforcement." Yet this lack does not imply that nothing was learned. Skinner to the contrary notwithstanding, human learning can occur in the absence of "conditioning"; it is for example noteworthy how many informants drew morals from the early stages of the Cultural Revolution, although these contradicted previous experience and were also disconfirmed by subsequent developments. On the other hand, if participants received systematic *negative* reinforcement from the mobilizational experience, as did its victims, it is not difficult to predict an adverse reaction. Few former victims, according to our interviews, really "repented". And those who deemed themselves "victims" were vast in number and sometimes exalted in status, forming a self-conscious political group of considerable solidarity and sense of mission. "I do not believe that there was any truly reformed person," opined one former target. "There is no need to give examples; they are everywhere, from Deng Xiaoping at the top to the masses at the bottom."[83]

It is also true that the campaigns of the Cultural Revolution were highly politicized, and the focus on polemical targets may have detracted from their pedagogical function. Yet politicization is quite typical of Chinese mass criticism campaigns. Actually, a case can be made that the campaigns of the late Cultural Revolution period were *insufficiently* politicized. In a successful mass criticism movement, the polemical and pedagogic functions are integrated: the teaching of the ideological "lesson" coincides with the unmasking of the ulterior target, resulting in a cathartic externalization of guilt and an enhanced resolve to adhere to the norms. But in the late Cultural Revolution period the delicate balance of power at the top that Mao preferred to any designated succession arrangement frustrated efforts to choreograph a criticism movement that would allow the villain to be climactically unveiled. The campaigns usually remained on an Aesopian level throughout, arousing a sense of peeved bafflement. Lacking an official revelation of the "real" meaning of a campaign, participants often reductionistically dismissed the whole ideological overlay: "I don't think Mao wanted to change thoughts at all— he just wanted power," inferred one former radical.[84]

83. Second interview, informant no. 29.
84. Male informant, born 1932 in Guangdong (Taishan), of poor peasant and revolutionary martyr family background, soldier individual class status (having "joined the revolution" when he was thirteen years old). He joined the Party when he was seventeen and was deputy leader of the CYL, a position equivalent to that of an eighteenth grade cadre. Left China illegally in 1973 because he was afraid he might be prosecuted for having committed manslaughter in the course of the Cultural Revolution. Interviewed May 30, 1977 (hereinafter informant no. 19).

There are three reasons why the later campaigns drew invidious comparisons with the initial outburst, however mixed the reaction to the latter. First, the "revolutionary breakthrough" model that made its debut in the spring and summer of 1966 had already exhausted its utility as far as the leadership was concerned by the summer of the following year. Though it exerted immense psychological appeal, it was intolerably destructive, and tended to escalate popular expectations well beyond realistic prospect of fulfillment. To the question, What next?, it provided little information, leaving matters to drift back to the *status quo ante*. The notion that "smashing frames" could suddenly solve problems that had eluded more patient and considered efforts gradually lost credibility. Thus this highly effective mobilizational device fell into disuse and even tacit disrepute.

Second, ten years of intensive and virtually incessant mobilization is after all longer than two years, and the constant repetition of clichés eventually led to surfeit. As one informant put it: "After hearing 'Grasp class struggle' too many times, we became desensitized [*mamuhua*]. It could not arouse our interest at all. To grasp class struggle had some deterrent effect, but it could only suppress the eruption of struggles without eliminating the source of troubles."[85]

Finally, the kaleidoscopically shifting ideological focus of the campaigns gave rise to great confusion. The masses were presented with a parade of campaigns, each raising different (and often mutually incompatible) critical themes, one following another, usually without clear resolution, in increasingly rapid succession. In brief review: the first wave of late Cultural Revolution campaigns (1968–70) was radically egalitarian and militaristic, fostering literal conformity with Mao's Thought. The second (late 1970–72) criticized Chen Boda and Lin Biao, attempting to repudiate "ultra-leftist" policies and promote a moderate policy line. The Criticism of Lin Biao and Confucius campaign (1973–74) essentially opposed Zhou Enlai and the moderate course he symbolized. The year 1975 began with a moderate initiative, was followed almost immediately by a radical attack upon it, followed in turn by a conservative mobilization of cadre support in the Dazhai Conference, then by another radical campaign in defense of the "new-born things" of the Cultural Revolution. And so it went. "Before the Cutltural Revolution, I would believe that Mao could reform people's thinking," confessed one informant. "After the Cultural Revolution, I did not know what kind of thinking Mao wanted to reform."[86] A medical doctor who had not been criticized expressed sympathy for those who had: "It is very difficult to say whether the thinking of those who were criticized and struggled [against] would be

85. Informant no. 24.   86. Informant no. 31.

reformed. If it was me, my thinking would change back and forth many times. I was afraid, therefore I would change."[87]

Mass mobilization, which had in the past been effectively employed by a unified elite for clearly stipulated objectives, proved to be a wasting asset in the hands of a divided elite committed at best to revolution for its own sake (and at worst to factional maneuvers). Mobilizational resources had been exhausted, and it proved impossible to reach consensus on a new target against which the masses could be usefully unleashed.

87. Informant no. 35.

SEVEN

Structural Fragmentation

During the post-1968 period, there was a shift from the paradigm of a residual "feudal-capitalist" counterpolity against which a revolutionary vanguard led the masses in a breakthrough toward a new utopia to a fragmentation of the revolutionary leadership into factional networks. The theoretical basis for this fragmentation was the discovery of an emergent "class conflict" within the leadership, corresponding to factional policy disagreements. This class *qua* factional antagonism quickly ramified among all social strata, each side vying for exclusive claim to the symbolism of revolutionary virtue.

During the late Cultural Revolution period, structural fragmentation went through three phases. In the first phase, experimentation with alternative "revolutionary" organizational arrangements (chiefly the Revolutionary Committee) quickly gave way to the reconstruction under military auspices of a monolithic emergent structure, complete with rigid organizational frames and a target definition derived primarily from residual class categories. This was in effect barracks communism, in which military hegemony was achieved by subjecting civilian political cadres to permanent reeducation and rusticating (or otherwise silencing) opposition.

Its collapse upon the death of Lin Biao made way for the second phase, in which a balance was sought between three factionally relevant social categories: rehabilitated civilian cadres, politically active soldiers, and radical activists. A synthesis between forces of order and forces of revolutionary vitality was sought not in new organizational forms, but in "affirmative action" recruitment policies within old forms.

For various reasons this balancing act collapsed, resulting in the formation during the third phase of *two discrete factional networks* based on a mix of ideological affinity, personal ties, and functional specialization. On the one side were the moderates, consisting of a coalition of military and rehabilitated civilian cadres, with a relatively broad and deep reservoir of career connections, who dominated the central and provincial administrative and planning bureaucracies. On the other side were the cultural radicals, consisting of a small minority of senior veterans and a somewhat larger group of relatively junior civilian cadres and supportive local publics. Radical leaders had relatively narrow and shallow bases, but managed to gain control of the central propaganda network and a number of auxiliary organizations. Both sides competed vigorously with all the organizational weapons at their disposal.

THE LIN BIAO SYSTEM

In November 1974, three students in the city of Guangzhou, under the collective penname "Li Yizhe," wrote a long, polemical big-character poster, the target of which they called the Lin Biao "system" (*xitong*). They explained:

> What is a "system"? It is the total entity of related things—thus a complete system. The Lin Biao system is the whole lot of Lin Biao's theories, programs, roads, lines, policies, measures, style of Party [building], style of study and style of work which has, in various spheres of politics, jurisprudence, military affairs, economy and culture, opposed the Party center and Chairman Mao and thus brought great disasters upon the whole people and spread poison over the whole country.[1]

The poster extended for a hundred yards in length, and attracted crowds of attentive readers. Local cadres were reportedly taken aback by the scope of the critique and by the sophistication of the argument, and somewhat at a loss about how to handle the incident. When the contents of the poster were referred to the CC for their instruction, Li Xiannian pronounced it "reactionary through and through, vicious and malicious to the extreme," and the three perpetrators were placed under arrest.[2]

The probable reason for Li Xiannian's indignation and for the harsh reaction of the authorities is that the focus of the attack by "Li" was so broad, conflating features peculiar to Lin's period with others characteristic of the pre- and post-Lin regimes. (Li's conception of Lin's regime as a seamless web is also obviously overstated, in view of the drastic shrinkage of his base in the final showdown.) Yet Lin Biao did leave his inprint upon the country. Within a very brief time span he constructed a structure of radical praetorianism or barracks communism that comprised one of the politically feasible futures that lay open to Maoism upon the termination of spontaneous mobilization.

Lin Biao's intervention into politics did not follow the typical pattern of the "man on horseback" in a less developed country, for it took place at

1. Li Yizhe, "Concerning Socialist Democracy and Law," pp. 11–20. Also translated in *IS*, vol. 12, no. 1 (January 1976): 110–49.
2. "Editor's Note," *IS*, vol. 12, no. 1: 111.

the invitation of the civilian political leadership. The PLA intervened massively at every level during the Cultural Revolution in order to fill the vacuum left by the destruction of the Party-state bureaucracies. The army expanded its power along two main organizational axes:

1. Military dominance was asserted following demobilization of the Red Guard and Revolutionary Rebel bands by dispatching "support-the-left" troops—or, to be more precise, troops implementing the "three-support" and "two-military" campaign.[3] Zhou Enlai told Edgar Snow that no less than 2 million soldiers were engaged in this campaign, including virtually the entire strength of the Regional Force troops, consisting of more than a million men. These troops were not normally sent as intact units, but were parceled out to form political work teams, or "soldiers' Mao Zedong Thought propaganda teams." Such teams were sent into all communes, enterprises, schools, offices, and state and Party organizations (including most State Council ministries) in which factional strife had disrupted normal administrative capacity, in order to supervise operations. As they began moving into troubled areas, the teams placed local police and public security personnel under their jurisdiction in the form of a so-called Military Control Commission (MCC), which exercised practically total control over the local civilian population. These temporary administrative organs were to prepare for the formation of RCs to succeed them, though in many cases the Mao Thought teams or MCCs declined to "fade away" following establishment of RCs. By the end of 1969, all organs, units, enterprises, and rural areas were thus governed by at least one (and perhaps all) of the following: a workers' unit, a PLA unit, a Mao Thought propaganda team, an RC preparatory group, and a Communist Party branch preparatory group—all of which were coordinated by the military and, in most cases, headed by an officer.[4] The various military work teams saw to it that the schools or factories to which they were assigned were organized in the same way that the army itself was organized, forming regiments, companies, platoons, and so forth, and teaching the "three-eight style of work" taught in the PLA.

2. As the civilian governmental (i.e., RC) and Party structures were reconstructed, the numerous leadership and staff vacancies were filled by professional soldiers. The same situation prevailed during the immediate post-Liberation period, but, unlike their predecessors, these soldiers did not demobilize. Local military leaders dominated the local and provincial RCs that were established between the summer of 1968 and the spring of 1969, and, because most delegates to the Ninth Congress were produced

3. The "three supports" were support for the broad masses of the left, industry, and agriculture; the "two militaries," military control and military training.
4. Ilsa Sharp, "The Saplings," *FEER* 69, no. 28 (July 2, 1970): 17.

by the RCs at various levels, the military also gained control of the Central Party apparatus. Only slightly more than 28 percent of the incumbents of the Eighth Congress (32 full members, 14 alternates) retained their positions in the Ninth. Of the 279 members elected, 132 (about 46 percent) were military commanders or political commissars (compared with 30.9 percent in the Eighth CC), 77 (27 percent) were cadres, and 56 (90 percent) mass representatives.[5] The CC also included 34 members of the central government (28 full members, 6 alternates, 18 percent of the total), thus serving as a major catchment basin for revisionist bureaucrats who had been washed out of the Politburo; among the Eighth CC incumbents who retained their positions were 15 full and 2 alternate members of the old Politburo, including Chen Yun, Nie Rongzhen, Chen Yi, and Xu Xiangqian. Of mass representatives elected, most were anonymous newcomers (only 2 were former Red Guards); if they received permanent functional positions outside the CC, these were usually subordinate positions in provincial RCs.

The Politburo was even more heavily weighted with military cadres than the CC (13 of the 25 total were military officers, only 3 of whom were members of the previous Politburo); 6 of these were Lin's personal protégés (Lin Biao himself, his wife Ye Qun, Li Zuopeng, Wu Faxian, Qiu Huizuo, and Huang Yongsheng), and the remainder were former marshals or provincial and regional military officials whose loyalties were not yet apparent. Five civilian radicals became Politburo members, 2 of whom (Kang Sheng and Chen Boda) sat on the Standing Committee. Only 2 State Council representatives survived (Zhou Enlai, Li Xiannian), leaving such veterans as Zhu De, Liu Bocheng, Ye Jianying, and Dong Biwu as a "swing" bloc.

The military's dominance was evident not only in its authoritative coordination of other units through PLA-dominated work teams and appointment of military officers into most commanding civilian political positions, but in the leverage the military continued to exercise over the two conceivable sources of opposition: rebel "mass organizations" and demoted civilian Party-state cadres. We have already noted the importance of the 1967 clash between Red Guards and PLA regional forces in splitting cultural and military radicalism and establishing the domin-

5. All eleven known MR commanders were elected, as well as all known MR chief commissars except for those from Tibet; all told, some 26 percent of the CC were drawn from the regional commands, including at least fifty-three general officers and some twenty-seven Military District (MD) or garrison officers. The chairmen of all twenty-nine provincial RCs (the majority of whom were military officers) were elected to full CC membership. The headquarters and staff departments were also quite well represented (12 percent) in comparison with the Eighth CC, though the real strength of this group was to be found in its domination of the CC's Military Affairs Commission (MAC). Ralph L. Powell, "The Party, the Government and the Gun," *AS* 10, no. 6 (June 1970): 441–72.

ance of the latter: whereas only two of the RCs set up before the Wuhan Incident were led by soldiers, nineteen of the twenty-three RCs established thereafter were. In addition to the prominent military role in the rustication of Red Guards that terminated spontaneous mobilization, there was an inherent class-based antipathy between soldiers (usually of "poor peasant" background) and young rebels (of urban middle-class background). This hatred was exacerbated when the PLA reverted to the "blood-line" theory of class origins in their implementation of such campaigns as the "great criticism," "cleansing of class ranks" or the "one-hit, three-anti" (yi da san fan—hit counterrevolutionaries; anti corruption/ theft, extravagance, and waste) in the 1968–70 period.[6] The radicals mobilized to protest their suppression in the wake of the Ninth Congress, becoming so troublesome that on August 28, 1969, the CC issued an eight-point Central Document banning struggle by force, dissolving all armed factions and mass organizations, and remanding all workers and peasants to their units of production.[7] Even when representatives of the "revolutionary masses" attained positions on RCs, these were usually not members of the disbanded rebel organizations but model workers or peasants receiving sinecures; being of inferior status and lacking political experience, they looked for guidance to the leadership, who encouraged them to remain at their units and "not divorce themselves from production."[8]

Purged cadres were disposed of in one of three ways: they were sent to May 7 cadre schools, sent to settle down on the farm as members of production teams, or sent to take part in manual labor for a specified period. As of January 10, 1969, nearly three hundred May 7 cadre schools had been set up in Guangdong alone, and more than a hundred thousand cadres had been sent for retraining. There they attended Mao Thought study classes, practiced criticism and self-criticism, and engaged in manual labor. Some groups of cadres were sent to the countryside to settle down indefinitely and receive reeducation from the masses. Shorter labor stints were more common: some units implemented the "three-thirds" system (one-third of the time doing manual work, one-third going down for investigation and study, and one-third engaged in routine office work), whereas some units spent half their time each day doing

6. Small meetings were held before and after work. Large meetings were usually held in the evenings, at which short articles of criticism written by the masses would be publicly discussed and linked to concrete problems. Dai Dan, " 'Da pipan' he 'yi da san fan' " [Great criticism and "one hit, three anti"] ZW, no. 209 (October 16, 1970): 8.

7. URS, vol. 56, no. 5 (July 15, 1959): 59; editorial, "Cadres Should Persist in Taking Part in Collective Productive Labor," RR, November 20, 1969, p. 1.

8. Nanfang Ribao, January 10, 1969, p. 1; RR, August 22, 1969, p. 2; RR, October 17, 1969, p. 2; RR, August 18, 1969, p. 2; HQ, no. 9, 1969.

manual labor, the other half doing their regular work. In each of these resocialization arrangements the military was in command and retained discretion to block the rehabilitation of cadres.

Lin was also energetic in organizing the masses into politically utilizable organizations, often introducing new organizational vehicles— partly because of ideological antipathy to the old ones, no doubt, but also because restoring the original organizations would necessitate rehabilitating their civilian leadership.[9] The masses were initially (mid-1968) organized along functional lines into various "congresses" (*daibiao dahui*): the Workers' Congress (*gong dai hui*), the Poor-and-Lower-Middle Peasants' Congress (*pin xiazhong nong daibiao huiyi*), and the Red Guards' (or University and Middle-School Students') Congress.[10] Article Fifteen of the Party Constitution adopted at the Ninth Congress alluded to the "Three Congresses" (*san dai hui*), and in fact some provinces held three-congress provincial meetings.

After the Ninth Congress such relatively unstructured assemblies fell into desuetude, to be replaced by a more militaristic pattern of organization. In schools, students were organized into battalions, companies, platoons and squads; in the factories, workshops, sections and work shifts were rechristened battalions, companies, platoons, and squads, each with its own "commander."[11] "Provincial activists' meetings" were introduced, under the direct jurisdiction of the PLA. Every functional group was to have its own catechism: there were the "four firsts," the "four-good company" movement, the "three-eight work style," and the directive to be "soldiers with five good qualities."[12] For the youth, there were

9. The Red Guards were no longer autonomous, of course, but placed under the supervision of the military. Functioning as a junior branch of the Red Guards were the "Red Little Soldiers" (*hong xiao bing*), including children between the ages of seven and fourteen or fifteen, which replaced the pre-Cultural Revolution Young Pioneers. Its activities included learning revolutionary songs and basic military drill or attending Mao's Thought study sessions. *CN* (Hong Kong), no. 370 (July 23, 1970); "Commentary," *HQ*, no. 7, 1970; *China Topics*, YB524 (May 6, 1969).

10. *RR*, May 31, 1969, p. 2; July 9, 1969, p. 2; August 22, 1969, p. 4.

11. *CNA*, no. 795 (March 20, 1970).

12. The "four firsts" (*sige di yi*) were: first priority for the human factor, for political work, for ideological work, and for living ideas. A "four-good company" was good in political-ideological work, in following the "three-eight" movement, in improving the organization, and in relation to the masses. (The four firsts and four-good company were Lin's summation of Mao's discussion of the priority of politics in his 1929 speech in Gutian.) The "three-eight work style" (*sanba zuofeng*) referred to one of Mao's directives consisting of three phrases and eight characters: The three phrases called for firm political attitudes, a simple and diligent work style, and flexible strategy and tactics. The eight characters constituted four words: unity (*tuanjie*), concentration (*xinchang*), seriousness (*yansu*), and liveliness (*huopo*). The "five goods" include the first three points of the four goods, plus two additions: good in production techniques, grasping scientific experiments and technical innovation, and good in patriotic sanitation. *JFJB*, January 22, 1964, as cited in Tilman

the five requirements for worthy revolutionary successors.[13] For cadres aspiring to rehabilitation, there were the "three criteria."[14] The meeting repertoire also reflected military influence. For example, on the basis of provincial "four-good" and "five-good" movements, exemplary individuals or units would be selected to attend provincial meetings, sometimes in conjunction with such meetings as the "congress of activists in the study of Mao Zedong Thought" (*huoxue huoyong Mao Zedong sixiang jiji fenzi daibiao hui*), or "meetings for the exchange of experience in the study of Mao Zedong Thought." Such meetings were held only after months of preparation and careful selection of participants at county-level activists' meetings. There was even some speculation that such meetings (which by early 1970 had been held in twelve of twenty-six provinces) might climax in a national congress, which might then replace the NPC (whose functions it in fact duplicated). But there were also reports of local and provincial resistance to the four/five goods campaign.[15]

Just as his economic initiatives jeopardized his relations with Zhou Enlai, Lin's organizational arrangements tended to alienate the radicals, isolating him in his showdown with Mao. His militaristic organizational preferences emphasized the reconstruction of tight organizational frames to which the radicals were opposed, due to their rebel constituency as much as to their abstract ideological commitments. The emphasis of Lin and the military politicians popularly associated with his rule on the restoration of discipline snuffed out the phase of radical organizational experimentation that flickered briefly in 1967–68. This emphasis precluded the possibility of an alliance with his most logical civilian collaborators, and possibly disquieted Mao as well. It seems to have also alienated any potential civilian mass constituency, for interview informants in Hong Kong were unanimous in their rejection of Lin's organizational arrangements.

Lin's demise allowed his contributions to radical reorganization to fall into swift and apparently unsung oblivion. Beginning in 1970 at Lushan,

---

Spengler, *Der Sturz von Lin Piao: Paradigm für militärisch-zivile Konflikte in der Volksrepublik China?* (Hamburg: Institut für Asienkunde, Mitteilung no. 76, 1976), p. 245.

13. Viz., (1) living study and (2) living application of Mao Zedong Thought; (3) act as a shock brigade in the Three Great Revolutionary Movements (class struggle, the struggle for production, and scientific experiment) in the countryside; (4) thoroughly implement mass criticism; and (5) take heroes as examples, conscientiously fighting self, criticizing revisionism, and remolding world outlook. *HQ*, no. 9, 1970.

14. Viz., (1) "Do they hold high the red banner of Mao Zedong's Thought? ... (2) Do they engage in political and ideological work? ... (3) Are they enthusiastic about revolution?" Spengler, *Sturz*. Lin considered the first criterion decisive whereas Mao deemed it less important, though he did not make his attitude clear until later.

15. *CNA*, no. 795 (March 20, 1970).

a national campaign was launched to "criticize revisionism and rectify work style" (*pixiu zhengfeng*). Its thrust was antiradical, enabling the moderates to criticize Cultural Revolution innovations without openly repudiating the Cultural Revolution itself. "Revisionism" was redefined in terms of the belief in "innate genius" (*tiancailun*) or the "hero in history" (*yingxiong shiguan*; i.e., Mao's personality cult), as counterposed to "materialism" and "the people make history."[16] The purpose of the campaign was to provide an appropriate public atmosphere for the introduction of more moderate policies; as Zhou explained to the national media in September 1972, "Without thoroughly discrediting the ultraleftist trend, you will not have the courage to implement Chairman Mao's revolutionary line."[17] Between late 1971 and the fall of 1972 a series of national planning conferences was convened on such topics as public security, economic planning, and science, taking as their framework for debate criticisms of previous "ultra-left" agricultural, industrial, and educational policies.

A DELICATE BALANCE

Contrary to popular misconception, the period from the death of Lin Biao until the polarization anticipating the succession crisis was not one of radical hegemony, but one in which a tenuous balance was briefly attained between mutually suspicious political groupings. This striving for balance was evident in the tacit agreement to divide political patronage equitably during the reconstruction of the central political structure, and by the observance of certain limits to inter-group competition. Adoption of this quota system was justified in terms of the desire to infuse a more revolutionary spirit into the existing structure through the recruitment of younger and more militant cadres, the aspiration to create a radically different structure having been implicitly abandoned with the shift from the RC to the reconstruction of the Party apparatus in 1969.

The fall of Lin Biao and his paladins created an organizational vacuum that the moderates and the radicals colluded to fill. As early as December 1970 a new definition of the "three-in-one combination" formula was advanced—instead of "soldiers, cadres, and masses," the formula that had been used since the establishment of the RCs beginning in 1967, the point was now to unite "old, middle-aged, and young people"—thereby tacitly excluding a military quota, permitting an increased proportion of rehabilitated cadres, and placing mass representatives in a position of

16. Xu Zhuanfu, "'Pi-Lin zhengfeng,'" pp. 5–8.
17. Theoretical Group, Heilongjiang Party Committee, and the Theoretical Department of RR, in *RR*, March 23, 1978, as cited in Ann Fenwick, "The Gang of Four and the Politics of Opposition: China, 1971–1976" (Ph.D. diss., Stanford University, 1983).

apprenticeship. The criteria for screening and "liberating" cadres were also relaxed in 1971, as the Party-building campaign accelerated at the provincial level. According to one estimate, by the end of 1973 military officers still held 46.5 percent of the positions (and nineteen of the twenty-nine chairmanships) on provincial Party committee secretariats, but cadres now held 44 percent and radicals 9.5 percent.[18]

At the central level, the post-Lin purge vacated fully one-third of the seats filled by the Ninth CC, three-fourths of which were PLA leaders, the other fourth formerly associated with the CCRG; 7 full and 1 alternate Politburo members were also dismissed.[19] At the Tenth CC, 100 of the 319 members (31.3 percent) were still soldiers, 91 (28.5 percent) cadres, and 107 (33.5 percent) mass representatives. In comparison with the allocation of seats at the Ninth Congress, this represents a slight gain in the proportion of cadres, a loss (of 12.8 percent) in the proportion of military, and a substantial gain (of about 9 percent) in the proportion of mass representatives. The radicals also claimed 9 of the 29 members of the Politburo, and 3 of the 9 seats on its Standing Committee. The number of vice-chairmen was increased from 1 (Lin Biao) to 5 (2 of whom, Kang Sheng and Wang Hongwen, were radicals), thereby signaling the "collective" character of the post-Lin succession arrangements.[20]

Whereas quantitatively considered the radicals made impressive gains at all central levels, if the quality of those gains is scrutinized they appear more modest, limited essentially to the Politburo, over which Mao wielded personal control. The reason has to do with the essentially honorific and acclamatory function of the CC, which meets too briefly and infrequently to function as a policy-making body.[21] To the extent that the CC has any political significance it functions as a talent pool for the co-optation of members of the various "standing" committees that actually make policy on a daily basis; aside from the Politburo Standing Committee, these include the various functional committees of the CC

18. "China," in *FEER Yearbook 1974* (Hong Kong), pp. 117–39.
19. An estimated 75 percent of the purged military cadres were members of Lin's Fourth Field Army, thereby bearing out Whitson's conception of the field army as a political loyalty group, at least in this instance. *FEER Yearbook 1974.*
20. The Politburo Standing Committee included Ye Jianying, Zhu De, Zhang Chunqiao, Dong Biwu, Li Desheng, Mao Zedong, Zhou Enlai, Wang Hongwen, and Kang Sheng. Of these, Zhang, Wang, and Kang could be considered cultural radicals. The new vice-chairmen were Zhou, Kang, Wang, Li, and Ye. Wang Hongwen had herewith vaulted from a mere CC membership to the Standing Committee and a Party vice-chairmanship, but inasmuch as he was the youngest and least powerful of the radicals, there was speculation that his was a showcase appointment.
21. This was especially true during the Cultural Revolution decade, when the CC met in plenary session only six times altogether. The Eighth CC met for its Eleventh Plenum in August 1966 and for its Twelfth in October 1968; the Ninth CC met for its First Plenum in April 1969 and for its Second in August–September 1970; the Tenth CC met for its First Plenum in August 1973 and for its Second (very briefly) in January 1975.

and the administrative bodies of the State Council.[22] Of the twenty-one full members of the Politburo, nine received no appointments to the Standing Committee, nor (so far as is known) to the CC departments then being formed,[23] nor to any government position.[24] That these nine included the prominent members of the radical grouping can hardly have been accidental. This pattern was even more evident in the appointment of mass representatives to the CC, a large proportion of whom were model workers without local political bases (or even necessarily radical ideological affinities): most of them were never heard from again after their election to the CC.[25]

Given the essentially ceremonial character of their positional gains in the post–Lin Biao reconstruction of the central Party apparatus, one might have expected the radicals to adopt Lin's orphaned military support base, seeking common ground ideologically with "military radicals." But any ideologically committed radicals in the military were purged along with Lin Biao, and the regional military leaders who had opposed Lin were unfavorably disposed toward radicals of any stripe, having fended off verbal and physical assaults by their confreres during the Cultural Revolution. The leading cultural radicals, utterly bereft of military experience or connections, offered no appeal to these veterans. The immediate military beneficiaries of Lin's demise were the old marshals whom he had shunted aside at the center, the MR commanders at the regional level. Ye Jianying replaced Lin as vice-chairman (and acting chairman) of the Military Affairs Commission, and was also appointed defense minister in January 1975.[26] By the end of 1974 Deng Xiaoping

22. See Dittmer, "The Formal Structure of Central Chinese Political Institutions," in Sidney Greenblatt et al., eds., *Organizational Behavior in Chinese Society* (New York: Praeger, 1981), pp. 47–76.

23. Reconstruction of the CC departments did not begin until after the Tenth Congress, and proceeded in almost total secrecy. The only department whose organization was made public was the Department for Foreign Relations; of the Departments for Organization and for United Front Work only rudiments could be identified, most of those mentioned in the press being newcomers unknown to the general public. See Wolfgang Bartke in *CA*, November 1976, pp. 598–603.

24. In the spring of 1972, reconstruction of the government apparatus accelerated; at least thirty-eight new ministers and vice-ministers appeared between September 1971 and December 1972. Deng Xiaoping was rehabilitated in April 1973. Yet this was so clearly Zhou's bailiwick that the radicals had little basis to intercede. Bastid and Domenach, "De la Revolution," pp. 126–72.

25. None of the mass representatives were first or second Party secretaries of their provincial Party committees, and twenty-eight of the forty-eight did not even have positions on the Standing Committees of their provincial Party committees.

26. According to Nationalist sources, the original suggestion was Zhang Chunqiao as defense minister, but Liu Bocheng pounded the table with his hand to express the vehemence of his opposition. To placate the left, Zhang was appointed director of the General Political Department. See J. P. Jain, *After Mao What? Army, Party and Group Rivalries in China* (New Delhi: Radiant Pub., 1975).

had been appointed chief of general staff. Later, any possibility of independent kingdom-building at the regional level was foreclosed by the military transfers effected by Mao and Zhou (through Deng Xiaoping) in January 1974. The moderates continued to strengthen their control over the military through the rehabilitation of veteran military cadres, with whom good informal connections had long been maintained.[27]

The optimistic interpretation to be placed upon all these developments is that the radicals could not have hoped to compete with veterans for policy-making positions on the various standing committees, in view of the priority customarily given to experience and seniority in such appointments, but that they were building for the future with their appointments of young people to the plenary assemblies, the candidate memberships, and other leadership "apprenticeships." The more pessimistic (and realistic) interpretation is that the radicals were being placated with showcase positions as a form of ideological window-dressing (from which they would in due course be squeezed out) while real power reverted to the same veterans who had monopolized it in the past.

It is true that the radicals made much more headway on the periphery of power, where they did not immediately threaten incumbents, than at the center. In their recruitment of activists into the Party as members or local leaders, for example, they achieved striking gains. The 1969 Party Constitution had omitted the previously required two-year probationary period for prospective Party members, facilitating an influx of no less than 8 million people into the Party between 1966 and 1973.[28] By the time of the Tenth Congress, Party membership had risen to 28.5 million (it would exceed 30 million by September 1976), representing an average increment of nearly one million members per annum since 1958; 25 percent of these were new recruits,[29] most of them under the age of 30.[30] Radical recruitment policies also had a noticeable affirmative-action com-

27. By February 1975, the moderates had succeeded in rehabilitating the pre-Cultural Revolution commanders of all twenty-five provincial MDs and eighteen of the twenty-five vice-commanders. *CA*, February 1975.

28. Zhou Enlai, "Report to the Tenth National Congress of the CPC" (August 24, 1973), in *The Tenth National Congress of the CPC* (Beijing: Foreign Languages Press, 1973), p. 8.

29. Y. C. Chang, *Factional and Coalition Politics: The Cultural Revolution and Its Aftermath* (New York: Praeger, 1976), quoting *Zhonggong Yanjiu* [Chinese communist studies] (Taibei), vol. 8, no. 4 (April 1974): 71.

30. A number of regional reports indicate that between 1966 and 1976, the majority of all candidates were under age thirty. For example, the overwhelming majority of the 60,000 who joined the Party in Beijing between 1966 and 1973 were under the age of thirty-five. Large numbers of the 33,600 recruited in Shanghai between 1969 and 1973 were less than twenty-five. In Liaoning province in the years 1965–76, 70 percent of all recruits were "young." *RR*, July 1, 1973; NCNA Shanghai, June 30, 1973; NCNA Shenyang, July 2, 1976.

ponent: whereas in the 1950s, only one in ten Party members was female, from 1966 to 1973, 27 percent of all new admissions were women.[31] At the brigade, commune, district, and county levels there was also an attempt to install young people into leadership positions; by 1972, reports of new cadres forming 40 percent of the leading bodies at or below county level were not uncommon.[32] Although the radicals probably lost a significant proportion of their mass constituency to the rustication program, this was to some degree a recoverable resource: those youths who proved themselves would be offered an enhanced likelihood of acceptance into the Party or Youth League,[33] special preference for admission to universities,[34] and good prospects for promotion to local leadership positions. Even more spectacular ascents were conceivable in exceptional cases (*vide* Zhang Tiesheng).[35]

Though in balance they were still losing the race for control of the central policy-making structure to an emerging coalition of civilian and military veterans, compensated only by gains of no immediate political utility at the lower levels, the radicals were not without recourse. In 1973 they played a major role in reviving the old mass organizations, as what seems to have been part of a considered strategy to build an independent

31. Joan M. Maloney, "Problems in China's Party Rebuilding," *Current Scene* 15, no. 3 (March 1977); see also Roberta Martin, *Party Recruitment*.

32. However, the pattern was to restrict new young recruits to lower positions. In a typical report, a county in Shanxi took a total of 564 young people into the brigade, commune, district, and county leaderships, but only 3 were taken into the leading county organs. Shanxi Radio, July 15, 1974, as cited in *CNA*, no. 968 (August 2, 1974).

33. Of the 8 million youths sent to the countryside between 1969 and 1973, at least 60,000 had been admitted to the Party by 1973, and another 830,000 had joined the CYL (as would be appropriate to this age cohort, and could normally be expected to lead to party membership). In January 1975, figures for the previous twelve-month period from fourteen provinces, special municipalities, and autonomous regions indicated that another 70,000 rusticated youths had joined the CPC within that time span. While on an average only 12,000 were accepted annually in the previous five years, the 70,000 accepted in 1974 would indicate a natural rate of increase based on maturation. NCNA Beijing, January 21, 1975; see also Maloney, "Problems."

34. In 1974, for example, Qinghua University graduated its first class of worker-peasant-soldier students. Over 500 of its 2,000 members had been admitted to the CPC while enrolled. If those already members when admitted to Qinghua are included, 70 percent of the 1974 class belonged to the Party. *PR*, no. 22 (May 31, 1974): 20.

35. Zhang finally passed his entrance exam "with distinction" and became something of a national celebrity, winning election to the NPC Standing Committee in 1975. Other notable climbers included Zhang Liguo, a former Red Guard who became vice-chairman of the Hubei RC in 1968 and secretary of the Hubei CYL in 1973; and Zhu Kejia, who graduated from middle school in Shanghai at the age of eighteen in 1969 and went down to the countryside in Yunnan, where he founded a school in an isolated mountain village and arranged to establish a factory there. At the Tenth Congress he became a candidate member of the CC (at the age of twenty-two) and at the Fourth NPC was also elected a member of the NPC Standing Committee. See Wolfgang Bartke, in *CA*, January 1977, pp. 724–30.

organizational base. Such a base coincided with radical ideological affinities, with its focus on China's relatively deprived social categories of youth, women, and workers. First heralded in the 1973 New Year's joint editorial, organizational efforts proceeded in proper radical sequence "from bottom to top": in April 1973 the General Trade Unions (GTUs) of Beijing, Tianjin, and Shanghai were established; Zhang Chunqiao and Yao Wenyuan (alone among the central leaders) were present at the Beijing congress, and Wang Hongwen attended the counterpart ceremony in Shanghai. By the end of 1973 all provincial GTUs, CYLs, and Women's Federations had been established (except Shandong, which set up its provincial organs in 1975).[36] In September 1973 the organization of the (armed) worker's militia began, with national media attention being focused on the Shanghai "model."[37] These mass organizations contained a considerable amount of "new blood," the leaders often hailing from the mass organizations of 1966–68—Ni Zhifu chaired the Beijing GTU, for example, and Wang Hongwen the Shanghai organ.[38] Although nominally controlled by the regional Party leadership, the mass organizations were often coordinated by political departments set up under provincial RC auspices, under de facto control of the radicals.[39]

The mass organizations proved to be politically useful. Whereas they had always figured prominently in the formation of local and provincial people's congresses, which in turn nominated the NPC, beginning with the Tenth Party Congress the mass organizations were also able to nominate about 20 percent of the members and candidates of the CC.[40]

36. The peasant associations, in contrast, were allowed to fall into desuetude; by the end of 1973 only four provinces (viz., Anhui, Hunan, Hubei, and Jiangsu) had set up provincial organs. *CNA*, no. 1087 (July 22, 1977). This neglect reflects an obvious gap in the cultural radical *Weltanschauung* that was also to plague them in the future—not surprisingly, given the distribution of China's population.

37. The campaign to establish an urban militia was heralded in a joint editorial entitled "Arm the Working Class" on September 29, 1973. The Shanghai model was distinctive in placing the militia directly under the Party committee, rather than under the local military garrison. But whereas other provinces talked of "learning from Shanghai in militia work," they were not at this time in fact following Shanghai in setting up an independent militia system. The purpose of the militia was to restore discipline among the working class and prevent factionalism; as such, it was expected to cooperate, not compete, with security organs and the army. *CNA*, no. 968 (August 2, 1974).

38. *FEER Yearbook 1974*, pp. 117–39.

39. In the middle of 1973, Hubei reports revealed the existence of political departments in the financial and commerce system and in the industry-communications sector of the provincial Party committee. In Qinghai the provincial RC's political department was in charge of propagating the films made of Jiang Qing's model operas, among other things. Hubei Radio, July 13, 1973; August 15, 1973; Qinghai Radio, August 20, 1973.

40. The provincial GTUs were best represented in the Tenth CC, with no less than twenty-two members and sixteen candidates, most of whom were model workers or peasants. Seven leading CYL officials became CC members, one a candidate; three members of the Women's Federation became members, seven candidates. At the provincial level, one

They were also effective mobilizational vehicles. When such radical slogans as "going against the tide" (*fan chaoliu*) appeared in the national media, the mass organizations of Shanghai, Beijing, Jiangxi, Zhejiang, and Xinjiang responded with conspicuous enthusiasm.[41] In February 1974, for example, these organizations held mass meetings to condemn Lin Biao and Confucius and "all conservatives who sought to turn back the wheel of history," in which the strongest voices stemmed from the workers.[42]

The radicals also began to take an active interest in the central propaganda apparatus at this time, focusing initial efforts on gaining control of the pace-making media outlets. They turned first to *Red Flag* magazine, the official Party organ, which offered a number of tactical advantages: control was relatively simple because of its compact organization (the editorial board consisted of only six persons), and it had enormous structural impact on the Chinese communication system—its title article in each issue had to be published on the front page of every newspaper, and an average of one-third of the articles in each issue were reprinted by the newspapers throughout the country.[43] The magazine was edited by Chen Boda from the date of its founding (at Mao's initiative) in 1957 until Chen became too preoccupied with mobilizational activities during the Cultural Revolution, whereupon he ceded control, first (informally) to Guan Feng and Lin Jie, then, upon the purge of Guan, Lin, and Qi Benyu as members of the May 16th Group in 1968, to Yao Wenyuan. Yao eventually appointed all six members of the editorial board. The radicals also launched their own theoretical publication at Fudan University in Shanghai on September 15, 1973, for the purpose of analyzing the struggle between Confucianism and Legalism. *Study and Criticism* (hereinafter *SC*) was a regional publication, hence free of the political constraints imposed upon central media; issues could be raised there more quickly and explicitly. Yet it was one of the few regional publications to have national (and even international) circulation, and for its first six months it displayed Mao's calligraphy on its masthead.[44]

Though the radicals were assiduous and relatively effective in culti-

---

hundred mass representatives have been identified as holding consequential positions: Forty were RC vice-chairmen and eighteen members of RC Standing Committees; eleven were secretaries and three members of the Standing Committees of the Party Secretariats. Half of these positions were held by GTU officials, nineteen by CYL officials, sixteen by Women's Federation officials and fifteen by peasant association officials. Helmut Martin and Wolfgang Bartke, *Die Massenorganisation der Volksrepublik China* (Hamburg: Institut für Asienkunde, Mitteilung no. 62, 1975), pp. 145–54.

41. *CNS*, no. 489 (October 18, 1973).

42. *CNA*, no. 952 (March 8, 1974): 5.

43. See the informative discussion of the politics of the press (specifically *HQ*) in *ZM*, no. 14 (December 1978): 32–34.

44. Fenwick, "The Gang of Four," chapter 4.

vating the central media, their influence at this point fell short of "hegemony." Zhou Enlai had acquired power over a wide range of activities upon the death of Lin Biao, and his access to the media remained excellent for as long as he was still active. He personally reviewed scripts to be broadcast over the central broadcasting network, correcting even wrong characters or faulty punctuation.[45] Zhang Chunqiao could not finalize the manuscripts of even unimportant articles in *People's Daily*, but sent them to Zhou without bothering with logic and grammar;[46] the premier once excused himself from a visiting American delegation to check the page proofs of the next day's *People's Daily*.

But it would also be misleading to assume that the media was factionalized at this point, attributing control of *People's Daily* and the broadcasting network to Zhou Enlai, say, and *Red Flag* and the Shanghai publications to the radicals.[47] Themes representing diametrically different ideological positions would appear whose factional origins were not hard to imagine: the emphasis on "taking the back door" (aimed against cadre malfeasance) and the emphasis on "class struggle" or "proletarian democracy"[48] probably all stemmed from the radicals; the emphasis on unity, discipline, and adherence to proper procedure from the moderates.[49] Yet there were continual shifts of nuance in all the media, even

45. In 1971 he once added the following marginal comment to a script of a sports broadcast: "Too long! I have already corrected it. Do not use so many adjectives." Before the broadcast of the news on the Tenth Congress on August 29, Zhou summoned the two announcers and told them at what speed they should read, and fixed the time of the broadcast. *GM*, January 12, 1977; *CNA*, no. 1070 (February 18, 1977).

46. Wang Ruoshui, "The Greatest Lesson of the Cultural Revolution Is That the Personality Cult Should Be Opposed," (February 13, 1979), in *Ming Bao Yuekan* (Hong Kong), no. 2 (February 1, 1980): 2–15.

47. Although criticism of Antonioni's documentary film "China" was widely construed to be a radical attack upon Zhou's State Council (Wu De's Cultural Group had allowed Antonioni to come to China, and the completed film was approved by Chinese diplomatic officials in Western Europe), criticisms were heavily featured in *RR*; the three radical journals did not publish a single article criticizing Antonioni, nor did any of the twenty-two identifiable pen names for radical writing groups. None of the thirty-three radical institutions is reported to have organized activities demonstrating against Antonioni. Simon Leys, *FEER* 87, no. 3 (January 17, 1975): 30–32; Brugger, *China*, p. 159; James Tong, "The Radical Elite and Anti-Americanism and Xenophobia in the PRC, 1974–1976," unpublished paper, Political Science Department, University of Michigan, 1978; Chen Fenghua, "Wei Antonioni fan'an" [Reverse the verdict on Antonioni], *ZM*, no. 11 (September 1978): 14–16.

48. For example, an article by Fang Hai in the December 26, 1973 *Xuexi yu Pipan* (*XP*) contended that "As long as a person is not anti-Party and anti-Socialist, he should be allowed to voice his own different opinion." As quoted in *CNS*, no. 501 (January 17, 1974).

49. At the beginning of February 1974 the CC issued its CD no. 12, an eight-point directive that urged restraint in order to prevent social disruption, noting that it was "strictly forbidden" to organize factions, attack individuals personally, engage in armed struggle, exchange experience (*chuanlian*, or "link up" with other radical groups elsewhere), display big-character posters in the streets, or stop work in order to hold criticism meetings.

SC, which gainsay any straightforward factional interpretation. In 1973 and 1974 the impression of Hong Kong analysts was that *People's Daily* took a more radical line than *Red Flag*, the opposite of what a factional model would lead one to expect.[50] Even within the same organ quite different construals of a given slogan would sometimes appear on alternate days, or even in different articles on the same day.[51] For example, in the fall of 1973 certain *Red Flag* articles interpreted "going against the tide" to mean that subordinates might selectively disobey superior directives if they violated Mao's Thought, obviously a radical interpretation. But other articles in the same journal took a quite different tack:

> Going against the tide is completely consistent with observing Party discipline. . . . In the course of the struggle between the two lines within the Party, our great leader Chairman Mao always unwaveringly abides by Marxist-Leninist principles and dares to go against the tide; he also firmly safeguards the Party's organizational principles and observes the Party's discipline. Chieftains of the opportunist lines within the Party, because they want to push the revisionist line, always sabotage and oppose the Party's discipline.[52]

What can be inferred from this confusion? The absence of clearcut ideological alignments among the media does not belie the existence of elite factionalism, for two clearly different interpretations of the main themes of the campaign were apparent, coinciding with the respective corporate interests of moderates and radicals. The apparently haphazard *appearance* of these two interpretations implies that all factions with seats on the Politburo probably held legitimate access to the pace-making media, and were entitled to give their views public hearing on the issues

50. In the February–April period both *RR* and *HQ* published their own editorials on the political situation—*RR* on February 2 and 20, March 15, and April 10; *HQ* (short commentaries) on February 5, March 6, and April 5—reflecting by their disparate schedules an inability to reach a consensus (as in joint editorials). Whereas on February 2 the *RR* editorial announced that the struggle against Confucianism must be "carried through to the end" (*ba pi-Lin pi-Kong de douzheng jinxing dao di*), on March 3 another *RR* editorial warned cadres that the campaign should not affect spring planting. The plea for unity was put forward by the Short Commentary (*xiao pinglun*) in the April *HQ* and in an article by Xie Zuo in the same issue; side by side with these pieces was however another article by Hong Yuan that criticized the argument that struggle would harm unity, advocating the use of the "four big weapons" in order "thoroughly to expose the contradictions." Not a single mention of "unity" can be found in the April *XP*. See the article by William Shawcross, *FEER* 83, no. 9 (March 4, 1974): 32–34.

51. *CNS*, no. 514 (April 25, 1974); *CNS*, no. 515 (May 2, 1974); *CNS*, no. 518 (May 22, 1974). In the April 1974 *HQ*, a strong plea for unity was put forward by the Short Commentary and in an article by Xie Zuo, reflecting the influence of Zhou Enlai. In the same issue there was, however, also an article by Hong Yuan, which criticized the argument that struggle would harm unity, and advocated using the "four big weapons" "thoroughly to expose the contradictions" and carry on struggle between them.

52. Fang Yanliang, "Going against the Tide Is a Marxist-Leninist Principle." *HQ*, no. 1 (December 1, 1973): 23–27.

of the day. Inasmuch as they were hardly inarticulate, it is likely that the moderates also cultivated their own "writing groups."

Second, regardless of who had operational control of specific media, the "democratic-centralist" decision-making model still appeared to obtain, meaning that all media were expected to reflect whatever consensus the leadership had reached. The selection of "models" for national emulation, for example, reflected this rolling consensus, shifting in the fall of 1974 from young rebels who "went against the tide" of received opinion to expose their parents and teachers to young martyrs of worker/peasant background who sacrificed themselves for the community.[53] Quite marked differences of line over time may reflect the tugging and hauling of leadership groups with different interests in response to constantly shifting circumstances, but do not necessarily imply that the rules of democratic centralism had broken down.

Third, there were periods of indecision or deadlock in this decision-making process, particularly during transitions from one dominant interpretation to another, when incompatible ideas could be publicly advanced. It is during such periods that factions might attempt to shape the new consensus by floating thematic trial balloons that deviated, subtly but perceptibly, from the previously dominant line. Success in such a consensus-shaping effort depends not only on access to the central media but on communications skills. It is particularly during such transitional phases that control of the provincial media by the provincial Party first secretaries may make a difference,[54] allowing provinces to sort them-

53. Zhang Tiesheng of Liaoning, who criticized the newly imposed requirement of university entrance exams for rusticated youth, received national publicity beginning in August 1973. His celebration was followed by that of Huang Shuai, a twelve-year-old who indicted her teacher for suppressing democracy (letter in *RR* on December 28, 1973); Chai Chunze, a rusticated youth who rejected "back door" aid from his father (letter in *RR* on January 5, 1974); Zhong Zimin, son of a soldier who rejected "back door" admission to college (letter in *RR*, January 18, 1974).

From the fall of 1974 until the spring of 1976, the nature of the models subtly changed, now exemplifying obedience, loyalty, and service to the Party. Zhou Risheng of Hebei, Chen Lazhen in Jiangsu, and Gosan Danceng of Tibet were all martyrs who died in service to the people; Wang Yalan, Wei Yixin, and Zhou Shishan were diligent in their work, integrating themselves with the workers and peasants. *RR*, November 17, 1974; February 9, 1975; May 30, 1975; July 11, 1975; see also *Current Scene* 13, nos. 3–4 (March–April 1975): 22–26. For a more general discussion of the use of models, see Donald J. Munro, *The Concept of Man in Contemporary China* (Ann Arbor: University of Michigan Press, 1977), chapter 6; also Anita Chan, *Children of Mao: Personality Development and Political Activism in the Red Guard Generation* (New York: Macmillan, 1985), pp. 68–69.

54. In 1966, a decision of the Central-South Bureau of the CC stated: "The first Party secretaries on all levels are responsible for the newspapers; the newspapers should become ever more useful for extolling politics and propagating the Thought of Mao Zedong." *Yangcheng Wanbao* (Guangdong), February 1, 1966. One provincial Party secretary (Hubei's Wang Renzhong) even had his own writing team. Hubei Radio, February 2, 1970.

selves out on the ideological spectrum in selective response to ambiguous signals emanting from the center.[55]

In addition to the keen interest they took in the conventional media, the radicals also proved to be highly resourceful in finding microcosmic "models" to embody and bespeak their values. These were ostensibly grassroots innovations which the radicals "discovered" and then highlighted in the media, although considerable attention (including financial subvention) had often been surreptitiously lavished on their cultivation. In contrast to such early model units as Dazhai and Daqing, the emphasis was not so much on production as on political culture and socialization, reflecting the radicals' own consistent focus on the cultural superstructure. In the army, the radicals endorsed the Fanghualian model army unit;[56] in agriculture, the Xiaojinzhuang-type political evening school,[57] the Chaoyang model agricultural college, and the May 7 peasant colleges;[58] in industry, they encouraged establishment of July 21 workers'

Thus when a first Party secretary is under a cloud, the provincial newspaper publishes no editorials. See *CNA*, no. 1070 (February 18, 1977).

55. An example of such a transitional phase is the period between the fall of 1972 and the spring of 1973, when Lin Biao's political crimes were redefined from "ultra-left" to "apparently 'left' but actually ultra-rightist." The metamorphosis began with vague warnings against a reversion to rightist policies in the fall of 1972 (see *HQ*, August 7, 1972), the anti-rightist orientation became more explicit in December (*HQ*, no. 12, 1972), and this formulation was adopted with increasing frequency thenceforth. *CNS*, no. 453 (January 25, 1973); no. 459 (March 15, 1973). Yet as late as March 1973 only half of China's provincial units accused Lin of ultra-rightism, while the other half remained silent.

A second transitional period was the spring of 1974, when the central media vacillated between struggle and unity. A survey of the provinces indicates that the majority echoed the call for unity; a minority sat on the fence, repeating leftist demands for struggle while also echoing moderate pleas for unity; and Shanghai alone advocated uncompromising struggle. *CNS*, no. 520 (June 5, 1974).

56. Fanghualian was a military company in Zhejiang that Jiang Qing (rather fruitlessly) hoped to induce the rest of the PLA to emulate. *CNA*, no. 986 (January 10, 1975).

57. Xiaojinzhuang was a brigade near Tianjin in which Jiang Qing took a special interest. All women learned to read and write, and the brigade sponsored poetry competitions (where anti-Confucian poems were written). Aside from promoting agricultural production techniques, the purpose of the political evening school was to teach the peasants how to use their spare time constructively—that is, for political study and "revolutionary recreation" (e.g., songs about the "two shining resolutions of the Party Center" of April 7, 1976)—so as not to become susceptible to the influence of bourgeois thinking.

58. The Chaoyang model started in Liaoning and was featured in a December 1974 *RR* editorial. The school adhered to Mao's instruction: "Half-work, half-study; work and study in diligence and thrift, not asking the state for a cent" (Hubei Radio, March 20, 1975). The idea came from a conference on the Chaoyang experience held by the Science and Education Group of the State Council and the Liaoning provincial Party committee in 1974. The school had no set curriculum, adapting courses varying in length to local agricultural needs. Students came from the communes and were expected to return to them. *CNA*, no. 1001 (May 23, 1975).

colleges.[59] To rusticated urban youth, they offered correspondence courses.[60] Here again, although the radicals predominated in the selection and advertisment of such model units, they had no monopoly over the process, as the moderates' selection of Dazhai as a conference site and symbol of their Four Modernizations would demonstrate in the fall of 1975.

FACTIONAL POLARIZATION

With the succession to the fading Mao and Zhou looming visibly ahead, all potential successors consolidated factional connections and bureaucratic or mass constituencies: the moderates began actively to mobilize the economic planning and management system by launching the Four Modernizations project, while the radicals made theoretical innovations to justify the mobilization of the masses toward the realization of communism. One of the chief features distinguishing this period from preceding periods is that *neither side* acknowledged adversary control of a chosen sphere of functional competence. However, each sought to penetrate and undermine the enemy base while defending one's own. Mao's efforts to balance and discipline the two sides continued, but grew increasingly whimsical, irresolute, and ineffectual. Whereas previously the central policy process registered feedback and arbitrated disputes accordingly, steering the ship of state on a zigzag course between obviously untenable alternatives, it now froze into a deadlock between moderates and radicals. The central government and the provincial power structure

59. The Shanghai Machine-Tool Plant set up the first "July 21 Workers' College" in September 1968, following "Chairman Mao's July 21 directive" for all factories to "train technicians from among their workers." By September 1974 there were 48 factory-run workers' colleges in Shanghai and more than 7,700 workers attended, among whom 2,663 completed their training. By early 1975 there were some 360 such colleges, by the end of the year 1200, and by August 1976 some 15,000, with 780,000 students. *RR*, July 21, 1974, p. 1. Factories in Liaoning also followed this model, though it does not seem to have spread far beyond that. Such colleges served only to make technology more generally available and not to raise its level, and to some extent the training overlapped with that provided in regular colleges; no degree (or higher wage) was offered, and about a third of the time was spent in manual labor. Lynn Yamashita, *FEER* 93, no. 35 (August 27, 1976): 26–27; *CNS*, no. 600 (January 28, 1976).

60. Study courses were extended to some thirty thousand rusticated youth in five rural provinces: Jilin, Yunnan, Jiangxi, Anhui, and Heilongjiang, lasting from six months to a year. Courses offered were in three categories: political and language studies, agricultural production techniques, medical treatment and public health. The fact that the courses were not sponsored by the State Council's Educational and Scientific Group, but by Shanghai, through its ten institutions of higher learning, suggests special concern on the part of the radical municipal leadership. NCNA, June 6, 1974; *CNS*, no. 521 (June 12, 1974).

were in effect co-opted into the moderate political base, whereas the central propaganda apparatus and the mass organizations and key educational institutions were integrated into the radical base. The two sides met in the central policy-making forums merely to trade invective and recrimination, yielding only superficially to attempts to impose central discipline.

The first signal of approaching polarization was the almost complete exclusion of the radicals from the central governmental apparatus established at the Fourth NPC. The radicals had expressed keen interest in gaining influential positions in the government after the somewhat disappointing outcome of their power play in the Party, turning first to Mao to plea for his intercession on their behalf. As he ignored their entreaties, they attempted to infiltrate the apparatus from bottom to top, by gaining a preponderant proportion of the delegates to the NPC Presidium via their control of the provincial mass organizations. Their (historically well-grounded) assumption was that the Presidium would comprise the talent pool from which cadres would be appointed to "standing" government positions. Whereas all members of the First through Third NPC Presidiums had been well-known veterans, the radicals succeeded in having forty-five newcomers nominated to the Fourth NPC Presidium, which, along with about forty-six other leftist nominees, comprised a plurality (about 40 percent) of the Presidium membership. This plurality in turn enabled them to wrest control of the Standing Committee, which is directly elected from the floor of the Presidium.[61] Yet the moderate leadership of the State Council, which nominates its own membership, ignored historical precedent and radical electoral machinations and appointed rehabilitated veterans to most vacancies. Three of the leading radicals, Jiang Qing, Yao Wenyuan, and Wang Hongwen, received no appointments whatever; Zhang Chunqiao was made second vice-premier (outranked by Deng), and played a formative role in drafting the State Constitution. The radicals could also claim three other of twelve total vice-premierships (viz., Ji Dengkui, Chen Yonggui, and Wu Guixian), though whether even these would support the Four in a showdown remained to be seen. Both the "Cultural Group of the State Council" and the "Group for Science and Education in the State Council" were disbanded under the pretext of their provisional status, and the radicals lost control of the latter to the moderates, who planned to "rectify" (purge) the education system for integration into their economic modernization project. Of the twenty-nine ministerial appointments, the radicals were

61. Of the 144 members of the NPC Standing Committee, 87 (61.6 percent) were mass representatives who rose as a consequence of the Cultural Revolution. Y. C. Chang, *Factional and Coalition Politics.*

able to claim only three: Yu Huiyong, minister of culture; Liu Xiangping, minister of public health; and Zhuang Zedong, chairman of the Physical Cultural and Sports Commission.

Throughout the summer and early fall of 1975, the moderates sought to augment their control of the central governmental apparatus by steadily rehabilitating cadres who had been purged during the Cultural Revolution. At least thirty-five important posts in the Party, army, and government were filled by purged cadres during this period.[62] At Zhou's banquet soiree preceding National Day on October 1, forty-nine of the seventeen hundred guests listed were pre-Cultural Revolution officials who had not publicly appeared since then. Military officers, particularly Deng's old army subordinates, were among those rehabilitated.[63] With only a few exceptions (e.g., Shanghai, Liaoning), the provincial Party and government apparatus remained securely in moderate hands.

Not until the death of Zhou Enlai and the virtually simultaneous abdication of Deng Xiaoping in January 1976 were the radicals able to make any headway at all in gaining government positions. Whereas at the Fourth NPC the Ministry of Culture was allotted no vice-ministers (others ministries receiving as many as ten), within two months of Zhou's death Jiang had succeeded in having two of her protégés, Hao Liang and Liu Qingtang (both Beijing opera performers), nominated vice-ministers of culture. At the same time, Lu Ying became editor-in-chief of *People's Daily*, filling a post that had been formally vacant since the purge of Wu Lengxi at the outset of the Cultural Revolution (probably due to the inability of competing factions to reach agreement on a successor).[64] With the purge of Zhou Rongxin as minister of education shortly before Zhou Enlai's death, Zhang Chunqiao instructed Chi Qun to take over the education ministry and set up a "temporary leading group"—as Zhang had no authority to name a new minister (and did not trust Deng or Hua to do so), he relied on informal arrangements.[65] After the fall of Deng, there were attempts to implant Party secretaries in the various military units as well, despite the fact that the military units already had Party

62. Kenneth Lieberthal, "Strategies of Conflict in China during 1975–1976," *Contemporary China* 1, no. 2 (November 1976): 7–14.

63. These included alternate Politburo member Su Zhenhua (former Navy commissar and shortly to reemerge as the Navy's first commissar), deputy army chiefs of general staff Li Da and He Zhengwen, Air Force commander Ma Ning, commander of the Xinjiang MR Yang Yong, senior PLA General Logistics Department commissar Guo Linxiang, and Chen Xilian.

64. Bartke, *CA*, April 1976, p. 140. In the years after the Cultural Revolution, a total of five "responsible functionaries" had run *RR*, including former editor Wu Lengxi (rehabilitated in 1972), former assistant editors Chen Jun and Wang Yi, and Pan Fei, former director of the International Press. Lu Ying was the only one who did not belong to the old team.

65. *CNA*, no. 1096 (October 14, 1977).

committees within them, with the apparent intention of supplanting mediated Party supervision with immediate political control by the left.[66] But generally speaking, although the radicals induced accelerated re- cruitment of many young activists, their attempts to gain a controlling influence at the middle or local levels of the power structure came to nought, succeeding only in raising the hackles of the veteran incumbents. And this failure (among other things) deprived them of a cooperative local support structure for their later campaigns.

They seemed on the verge of more substantial success in their efforts to colonize the auxiliary organizations. No sooner had the Fourth NPC adjourned than preparatory meetings for future convention of the Ninth All-China Congress of Trade Unions, the Tenth All-China Congress of the CYL, and the Fourth All-China Congress of Women were held in Beijing. Work reports were drafted, the revision of charters and the apportioning and selection of delegates were discussed. The press con- firmed reports on June 3 that national congresses for these organiza- tions would be convened soon to elect a new central leadership.[67] Between March and the summer of 1975, one province after another held joint meetings of the three mass organizations and announced forthcoming national congresses, also selecting preparatory committees (usually domi- nated by the radicals)[68] for projected national organizations. But, myster- iously, national congresses were never convened, national organizations never established—until after the arrest of the Gang of Four.

The political advantages of nationwide vertical organizations coordi- nated by a headquarters and national officers in Beijing are so obvious that one wonders why the process leading to this outcome was left hanging in abeyance. One is tempted to infer that the process was stymied by moderate adversaries at the center. At least equally likely, however, is that the radicals themselves simply lost interest: centralized hierarchical organizations after all contravened radical organizational principles, which emphasize informality and grassroots autonomy, and in any case the establishment of national hierarchies would have only led to cen- tralized *Gleichschaltung* by their Party superiors. Similarly, the radicals argued with Deng in favor of decentralization of the economy in 1975,

---

66. *CA*, September 1976, pp. 434–36.

67. Oskar Weggel, *CA*, April 1974, pp. 171–81.

68. Young activists emerging from the campaigns of the Cultural Revolution found un- usually good prospects for upward mobility in the new mass organizations. Among the 571 officials whose backgrounds had been identified as of 1975, none had held their posts be- fore 1966. Two-thirds were political neophytes—i.e., their names appeared for the first time. The other third were known because they held posts on provinical RCs and Party Secretariats, or were members or candidate members of the CC. Martin and Bartke, *Massenorganisation*, pp. 145–54.

seeking to detach organizational sectors from hierarchical control so that they could more easily respond to radical propaganda initiatives.

The radical attempt to establish the workers' militia as a sort of radical storm troop was equally inconclusive. The new "armed" workers' militia began as an experiment in late 1970 at the Shanghai No. 21 Cotton Mill, where Wang Hongwen (who had served as a petty-functionary cadre at the mill) may have had a hand in its development. The new organization was conceived as an "armed defense group" merging groups responsible for civil defense, firefighting, and policing activities. The organization was sanctioned and spread throughout Shanghai in April 1971, and the "Shanghai experience" was nationally advertised in a joint editorial in September 1973. Beijing and Tianjin followed suit in establishing the new militia, as did Anhui and Guangdong provinces. Rather than the militia's being directed by the PLA People's Armed Department (*renmin wuzhuang bu*) as in the past, its command was to come under the direct leadership of the municipal Party committee and participate actively in the movements of the day. Deng reportedly opposed this politicized conception from the beginning, emphasizing the militia's civil defense and production tasks and the exclusion of "class struggle."[69]

In the end, it proved impossible to separate the militia from the army, for two reasons. First, even when the Party committee had nominal "command," the PLA remained in charge of training and staffing. Thus different emphases could be detected in different reports, sometimes stressing Party leadership, sometimes the PLA's continued training role, betraying uncertainty over chain of command. Second, militia participation in mass campaigns opened deep cleavages within the militia when the mass movement split, exacerbating the intensity of the conflict by providing weapons to the contending factions. The Hangzhou Militia Command, for example, was established early in 1974, at a time of factional rivalry between the so-called Mountain Top and Mountain Base factions, which it was meant to control. But the command split into rival militia units coaligned with the rival factions, and armed clashes occurred in Hangzhou, Wenzhou, and Jinhua. The militia was officially disbanded there in March 1975, yet hostilities continued until July, when Deng sent in regular army units to disarm militiamen and maintain production in the factories.[70] By September 1975 there was no mention anywhere of the second anniversary of the founding of the workers' militia, and Ni Zhifu and other city militia commanders kept a low profile. The militia regained face somewhat as a result of its contribution to the suppression of the Tiananmen rioters in the spring of 1976,[71] but

69. *China Topics*, YB600 (September 1976).
70. Ibid.
71. Richard von Schirach, *CA*, May 1976, pp. 210–21.

it remained under the control of the PLA in all but a few places, and received little publicity for its role in alleviating suffering during the Tangshan earthquake that summer.

In consolidating their hegemony over the cultural-propaganda apparatus the radicals were more successful. Jiang Qing chaired the ad hoc campaign committee established in January 1974 to lead the campaign to criticize Lin Biao and Confucius, presiding over a network of *pi-Lin pi-Kong* offices paralleling Party organizations at all levels; and Wang Hongwen utilized his position as Party vice-chairman to convene two ten-thousand-person "mobilization rallies" in late January, putting the full authority of the center behind the campaign. By the end of 1974 the radicals had gained effective control over *People's Daily* using a campaign to "criticize the unhealthy influence" in order to eliminate those who had been involved with the paper's 1972 critique of ultra-leftism and place their own lieutenant, Lu Ying, in editorial control. All the major media organs, including *Enlightenment Daily*, the Central Broadcasting Administration Bureau, New China News Agency, and Beijing Television, were to feel the influence of the radicals. So too would the publication of literary and artistic magazines, university journals, books, and pamphlets in the publishing centers of Beijing and Shanghai.[72] Among these were *Philosophical Studies* and *Historical Studies*, both revived with Mao's approval in 1973 after a seven-year suspension, initially under the aegis of the Philosophy and Social Sciences Department of the Academy of Science, but then (on June 14, 1974) taken over by Zhang Chunqiao's colleagues on the Science and Education Group of the State Council (and ultimately by Liang Xiao), "because the [Social Sciences] Department was unable to do the work."

To engage in polemics in China it is not enough to have a target, for the identity and actual faults of the target cannot be disclosed until its political destruction. It is also necessary to have a didactic historical or literary theme in which the target may be respectably clothed until the appropriate time for its exposure. For help in concocting scholarly allegories, the cultural radicals were able to draw upon a talent pool of ambitious young intellectuals who had been politicized by the Cultural Revolution. Thus the campaign to criticize Confucius got its start in the Philosophy Department of Beijing University, where the class of 1970, the first graduating class since the universities began to reopen, produced a critically annotated version of the *Analects* as its graduation exercise. But a more permanently organized brain trust was needed. In 1972, Zhang Chunqiao began to recruit able "pens" to write articles.[73] In due

72. *China Record* 1, no. 11 (November 1976).
73. Han Suyin, *My House*, p. 579.

course numerous "writing groups" (*xiezuo zu*) were formed, each with one or more distinctive pseudonyms, each usually attached to specific publication outlets. In Shanghai, Luo Siding, pseudonym of the writing group of the Shanghai Municipal Party Committee, dominated *SC* and seven other major journals;[74] in Beijing, Liang Xiao, penname for the "Great Criticism Group of Beijing and Qinghua Universities," dominated *Historical Studies*, the *Beijing University Journal* (a fortnightly inaugurated on February 20, 1974), and contributed to *Red Flag*.[75] Other contributors to *Red Flag* included Chi Heng, a group attached to the *Red Flag* editorial board; Tang Xiaowen, the writing group of the Central Party School;[76] Jiang Tian and Chu Lan, both pseudonyms for the writing group of the State Council's Cultural Group (*wenhua zu*);[77] and Hong Zhansi, the writing group of the Beijing Municipal Party Committee. From the time of their formation until their abrupt demise in 1976 (Liang Xiao was among the first arrested, on the same night as the Four), these writing groups had a prolific and relatively high-quality output, which was consistently left of center. Their research extended to highly sensitive current issues as well as historical allegories; for example, reference materials on foreign trade and on the ship-building industry collected by

74. The Shanghai Municipal Party Committee writing group was established in July 1971 at the suggestion of Zhang Chunqiao and Yao Wenyuan. The head of the group was Zhu Yongjia, and vice-chairmen were Wang Zhichang and Xiao Mu. In addition to Luo Siding, the group used more than a dozen other pseudonyms, publishing more than a thousand articles in *XP*, *Jiefang Ribao*, *Wenyi Bao*, and other Shanghai publications. The group also controlled Shanghai's culture and education, science and technology, wielding influence over industry, even over part of the army. For a comprehensive account of the writing groups, see Hua Yang, "Wenge moqi Zhonggong de xiezuo banzi" [The Chinese Communist writing groups at the end period of the Cultural Revolution], *Zhonggong Yanjiu*, January 1981, pp. 138–50.

75. Liang Xiao was formally established in October 1973, under the leadership of the chairman and vice-chairman of the Beijing University RC, Chi Qun and Xie Jingyi, with Feng Youlan acting as academic adviser. During the 1973–76 period, using the name Liang Xiao (or one of its dozen other pseudonyms) the group wrote 219 major articles, of which 181 were published, concerning history, literature, art, education, science and technology, economics, and international politics. Hua Yang, ibid.; for a participant-observer's account, see Yue Daiyun and Carolyn Wakeman, *To the Storm* (Berkeley: University of California Press, 1985).

76. Tang Xiaowen was organized at the Central Party School by Kang Sheng in 1972; when Kang retired in June 1973, Jiang Qing and Chi Qun assumed control. Hua Yang (see n. 74 above).

77. Chu Lan, which had a total of twenty-eight different pseudonyms (including Xiao Qiu, Xiao Luan, Hong Tu, Fang Jin, Su Yan, Wang Pu, Cai Yue, and Jiang Bo), was founded in 1972; the group wrote a total of 165 articles over the next four years, all but 9 of which were published. Hu Yongnian and Xu Wenyu, "Exposing Chu Lan," *Anhui Wenyi* [Art and literature] (Hefei), no. 12 (December 1977): 3–11. Whereas Luo Siding wrote on a broad range of topics in literature, philosophy, science, history, education, politics, and economics, Chu Lan confined itself for the most part to fine arts and cultural topics.

Luo Siding facilitated a well-documented radical critique of moderate trade and investment policies.[78]

This control over media outlets and intellectual inputs gave the radicals hegemonial control over the media system by the end of 1975. Upon Zhou Enlai's death, Yao Wenyuan could reduce newspaper coverage to one page of commemorative photos (from a proposed four) and effectively mute his commemoration by Chinese radio and television, in the face of a reported 1,000 telephone calls and 130 letters urging this.[79] As Yao Wenyuan noted without demur in a diary entry dated February 26, 1976:

> The foreigners all say: "The propaganda instruments are in the hands of the leftists, 'propagating Mao's line' and the 'theory of continuing revolution,' while those who do 'economic work are the pragmatists.'" When can economic work be done under the leadership of genuine Marxists?[80]

This formidable accumulation of intellectual capital and media outlets could hardly be said to have resulted in a cultural renascence. Control over media channels was tightly centralized: in 1960, 1,330 official periodicals had been published in China; in 1966, the number was cut to about 648, and by 1973, it had been further reduced to about 50.[81] Mass entertainment was essentially reduced to Jiang Qing's "ten great theatrical productions," and the songs, movies, and productions in local dialect that could be derived therefrom. The cultural and informational policy of the radicals was to pursue intellectual "monolithicity" (*yiyuanhua*), meaning that a narrowly orthodox conception of truth should prevail. Justified among other things was the transformation of the educational system into intellectually sterile vocational institutions *qua* labor camps and the banishment of every cultural artifact that did not fit the radical Procrustean bed.

Yet despite the disintegration of the central policy-making process in the course of this factional polarization, procedural rules apparently continued to place certain limits on radical exploitation of the media for partisan purposes. Many critiques (and no defenses) of Deng Xiaoping were published between his unofficial retirement in early February and his official purge on April 7, for example, but few of them were editorials

78. *Lishi de Jilu* [The historical record], ed. by Institute of History, Chinese Academy of Social Sciences (Beijing: Beijing chubanshe, August 1, 1973), p. 3; as cited in Fenwick, "The Gang of Four," chapter 4.

79. The disproportion presumptively owes to the fact that phone calls may be made anonymously, avoiding possible retaliation. *GM*, January 12, 1977, as cited in *CNA*, no. 1070 (February 18, 1977).

80. Quoted in CD no. 37 (1977), trans. in *IS*, vol. 14, no. 11 (November 1978): 98–110.

81. Helen F. Siu and Zelda Stern, eds., *Mao's Harvest: Voices from China's New Generation* (New York: Oxford University Press, 1983), pp. xlv–xlix.

or commentaries, suggesting that the latter presuppose a Politburo consensus.[82]

The moderates lacked the command of the media that might have permitted them directly to confront the radicals in the public arena, but with the Four Modernizations campaign they were able to seize control of the national political-economic agenda and to generate widespread bureaucratic support under the pretext of convening planning meetings. The Fourth NPC was only the beginning of this type of mobilization of the moderate constituency. Deng alone attended at least seven national conferences between March and October 1975, each of which convoked hundreds, sometimes thousands of Party, administrative, and non-Party professional cadres. These included a Conference of Representatives of the Iron and Steel Industries (May 29), an enlarged Military Affairs Commission meeting (July 14), a Conference of "National Defense Industry Key-point Industries" (probably in early August), the first "Learn from Dazhai" conference, a Conference of Party Secretaries from Twelve South China Provinces (in September-October), a Conference on the Work Plan of the Academy of Science (September 26), and a National Coal Conference (October 30–November 11). Deng is also known to have convened other conferences—for the secretaries of national industies, on rail transport (both in March), and in state accounting. These conferences greatly enhanced the visibility and influence of Deng and his colleagues, who read reports and gave speeches for national dissemination and "study." Each national conference was followed by an upsurge of smaller meetings, regional post-conference information transmission meetings (*chuanda huiyi*), symposia, individual speeches, and preliminary reports and articles (usually published internally and in the regional media).

The policy import of these meetings was partly to prepare for the Fifth FYP (due to commence at the beginning of 1976), but beyond that to draft documents for the more ambitious long-term developmental plan that was to guide all work over the next twenty-five years. The three key documents for this master plan were "On the General Program

82. Many articles by the cultural radicals appeared in *RR*, *GM*, *HQ*, but at most eleven of these were signed by individuals or criticism groups, and only a few by low-level official organizations within the formal apparatus. Between January and March 1976, the only editorial on the anti-Deng movement was an *RR* editorial on February 24, which devoted equal space to the need to criticize capitalist-roaders and to the promotion of spring farming. In contrast, when the campaign to criticize Lin Biao and Confucius was launched in February 1974, or the campaign to study the theory of proletarian dictatorship in early 1975, or even the campaign to study *Water Margin* in August 1975, there were many *RR* editorials and *HQ* commentaries. Central Documents were reportedly issued for the campaign, however, though their contents have not been disclosed. Guizhou Radio, February 17, 1976.

for All Work of the Party and the Nation," prepared in the summer of 1975 under Deng's guidance and completed in draft form on October 7; a twenty-point "Decision Concerning Certain Problems in the Acceleration of Industrial Development," promulgated in August and September; and "Report Outline for the Academy of Sciences," designed to guide the nation's scientific-technological establishment. By September these draft documents were ready for formal approval and promulgation at forthcoming national conferences and through the media. Educational policy had also been under assessment throughout the summer, and in early October the results were to be formalized in a policy planning document.

All of these documents gave pride of place to economic development, reconstruing cultural or ideological concerns to coincide with developmental priorities. Radical efforts to "continue the revolution" that did not jibe with these priorities were due to be squelched. Already in the Fourth NPC Constitution public security organs were granted greater discretion to arrest Chinese citizens, and later documents made the identity of the likely targets fairly transparent:

> These persons, completely ignorant of politics and totally inexperienced in production, are cavilling and carping, doing nothing but purging others, chanting bombastic words, while doing nothing concrete, and constantly tagging others with the labels of "restoration of the old," "retrogression," "conservative force," and "only pulling the cart ahead without looking at the road" to suppress the initiative of the broad cadres and masses.... All those who use "rebellion" and "going against the tide" as assets to stretch out their hands to the Party demanding Party membership or official posts will be denied satisfaction—not only will their demand be denied but they will be criticized.... Egalitarianism will not work now, nor will it work in the future.[83]

By the fall of 1975 the plan to get rid of radical troublemakers had already been initiated in some places. In the "Study Dazhai" campaign that followed the conference, many cadres—most of them young radicals—were sent down to the countryside, leaving older cadres in the cities to keep the offices running. For example, 80 percent of the cadres in the Hangzhou area were sent down to the countryside in this connection.[84]

The extent to which the administrative apparatus had become polarized into rival factional networks (and who belonged to which network) tended to become manifest in response to agenda-setting initiatives

83. "Some Problems in Speeding Up Industrial Development" (September 2, 1975), compiled as reference material for further discussion after a special meeting convened by Deng on May 18, 1975, later revised into the "twenty points." Trans. in *IS*, vol. 13, no. 7 (July 1977): 90–114.

84. David Zweig, "A View from Beida," unpublished seminar paper, University of Michigan, 1978.

emanating from the center. Whereas during the Criticism of Lin Biao and Confucius the worker-peasant Mao Thought propaganda teams continued to support movement activities, even receiving reinforcements in June 1974 in order better to maintain order and prevent confrontation between movement participants and authorities,[85] these teams were apparently withdrawn from the 1975–76 campaigns. In consequence, mass response to central media initiatives became increasingly fragmented, depending on whether the vertical network to which the masses in question were attached was under moderate or radical leadership.

This differentiation first clearly manifested itself in the aftermath of the Dazhai Conference. The Party Committees of most provinces responded promptly, sending out large numbers of propagandists to explain the meaning of the conference (Anhui province, for example, sent out one hundred thousand propagandists). Whereas only four provincial Party secretaries appeared at concurrent meetings at which the "capitalist-roaders" were criticized, a large number of Party provincial leaders appeared at similar meetings in support of the Dazhai program.[86] A few months later, when the radical campaign in defense of the "newborn things" was launched (late November 1975), the provincial authorities fell mute and the radical constituency was activated: Xiaojinzhuang Brigade's political evening school, July 21 Shanghai Lathe Factory-type universities, Chaoyang-type colleges, the Beijing and Qinghua University student bodies (now consisting preponderantly of worker-peasant-soldier students, who owed their access to higher schooling to radical education policies) all participated in the upsurge. The Preparatory Committee of the Ninth National Congress of Trade Unions published an article criticizing Deng, and some provincial GTUs convened conferences to criticize him.[87] Within the formal Party-state regional apparatus, Shanghai and Liaoning were most active; other provinces remained tepid, with few reports of Party meetings, mass rallies, or editorial comment.[88] From the PLA there came virtually no response at all.[89]

85. *URS*, vol. 74, no. 7 (January 22, 1974): 86; vol. 76, no. 2 (July 5, 1974): 11.
86. *CNA*, no. 1028 (January 23, 1976); *CNA*, no. 1035 (April 2, 1976).
87. *CNA*, no. 1087 (July 22, 1977).
88. From January 1, 1976 to the end of March, only two provincial and one municipal Party committee convened plenary sessions, and only one prefecture and one municipality convened Party Congresses—only one of which had anything to do with the campaign. Jilin held a Party committee plenum on January 9–19, whose purpose was to carry out the "spirit" of the National Conference on Learning from Dazhai. The Nanjing Municipal Party committee held a plenum to criticize "taking the three instructions as the key link." Jiangsu Radio, February 23, 1976. Anhui Provincial Party committee held a plenum March 8–15, at which First Secretary Song Peizhang, alone among provincial leaders, denounced the "unrepentant capitalist-roaders."
89. Aside from three articles on February 21 signed by one deputy squad leader and two ordinary soldiers from the sixth company of a certain unit in the Beijing Garrison, there was no manifestation of military support for the campaign.

As the formal administrative structure became polarized into opposing factional networks, each with its own agenda, constituency, and resources, both sides resorted to political espionage to penetrate and expose enemy plans, also using counterintelligence to deter such penetration. If the moderates shut the radicals out of their Four Modernizations conferences, the radicals would stage "walk-ins." Jiang Qing was not invited to make a speech at the opening ceremonies of the Dazhai Conference, for example, but she launched a "surprise attack" by speaking anyhow (about *Water Margin* and the danger of capitulationism), even requesting (unsuccessfully) that the text of her speech be published and distributed along with the conference documents. At a rural planning conference in July 1976 some radicals attended under the auspices of the Criticism of Deng campaign, availing themselves of the opportunity to criticize the cadres present. The leading radicals also utilized their official access to documents and minutes of the meetings of the State Council, the CC Military Affairs Commission, and the National Defense Ministry office (Jiang Qing once boasted that she read more documents than anyone) to collect and edit a large quantity of "black material" in order to bring charges against their opponents, "leaking" this material through such channels as NCNA, *People's Daily*, or one of their writing groups.[90] They endeavored to insert investigative reporters into the organizational networks controlled by their opponents at both central and provincial levels to intercept and publicize incriminating materials.[91] They utilized internal communications channels to circulate messages among faction members, disregarding accepted routing procedures.[92] The moderates complained on procedural grounds, and were sometimes successful in bringing disciplinary sanctions to bear.[93]

In attempting to counter the radical hegemony over the levers of

90. CD no. 24 (1976), trans. in *IS*, October 1977, pp. 79–112.

91. Kenneth Lieberthal, "Introduction" in *Central Documents and Politburo Politics in China* (Ann Arbor: University of Michigan, Center for Chinese Studies Monograph no. 33, 1978), pp. 1–111; see also David Bonavia, *Verdict in Peking: The Trial of the Gang of Four* (New York: G. P. Putnam's Sons, 1984), pp. 57–60.

92. They allegedly sent letters and materials to the Ministry of Foreign Affairs, the Liaison Department of the CC, the Air Force Department of the MAC, the National Defense Science Commission, the Chinese Academy of Science, the Chemical Defense Company of unit 2081, the "wide prospects and far room" commune, among others.

93. "All the documents sent to the lower levels should be issued under the name of the center, not individuals," Mao reproached Jiang Qing. "For example, don't issue such things in my name, I would never send any materials." Apparently deterred by such criticisms, Jiang told her supporters at Xiaojinzhuang: "I dare not send materials to you, because sending materials also constitutes a criminal offense. My sending out some materials for criticism of Lin Biao and Confucius was an open act, not a secret, but [etc.]" Mao's letter to Jiang Qing and Wang Hongwen is cited in CD no. 24 (1976), pp. 80–110; Jiang's talk at Xiaojinzhuang (August 28, 1976), in CD no. 37 (1977), trans. in *IS*, February 1979, pp. 94–111.

propaganda and culture, Deng Xiaoping abandoned Zhou Enlai's subtle tactics of sidestepping or reconstruing radical rhetoric in more innocuous terms in favor of a more openly belligerent, uncompromising stance. On January 6, on the threshold of his appointment as CPC vice-chairman and first vice-premier (acting premier) of the State Council, Deng sent for an unnamed "theoretician," said to have been a former collaborator of Liu Shaoqi (and who can now be identified with reasonable certainty as Hu Qiaomu, a veteran philologist, educator, and journalist, who had been purged along with Liu and Deng in 1968 and since rehabilitated); Deng told him that there were "many questions" that "the broad masses at home and abroad urgently want systematically resolved," and discussed plans for preparation of a suitable ideological climate for the Four Modernizations program. He should write a series of articles, Deng suggested: "Look for help from more people. Recruit more disciples, and organize a writing team." He added pointedly: "What we have talked about today has not been discussed by the Party CC and the State Council, and is just an informal exchange of views." Six months later Deng asked Hu to "gather materials related to the implementation of the policy of 'Let a hundred flowers bloom, let a hundred schools of thought contend' in the fields of culture, education, science and publishing." In this connection he also directed He Long's daughter, one He Jiesheng, to recruit informants to make a clandestine investigation of Jiang Qing's administration of the field of art and literature.[94] It was precisely at this time that Deng proceeded to rehabilitate cadres previously active in the cultural and propaganda sector, with the apparent intention of restoring them to high positions in that sector where they might prove useful to him.[95] By the fall of 1975, applications had been sent out to the post offices for subscription to a new moderate theoretical journal equivalent to *Red Flag* or *Study and Criticism*. Only the January 1976 eclipse of Deng and the burgeoning criticism campaign against him prevented its inauguration.[96]

All this seems to have been part of a centrally concerted counterattack

94. David Bonavia, *FEER* 93, no. 32 (August 6, 1976): 18–20; also see *Ming Bao*, August 6, 1981, p. 3.

95. Of the forty-eight rehabilitated cadres to reappear on National Day in 1975, more than 20 percent were previously active in the culture and propaganda sector. These included four former vice-ministers of culture, two vice directors of the CC Propaganda Department, two assistant editors of *HQ*, a vice director of the propaganda department in the PLA General Political Department, and three former cultural functionaries in the Shanghai Party committee.

96. When subscriptions for reviews were being accepted at the end of 1975 for the following year, one could subscribe to a new review entitled "Ideological Front" (*Sixiang Zhanxian*), advertised to appear beginning in April 1976. By that time, of course, the tables had turned and no more was heard of this publication. *CNA*, no. 1044 (June 18, 1976).

STRUCTURAL FRAGMENTATION ★ 205

upon the predominating influence the radicals had gained over culture and propaganda in the past several years. The results of moderate espionage *qua* "research" indicated that the radicals had been excessively rigorous in their definitions of ideologically acceptable cultural fare, with a concomitant decline in creativity. This line of attack coincided with the moderate appeal to the interests of specialized professional groups in greater functional autonomy (as well as with broader audience desires for more varied entertainment). A series of cases in which the radicals had, for allegedly petty and vindictive reasons, censored the appearance of some promising movie or book was raised in inner-Party councils and simultaneously leaked to the public in the form of "rumors" (inasmuch as the moderates lacked publication outlets), replete with verbatim quotations of relevant *in camera* conversation snippets.[97] In response to this well-orchestrated chorus of complaints, radical culture minister Yu Huiyong mobilized his own staff and writing groups, publishing an investigation report in early September that purported to document that the number of novels published in the three years following the advent of the Cultural Revolution exceeded those published in the previous three years (not, however, mentioning the subsequent three years), and that aggregate indices of cultural productivity remained high.[98]

In addition to such bureaucratic infighting, both sides prepared to take recourse to their factional networks for more clearly illegitimate expedients if worst came to worst. The radicals seem to have been first to engage in conspiratorial discussions and informal pooling of efforts, perhaps due to their lack of a strong foothold within the formal organizational structure and/or "radical" contempt for established procedure. Their factional activities, however, were perhaps no more than a politically ineffectual mirror image of the activities of their opponents. There is evidence from as early as the fall of 1974 that the moderates had begun to caucus informally in preparatory meetings for the Fourth NPC (from

97. In March 1975, the movie "Chuangye" (Pioneer) was criticized on ten grounds and barred from production. On July 25, Mao wrote Zhang Tianmin, script writer for the film, that "this film contains no great mistakes. Recommend that it be accepted for publication. Don't demand perfection." Copies of his letter were provided to the Department of Culture and the parent unit of the recipient, and Jiang Qing beat a retreat. In another case, Zhou Enlai approved the movie "Haixia" (Sea clouds) in the spring of 1975, but the radicals sought to bar its appearance, allegedly for petty reasons: "They did not send it to me to preview, but first to Deng Yingchao and her group to see," Jiang Qing complained. CD no. 37 (1977), trans. in *IS*, vol. 15, no. 3 (March 1979): 87–107.

98. The report indicated that by the end of September 1975, more than fifty-one kinds of literary and artistic publications had been published at the central, provincial, municipal, and autonomous regional levels. But only four of these appeared at the central level, with the remaining forty-seven emerging from the provincial, municipal, and autonomous regional levels. Yu Huiyong, "Investigation Report" (September 9, 1975), in CD no. 37, trans. in *IS*, vol. 15, no. 2 (February 1979): 94–111.

which they excluded the radicals), initiating the discussion of cabinet formation that would prompt Jiang Qing to try to assemble a rival "slate." Zhou's retirement to the hospital in the spring of 1974, by making him inaccessible except on an informal basis, may have contributed to this tendency to resort to factional networks, much as Mao Zedong's later withdrawal from public activity restricted access to the Chairman to those who could claim personal intimacy.

As both Zhou and Mao faded from the scene their arbitrating capability vanished with them, and factional polarization proceeded apace. The moderates first contemplated eliminating their radical rivals (necessarily a factional aim) while at the height of their power in the fall of 1975, according to surviving moderate Zhang Pinghua:

> The October 6 action the year before last [i.e., the arrest of the Four] was by no means an accident. About two or three months before Premier Zhou's death, many of us realized that if we did not make a desperate effort to deal with the Gang of Four, the resulting situation would have been hard to imagine.[99]

Later, after Deng was again purged from all formal positions, it was his turn to rely upon factional ties and clandestine schemes—including, when push came to shove, some of those once considered by Lin Biao. Zhang continues:

> After the Tiananmen Incident, Vice-premier Deng went to the south under the escort of Commander Xu. Marshal Ye also returned to Guangdong shortly thereafter.... Deng once said at Conghua, "If we win, everything can be solved. If we lose, we can go up to the mountains as long as we are still alive or we can find protection in other countries to wait for another opportunity. At present, we can at least use the strength of the Guangdong MR, the Fuzhou MR, and the Nanjing MR to fight against them." ... At that time the Gang of Four used to send secret agents everywhere, and the responsible persons of the center in Guangzhou, Conghua and Shaoguan were consequently forced to hold meetings secretly. Once, when Vice-premier Deng decided to go to Meixian to see Marshal Ye, he could not go there by car. To escape notice, Commander Xu used a paddy wagon, all the windows of which were closed.[100]

That the period immediately before and after Mao's death was one of frantic radical plotting has been generally acknowledged, and thus the details need not be reiterated. But parallel conspiratorial activities on behalf of Deng, geographically based in the South China MRs and organizationally coordinated by Xu Shiyou and Ye Jianying, have hitherto received less attention.[101] The reason has to do with the moder-

99. "Chang P'ing-hua's Speech to Cadres on the Cultural Front" (July 23, 1978), trans. in *IS*, vol. 14, no. 12 (December 1978): 91–119.
100. Ibid.
101. Dittmer, "Bases of Power," pp. 26–61.

ate conspirators' greater discretion and more broadly based factional network—and, of course, their ultimate victory.

CONCLUSION

Two aspects of the late Cultural Revolution's impact upon structure may be distinguished: first, there was the attempt to construct less aversive emergent structures, thereby facilitating a transcendence of the impermeable barrier between inner and outer, permitted and forbidden, and so forth. Second, there was the drive to continue to smash the structure of "counterrevolution" as a way of sustaining the revolutionary animus.

The attempt to construct new and less aversive structures went through three stages. In the first stage, incipient experimentation with organizational innovations such as the RC in the context of chaotic factional violence that seemed otherwise uncontrollable led rapidly to the subordination of such experiments to that organization most capable of reestablishing order: the PLA. A structureless situation thus gave way to the imposition of a structure more rigid and absolute than before. And this political structure became attached to a viable but relatively inefficient economic platform. Widespread aversion to such a prompt restoration of the worst features of the pre-1966 structure may have played some role in the ouster of Lin Biao, albeit probably subordinate to elite power-political considerations.

During the second phase, the prospect of erecting new and more ideal structures was abandoned in favor of the more modest objective of achieving a personnel balance within the existing structure among representatives of various functionally significant groups. Two different formulations for the allotment of quotas were tried, the first based on professional specialization (the military, the revolutionary masses, and rehabilitated civilian cadres), the second based on generation (the old, the middle-aged, and the young). Yet neither formula was able to prevent rehabilitated civilian cadres from gradually reestablishing their dominant position in the formal hierarchy and reducing representatives of other groups to parliamentary tokens. Radical affirmative action recruitment policies had a significant and enduring impact on the periphery of power, where they were able to promote upward mobility for young people, women, and the relatively disprivileged classes, and to establish organizational vehicles disconnected from the center that would link their own interests to those of these client publics. But the increasing weakness of radicals at the center outweighed these peripheral gains in the power-political calculus, tending to discredit the strategy of affirmative action recruitment.

In the third phase, structural innovation and balanced recruitment policies gave way to an intense effort to organize, expand, and protect factional networks and to penetrate and discredit opposing networks. Factional loyalties usurped loyalty to the central policy process, and faction leaders remained practically impervious to central discipline. Marginally legitimate espionage, counterespionage, and public mudslinging activities were conducted within the formal organizational structure; obviously illegitimate coup plots were discussed and elaborated through factions. Although structural innovation was by this point completely eclipsed by more pressing tactical considerations, a novel structural configuration coincidentally emerged, consisting of a functionally differentiated sort of "dual rule" in which organization and ideology operated at cross purposes. The formal political apparatus, except for a brief surge of activity following the Fourth NPC in 1975, became paralyzed: whereas Lieberthal was able to document the convention of 271 centrally sponsored and organized meetings between March 1949 and August 1966, he could find evidence for just 26 equivalent centrally organized events between August 1966 and January 1977, only 9 of which occurred after October 1968.[102]

Conceptualization of the revolutionary target structure abruptly reverted under Lin Biao from the tendency to conflate residual and emergent structures during the early Cultural Revolution to a focus on the residual (prerevolutionary) class structure, thereby reviving the pre-1966 conception of frames. This conceptualization, however, conflicted not only with the radical emphasis on ideology as a determinant of class but with the moderate need for functional experts of dubious class background to run the economy. Following the death of Lin Biao, the radicals reverted to emergent ideological criteria for their conceptualization of the opposing class structure in order to mobilize popular discontent against the reestablished Party-state apparatus, whereas the moderates in self-defense sought recourse in residual criteria that justified all (military and civilian) cadres.

Fragmentation of structure in the final period resulted in elite controversy and mass bewilderment over conceptualization of the residual structure. Both radicals and moderates became concurrent framebuilders and frame-smashers: the moderates sought to rebuild the organizational frames, railing against the Inquisitorial sterility of radical thought control; the radicals for their part seized every opportunity to encourage the smashing of organizational frames, only to impose even more severe constraints on intellectual mobility. Both sides actually shared the value premise that truth is exclusive and inherently intolerant in the long run. The contest between them created constantly oscillating

102. Lieberthal, *Central Documents*.

opportunities for repression on the one hand and anarchic revolt on the other.[103]

Structurally considered, the impact of a decade of Cultural Revolution was paradoxical, leading to a collapse of the old distinction between emergent and residual structures, while demonstrating the folly of any facile attempt to merge the two. The old distinction became untenable as much due to the unblinkable salience of problems deriving from the emergent socialist structure—problems such as bureaucratic stagnation, arrogance, corruption, secrecy-mongering—as because of the cumulative discrediting of the notion that all social ailments could be traced to the pre-Liberation class structure. Yet the attempt to merge residual and emergent structures into a target for continuing revolution foundered on the theoretical difficulty of distinguishing this target from those features of "proletarian dictatorship" still to be protected and preserved.

103. It is not entirely fair to claim that the Four fomented anarchism, for they did take some pains to distinguish theoretically between "proletarian revolutionary" leaders (such as themselves) and representatives of the "capitalist road," but these distinctions were often based on circular reasoning and were in any case too subtle to be understood by the broad masses. Thus, *in effect*, the radicals did give rise to anarchistic tendencies. During the 1973–74 period of balance when both sides remained responsive to the central policy process, this endowed the movements they promoted with a yo-yo-like dynamic, in which the masses would be aroused by a centrally initiated publicity blitz, encouraged to link central slogans to local political grievances, and permitted to mobilize until they came into conflict with local authorities or rival factions. When the movement reached a threshold of violence or property damage, the authorities would proceed to suppress it. During the 1975–76 polarization, as rival fractions became unresponsive to the central decision-making process, this dynamic threatened to escalate unremittingly.

EIGHT

Beyond Continuous Revolution

This study has been based on the premise that continuing revolution after the seizure of sovereignty has three functional requisites. The first is charismatic leadership, consisting of an inspiring leader and an inspired staff, successfully performing a revolutionary mission. The second is effective mass mobilization, which presumes access between elite and masses and some judicious combination of material and normative incentives. The third is a structure of opposition against which the forces of revolution may reflexively define themselves through "struggle." These three functional requisites have historically been combined, with varying selective emphases, into two distinct approaches to revolution. The "storming" approach, with its characteristic emphasis on simultaneous, egalitarian, and spontaneous elements, has been relatively infrequently applied, but it retains a strong hold on the revolutionary imagination and is often evoked in propaganda. The "engineering" approach, which emphasizes the sequential, elitist, and well-organized aspects of the revolutionary experience, has figured prominently in the practical socialization of cadres in the post-Liberation era.

During roughly the first decade after Liberation, the engineering approach had its heyday. Revolutionary ideology and the charismatic leadership of Mao Zedong formed a complementary union with the administrative staff of the Chinese Communist Party and the incipient government, belying the assumption that there is an inherent contradiction between charismatic leadership and bureaucratic organization. Making ample use of purges and swift promotions to motivate cadres and informally linking cadres with activists during implementation all helped to maintain the revolutionary dynamic of the organization; although admittedly there were occasional clashes between the more impatient and driving leader and those colleagues more attentive to organizational maintenance and enhancement needs, these were resolved according to the norms regulating intra-Party conflict.[1] The masses were mobilized by

1. See Teiwes, *Politics and Purges in China.*

a combination of material and normative incentives so closely calibrated that the latter acquired legitimacy per se, with the result that for several years afterward the masses would respond to normative incentives alone. The structure of opposition consisted of empirical representatives of the former ruling classes who could still be said to pose a credible threat of restoring the old order if not vigorously repressed, though they had lost political power. Thus the contrast between old and new, pre- and post-revolutionary, counterrevolutionary and revolutionary, could still be credibly dramatized within a bipolar rhetoric of inner/outer, permitted/forbidden, and so forth, and evocation of this symbolic cleavage gave a semblance of moral order to a swiftly changing political reality.

Before the first decade had elapsed, the socialist transformation of the means of production and the restructuring of primary group relationships marked successful achievement of the first phase of continuing revolution. The period from 1957 to 1966 was a period of transition, consisting of a number of false starts interspersed with inconclusive floundering for a new theoretical direction. The first attempt to turn the revolution against vestiges of traditional Chinese political culture in the Hundred Flowers movement collapsed swiftly as the burgeoning movement revealed contradictions in the actors' notions of which aspects of the cultural and political superstructure most needed to be transformed, and the leadership recoiled from this flirtation with liberalism to a more repressive stance vis-à-vis society. Material incentives were not employed, hence only "intellectuals," who proved to have been inadequately resocialized, responded. The attempt the following year to shift the revolution from redistributive and transformative tasks to economic development was both badly conceived and meteorologically unlucky, and the Great Leap Forward took a big step backward, permanently discrediting the direct transposition of storm tactics to economic objectives. The Socialist Education movement of the early 1960s coincided with recovery but foundered on the incongruence between revolutionary ideological rhetoric and "revisionist" economic policies.

By the mid-1960s the functional requisites of revolution had so changed in character as to facilitate a transition from the engineering to the storming approach for the first time since the late 1920s and early 1930s. The charismatic leader and his personal staff had become detached from the administrative apparatus, as the latter became increasingly absorbed in the satisfaction of organizational interests and mistrustful of mobilizational techniques and the former became preoccupied with finding a new theoretical direction for the revolution. Therefore, when the Cultural Revolution erupted, it did so with minimal organizational guidance from the central or local leadership (many of whom became its targets), thereby achieving unprecedented spontaneity. Although there was thus no systematic linkage of normative and material incentives, the masses participated avidly and in great numbers in order to take advantage of this unwonted freedom to raise new issues and vent long-repressed grievances. By daring to air such sensitive issues publicly, the supreme leader momentarily recovered his claim to charismatic boldness and vision. The opposition structure took the form of personalized condensation symbols (viz., Peng Zhen, Liu Shaoqi, Deng Xiaoping) who were polemically associated with a theory of socialist degeneration that conflated residual ("capitalist") and emergent (socialist) contradictions. The thinking on which the Cultural Revolution was based was so loose and question-begging that the great movement it precipitated soon threatened to devour itself, however, requiring the intervention of a *deus ex machina* (namely, the PLA "aid-the-left" troops and Mao Zedong Thought worker-peasant-soldier propaganda teams) to terminate it.

The period from the suppression of spontaneous mobilization and the rustication of Red Guards in 1968–69 until the fall of the leading cultural radicals in September 1976 might be characterized as one of revised storming. The storming approach in its 1966–68 form could not be sustained without tearing the country apart, and so an attempt was made to institutionalize its iconoclastic animus. But, partly because of irresolvable contradictions between the two approaches, partly because these contradictions coincided with factional rivalries at a time of succession crisis, this attempt at fusion fell apart. The radicals were frustrated by the inherent contradictions between the dynamics of storming and their own stake in the new order, whereas the moderates were stymied by the superficial similarity between engineering and "revisionism."

In the post-Mao period, a brief and abortive attempt to revive the engineering approach under Hua Guofeng gave way under Deng Xiaoping to an unprecedentedly explicit attempt to adapt to a postrevolutionary era. Although the final form that this adaptation will take is still at issue at this writing, the transformation of the erstwhile functional requisites for continuing revolution has been so profound that the likelihood of reconstituting them seems remote. These changes will be examined as they have affected charismatic leadership, mass mobilization, and the structure of opposition respectively.

THE ROUTINIZATION OF CHARISMA

In the course of post-Liberation CPC history, Mao initially exercised the personal charisma that had accrued to him as a result of his successful leadership of the revolution on behalf of the corporate interests of the Party-state apparatus. But then in the wake of the split occasioned by essential completion of socialization of the means of production, he began to exercise charismatic leadership in defiance of all organizational mechanisms erected to contain it, in time appropriating ideological innovation on behalf of a highly personal revolutionary vision. His performance record hence declined measurably from that which he had been able to claim as spokesman for the Party-state apparatus as a whole, at first simply because of the inefficacy of the policies he espoused, which were vigorously implemented with catastrophic results, later (in the early 1960s) because of poor execution as well, as the bureaucracy lost faith in his initiatives and passively resisted them. Yet Mao still had faith in his own vision and, with the help of Lin Biao and a successful propaganda campaign that reasserted the infallibility of his "line" and blamed misfortunes on ideologically defined scapegoats, he was able to retain mass support. Then in the early Cultural Revolution Mao reclaimed genuine charisma by boldly assailing the structures of authority in the emergent socialist regime, bidding promise of salvation to the many who had resented the constraints of these "frames." His vision once again seemed to fail him in the late Cultural Revolution period, however; unable to synthesize the conflicting requirements of economic production and continuing revolution, or to balance the mutually antagonistic factions that competed for his blessing in the anticipated succession crisis, he equivocated, shifting lines as he shifted alliances, ultimately failing either to preserve or to transmit charisma.

Apparently unaware of the tenuous condition of charisma and the inauspicious circumstances confronting its prospective revival, Hua Guofeng attempted to "inherit" Mao's charismatic mantle by publicly embracing his Thought. Yet the ultimately prevailing tendency in the successor leadership was not only to abandon such efforts but to adopt institutional safeguards *against* charismatic effervescence. Three aspects of this tendency may be distinguished: a repudiation of the personality cult, evacuation of revolutionary mission, and diffusion of leadership responsibility.

Repudiation of the Personality Cult

A useful preliminary to any attempt to inherit charisma as an instrument of personal hegemony is an enhancement of the prestige of one's predecessor—such had been Stalin's ploy in launching a movement to honor the dead Lenin—and Hua Guofeng followed suit. It was particularly in Hua's interest to refurbish the cult, for his own emergence as Mao's successor could be justified by the infallibility premise and by little else. Hua's previous career had demonstrated him to be a competent implementer of radical policies at the provincial level and a political maneuverer capable of surviving in a chaotic political milieu without accumulating enemies. He had not distinguished himself as a policy innovator, however, and his arrest of the Gang of Four offered the first hint of political imagination or even inordinate ambition. His strategy for

214 ★ BEYOND CONTINUOUS REVOLUTION

legitimating his seizure of power seems to have been to arrogate to himself the superficial trappings of the cult, while reaffirming the infallibility premise with regard to the now-disembodied Thought of Mao Zedong, hoping thereby to establish an equation of himself with the late Chairman. Hua's first official act upon taking the helm was thus to appoint himself chairman of the committee to edit volume five of Mao's *Selected Works* and the committee to plan construction of a mausoleum to house Mao's crystal sarcophagus (like Stalin, Hua mummified his predecessor contrary to the latter's express wish). Pictures self-consciously associating Mao with Hua promptly appeared in public places, and Hua began to emulate Mao by adopting his hair style, bestowing exemplars of his calligraphy to various journal mastheads, visiting prominent sites in Mao's career itinerary (such as Jinggangshan), and otherwise appropriating his persona.

With respect to Mao's Thought, Hua ignored the dilemmas and theoretical dead ends into which it had gravitated during its terminal phase and reaffirmed its infallibility as of that time in which it could claim its greatest popular consensus: the 1950s. Within a year and a half after Mao's death no less than eight hitherto-unpublished Mao texts had made their appearance in *People's Daily*; except during the Cultural Revolution itself, no previous period in PRC history had witnessed the publication of so many new texts.[2] In the first stages of the campaign to criticize the Gang of Four, the latter were accused of being "apparently left, but actually right," and placed in the Maoist framework of "two-line struggle" in direct line of descent from their old nemesis, Liu Shaoqi.[3] At the apparent instigation of Wang Dongxing,[4] Hua sponsored a joint editorial containing the famous "two whatevers": "Whatever policies

2. Helmut Martin, *Cult and Canon*; see also Krishna Prakash Gupta, "Mao after Mao: A Marxist Debate in China," in V. P. Dutt, ed., *China: The Post-Mao View* (New Delhi: Allied Pub., 1981), pp. 162–81.
3. The continuing antirevisionist animus is also apparent in the editing of volume 5 of Mao's *Selected Works*. See Lu Shi, " 'Mao xuan' wu juan yingdang chong shen chong bian" [The fifth volume of 'Mao's Selected Works' should be reexamined and reedited], *ZM*, no. 24 (October 1979): 16–17.
4. In a self-examination presented at the preparatory meeting of the Fourth Plenum of the Eleventh CC (December 10, 1979), Wang said: "I proposed the 'two-whatever' theme when I was concurrently placed in charge of the *Red Flag* journal. This proposal came to my mind shortly after the downfall of the Gang of Four. . . . I believed that the overliberalization of the discussion on practice as the sole criterion for truth may lead to trouble. This belief was corroborated by incidents that erupted in various localities since the beginning of January this year as a result of the overemphasis on the emancipation of people's minds. Eventually, the bourgeois democracy and anarchist trend of thought flooded our country. As soon as the CC noted this, it proclaimed the four basic principles as 'an emergency measure' to stop this trend." Text of Wang Dongxing's Self-examination Paper Read at the Preparatory Meeting for the 4th Plenary Session of the 11th CCP CC," *Dong Xi Fang*, no. 12 (December 10, 1979): 10–12.

Chairman Mao had decided, we shall resolutely defend; whatever instructions he issued, we shall steadfastly obey."[5]

Hua's position unfortunately placed him at cross-purposes with Deng Xiaoping, for in the same "infallible" decision in which he appointed Hua to the heir-apparent positions of premier and first vice-chairman, Mao had also evicted Deng from all his Party and government posts. Deng therefore had an interest in negating the infallibility premise on which Hua was attempting to build his own legitimacy. Having just purged Mao's most enthusiastic supporters, and lacking any political base of his own, Hua was however thrown into the arms of the moderate senior Party-state cadres, most of whom had stronger bonds to Deng than to Hua. Aware of the threat that Deng posed to his position, Hua fell back on assertions of Mao's infallibility; for example, his "two whatevers" statement, issued on the anniversary of Hua's appointment as acting premier, seems to have come in response to strong pressure for Deng's rehabilitation in the public expressions of bereavement surrounding the first anniversary of Zhou Enlai's death. Deng adopted the tactic of expressing contrition and exaggerated deference in order to ingratiate himself with Hua, but he also took issue with the "two whatevers," before he had even been rehabilitated.[6] He seems to have permitted his criticisms to leak through the rumor network, for by April a group of military supporters in Guangzhou had drafted a manifesto evoking them.[7]

In response to this combination of blandishment and pressure, Hua finally agreed to rehabilitate Deng to all former positions, a decision formalized at the Third Plenum of the Tenth CC in July 1977. In his maiden speech to the CC, Deng questioned the common practice of quoting Mao out of context: "We must not distortedly take one sentence and use it as a slogan," he said. "Mao Zedong Thought must be taken as a whole and cannot be unilaterally applied. Chairman Mao's style is very

5. "Study Well the Documents and Grasp the Key Link," *RR*, February 7, 1977.
6. See Deng Xiaoping, "The 'Two Whatever' Policy Does Not Accord with Marxism" (May 24, 1977), in *Beijing Review* (hereinafter *BR*), no. 33 (August 15, 1983): 14–15.
7. "We have the Party Statutes and the Constitution before us; there are precise regulations as to how the Chairman of the Party, who will also be the commander-in-chief of our army and chief of state, is to be nominated.... The fact that comrade Hua Guofeng assumed the chairmanship of the MAC without calling the NPC into session, indeed without even calling a plenary session of the CC, can only be described as an emergency solution forced upon him by the circumstances, and also as a consequence of the struggle against the anti-Party clique, the Gang of Four.... We need not emphasize the point that Hua Guofeng assumed Chairmanship of the CC based on Mao's written remark, 'with you in charge, I am at ease.' These words, be they glittering as gold, cannot represent anything but the personal opinion of Chairman Mao; they can by no means be rated as the expression of the will of the Party, army or people." "Proposal of the Canton PLA Party Committee and the Guangdong Provincial Party Committee Concerning Certain Topical Questions," trans. in *Der Spiegel* (Hamburg), April 18, 1977, pp. 161–64.

lively and popular and sometimes he liked to say something humorous."[8] Deng's influence was perceptible in a series of articles that appeared at the time of the first anniversary of Mao's death, stressing the same theme, and in a gradual change in the public handling of Mao's writings and statements. Nie Rongzhen, for example, wrote an important article arguing that Mao Zedong Thought should be studied only in terms of its spirit, and not through isolated quotations that disregarded their spatial and temporal context.[9]

By December 1977 it had become apparent that tighter constraints were being placed on the publication of Mao texts. By April 1978, the press had ceased printing all Mao quotations in boldface type, and at about the same time *People's Daily* desisted from carrying a daily quotation in a special nameplate at the top of the page.[10] There were fewer quotations, and Mao's name was not inevitably invoked in support of particular policies. Only three major writings by Mao were released in 1978; one was his 1962 speech to seven thousand cadres, in which he discussed the importance of democratic centralism and offered his own self-criticism (hitherto unpublished) for errors committed during the Great Leap; the second (a 1958 piece entitled "Uninterrupted Revolution") actually stressed economic reconstruction through technological revolution (Mao's two letters to his sons, published at about this time, also stressed the need for science and technology); and the third, Mao's 1941 talk to a women's group, upheld the primacy of actual practice and investigation in justifying a theoretical viewpoint. On the second anniversary of Mao's death, only three poems were released; by the fourth anniversary, Mao was totally ignored in Beijing.[11]

But Deng's most explicit and theoretically ambitious challenge to the doctrine of charismatic infallibility took the form of a seemingly academic debate concerning the epistemological issue of the correct "criterion of truth" (*zhenli de biaozhun*).[12] The origins of this debate can be traced all the way back to Deng's brief concluding speech at the Eleventh Party Congress in September 1977, in which he emphasized the need to "revive . . . the practice of seeking truth from facts."[13] This theme was reflected in the article "Practice Is the Sole Criterion of Truth," which first

8. *Ming Bao*, August 16, 1977, p. 1; and August 17, 1977, p. 1.

9. Nie Rongzhen in *RR*, September 5, 1977; see also *GM*, August 29, 1977, as trans. in *Survey of the People's Republic of China Press* (hereinafter *SPRCP*), no. 6431 (September 27, 1977): 77–80.

10. AFP Hong Kong, January 10, 1978.

11. NCNA, June 30, 1978; NCNA, December 25, 1978; NCNA, December 12, 1978; *RR*, January 16, 1979; NCNA, September 8, 1978; NCNA, September 7, 1978; all cited in Gupta, "Mao after Mao."

12. See *CNA*, no. 1134 (September 22, 1978).

13. Deng Xiaoping, "Concluding Speech," in *The Eleventh National Congress of the Communist Party of China* (Documents) (Beijing: Foreign Languages Press, 1977), pp. 192–93.

appeared in *Guangming Daily* on May 11, 1978, and was reprinted shortly thereafter in *People's Daily*. Although most such articles were composed by the Theory Study Group at the Central Party School in Beijing under the patronage of Hu Yaobang (deputy director of the school under Hua), it was (ten months) later revealed that the "special commentator" who wrote this seminal article was one Hu Fuming, director of the philosophy department at Nanjing University and deputy secretary of the department's general Party branch, who voluntarily submitted it to *Guangming Daily*. The newspaper in turn referred it to Hu Yaobang, who edited it in consultation with the author and published it.

The central issue dealt with in this article was whether dogma might be revised. The answer, the author declared, was that it could: Marxism recognized no "forbidden zones," and those that had been erected by Lin Biao and the Gang of Four (or Hua Guofeng?) were anti-Marxist. Hu Fuming later explained that the article had become necessary because after Mao's death many of his colleagues were constantly on tenterhooks about possible violation of one Mao quotation or another at a time when no authoritative arbiter remained available to resolve such uncertainties, leaving them unable to decide the correctness of any policy strictly on the merits of the issue. Truth cannot become its own yardstick, he argued, but must constantly be validated anew in the course of practice. The implications of this line of thinking, if taken to its logical conclusion, was that "practice" exists independently of any revolutionary theory, that "facts" are value-free, and that Mao's Thought was valid only with reference to the historical milieu that had produced it.[14]

Opposition quickly materialized, led by Wang Dongxing, Zhang Pinghua (director of the Propaganda Department), Wu Lengxi (former *People's Daily* editor), and Xiong Fu and Hu Sheng (*Red Flag* editor and assistant general editor, respectively).[15] But opposition never became

14. See Oskar Weggel, "Ideologie im nachmaoistischen China: Versuch einer Systematisierung," *CA*, January 1983, pp. 19–40.

15. Wu Shengzhi's "Zhonggong dui Mao Zedong sixiang pingjia de xin fazhan" [New developments in the evaluation of Mao Zedong thought], *DX*, no. 1 (October 1978), lists the other important articles in the discussion of the criterion of truth through the fall of 1978. The opponents of "practice as the sole criterion" held Mao's Thought to be, if not the sole criterion, certainly a relatively definitive one. They controlled *HQ*, and the Party journal conspicuously avoided endorsing this epistemological line (until the summer of 1979; see the self-criticism published at that time, "Conscientiously Make Up the Missed Lessons in the Discussions of the Criterion of Truth," *HQ*, no. 7 [July 1979]). On National Day (October 1, 1978), for the first time since 1967 there was no joint editorial, signaling the gravity of the split. See Chen Chi, "'Hongqi' zazhi qiguai de chenmo" [The strange silence of *Red Flag*], *ZM*, no. 13 (November 1978): 16–17. In September 1978, Wang Dongxing and Zhang Pinghua went so far as to impound the first issue of *Zhongguo Qingnian* [China youth] since the Cultural Revolution for its selection of the participants in the Tiananmen demonstrations as model activists against the Gang of Four (both Hua and Deng happened to be out of the country at the time). See Qi Xin article in *QN*, no. 106 (November 1978): 6–13.

theoretically articulate (this had been ingeniously precluded by the use of Mao's own words to underpin this delimitation of their theoretical significance), whereas Deng Xiaoping publicly announced his approval in a speech to a PLA work conference on June 2 (published a week later).[16] Deng's cue elicited a series of echoing affirmations from his supporters throughout the summer and fall. At the Chinese Academy of Sciences, Deng Liqun and Zhou Yang (a vice-chairman and an adviser, respectively) gave speeches of endorsement. The first secretaries of the various provincial Party committees and the MR commanders each contributed an article on the importance of practice as a criterion of truth. Many organizations and provinces held a large educational conference for cadres, using Hu's article and Deng's speech as study documents. The journals *Philosophical Studies* and *Economic Studies* convened conferences on the topic. Beginning in October, ancillary themes were introduced, such as the critique of the "theory of genius"—the notion that thought can transcend historical circumstances and apply to all times and places.[17] In terms redolent of Marx's attack on religious authority, reformers began to characterize the belief in infallible leadership as a "superstition" or "fetish" devoid of "scientific" basis. For example, one article drew implicit parallels between the European Inquisition and thought control in China during the period of the Gang of Four.[18] In repudiating the "Gang's" notion (actually Mao's) that "the political line decides everything," or that there were certain transitional periods when "spirit, not the material foundation, is the primary condition," reformers tended to derogate the role of political leadership to that of the competent management of socio-economic interests.[19] One article even lampooned the "foolish old man who moved mountains" for his "imbecilic" lack of realism, pointing out that the happy ending to the tale requires a leap into "superstition" (i.e., two angels come and bear the mountain away).[20]

The Third Plenum, held in Beijing in December 1978 after a long and apparently contentious central work conference (November 10–December 13), heralded a breakthrough in the critique of the cult in at least three respects. First, the CC "highly appraised" the discussion

16. Editorial, *RR*, June 10, 1978, p. 2.
17. The major article on this theme is by Special Commentator, "The Struggle of the Theory of Genius and the Theory of Practice," *RR*, October 30, 1978, p. 2.
18. Yan Jiaqi, "Religion, Rationality, and Practice: Visiting Three 'Law Courts' on the Question of Truth in Different Eras," *GM*, September 14, 1978, pp. 3–4.
19. See Hong Yuanpeng, "Hypotheses on the Inner Springs of Productive Forces," *Sixiang Zhanxian* [Ideological front] (Kunming), no. 5 (October 20, 1978): 1–16; see also Brantly Womack, "Chinese Political Economy: Reversing the Polarity," *Pacific Affairs* 54, no. 1 (Spring 1981): 57–82.
20. Liu Maoying (commentator), "A New Explanation of the Story of Yu Gong Who Removed the Mountains," *Wenhui Bao*, August 15, 1980.

on the criterion of truth and affirmed such guiding principles as the emancipation of the mind and seeking truth from facts. Second, Mao's infallibility was denied, both in the abstract (by criticizing the "two whatevers") and by implication, overruling his verdicts in various specific cases: the Tiananmen Incident was deemed "revolutionary" rather than "counterrevolutionary," and some five hundred thousand victims of the 1957 Anti-Rightist movement were rehabilitated, as were such high-level purge victims as Peng Dehuai and Peng Zhen. Third, Hua Guofeng publicly forswore the cult he himself had attempted to appropriate, advocating that all members of the leadership henceforth be addressed as "comrade" rather than by title, and that no opinion expressed by Party leaders should be called an "instruction" (*zhishi*).[21]

Throughout 1979 and 1980, as the frequency of public references to Mao or his Thought underwent a steady secular decline,[22] elite critiques of his leadership escalated with seeming inexorability. Whereas the Third Plenum had merely deferred discussion of Mao's responsibility for the Cultural Revolution, in the spring of 1979 Wang Ruoshui gave a devastating internal speech, "The Important Lesson of the Great Proletarian Cultural Revolution Is the Need to Oppose Individual Superstition" (*geren mixin*), which attributed that movement (now evaluated in purely negative terms) to Mao's ideological imbalance and to the overweening personal power he had arrogated.[23] In Ye Jianying's public address on the occasion of the thirtieth anniversary of the founding of the People's Republic in October 1979 (reportedly drafted by Hu Yaobang after months of mutual consultation and approved by the Fourth Plenum prior to delivery), Mao's errors—now referred to as "faults" rather than "shortcomings and mistakes"—were referred to on six points: (1) broadening the scope of the attack against the rightists in 1957; (2) encouraging the "Communist wind" during the Three Red Banners (1958–60); (3) leading the intra-Party struggle against Peng Dehuai in 1959; (4) launching the Cultural Revolution; (5) artificially creating or widening the scope of class struggle; and (6) indulging the personality cult.[24] At the Fifth

21. See Wang Jienan, "Why We May Call the Third Plenum a Great Turning Point of Far-reaching Significance in the Whole History of Our Party since the Establishment of the People's Republic of China," *Wenhui Bao* (Shanghai), July 17, 1981, p. 3.
22. See L. Dittmer, "Charismatic Leadership and the Crisis of Succession: Changing Conceptions of Legitimacy in the PRC," unpub. paper presented at the Association for Asian Studies, Los Angeles, Calif., February 1979.
23. Wang Ruoshui, "The Greatest Lesson of the Cultural Revolution Is That the Personality Cult Should Be Opposed," *Mingbao Yuekan*, no. 2 (February 1, 1980): 2–15.
24. Ye Jianying, at Fourth Plenum of the Eleventh CC, *Speech at the Meeting in Celebration of the 30th Anniversary of the Founding of the People's Republic of China* (Beijing: Foreign Languages Press, 1979), pp. 5, 16–17, 19, 20–21, *et passim*. After Hu drafted the report, the draft was sent to leading strata in various localities, to various ministers, secretaries of

Plenum of the Eleventh CC (February 1980), Mao's old nemesis Liu Shaoqi was posthumously rehabilitated, and although the "mistakes" of this erstwhile "top Party person in authority taking the capitalist road" were not unreservedly absolved, this reversal of verdicts inevitably reflected adversely on Mao's judgment (Mao's own "faults" had meanwhile come to be referred to as "serious mistakes" [*yanzhong de cuowu*]).[25] Finally, the Gang of Four and six surviving participants in the Lin Biao conspiracy were placed on public trial in the fall of 1980, and although some care was taken (in deference to Hua Guofeng) to limit the process to the defendants (who had committed "crimes," as distinct from "political errors"), Jiang Qing herself sought refuge in an Eichmann defense, referring to herself as the Chairman's running dog.[26] These object lessons destroyed Mao's symbolic utility for those seeking to salvage some ideological flotsam from his radical platform, as well as fatally undermining the legitimacy of Hua Guofeng's "feudal" succession. The latter formally retired from his chairmanship at the Sixth Plenum.[27]

In the spring of 1981 the regime attempted to call a halt to the process of de-Maoization and formulate a final verdict on the Chairman's histor-

---

provincial committees, and secretaries of Party committees of institutes of higher learning, a total of more than a thousand persons, who made suggestions (the entire drafting process took three months). Then Deng and Ye revised it, whereupon it was taken to the Fourth Plenum for discussion and passed. Amid many favorable comments about Mao and some fairly low-key criticisms (e.g., "we had become imprudent"), the speech introduces the notion that Mao Zedong Thought is a collective rather than an individual product.

25. Although Liu was honored at a memorial service two months later as "the first to advance the concept of Mao Zedong Thought," the impression of a theoretical "contradiction" between Mao and Liu was not easily allayed. Among the top leaders involved, such a contradiction was explicitly acknowledged. The memorial ceremony reportedly had to be postponed for two weeks because of the objections of Liu's widow, Wang Guangmei, to a line in the eulogy referring to her late husband as Mao's "close comrade-in-arms." The phrase was deleted. *NYT*, May 18, 1980, p. 13; see also Dittmer, "Death and Transfiguration: Liu Shaoqi's Rehabilitation and Contemporary Chinese Politics," *Journal of Asian Studies* 40, no. 3 (May 1981): 455–80.

26. Perceptive reportage on the "great trial" may be found in Luo Bing, "Da shenxun taiqian muhou" [On the stage and behind the scenes of the great trial], *ZM*, no. 38 (December 1980): 7–11; Luo Bing, "Beijing da shenxun zhongzhong" [About Beijing's great trial], *ZM*, no. 37 (November 1980): 8–10; Liu Ying, "Tingqian muhou de Jiang Qing" [Jiang Qing at court and behind the scenes], ZM, no. 40 (February 1981): 18–21; Li Mingfa, "Zhonggong gaoceng dui panjue Jiang Qing de zhengyi" [The dispute among high-ranking Chinese Communist officials concerning the sentence of Jiang Qing], *ZM*, no. 40 (February 1981): 22–24; Qi Xing, " 'Shirenbang' da shen de youguan wenti" [Issues concerning the trial of the 'Gang of 10' "], *Qishi Niandai*, December 1980, pp. 8–14; Ding Wang, "Beijing 'da shen pan' de falü genju boruo" [The legal basis of the Beijing 'Great Trial' is weak], *Dangdai*, no. 3 (November 15, 1980): 28–30.

27. See Luo Bing, "Hua Guofeng cizhi muhou" [Behind the scenes of Hua Guofeng's resignation], *ZM*, no. 39 (January 1980): 7–10; and Luo, "Shei yao qudai Hua Guofeng diwei" [Who will replace Hua Guofeng?], *ZM*, no. 39 (January 1981): 12–13.

ical contribution, thereby establishing an ideological consensus upon which to consolidate its legitimacy. The main components of this consensus consisted of a selective restoration of Mao's reputation and a more flexible interpretation of his Thought. The result has been a balanced and multidimensional portrait unique in the annals of Chinese political hagiology.

The article by Huang Kecheng (who had been purged along with Peng Dehuai in 1959), "About Mao and Mao's Thought," published by *Liberation Army Daily* on April 10, 1981, to coincide with a major resurgence of military leftism (including the criticism of Bai Hua, to be examined later), set the basic themes for this more "balanced" interpretation. Huang did not deny Mao's errors ("in his later years, Chairman Mao had some shortcomings and made some mistakes, even some serious mistakes.... When I had the chance of being with him in 1958, I felt that he had overtaxed his brain."), but he did attempt to compensate for this by celebrating his virtues, placing errors in a secondary position.[28] Huang's article, reportedly written at the instigation of Deng Xiaoping, prompted a small freshet of similar memorials, usually from former military figures such as Xiao Hua, Wei Guoqing, or He Changgong (deputy commander of the PLA Academy), whose usual pattern was to devote nine-tenths of the essay to a recollection of some particular episode that revealed Mao's heroic or endearing qualities and then insert a few sentences adverting to errors in his "later years."[29]

The Sixth Plenum endorsed the reevaluation inaugurated by the PLA in its *Resolution on CPC History (1949–81)*. This epoch-making document, reportedly drafted by Deng Liqun (Liu Shaoqi's former secretary, now chairman of the CC Propaganda Department) on the basis of a year's

28. Translated in *FBIS*, April 10, 1981, pp. K5–14. Also see Jiang Xinli, "Cong Huang Kecheng zhuanwen kan Zhonggong pi-Mao yundong" [Looking at the criticize Mao movement from the perspective of Huang Kecheng's speech], *Feiqing Yuebao* 23, no. 11 (May 1982).

29. Thus Yang Dezhi, in a July 1981 *HQ* article: "After the decade of disorder in the country, some comrades have a misunderstanding that Comrade Mao Zedong made mistakes in the 10-year 'Great Cultural Revolution.' However, if we judge his activities as a whole, he made indelible contributions.... Our Party and the people of all nationalities in the country would have had to grope in the dark much longer had it not been for comrade Mao Zedong and the Party CC he led more than once to rescue the Chinese revolution from grave danger and chart the firm, correct political course for the Party and the army.... Of course, our advocacy of upholding Mao Zedong Thought is by no means an attempt to restore the erroneous leftist ideology which prevailed prior to he Third Plenum." *HQ*, July 1981, translated in *FBIS*, July 7, 1981, pp. K9–K10. Other contributors to this wave of more favorable reevaluations include Song Renqiong (member of the Secretariat and director of the CC Organization Department), in a *RR* article, June 30, 1981, trans. in *FBIS*, July 16, 1981, p. K8; Xu Xiangqian (MAC vice-chairman), *HQ*, October 1979, trans. in *BBC Summary of World Broadcasts Part 3 Far East*, no. 6249 (October 19, 1979), p. BII/4.

discussion and widespread consultation before submission to the CC, attempted to stake off limits to further erosion of Mao's reputation[30] and to define the "living soul of Mao Zedong Thought" from the "correct" perspective of the post-Mao leadership. The "key link" was no longer class struggle, which was subordinated in importance to the contradiction between "advanced" and "backward" sectors of the economy. Mao's Thought could "boil down" to three basic points: "to seek truth from facts, the mass line, and [national] independence."[31]

Mao's personal role in the formulation of his Thought is relegated to far more modest proportions. Mao's contribution, the resolution makes clear, has only historical reference; his more sweeping generalizations conceivably have contemporary relevance but may only be construed with the exegetical assistance of the Party. Mao's Thought is not a set of fixed principles but a "scientific system"; that is to say, its content is open to periodic reinterpretation in the light of subsequent "scientific" (i.e., authoritatively validated) experience. It is by no means a "work of genius" by a single heroic leader, as had successively been alleged by Lin Biao and by the Gang of Four (as in their allegorical apotheosis of Qin Shihuang), but rather the by-product of the "collective struggle of the Party and the people," to which "many outstanding leaders of our Party" also made contributions, including such erstwhile renegades as Liu Shaoqi. Mao Zedong himself is thus conceptually distinguishable from his Thought and indeed sometimes violated his own correct line.

Thus the leadership's handling of the infallibility premise seems to have gone through three phases in the post-Mao period. The first phase was marked by an attempt to maintain the popular belief in Mao's flawless decision-making capability and in the privileged epistemological status of his Thought, in order to justify his succession arrangements and in hopes that this infallibility might in time be imputed to the next Chairman. This attempt failed, for several reasons. First, it failed to take into account that popular belief in Mao's infallibility had already eroded over the previous decade. Second, it revised the content of Mao's Thought in a more moderate (and less distinctive) direction even while claiming unadulterated commitment to it. And finally, the new defender of the faith lacked the political base and skills to maintain his position when challenged by a stronger adversary—the presumption of infallibility proved to be based upon power rather than vice versa.

30. See the analysis in *Feiqing Yuebao* 24, no. 1 (July 1981): 1; see also Zhang Zhenbang, "Analysis of the 6th Plenum of the 11th CC," in ibid., pp. 9–14; and David S. G. Goodman, "The 6th Plenum of the 11th CC of the CCP: Look Back in Anger?" *CQ*, no. 87 (September 1981): 518–28.

31. *Resolution*, p. 67 *et passim*; see also Editorial department, "The General Content and Far-reaching Significance of the 'Resolution,'" *Banyue Tan* [Semimonthly talks], no. 13 (July 10, 1981): 3–9, 26.

The second phase witnessed displacement of the infallibility premise by pragmatism of a relatively pure form, as rationalized in the defense of practice as the sole criterion of truth. This motto legitimated an outburst of political and intellectual experimentation, which soon trespassed the threshold of official tolerance, unleashing an ideological backlash to be examined later.

During the third and so far final phase, the leadership has sought to reclaim and institutionalize at least a *prima facie* assumption of infallibility, vested however in formal offices rather than in their incumbents. The ongoing critique of Mao Zedong's policy errors has been arrested in order to preserve popular faith in the political order he after all did much to create. Although Deng Xiaoping has clearly emerged as first among equals in the successor regime,[32] he seems to have adhered to the discipline of collective leadership (as evinced, for example, in his policy zigzags, which conform to a shifting Politburo majority), and there are no signs of any attempt to resuscitate the cult of personality.

Evacuation of Mission

The tendency for the concept to lose its content and become equivocal, vague, "vacuous" is referred to as "evacuation of mission." The tendency in the post-Mao period has been for the mission or "line" to shift its function from that of indicating a broad but relatively clear policy direction *ex ante* to that of providing an *ex post* legitimating umbrella for high-priority system requirements. The successor leadership emphatically still has a mission, consisting of the achievement of economic modernization, but this mission is no longer "salvationary" by our criteria: it is not unique (not even distinctive), and it is not utopian. Modernization is not really an ideologically derived objective, as was socialization of the means of production or creation of a revolutionary culture and New Man, but rather a goal shared by various classes in any less-developed country: non-Party elites are also likely to desire the prestige of major power status (for which modernization is *sine qua non*), for example; non-Party masses to desire the material improvements of mass consumerism. If the mission is widely shared, so too are the resources and skills necessary for its achievement. This sharing permits the leadership to shift from the invidious mobilization of a "class" constituency to the inclusion of all interested social groups in a common project. But it also means the Party risks losing its claim to a monopoly of insight into the scientifically "correct" means of achieving a mission so widely shared and eclectically de-

32. As Hu Yaobang put it, "over the past years four comrades have been of major usefulness: Jianying, Xiaoping, Xiannian, and Chen Yun—especially Comrade Xiaoping. This is no secret. Even foreigners know that Comrade Xiaoping is the primary decision-maker in China's Party today." "Comrade Hu Yaobang's Speech to the Closing Session of the Plenum" (July 29, 1981), as trans. in *IS*, December 1981, p. 75.

fined. What is thus threatened is not only the claim to charismatic in-fallibility of an individual hero-leader, but the "leading role" of the Party itself, whose ideological competence is no longer uniquely relevant.

Hua Guofeng's statement of mission was essentially Maoist, designed to coincide with his attempt to assume sponsorship of the personality cult; at the same time, he could not afford to alienate the senior cadres who provided his base of support. The result was something of a mélange—inchoate "evacuation." Thus he reaffirmed the Maoist motto of "con-tinuing the revolution under the dictatorship of the proletariat" but tended to downplay "class struggle" in favor of achieving "great unity under heaven."[33] He adopted the Four Modernizations, the final fruits of the engineering approach to continuing revolution, with minimal or no revision of the documents Zhou and Deng and their supporters had drafted in 1976 (Deng's "three poisonous weeds" were rehabilitated even before Deng himself was, in June 1977), but then implemented them in a storming fashion reminiscent of the Great Leap Forward. In his report to the Eleventh Party Congress, Hua averred that the Cultural Revolution reflected Mao's correct analysis of the danger of capitalist restoration in the Party via revisionism, but expressed regret that the movement had been led astray by the machinations of Lin Biao, Chen Boda, and the Gang of Four. Declaring the Cultural Revolution to have been victori-ously concluded, he however reserved the option of repeating it, and reasserted the themes Mao had used to justify the purge of Deng: that "class struggle is the key link," and "stability and unity do not mean writing off class struggle."[34] Such comments can have only aroused the anxieties of veteran cadres about the prospects of coexistence with Cul-tural Revolution beneficiaries in the post-Mao era.

The outlines of Hua's syncretic strategy were first announced at the Eleventh Congress and presented in more elaborate form at the Fifth NPC in February 1978, after a series of professional conferences similar to those held in 1975. Hua's mission was characterized by excessively ambitious production targets and an uncoordinated effort to achieve striking results in many different directions at once: 60 million tons of steel, production of 400 million tons of grain, 85 percent mechanization of all farmwork, 10 new oil fields, 120 large-scale industrial projects to be completed by 1985. "In these eight years [viz., 1978–85], state revenues will be equivalent to the total for the past 28 years," Hua announced.[35]

33. Hua Guofeng, "Continue the Revolution under the Dictatorship of the Proletariat to the End," *PR*, no. 19 (May 6, 1977): 15–27.
34. Hua Guofeng, "Political Report to the Eleventh National Congress of the Communist Party of China" (August 26, 1977), *PR*, September 2, 1977, pp. 16–23.
35. Hua Guofeng, "Unite and Strive to Build a Modern Powerful Socialist Country: Report to the Fifth National People's Congress" (February 26, 1978), *PR*, no. 10 (March 10, 1978): 39.

Dispensing with extensive mass mobilization because of its manifest drawbacks, Hua's long-term plan seemed to rely upon foreign investment as a functional substitute for cheap labor, and it rapidly incurred a balance-of-payments deficit, an ill-prepared round of plant construction, inflation, and other problems. The fact that Hua's program failed so resoundingly that it had to be substantially revised within a year of its unveiling and publicly repudiated within two[36] crippled any further thought of harnessing economic production to continuing revolution.

Deng's rise was unique in that it promised not to "grasp" a "line," whether new or refurbished, but an end to untested "lines," announced *a priori* and implemented with "one slice of the knife" (*yi dao qie*). In place of a clear-cut positive program he offered a critique of the contradictions and inadequacies of Hua's line and a commitment more effectively to harness the innovative and managerial capacities of China's bureaucratic-intellectual elite to the broad goal of modernization. Thus in April 1979 the Four Modernizations project was placed in abeyance for a three-year period of "readjustment," during which the administration would rely upon short-term planning and improvisation. The ambitious goals of the "great plan" of 1978–85 and 1985–2000, in the course of which China was to "join the ranks of the foremost economic powers of the world," have since been cut back from a per capita GNP of U.S. $2,000 in 1978, to $1,000 in 1980, to the still-ambitious objective (proclaimed by Hu Yaobang in September 1982) of quadrupling the GNP and achieving a per capita GNP of $800 by the year 2000.

Deng Xiaoping has, since his accession to power, consistently advocated a more open, "vacuous" notion of mission. While declining to disavow the concept of "line" altogether, Deng has sharply curtailed its usage, suggesting, for example, that the concept of "line struggle" has little applicability.[37] At the same time, observing in 1978–79 that the absence of line gave rein to uncontrollable experimentation, Deng also moved quickly to delimit the range of freedom, as we shall see. In place of line, the leadership seems to be moving toward a notion of a "struggle on

36. By Hua himself, at the Third Session of the Fifth NPC (September 1980), where he conceded that the Ten-Year Plan he had sponsored was unrevisable and would have to be scrapped.

37. See Liu Mouyin, "Why Are We Going to Avoid Mentioning 'Struggle between the Two Lines' and Also Shun the Term 'Line' Hereafter?" *Zhejiang Ribao* (Hangzhou), August 12, 1981, p. 4. Also see Jin Wen, "The Struggle within the Party and the Unity of the Whole Party," *HQ*, March 6, 1979, trans. in *FBIS*, no. 79070 (April 10, 1979). According to Jin, inner-Party struggle should not be equated with two-line struggles (although there may be some relationship), and two-line struggle should not be regarded as class struggle (though it may to some extent reflect it). As a nonantagonistic contradiction, the method of "unity-criticism-unity" is appropriate. See also, however, Liang Xuechu, "CCP Power Struggles as Seen from the 'Selected Works of Deng Xiaoping,'" *Qishi Niandai* (hereinafter *QN*), no. 8 (August 1983): 60–63.

two fronts," in which both "left" and "right" deviations are clearly delineated but the precise outlines of correct policy hover vaguely somewhere in the "middle of the road."[38] Though the concept of line thus seems to have retained its negative function of proscribing deviation, it has lost its positive function of prescribing the general direction of movement. As one recent commentator observes, "one cannot speak at the present time of any durable national consensus or common outlook on development among the overall Party and state leadership."[39]

Diffusion of Leadership Responsibility

This term approximates what the Chinese call "collective leadership," a political counterpart of the diffusion of economic responsibility (via such vehicles as the "responsibility systems" in agriculture and industry). Diffusion of responsibility in this broader sense has been among the pervasive tendencies of the past two decades, antedating the death of Mao to some extent in the form of decentralization and the "cellularization" of self-sufficient local units, but accelerating even more rapidly since then. Nor has this diffusion of responsibility been entirely welcome, contributing among other things to a loss of financial control over investment. Thus far, it does seem to have been irrevocable.[40]

The political import of this trend has been a transition from the concentration of formal power and diffusion of informal power in the immediate post-Mao period to a diffusion of formal power and concentration of informal power in the period since 1980. During the Hua Guofeng interregnum, the positions of chairman of the Party, chairman of the CC Military Affairs Commission (MAC), and premiership of the State Council were all in the hands of one man—Hua Guofeng—for the first time in the history of the People's Republic. This concentration of formal power coincided however with a diffusion of informal power, as, due to his brief tenure in office and lack of base (*zhengzhi jichu*), credentials (*zige*), or seniority, Hua was obliged to seek the support of those who informally outranked him (e.g., Ye Jianying, Li Xiannian)—at the price of an obfuscation of mission and rehabilitation of those with whom he had a clear conflict of interest (Deng Xiaoping, Hu Yaobang). Following the

38. See Xin Cheng, "Grasp Firmly the Central Line," *HQ*, no. 11 (June 1, 1982): 34–36.
39. Ruediger Machetzki, "The People's Republic of China: The Condition of Its Economy and the Limits of Reform," *Vierteljahresberichte* (Bonn: Forschungsinstitut der Friedrich-Ebert-Stiftung) 92 (June 1983): 123–35.
40. See Barry Naughton, "The Decline of Central Control over Investment in Post-Mao China," unpub. paper, December 20, 1983; also Christine Wong, "Material Allocation and Decentralization: Impact of the Local Sector on Industrial Reform," in Elizabeth J. Perry and Christine Wong, eds., *The Political Economy of Reform in Post-Mao China* (Cambridge: Harvard University Press, 1985), pp. 253–78.

triumph of Deng at the Third Plenum, the growing discrepancy between formal and informal power forced Hua into the role of a figurehead who announced policies made by a collective leadership.[41] Even this role was eventually to be denied him, as this hapless and unlikely relict of the age of individual heroism was progressively divested of his premiership (at the Third Session of the Fifth NPC, in September 1980), his chairmanship of the Party and the MAC (Sixth Plenum of the Eleventh CC, June 1981), and finally of his Party vice-chairmanship (Twelfth Party Congress, September 1–11, 1982).

Deng Xiaoping's reforms were designed to preclude the possibility of any future recurrence of the cult of personality by institutionalizing the principle of collegiality and by diffusing power throughout the governmental structure. The first stage in this effort consisted of reestablishment of the Central Party Secretariat at the Fifth Plenum of the Eleventh CC (February 1980) under the leadership of Hu Yaobang. Deng Xiaoping unveiled the general outlines of a more comprehensive reform in his August speech to an expanded Politburo meeting, extended and elaborated two months later in the still more ambitious proposals of Liao Gailong, a Party historian and member of the CC Policy Research Section. This platform has since become known as the "Gengshen reform" (1980 is "Gengshen" in the traditional Chinese sixty-year cycle, an obvious reference to the "100-Day Reform" of 1898). With specific regard to the redefinition of leadership entailed (other aspects of these reforms will be examined later), the Gengshen reforms envisaged a functional division of authority (the separation of Party and state and an independent judiciary in particular, but also including autonomous economic/financial, cultural, educational, and scientific and technological organizations), a system of "checks and balances" (zhiheng) among different leadership organs, even the abolition of the Politburo as the central decision-making forum (to be replaced by a Central Executive Committee, staffed by representatives of these larger bodies).[42]

In the course of discussion and ratification, the Gengshen reforms seem to have encountered strong resistance, for they were watered down considerably. Still, their intent is discernible in the Party and State Constitutions approved by the Twelfth Party Congress (September 1982) and the Fifth Session of the Fifth NPC (December 1982), respectively. Whereas a Central Advisory Commission was introduced to fill out the troika of CC, Central Disciplinary Inspection Committee (already introduced at the Third Plenum), and CAC, for example, it was not

41. See for example his report to the Third Session of the Fifth NPC, which closely echoes Deng Xiaoping's speech on reform to an enlarged Politburo meeting in mid-August. Hua Guofeng, "Report on the Work of the Government," BR, no. 38 (September 22, 1980): 21.
42. Xu Xing, "Conservative System Reforms," ZM, no. 73 (November 1983): 54–57.

vested with meaningful political functions,[43] and the idea of a check-and-balance relationship among the three organs yielded to the notion of "consultation and assistance" that has historically governed the relationship between CC and CPPCC (that is to say, the CC is to retain primacy). The Politburo also survived, but the "chairmanship system" (i.e., the positions of Party chairman and ranked vice-chairmen) was eliminated, to prevent the chairman from accumulating too much power. This change leaves the Party general secretary as de facto chair of the CC and its Politburo and Standing Committee, though formally he chairs only the Secretariat, having the right to "convene" (*zhaoji*), but not "preside over" (*zhuchi*) these other organs. In terms of informal power, Hu is at this point not even first among equals in the collective leadership of the Politburo or its Standing Committee. For the first time since the founding of the PRC, leadership of the Party has been separated from chairmanship of the MAC, in effect dividing executive control over Party, state, and army among three leaders—and coincidentally obscuring the succession picture, by making it unclear which position it is most relevant to inherit. As at the center, the leadership has stressed that the system of collective leadership should be fully implemented at all levels throughout the Party structure. Within the Party committees, decisions must be made by majority vote and not unilaterally by the first secretary. If a first secretary departs from the system of collective leadership, all members of the Party committee (and not the secretary alone) must bear responsibility.[44]

In view of the cultural propensity to defer to strong leadership and the long and rather discouraging history of constitutional engineering in modern China, the efficacy of this diffusion of leadership responsibility is uncertain. As noted at the outset, its purpose has been ambiguous, serving at once to inhibit the concentration of power in a general sense and to undermine the position of Hua Guofeng in particular. The articulation of a complex system of organs and offices both superannuated Hua's functionaries and provided new sets of offices for Deng and his lieutenants to fill with their protégés, with the paradoxical effect that the formal diffusion of power coincided with an informal concentration of power, as Deng's factional rivals were slowly squeezed out of the emergent formal network. Whether this reorganization actually results in an elaborate façade for the reconcentration of leadership under a single head

43. It is not equipped to prepare resolutions, and is not staffed on any principle of functional specialization, but rather on power-political considerations. Deng once even suggested that the CAC was a transitional institution, to be abolished within ten to fifteen years. *Wenjian Huibian*, p. 171; as quoted in Tang Tsou, "Reflections on the Formation and Foundation of the Communist Party-State in China," unpub. paper, University of Chicago, 1983.
44. Tsou, "Reflections."

thus remains to be seen. The operating assumption of the reformers seems to have been that "structure is fate"—that although the current leadership may still be more hierarchically ordered at an informal level than appears on the surface, ultimately the constitutionally diffused distribution of functional authority will enable a balance of power to emerge. Informal relationships, it is assumed, will eventually come to complement rather than undermine formal structure, as they are usually found to do in studies of Western bureaucratic behavior. The real test of the efficacy of these reforms must await a clear-cut divergence between factional ambitions and the constitutional distribution of power.

FROM MOBILIZATION TO PARTICIPATION

In rethinking the role of the masses in Chinese politics, the post-Mao leadership found itself faced with three questions: what priority should mass political involvement have, how should it be organized, and toward which objectives should it be directed? The dominant tendencies since 1976 have been in the direction of declining priority for mass participation in general, a shift from concerted mobilizational efforts toward more routinized arrangements, relying by default on voluntarism. There has been a parallel shift from economic or cultural transformation of a maximally inclusive constituency to the indirect representation of publics in political activities functional to their specific interests. Mass involvement in politics has gone through three distinguishable phases: the Campaign to Criticize the Gang of Four in 1976–79, the Democracy Wall movement in 1978–81, and the implementation of liberalized electoral procedures in 1980–82.

The Campaign to Criticize the Gang of Four

The anti-Gang campaign was initiated shortly after Hua's accession to the chairmanship and lasted until it was declared "essentially completed" at the Third Plenum in December 1978.[45] Hua Guofeng assigned fairly low priority to the campaign, both because criticism of the Gang raised the delicate question of their relationship to Hua's patron, Mao, and because Hua stood in an opportune position to inherit the orphaned radical constituency. "All slanders and charges levelled at anyone by the 'Gang of Four' should be repudiated and cancelled," as he put it in September 1977. "On the other hand, our comrades, and especially those who have been screened, must take a correct [i.e., basically positive]

45. The only analysis of the campaign I have found is an unpublished paper by Constance Squires Meany, "Political Conflict in China: 'Reversal of Verdicts' and the Campaign to Suppress the 'Gang of Four's Bourgeois Factional Setup,' 1977–1978," Berkeley, Center for Chinese Studies, 1980.

attitude toward the Great Proletarian Cultural Revolution, toward the masses and toward themselves."[46] Upon being restored to his previous positions in July 1977, Deng reportedly requested and was granted leadership of the campaign, giving it higher priority—and a more vindictive thrust.

As a result of the decoupling of mobilization from organizational coordination in the last years of the Cultural Revolution decade (see chapter 7 above), mobilization had grown increasingly spontaneous and disruptive. Deng's organization of the movement was thus rather tight, hearkening back to pre-Cultural Revolution techniques: "work teams" were dispatched from higher levels to lead the struggle in local units, an ad hoc campaign committee was established, and mass criticism of human "targets" was arranged by cadres with punishment for the recalcitrant. The objectives of mobilization were to motivate neither economic production nor economic/cultural transformation, but (1) to restore order, and (2) to settle factional scores.

The campaign literature suggested that mass mobilization as practiced during the ten years of upheaval had become a pretext for widespread corruption, looting, vandalism, and other forms of criminal activity. As a major article on the movement put it in the spring of 1978:

> [The] industry, communications and other fronts have launched step by step and on a large scale a movement to deal blows at both the sabotage activities of class enemies and at the frenzied assaults of capitalist forces, and have combined this movement with the great struggle to expose and criticize the "Gang of Four." . . . The Gang of Four's scheme to usurp Party and state power had a close bearing on the sabotage activities of class enemies and capitalist forces. A large number of persons of the bourgeois factional setups were "two-faced tigers." They were at once the background elements of bourgeois factional setups and the bad elements engaged in corruption, theft and speculation.[47]

Deng's movement, by conflating this dragnet against "smash-and-grabbers" with the criticism of the Four, magnified the crimes of the latter even as it permitted the acts of the former to be punished under ideological sanction. Such a condensation of evils gave impetus to the crackdown: Thus newspapers teemed with reports of executions during the first eighteen months of the campaign.[48]

46. Hua, "Political Report to the Eleventh Congress," p. 56.
47. "It Is Necessary to Unfold the 'Two Blows' Movement on a Large Scale," *RR*, April 7, 1978, p. 1; as trans. in *FBIS*, April 20, 1978, p. E6; as quoted in Meany, "Political Conflict."
48. Nigel Wade reported that executions in Kunming (Yunnan) and Beijing in the first nine months of 1977 alone ran into the thousands. *Sunday Telegraph*, London, October 30, 1977, p. 1; see also Georges Biannic, AFP, Hong Kong, October 29, 1977, as trans. in *FBIS*, October 29, 1977, pp. E15–E16.

It also permitted Deng to utilize the campaign for factional gains. Both the purge of upwardly mobile cultural radicals and the rehabilitation of their erstwhile victims served Deng's political interests, and he pressed the campaign in order to legitimate such personnel shifts in the teeth of Hua's evident discomfiture. While vulnerable to Deng's mobilization of the anti-Cultural Revolution right, Hua's political position precluded any defensive countermobilization: he could hardly appeal to the right while claiming the aegis of Mao's Thought, and yet his arrest of the Four had placed radical support beyond his grasp. Beyond intimidating such residual "Maoists" and facilitating the wholesale rehabilitation of veteran cadres, however, Deng did not press for a sweeping purge of radicals from the middle and lower bureaucracy at this time, for prospective targets were so numerous that such a purge would surely have split the Party.[49]

Democracy Wall

The so-called Democracy Wall movement arose in China's leading urban centers in the fall of 1978 as a direct outgrowth of the attempt by victims of the Tiananmen Incident to gain official rehabilitation. The success of that attempt immediately triggered a mushrooming of analogous appeals by victims of various other radical policies. Although participants were thus defined by opposition to the Cultural Revolution and articulated liberal rather than radical values, their participatory mode was "leftist in form": it consisted of a spontaneously assembled ideological constituency with informal links to a sympathetic elite patron, expressing itself through big-character posters, unofficial tabloids, and mass demonstrations.

There is little question that Deng Xiaoping was the foremost "backstage backer" of the Democracy activists' self-emancipatory activities through the fall of 1978. He expressed himself clearly in this regard in interviews with a number of foreign visitors, allowing his comments to be

49. This is an inference based on the lack of evidence of any extensive purge. Thus when the Party rectification campaign was launched at the Second Plenum of the Twelfth CC in October 1983, the chief targets were still defined as the "three types of person" (san zhong ren): those "who rose to prominence by following the counterrevolutionary cliques of Lin Biao and Jiang Qing in 'rebellion,'" those who are seriously factionalist in their ideas, and those who indulged in beating, smashing and looting"—each of whom had a clear line of descent from the Cultural Revolution. Statistics indicated that of the 40 million members in the Party at this time (including ca. 9 million cadres), about 18 million had been recruited before the Cultural Revolution, while 4 million had been recruited in the post-Mao period, leaving 18 million who had been admitted during the Cultural Revolution decade. "The Decision of the CC of the Communist Party of China on Party Consolidation" (adopted by the Second Plenary Session of the Twelfth Party CC, October 11, 1983), BR 26:42 (October 17, 1983): II. Clearly, Cultural Revolution recruits at the middle and lower bureaucratic echelons had not yet suffered serious attrition, despite the elimination of their patrons at the higher levels.

232 ★ BEYOND CONTINUOUS REVOLUTION

leaked to the masses. "We have no right to deny this or to criticize the masses for making use of democracy," he said on one such occasion. "If the masses feel some anger, let them express it."[50] In view of Deng's status as one of the leading victims of the Cultural Revolution his patronage seems somewhat surprising, inviting suspicions of Machiavellianism. In fact this liaison of strange bedfellows seems to have been based on an opportunistic coincidence of tactical objectives—both sides wanted a reversal of the Tiananmen verdict—rather than on any considered convergence upon a long-term strategy for mass participation. Upon achievement of this tactical objective,[51] the confluence of interests quickly dissolved.

Deng Xiaoping seems to have expected the mass movement to recede following his victory at the Third Plenum, granting time to consolidate his gains. The masses, on the other hand, seizing upon these verdict reversals as a quasi-judicial precedent, hastened to crowd through the window of opportunity before it closed. The result was a chain migration of petitioners from the countryside to the capital cities (Beijing, Ji'nan, Hefei), where they staged sit-ins in government offices, blocked street traffic, damaged public property, and congested the railroads. Aggrieved dissidents like Fu Yuehua led bands of demobilized soldiers, rusticated urban youth, poor peasants, and other disprivileged marginal groups in urban protest marches, raising the specter of a Solidarity-like alliance between intellectuals and proletariat. Big-character posters proliferated in urban centers, most consisting of individual petitions for redress of grievances irresolvable at the unit level.

Whereas the masses were primarily concerned with the application of the new verdicts to their individual cases, the movement quickly spawned intellectual dissidents who sought to elaborate and generalize these principles, to push the movement's logic as far as it would go. As in the Cultural Revolution, big-character posters led to the proliferation of

50. From an interview with Ryosaku Sasaki, chairman of the Japanese Socialist Party, as quoted in *NYT*, November 26, 1978. "Wall posters are guaranteed by the Constitution," Deng pointed out, also noting that "my talk to you today is based on a decision of the CC." "Foreigners make a fuss about the posters. But we have no intention of suppressing them or denying the right of the masses to express their views by pasting up wall posters." In another interview, with American columnist Robert Novak, later relayed to crowds at Tiananmen by John Fraser, he said the posters were a "good thing," though some statements were not correct. See Fraser, *The Chinese: Portrait of a People* (New York: Summit Books, 1980).

51. On November 16, 1978, the Beijing Municipal Party Committee reversed verdicts on the Tiananmen Incident; on November 21–22 *RR* published a comprehensive rationalization, "The Truth about the Tiananmen Incident." See Jian Yan, "Tiananmen shijian de an fandingle!" [Reversal of the case of the Tiananmen Incident], *DX*, no. 1 (October 1978): 30–33.

unofficial "people's publications" (*minkan*), expanding their authors' range (to include the international wire-service public and beam back to a domestic audience over the Voice of America, thanks to foreign correspondents) and facilitating more intensive analysis of issues. Intellectual liberation remained the movement's central leitmotif, now ramifying into other functional realms. Science was idealized as an antidote to the masses' susceptibility to charismatic leadership, in a conception that emphasized an inductive, trial-and-error methodology congenial to emerging notions of a free market of ideas.[52] In economics, a case was made not only for expanded free markets, but for the dissolution of agricultural communes and state enterprises, based on the argument that "whole people's ownership" did not involve the assumption of popular control so much as "étatization"; collectives accordingly offered greater ambit for the realization of socialism.[53] The legal system was scrutinized, some attention being given for the first time to the delicate question of why laws were made and then not enforced.[54] Even the prison system received some attention for the first time.[55] There were radical critiques of socialist bureaucracy.[56] There was a widespread "blooming" of poetry, short stories, and other literary "flowers," including the most inventive experiments and theoretical formulations since the early 1960s. There was at this juncture a tacit alliance between democracy activists and elite members of the "practice faction,"[57] and many of the ideas at the cutting edge of Deng's reform program may be traced to the democracy movement.

Yet, notwithstanding their affinity for many aspects of Western pluralism, the democracy activists still exhibited a "breakthrough" style of

---

52. See Hu Ping, "On Freedom of Speech," as reprinted under the title, "Selections from the Political Views of China's New Generation of Politicians," *QN*, no. 3 (March 1, 1981): 68–82; no. 4 (April 1981): 57–75, and no. 6 (June 1981): 67–76.

53. Commentator, "On Collective Ownership and Its Future," *Siwu Luntan* [April fifth forum], no. 12 (September 9, 1979): 1–8; trans. in *JPRS*, no. 74909 (January 11, 1980): 22–35.

54. Qiu Mu, "Why Laws Are Made but Difficult to Enforce," *Tansuo* [Exploration], September 9, 1979, pp. 9–14.

55. Liu Qing, "Prison Memoirs," ed. Stanley Rosen and James D. Seymour, *Chinese Sociology and Anthropology* 15, nos. 1–2 (Fall-Winter 1982/3), 181 pp.

56. E.g., Lu Min, "Gradually Abolish the Bureaucratic System and Establish the Democratic System Modeled after the Paris Commune," *Beijing zhi Chun* [Beijing spring], no. 1 (January 9, 1979): 17–21; and no. 2 (January 27, 1979): 43–45. See also Lu Min, "Do Away with the Power of Administrative Leadership of Basic Level Party Organization in Factories, Mines, and Other Enterprises," ibid., no. 2 (1979), pp. 17–21.

57. Thus the people's publication *Beijing Spring* was able to publish one issue in the regular press, and in the middle of 1979 the Beijing People's Press even prepared a reprint of important articles from various unofficial publications. Three members of the CYL Central Committee even participated in editing *Beijing Spring*. Opletal, *Die Informationspolitik der Volksrepublik China*, p. 185.

mobilization that polemically exaggerated the defects of the target as well as the relief its destruction would bring, generating a powerful, consuming momentum bound to frighten former targets of mass criticism—especially as the focus shifted from past iniquities to their structural residues in the present. Cadres also found the activists' tendency to generalize an abstract principle to every functional realm—another aftereffect of the Cultural Revolution polemical style—quite unnerving. As the most outspoken advocate of "taking the lid off," Deng bore the brunt of inner-Party recriminations.[58] Unlike Mao, however, he responded to criticism by reversing course, depriving his adversaries of this issue while continuing to pursue reform in less problematic areas.[59] In his public statements on the question he backed away from his previous stand that democracy was prerequisite to modernization toward an assertion that modernization was prerequisite to democracy—a position redolent of Sun Yat-sen's "tutelage."[60] Democracy activists were no longer the Cultural Revolution's victims but its reincarnation. Between October and November 1979 the two most prominent activists in the capital, Wei Jingsheng and Fu Yuehua, were tried and convicted, and (after transcripts of Wei's "public" trial had been posted and circulated there), Xidan Wall was closed. Annoyed by dissidents' tendency to appeal to "constitutional rights," the authorities proceeded to rewrite the Constitution: the "four big freedoms" were rescinded at the Third Session of the Fifth NPC, and henceforth movement activists were invariably referred to as "illegal organizations" and "illegal publications."[61] Early in 1981 the CC transmitted a series of documents, beginning with CD no. 2 and

---

58. Yielding reluctantly on substance, Deng complained (in a speech made March 16, 1979) about the timing of the criticisms. "I never concealed my opinions. But in the past ten years a bad habit has developed in the Party. . . . It is that, at the start, no one opposes a resolution. But as soon as something goes wrong, no matter how small, they either drop a stone on someone who has fallen into a well or stick a knife in your back, eager to find a scapegoat." *NYT*, May 26, 1979, quoting Nationalist intelligence sources.

59. At a March 1979 expanded Politburo meeting he introduced his own counterpart of the "two whatevers" to define the limits of dissent, the "four fundamental principles" (*si xiang jiben yuanze*): Uphold the socialist road, uphold the dictatorship of the proletariat, uphold the leadership of the Chinese Communist Party, and uphold Marxism-Leninism and Mao Zedong Thought (thus sometimes dubbed the "four upholds"). "Summary of Deng Xiaoping's March 1979 Speech at a Discussion of Theoretical Issues," *Guang Jiao Jing* (Hong Kong), no. 85 (November 16, 1979): 4–10.

60. "We can never achieve the Four Modernizations without a political situation of stability and unity, because people cannot embark on modernization without peace of mind. Therefore, we are opposed to those people and things which create disturbances. Take, for example, the method of allowing the existence of the 'Xidan Wall.'" Quoted in Bai Renqiong, "Some Movements in the Political Situation of the PRC," *DX*, no. 16 (January 16, 1980): 4–6.

61. E.g., see the commentator article in *Jiefang Ribao* (Shanghai), January 10, 1981.

culminating in CD no. 9, which instructed all departments concerned to interdict "two illegal" activities.[62] Throughout the spring of 1981, the police made one arrest after another, dealing a final crushing blow to this singular amalgam of revolutionary tactics and democratic objectives.[63]

Electoral Reform

Whether in order to co-opt the democracy issue or as a token of the sincerity of his professions of support for greater popular input, Deng proffered expanded opportunities for participation through formal electoral mechanisms even as he proceeded to eliminate intra-Party opposition and crush the democracy movement. "The Electoral Law of the PRC for the NPC and Local People's Congresses at All Levels" was one of seven major laws passed on July 1, 1979, by the Second Session of the Fifth NPC, to take effect on January 1, 1980. It departed from the previous (1953) electoral law in at least three respects: a policy of more candidates than positions (*cha e xuanju zhi*) was adopted, delegates to county people's congresses were subject to direct election (previously only local officials up to the commune had been directly elected), and the nominating process was opened for the first time to (non-Party) mass participation, allowing any organization or individual with three seconds to submit candidates for the initial list (though they would not necessarily be placed on the final list).[64]

The first test of the new law came during the nationwide county-level elections that were conducted on a staggered timetable through the summer and fall of 1980, and it soon became apparent that despite the liberalization of procedure, any attempt to use the electoral process to manifest dissent or even to aggregate popular demands was fraught with risk. In most of the nation's nearly three thousand counties elections

62. Central Document no. 9 reportedly included provision for arrest of activists, exposure of those supplying or otherwise supporting them, and eviction of cadres involved from the Party. Ge Zhili, "People's Publications under 'Central Document no. 9,'" *ZM*, no. 5 (May 1, 1981): 50, 90; also Liang Mingjun, "The Chinese Communist CC's Documents no. 4, 7, and 9," *Dangdai* [Contemporary monthly] (Hong Kong), no. 8 (April 15, 1981): 43.
63. Xu Wenli and Yang Jing, members of *Siwu Luntan*, were arrested by public security personnel in their Beijing homes. Also arrested at his home was Sun Feng, editor of *Hailang Hua* [Sea waves], a private publication in Qingdao, Shandong. Wang Xizhe, chief writer of the Li Yizhe trio, was arrested in his factory on April 10. Fu Shenqi of Shanghai and He Qiu, editor of *People's Road* in Guangzhou, were arrested in Beijing. Zhong Yueqiu, responsible person of *People's Voice* (Shaoguan), was arrested in that city. See Miao Xiao, "The Current Situation of the Beijing People's Publications," *ZM*, no. 28 (February 1980): 44–45.
64. See Li Zaizao and Chen Jinluo, "The Fundamental Spirit of Electoral Law and the Significance of Direct Elections of People's Assemblies at the County Level," *Faxue Yanjiu*, no. 2 (1980): 12–15; and Zhang Qingfu, "China's Electoral System," *Faxue Yanjiu*, no. 6 (1980): 42–46.

proceeded smoothly, the vast majority of the nation's 540 million voters apparently voting in accord with the wishes of the leadership.[65] A number of well-publicized incidents revealed, however, both that local constituencies were sometimes prepared to use the new game rules to articulate local interests in defiance of Party guidance, and that local authorities were apt to bend the rules if necessary to ensure continued dominance. The position of the center toward these developments was ambivalent; sometimes it denounced illegal attempts by local authorities to revise unfavorable electoral outcomes, but in other cases it reproved the sponsors of unofficial candidates for allowing campaigns to degenerate into anarchy.[66] In the Haidian electoral district containing Beijing University, for example, 8,000 students nominated no fewer than 29 candidates for the two vacant seats to the district people's assembly; candidate support committees were organized, surveys were conducted, wall newspapers appeared, and a veritable election campaign was staged, replete with unrealistic campaign promises. In an electoral district containing 6,084 voters, public discussion meetings allegedly involving 20,000 people were convened in the halls, canteens, and classrooms.[67] One of the successful candidates, a Beijing University graduate student (in philosophy) named Hu Ping, was met by CC charges of having precipitated a "Cultural Revolution–style movement" when he tried to assume his seat in the Haidian People's Assembly. As of the spring of 1982, he was still living in a dormitory on campus "waiting for placement." In Changsha, students at Hunan Teachers' College succeeded in nominating one Liang Heng as a non-Party candidate only after staging a hunger strike, "rioting," and sending a protest delegation to Beijing. Liang's campaign was

65. Brantly Womack, "The 1980 County-level Elections in China: Experiment in Democratic Modernization," *AS* 22, no. 3 (March 1982): 261–78. See also Womack, "Modernization and Democratic Reform in China," *Journal of Asian Studies* 43, 3 (May 1984): 417–41; and Andrew J. Nathan, *Chinese Democracy* (New York: Knopf, 1985).

66. Press reports indicated that it would be wrong for leading cadres to blame the voters for electing the wrong representatives or arbitrarily to invalidate the electoral results, but if proper preparations were made doing so should not be necessary. If incumbents do not get placed on the candidate list they should do public self-criticism and ingratiate themselves with their constituency. Zhang Zeng, "Adopt a Correct View toward Failing to Get Elected," *Nanfang Ribao*, December 17, 1980, p. 3; Liu Xin, "Analysis of 'An Old Honest Fellow!'" ibid., December 20, 1980; Gen Niu, "In a Production Team Election, All Party Member Candidates Are Defeated," *Dong Xi Fang* [East and West] (Hong Kong), no. 24 (December 10, 1980): 18–20.

67. Su Rong, "The Strange Record of Beijing's Cold Spring," *ZM*, no. 5 (May 1, 1981): 10–12; "Selections from the Political Views of China's New Generation of Politicians," *QN*, no. 3 (March 1, 1981): 68–82; Gong Bo, "Summary of the Student Election Campaign at Beijing University" (in "Letters from Readers" column), *ZM*, no. 42 (April 1, 1981): 87–90; Wei Ming, "Zhongguo xin yi dai de zhengzhijia" [China's new generation of politicians], *QN*, no. 2 (February 1981): 15–20.

ultimately unsuccessful, and Tao Sen, the central figure in the student protest, was subsequently arrested.[68]

In a speech on December 25, 1980, Deng Xiaoping complained bitterly about those who exploited the elections to make speeches attacking the Party leadership and the socialist system.[69] In early 1981 the official press began to fulminate against "ultra-democracy" and "dissidence," eventually leading to a general Party drive against "bourgeois liberalization." In a report published in September 1981 summarizing the electoral experience over the previous year and a half, Cheng Zihua, minister of civil administration and chairman of the National County Election Office, complained that a "tiny minority of people" had spread anarchy, conducted secret "linkups," expressed "outrageous and inflammatory views," and otherwise contravened the four basic principles. Cheng put forth a series of proposals for tightening up the Election Law that would transfer final power to determine lists of formal candidates to a new body not specified in the 1979 law, an "Electoral District Leadership Group." Such changes would presumably have the effect of precluding genuinely independent candidates from participating in the electoral process.[70] Moreover, the right to promulgate campaign propaganda was taken from the candidate and reposited in the election committee. The fact that a second round of national elections for representatives to county assemblies was held in April–May 1984 with minimal publicity tends to confirm apprehensions that the process has been eviscerated.

In sum, the mobilizational approach to mass involvement suffered a surprisingly swift and unsung demise, but transition to a participatory style still hangs in abeyance. In previous chapters we have contended that mobilization functioned most satisfactorily when the masses were motivated by an optimum mix of normative leadership and material incentives, though it could also be provisionally sustained by a plausible deferment of the latter. This mix was obtained only during the first decade of CPC rule. Completion of socialization of the means of production deprived the leadership of its cheapest source of material incentives, and the attempt to replenish these through hypergrowth failed. Mobiliza-

---

68. Robin Munro, "The Chinese Democracy Movement, 1978–1982," unpub. paper, 1983.

69. On the case of Liang Heng, see Zong Lei, "Hunan xuesheng zheng minzhu fan guanliao de xingdong" [Hunan student movement for democracy against bureaucratism], *QN*, December 12, 1980, pp. 19–20.

The CC also dispatched a directive forbidding newspapers and journals from publishing Hu Ping's writings. Because it published Hu's article on freedom of the press, *Qingnian Wengao* [Youth draft articles], published internally by the Chinese Academy of Social Science, came under criticism. Su Rong, "The Strange Record," pp. 10–12; "Selections from Political Views," pp. 68–82.

70. Munro, "Chinese Democracy Movement," pp. 18–19.

tion revived in the Cultural Revolution by dint of fresh normative/ political appeals, but when these extravagant promises could not be kept the rhetoric lost credence; in any case, the leadership found it to be dangerous and unpredictable to mobilize the masses with so little control over their movement. Mobilizational efficacy declined steadily during the late Cultural Revolution, as elites sought in various ways to control and direct the movement to their own ends, without offering to replenish the fund of material incentives or providing a credible, fresh, or broadly appealing normative vision. In the post–Cultural Revolution period, additional material incentives became available through the reallocation of funds from investment to consumption, but these incentives were linked to production rather than mobilization, as modernization usurped priority. The democracy activists offered a compelling normative vision, which was, however, deemed intolerably threatening by bureaucratic elites. Only mobilization against negative targets remained viable, and it proved impossible to ensure that the demands and grievances thereby evoked would be delivered to the authoritatively stipulated address (scapegoat) without damaging spillover (of which more later).

The transition to a participatory mode has heretofore been inhibited by two deeply ingrained propensities. On the one hand, bureaucratic elites seem no less paralyzed by "fear" than when Mao lambasted this "mental encumbrance" in days of yore, tending to panic at the first sign of disagreement. Democracy Wall aroused anxiety, so it was replaced by elections, which could be more easily controlled; but cadres also felt uneasy at the tendency for electoral campaigns to get out of hand. From the elite perspective it remains difficult to open any forum to mass participation (and thereby engender the support and feedback still deemed necessary) without running unacceptable risks of losing control, and there is a consequent tendency to "Procrusteanize" participation. On the other hand, the masses continue to exhibit a "breakthrough" mentality, giving rise to two tendencies: a flagrantly hyperbolic rhetoric, which sharpens rather than conciliates differences; and the propensity to treat every concession as an opening for additional demands, so that the slightest "spark" of political entitlement can easily start a "prairie fire" of rising and eventually unfulfillable expectations. It is still too early to tell whether some form of meaningful mass participation will survive the Scylla of mass anarchy and the Charybdis of an empty formalism.

THE CONQUEST OF STRUCTURE

The two opposition structures against which the continuing revolution had been mobilized consisted of the residual and the emergent structures.

The former consisted of class contradictions, which had survived socialization of the means of production on which they were based. The latter consisted of emergent contradictions, deriving from the structural features of socialist society. The lesson of ten years of Cultural Revolution was ambiguous: from the fact that the uprising had occurred, one could infer that no rigid or impermeable structures should be constructed, for these had, after all, contributed to its explosive cathartic force. Those most committed to political reform touted this inference. From the fact that it had failed, on the other hand, one could draw the inference that frames should be respected and preserved, or at least never simply smashed—an interpretation to which the more conservative forces were partial. Despite a tendency to vacillate between uncritical restoration of pre–Cultural Revolution structures and terminal iconoclasm, the overall direction of movement seems to have been toward a synthesis: structure is an essential facet of social life, but it must be sufficiently flexible and permeable to permit innovation, communication, change.

The dominant current during the Hua Guofeng interregnum was one of indiscriminate restoration of all structures, probably due as much to the public mood at the time as to Hua's theoretical eclecticism. Thus Hua endorsed the residual conceptualization of class and class struggle (however tepidly), and also moved to rebuild the state apparatus and otherwise reaffirm emergent structures.

Deng Xiaoping, on the other hand, renounced residual structures outright, thereby lifting that historical burden from his bureaucratic-intellectual constituency, while adopting a meliorist stance toward emergent structures. The revolution had succeeded, he implied, in destroying the original counterrevolutionary opposition, but it was unsuited for the rectification of emergent contradictions. Emergent structures should be qualifiedly affirmed rather than smashed, their objectionable features rectified gradually through proper channels.

Eliminating the Residual Structure

First to be emancipated were overseas Chinese, many of whom were of bourgeois background or at least had kinship ties with capitalists, but also had access to overseas remittances, high educational attainment, and useful managerial/technical talents. In January 1978, the regime promised to cease all discrimination, return confiscated houses, and reopen the special shops for overseas Chinese to service their "special needs." The intellectuals were next in line for rehabilitation: Deng Xiaoping, in his March 1978 speech to the National Science Conference, was first to include this category, previously grouped among the petty bourgeoisie, within the proletariat: "Generally speaking the overwhelming majority of them are part of the proletariat. The difference between them and the manual workers lies only in a different role in the division of labor."[71] In early 1978 Deng also instructed the Party to stop using the label of "rightist," a political label equivalent to bad class categorization. In order to implement this instruction, the Organization, Propaganda, and United Front Departments of the CC and the Public Security and Civil Affairs Ministries jointly convened a meeting from June 16–22, 1978, in Shandong. After a heated debate between Deng's supporters and representatives of the "whatever" group, the meeting approved "Concrete Measures to Implement Thoroughly the Decision to Remove All Hats of the Rightists."

Responsibility for checking the correctness of the original label fell on the unit that had made the decision to apply it, regardless of whether the person in question was still in the unit. The Party committee in each unit typically organized one or several special investigation teams to look into the case, after which an internal Party meeting would be convened to write up the organizational conclusion and enter it into the person's dossier. This conclusion might include such statements as "no rightist remark was found," or "should not be considered a rightist." The conclusion would then be shown to the person, and if he or she agreed, forwarded to the next higher level for approval. Once approved, the unit would issue a certificate correcting or removing the rightist designation, sending one copy to units where the person's spouse or children worked as well (to relieve the latter of the onus of "connection" to a rightist). Then the person would be eligible for job reassignment and restoration of salary. Rehabilitated rightists were not automatically entitled to return to their previous positions—their new assignments were to be based on ability, physical condition, and unit needs—but the original salary scale was usually restored in any case. The process of removing the rightists' "hats" was successfully completed by November 1978.[72]

Immediately following completion of the rehabilitation of rightists, the regime proceeded to remove the designations of "four-category elements" (i.e., landlord, rich peasant, counterrevolutionary, and bad element).[73] Removal of these designations was not categorical, for "extremely small numbers of those who are stubbornly upholding the coun-

71. Deng, "Speech to the National Conference on Science and Technology," PR 21, no. 12 (March 24, 1978): 11.

72. See Hong Yung Lee, "Changing Patterns."

73. RR announced in an editorial on January 29, 1979, that former landlords and rich peasants would have "citizen's rights" restored, and restoration of rights was formally confirmed by the CC on June 28. It was also announced that China's "national bourgeoisie" would get back the property, titles, and money that had been seized during the Cultural Revolution—with interest. NYT, January 29, 1979.

terrevolutionary standpoints and those who are not yet properly re-molded" must continue to carry the labels. It is estimated that only 1 to 2 percent of former four-category elements failed to have their "hats" removed.[74] Rehabilitation was formalized in the 1982 State Constitution, Article 33 of which guarantees equality of all Chinese citizens before the law. The label of "class enemy" is henceforth to be limited to five fairly restrictive categories.[75] Once the government rescinded its sanctions against the old bad classes, social discrimination quickly evaporated. Class origins no longer count even in the arrangement of marriages; more important is the wealth and income potential of the prospective groom's family.[76]

An equally important aspect of the emancipation of the residual structure has been the leadership's renunciation of its right to lead criticism campaigns against it. Thus at the Third Plenum, the CC announced that turbulent class struggle on a large scale had been "basically concluded." Although "class struggle will continue to exist, within certain limits, for a long time to come," it is no longer held to be the "principal" form of contradiction in socialist society.[77] With certain qualifications, the mass movement has been disavowed.

The policy toward emergent contradictions has been two-tiered. With regard to *political elites*, the most notorious emergent structure, the "Party persons in authority taking the capitalist road," a concept imply-ing the possibility of the political procreation of class, has been unequivo-cally repudiated. As Deng put it in March 1979: "We do not admit that

74. *Zhongguo Qingnian Bao*, September 8, 1979. Another source estimated that only about fifty thousand people still carried the labels of landlords and rich peasants. *BR*, January 21, 1980, pp. 14–20; as quoted in Hong Yung Lee, "Changing Patterns."

75. They are (1) counterrevolutionaries and enemy agents; (2) remnant elements of the Lin Biao and Jiang Qing cliques; (3) criminals who have gravely upset the socialist order; (4) new exploiters; and (5) old exploiters. They will be handled according to the law. *JFJB* commentator, "Scientifically Understand and Handle Class Struggle in China," *BR*, no. 49 (December 6, 1982): 18.

76. Chan, Madsen, and Unger, *Chen Village*, p. 283. Within two years one production team (in rural Guangdong) had elected a former rich peasant to serve as team leader, while another team elected the son of the ex-guerrilla "bad element." Jonathan Unger, "The Class System in Rural China: A Case Study," in James L. Watson, *Class and Social Stratification in Post-Revolutionary China* (Cambridge: Cambridge University Press, 1984), pp. 121–42.

77. Thus whereas the concept continues to be used to legitimate police suppression of criminality and the enforcement of political consensus, its relationship to economic stratifi-cation has grown increasingly obscure. There has even been a tendency to assert that class is now simply an economic category with no necessary political significance. See Wang Zhenping, "Is Class Merely an Economic Category?" *RR*, January 4, 1980, p. 5 (in which Wang concludes that it is); also Zhao De, "Should the Method of Class Analysis Continue to Be Upheld?" Xinhua Ribao (Nanjing), April 21, 1981, p. 3; *China Record*, no. 197 (June 17, 1981): 20–23.

there is a bourgeois class in the Party. We also do not admit that under a socialist system after the effective elimination of the exploiting class as well as the conditions making exploitation possible, a bourgeois class or any other exploiting class can be produced."[78] The somewhat weaker concept of "line struggle" to refer to leadership disputes within the Party has not been disavowed in principle, but it has been generally avoided in practice, as noted above.

As for the *masses*, the approach has been more circumspect. The dominant effort in the post-1978 period has been to "build down" the existing sturcture, introducing various reforms to make it more flexible and permeable. A second and conceptually more ambitious approach has been to shift from the exclusive reliance on socio-political structures to the "rule of law"; this approach offers even greater potential for flexibility and permeability.

Building Down Emergent Structure

Efforts to reform emergent structure may conveniently be grouped into three categories: (1) those seeking to relax constraints on horizontal mobility; (2) those making structure more permeable through the proliferation of communications; and (3) those facilitating greater vertical mobility via bureaucratic reorganization.

1. One of the major constraints on horizontal mobility has been the system of central labor allocation to jobs followed by lifetime employment in the unit to which one has been assigned. As already noted in chapter 3, this system tends to result in the ghettoization of everyone, fostering petty tyranny by local cadres over subordinates who have neither voice nor exit, and sometimes forcing protracted marital separation. It was already proving increasingly difficult for the authorities to enforce labor allocation in the post-Mao interregnum, as indicated for example by cases of university graduates refusing to accept their (usually rural) job placements—a previously unheard of phenomenon that authorities blamed on the influence of "Existentialism." A symptom of these difficulties was the unprecedented announcement in early 1979 that 20 million urban residents, just over 20 percent of the urban work force, were unemployed—a figure that would rise to 26 million by early 1981.[79] This level of unemployment would be inconceivable in a planned labor

---

78. See Jie Wen's article in *HQ*, no. 20, 1981, p. 27; see also Lin Boye and Shen Che, "Ping suowei fandui guanliao zhuyizhe jieji" [Criticizing the so-called overthrow of the bureaucratic class], *HQ*, no. 5, 1981, pp. 12–18; as quoted in Tsou, "Reflections."

79. Nicholas R. Lardy, *China's Economic Readjustment: Recovery or Paralysis?* (New York: China Council of the Asia Society, March 1980); see also Gorden White, "Urban Employment and Labor Allocation Policies," in G. White et al., eds., *Revolutionary Socialist Development in the Third World* (Sussex, England: Harvester Press, 1983), pp. 257–87.

allocation system without assuming massive noncompliance. Part of the problem is that the most ambitious instance of ideologically inspired labor allocation, the "up to the mountains and down to the countryside" (*shangshan xiaxiang*) campaign, had been "basically concluded"[80] by 1979 without adequate alternative facilities to absorb surplus urban labor. The more fundamental difficulty (to which rustication itself was originally thought to be the solution) is the tendency (hardly unique to China) for rural inhabitants to migrate to the cities faster than housing or jobs can be found to accommodate them. This problem has been so serious even under state labor allocation that Shanghai shut its doors to further in-migration in 1973, Beijing in 1982.

Two reforms have been proposed and, to some extent, implemented, which intend to facilitate greater "personnel mobility" (*rencai liudong*). The first is the creation of a collective and private enterprise sector relatively independent from the state labor allocation system, in which there would be much greater individual autonomy in the allocation of employment. In November 1981 the Party-government authorities issued a joint directive urging unemployed Chinese to create their own jobs, either in collective enterprises or in the private sector. The directive also made clear that young people would no longer be guaranteed job tenure in a state enterprise, a practice nicknamed the "iron rice bowl." Hao Haifeng, chairman of the Individual Enterprises Department of the State Industrial and Commercial Administration, claimed at a news conference in March 1984 that the number of self-employed Chinese had risen from one hundred forty thousand in 1978 to more than 7.5 million in 1983.[81] It was projected that of the 6 million who enter the urban labor force each year, perhaps a quarter will have to find jobs on their own, and most will be hired on a competitive basis rather than through state assignment. According to statistics, nearly four-fifths of the restaurants, retail stores, and service shops set up since 1978 have been privately owned; such businessmen are permitted to hire up to seven apprentices and helpers, not including family members. New labor contracts will also provide, for the first time, for dismissals and layoffs.[82] In the countryside, even greater latitude has been granted for job-related mobility, including short-term migration.

The second attempt at reform would involve the "destatification" of the system of labor allocation, both for initial placement and subsequent mobility. Labor bureaus would hand over part of their functions to local

---

80. According to an informant from the Economics Institute of the Chinese Academy of Social Sciences, in private conversation, Berkeley, Calif., 1981.

81. Christopher Wren, *NYT*, September 15, 1984.

82. Wren, September 15; also Michael Parks, in *The Los Angeles Times*, April 25, 1983, part 4, pp. 1–2.

non-state agencies; for instance, collectively owned "labor service companies," under the supervision of street committees, schools, or offices, might arrange placements in the collective and private sectors. The enterprises themselves would be permitted to advertise for new workers or even to hire labor away from other units, by offering higher wages; they should also have the right to fire, thereby curtailing overstaffing and raising productivity.[83]

Whereas success in the area of employment creation has been impressive, innovations in the system of labor allocation have hitherto been less successful. To attempt to introduce greater flexibility into the labor allocation system at a time when high unemployment precipitated fear of dismissal and other insecurities among workers proved ill advised. Thus the state labor bureaus have heretofore continued to monopolize the allocation of labor to state enterprises, sometimes even forcing enterprises to accept labor quotas above their own estimated labor requirements in order to help alleviate unemployment. The proposed power of dismissal has remained a dead letter, with the exception of joint venture companies in the Special Economic Zones.

The foreseeable outlook is for a dual structure of lateral occupational mobility, in two senses: (1) within the state sector, a differential between entrenched, "fixed" workers on the one hand (entitled to all welfare benefits), and short-term contract workers on the other, the latter providing management with some flexibility in the disposition of labor; (2) another differential between the state sector on the one hand and the collective and private sectors on the other. In each case, the differential involves a trade-off between mobility and security, implying that progress toward a free labor market will be contingent upon continuing assurance of reasonably favorable prospects for venture entrepreneurialism and limited employment opportunities within the state sector (meaning low opportunity costs in terms of job security).

Whereas employment restrictions constitute the most egregious deterrent to lateral mobility, lesser barriers have also been subjected to piecemeal reform. Amid the general cultural liberalization there has been somewhat greater courtship mobility, including the opening of "marriage introduction institutes" in the larger cities (since 1980) to introduce eligible mates. Most ration coupons have been dispensed with, given the greater emphasis on light industry and increased availability of consumer goods, with even some discussion (so far inconclusive) of "canceling the rice coupon" (*chuxiao liangpiao*); similarly, there has been a move to eliminate the congeries of identity cards most Chinese citizens must carry

---

83. The rights of fired workers would be protected by involving enterprise workers' organizations, trade unions, and workers' congresses in the decision to fire. Formal approval would be required from higher organs as well. There might be special welfare provisions for a period of transitional unemployment organized by state labor agencies.

in favor of a single residence identity card.[84] In addition, the expansion of the private sector has considerably facilitated commercial travel.

In the face of these pressures for mobility arising from a combination of cultural liberalization and economic commercialization, the local unit has gradually been losing its grip. In urban areas, industrial managers have lost power over matters extraneous to their professional competence, such as the right to "stop work for self-criticism" (*tingzhi fanxing*; tantamount to the power of house arrest), the right to transfer, and the right to examine incoming or outgoing mail; to be sure, managers retain great power over matters within their spheres of competence, such as bonus allocation. Some units have introduced work councils or other representative bodies in an effort to harness unit authority to popular control.[85] In the countryside, the team has been severely weakened by the devolution of power to the family in the "responsibility system"—and the family has been concomitantly strengthened, once again becoming the basic unit of production as well as consumption. The commune has given way to a three-way functional division of labor in which it must share jurisdiction with the commune, the commune Party committee, and the *xiang* (township) government. As such functional differentiation becomes more general, the neo-feudal power of local authorities may be expected to yield to overlapping spheres of competence and crosscutting membership obligations.

2. Even more far-reaching in its implications than the still limited expansion of the ambit of physical mobility has been the proliferation of communications that has occurred since 1976. This was in part a response to the sudden removal of constraints on repressed demand after ten years of media deprivation: Whereas in 1960, 1,300 official periodicals were published in China, in 1966 the number was cut to 648, and by 1973 the number had further dwindled to about 50. During this period, not only almost all foreign literature but also traditional Chinese literature and the modern Chinese classics of the 1920s and 1930s were barred from publication, distribution, and library circulation; about the only works widely available were political tracts, technical manuals, a few novels, and the collected works of Marx, Lenin, and Mao.[86] In 1978 some 890 magazines were publicly available, selling a total of 76 million copies; in 1979 the number of titles rose to 1,200 (with a circulation of 118 million); and by 1982 it was possible to subscribe to no less than 2,100 reviews and magazines.[87] The best-selling periodical is still the authoritative Party publication *Red Flag*, which distributes 9.7 million copies, but it is

---

84. Julian Baum, in *Christian Science Monitor*, September 6, 1984.
85. Whyte and Parish, *Urban Life*, p. 297.
86. Siu and Stern, *Mao's Harvest*, pp. xlv–xlix.
87. John Howkins, *Mass Communication in China* (New York: Longman, 1982), pp. 86–87; also *CNA*, no. 1223 (January 1, 1982).

closely rivaled by "specialty" publications such as *Xiaoshuo Yuebao* (Fiction monthly), *Dazhong Dian Bao* (Popular film), *Kexue Huabao* (Science illustrated), and *Lianhuan Huabao* (Cartoons), each of which published 2 to 3 million copies in 1978. Non-Party newspapers such as the *Beijing Evening News* and Guangzhou's *Yangcheng Evening News*, somewhat more open in their reporting, have resumed publication. Since 1979, there has been an explosive growth of self-published newspapers in rural areas: most of China's more than 400 provincial and county papers (which account for half the newspaper circulation nationwide) are published without state subvention, and their editorial policies reflect efforts to boost circulation.[88] Even within the Party newspapers, the content is more varied than before, emphasizing information over propaganda and gradually minimizing "taboo areas." The most rapidly growing sector of the publishing industry has been literary magazines—there are 71 of them in Beijing, 38 in Shanghai, and 16 in Guangzhou, and many provinces have their own literary magazines.[89]

The impact of this communications explosion has been felt in every media sector. From 1966 to 1977 barely half a dozen new feature films were approved for release, and almost no new directors or actors were trained; in 1977, 28 feature films were produced, increasing to 40 in 1978, 65 in 1979, more than 100 in 1980.[90] The increase in the availability, variety, and aesthetic quality of films, with more cinemas open longer hours, has increased attendance from 50 million daily in 1977 to 70 million in 1980 (30 billion per year), giving China the world's largest moving picture audience.[91] After 1977 radio jamming ceased, and it became legal to listen to foreign broadcasts; the BBC, Voice of America, Radio Japan, and other stations began to provide a regular diet of news about events inside and outside China. With new satellite reception stations, film clips from American television became a regular staple on China's evening news broadcasts, and television sets became more widely available.[92] At the beginning of 1980 one in every 280 Chinese reportedly had a television set, compared with one in 16,400 people in 1970, with 38 television centers and 238 transmitting and relay stations.[93] The fare includes, in addition to (traditional) Beijing opera and educational programs, the American series "Man from Atlantis," and the BBC series

88. *FEER*, April 5, 1984, p. 44.
89. *Zhengming Ribao* (Hong Kong), July 25, 1981; quoted in *CNA*, no. 1223.
90. Moreover, about seventy foreign films were imported for exhibition and "study" in 1979, including "Death on the Nile"—which became the most popular film in China— "Cabaret," "The Sound of Music" (because it was "anti-fascist"), "Nightmare in Badham County," and "Convoy." Howkins, *Mass Communication*, pp. 67–68.
91. Mathews and Mathews, *One Billion*, pp. 279–81.
92. Whyte and Parish, *Urban Life*, p. 298.
93. Xinhua, February 18, 1980; as cited in Howkins, *Mass Communication*, p. 31.

"David Copperfield" and "Anna Karenina." The publishing sector has also expanded, from 103 publishers in mid-1978 to 158 by the end of 1980. As it has expanded, publishing has become more decentralized: previously publishing tended to be concentrated in Beijing and Shanghai, but by 1980, half of the publishers were located in the rest of the country. In 1978 they published about 15,000 books (with an average run of about 200,000 per book, this amounted to 3 billion copies), increasing to 17,000 titles (and 4.2 billion copies) in 1979.

This quantitative increase in communication flows has helped to erode the "honeycomb" system of internal constraints in at least three respects. First, it has swamped internal communication channels by sheer volume, no doubt similarly overloading censorship and control mechanisms. Subscriptions to magazines and newspapers are managed through the post offices; for example, in January 1982, the Beijing post office was dispatching some 512 periodicals, with 35 million copies; in addition, it must handle over 200 periodicals coming in from elsewhere.[94] Vast quantities of paper were used, straining the transport capabilities of the railways.[95] Yet even such an increase has not satisfied consumer demand. Popular literary magazines are sold on the black market at prices above the original, and government publishers estimate that each book they print reaches ten to twenty readers—all the more remarkable when libraries are so few and crowded.[96]

Second, consistent with general tendencies toward devolution of managerial and financial control to producing units and greater responsiveness to consumer demand, political authorities have to a considerable degree abdicated responsibility for the content of publications, making way for a tendency toward commercialization of the media. In 1979 it was decided that publishing houses would print runs based on estimated demand, arriving at such estimates by aggregating advance orders from local bookstores. Each bookshop is seen as a profit center and must fill a quota for sales, revenue, and expenditure (and pay taxes on its profits). This policy has resulted among other things in the publication of 1,750,000 copies of a three-volume translation of *Gone with the Wind*; no fewer than 45 Agatha Christie novels were slated for publication in 1980,

94. *Beijing Ribao*, August 3, 1981, p. 2; as quoted in *CNA*, no. 1223.

95. In 1981 the printing offices in Beijing used 7.5 million reams of paper, most of which (4.9 million reams) was however used for official publications. Some two thousand sacks of the periodical *Dazhong Dian Bao* are directed to the northwestern provinces, but the trains can haul only two hundred fifty sacks per day, and when other transport has priority, the masses must wait. *CNA*, no. 1223.

96. A survey of university students in Canton found most of them spending at least five hours a week reading novels and short stories. Some claimed that they spent as much as twenty-three to thirty hours a week reading books that had little to do with their schoolwork. Mathews and Mathews, *One Billion*, p. 296.

following the 1979 cinematic success of "Death on the Nile." Similarly, the success of the American film "Futureworld" in ′1980 excited an interest in publishing science fiction. In February 1979 the Ministry of Culture's Film Bureau likewise relinquished its right to review film scripts prior to filming, permitting studios to move directly to production on the basis of self-censorship. Troupes of actors and Beijing opera performers have been dispatched to the countryside with the exhortation to become economically self-supporting, resulting in the depoliticization of their repertoire (also in a deterioration in quality). Regional media seem most sensitive to commercial considerations; the central media establishment in Beijing, while attuned to political nuances, is also more willing to take a principled stand on given issues.

Third, emergence of a large-scale, commercially remunerative media network, and an enthusiastic public whose demand seems capable of consuming all that this network can produce, seems to have enhanced the autonomy and even the sense of self-importance of the literati whose creations it reproduces, and self-selected representatives of the literati have shown an increasing willingness to confront authorities who threaten to restrict the media for political reasons. To be sure, their assertiveness is attributable only partly to the growth of their media "base," and partly to their conviction that cultural liberalization is a legitimate construal of the administration's "double hundred" (let a hundred flowers bloom, let a hundred schools of thought contend) and "emancipation of mind" policies.

Confrontation between dissident literati and authorities did not erupt abruptly, but emerged only gradually in the course of emancipation from past repression. The Hua Guofeng position toward intellectual liberation had after all been quite conservative, inheriting the censoriousness of cultural radicalism without sharing any of its populist proclivities; the literati for their part remained deeply traumatized, not venturing any statements that might be misconstrued. In a speech made as late as July 1978, Zhang Pinghua, erstwhile CC Propaganda Department director, continued to defend Jiang Qing's revolutionary model operas, for example, opposing even aesthetically superior productions if they reflected badly upon socialism. "We should persist in one principle, that is, report on the bright side of society and the mainstream of socialism," he said. "Defects and mistakes are only minor things that can be overcome." [97]

The first significant departure from radical orthodoxy was signaled by publication of Liu Xinwu's short story "Class Counselor" (*Banzhuren*), just after adjournment of the Eleventh Party Congress in September

---

97. "Chang P'ing-hua's Speech to Cadres on the Cultural Front," trans. in *IS* 14, no. 12 (December 1978): 99–108.

1977. This introduced the so-called wound literature (named after a short story, "The Wounded," by Lu Xinhua), which exposed to sympathetic diagnosis the scars left by the Cultural Revolution, focusing primarily upon young people and intellectuals—thus harmonizing well with the concurrent campaign against the Gang of Four.[98] By 1979, spurred by the rehabilitation of the authors of the Hundred Flowers period, the critique of the Cultural Revolution had graduated to criticism of the shadow side of contemporary political reality, introducing the novel possibilities of tragedy. In film scripts, reportage, or plays such as "In Society's Files," "People or Monsters?" and "What If I Really Were?" such issues as cadre privilege or corruption were bruited.[99]

The Party and army cadres most frequently skewered in such satirical sallies resented this artistic license—one PLA representative (to the Fourth Session of the Fifth NPC) was heard to remark that the intellectuals were becoming "cocky" (literally, "sticking up their tails"— qiao weiba).[100] Yet there was no immediate crackdown, but rather a preliminary effort by authorities to signal that the bounds of tolerance were being trespassed. The first such signal took the form of quasi-official redefinition of the ambit of intellectual competence. Hu Qiaomu's July 1978 speech to the State Council contending that economics should be governed by "objective economic laws" was justly hailed as a landmark in claiming autonomy for the social sciences,[101] but after further debate the conclusion was reached that whereas the natural sciences consisted of truths that were independent of class standpoint, in the humanities and social sciences truth remained subjective and therefore under the ultimate jurisdiction of the Party.[102] In another academic discussion of the limits of freedom of speech, it was concluded that "thought activity" was not punishable by law, only "acts" were; the former did not, however, include the right to express thoughts freely if they were deemed harm-

98. See Lu Xinhua et al., The Wounded: New Stories of the Cultural Revolution, 1977–78, trans. Geremie Barme and Bennett Lee (Hong Kong: Joint Pub., 1979).

99. Jiang Youbei, "Wen tequan tiaojian de Zhonggong wenyi" [Chinese Communist literature that challenges special privileges], ZM, no. 26 (December 1979): 27–29; Huai Bing, "Ping 'Zai shehui de dang'an li'" [Criticism of "In the files of society"], ZM, no. 28 (February 1980): 78–79; in Jin Fang, "Zhonggong huaju mianshang de fengfeng leilei" [Storm in Chinese drama], ZM, no. 28 (February 1980): 32–33, 66.

100. Luo Bing, "Renda de muhou xinwen" [The inside story of the People's Congress], ZM, no. 51 (January 1982): 8–13.

101. Hu Qiaomu, "Act According to Economic Laws, Accelerate the Four Modernizations" [Anzhao jingji guilü ban shi, jiakuai shixian sige xiandaihua], finally published in RR on October 6, 1978.

102. See He Zuoxiu, Zhao Hongzhou, and Guo Hanying, "Criticize the 'Science and Technology Superstructure Theory,'" pp. 13–22; also "Implement the Policy of 'Let One Hundred Flowers Bloom and One Hundred Schools of Thought Contend,' Promote Academic Research," Nanfang Ribao (Guangzhou), January 13, 1979, p. 2.

ful.[103] Only after such signals fell on deaf ears did the authorities resort to more familiar and severe tactics to discipline errant literati (to be reviewed later).

In sum, the proliferation of communications seems to have been highly successful in permeating the internal gridwork of lateral constraints, qualified only by two considerations. First, notwithstanding the breaching of many geographical barriers, the general distinction between "inner" and "outer" remains a formidable one, and the authorities have made clear their determination to shore up the *neibu* communication system against further erosion.[104] This distinction reflects and tends to reinforce the persisting elite-mass cleavage in society. Second, although the regime's ideological justification of continuing political control over communication is logically vulnerable, the political strength of the literati and assembled intelligentsia, though growing, is still too weak to pose a serious challenge.

3. Vertical (hierarchical) structures have long been considered problematic in Chinese politics, although the nature of the problem has been defined differently from time to time. The early Cultural Revolution vision of an end to bureaucratic authority had by the late Cultural Revolution given way to an embrace of strict proletarian dictatorship, for example. The post-Mao critique of vertical structure, while more tolerant of hierarchy and more critical of autocracy, continues to embrace many elements of the radical polemic, such as its animus against cadre "privilege" and gerontocratic ossification. Having forsworn iconoclastic approaches to structural change, the post-Mao regime has, however, opted for nonconfrontational (indeed, elaborately consultative) change via constitutional engineering, proceeding "from the top down." Three aspects of these reforms are noteworthy: the co-optation of functional specialists into the state structure, the introduction of limited tenure and other devices designed to facilitate vertical mobility, and the institutionalization (and concomitant propensity for depoliticization) of elite monitoring devices.

103. See Yu Yiding, "On Emancipating the Mind and Opposing Bourgeois Liberalization," *HQ* no. 23 (December 1, 1981): 23–28, which supports a restrictive interpretation. Taking a more liberal tack are Gu Bing, "The Theory of the Vitality of Faith," *Jiefang Ribao*, February 28, 1980, p. 4; and Wang Ruoshui, "It is Permissible to Criticize Mao Zedong Thought" (part of a speech given in Shanghai in August 1979 but never published in the PRC), *ZM*, no. 31 (May 1, 1980): 27–29.
104. Albeit not without controversy. Noteworthy are several articles in which *neibu* book publishing and the difficult access to libraries have been criticized. See Yu Zhen, "Jiefang 'neibu shu' " [Liberate internal books], *Dushu* [Reading] (Beijing), no. 1 (1979); also Feng Yumin, " 'Tushuguan' bixu si men da kai" [The libraries must be opened on all sides], *Dushu*, no. 2 (1979). But the issue appears dead at this writing.

Co-optation of functional experts entails restoration of the power and status of the state bureaucracy, which remains the principal institutional channel through which these experts have input. During the Cultural Revolution era, although Zhou Enlai managed to keep the State Council intact and finally to convene the Fourth National People's Congress, the governmental structure below the central level was merged into the Revolutionary Committees, where they were subordinated to de facto military hegemony much of the time. This measure was theoretically justified in terms of the "withering away" of the State and its replacement by proletarian dictatorship as represented by the direct leadership of the Communist Party. In retrospect, however, the reformers deem it premature to have reduced the role of the governmental apparatus in the context of economic underdevelopment. As modernization assumed top priority in the post-Mao ambience, the State's functional significance grew. Thus the National People's Congress met annually in 1978 and 1979, for example, and its Standing Committee convened as many as eight sessions during the intervening period; several state commissions became engaged in working out various proposals. The State Council busied itself with numerous new projects, including calling national conferences in almost every important functional field for the formulating of guidelines relevant to the Four Modernizations.[105]

Despite the persistence of problematic elite-mass relations, the regime has granted increasing autonomy to vertically defined sectors, be they functional sectors or parallel bureaucracies.[106] The CPPCC has been revived at both central and local levels, and the Bourgeois Democratic Parties claim to have exhibited a certain popular appeal in attracting new members, though recruitment remains necessarily low-key.[107] The mass organizations have all been revived: The All-China Federation of Trade Unions held its Ninth Congress in Beijing October 11–21, 1978, after a hiatus of twenty-one years; the Tenth Congress of the China Youth League was held October 16–28, 1979, for the first time since 1964; the Fourth National Women's Congress was held in September 1978; and in October–November 1979, the Fourth Congress of Writers and Artists

105. Manoranjan Mohanty, "Party, State and Modernization in Post-Mao China," in V. P. Dutt, ed., *China: The Post-Mao View* (New Delhi: Allied Pub., 1981), pp. 45–67.
106. Hong Yung Lee, "Changing Patterns."
107. Many have joined the Bourgeois Democratic Parties, including young people. *Tuan-jiebao*, the newspaper of the Revolutionary Committee of the KMT, has been allowed to publish in Beijing, and has a circulation of more than fifty thousand per day. See He Wenxing, "Beijing, kexi, keyou" [Happiness and worry about Beijing], *ZM*, no. 49 (November 1981): 13–15; Xiao Ying, "Bei hang jian wen suo ji" [Miscellaneous information from my trip north], *ZM*, no. 28 (February 1980): 29–30.

met for the first time in nineteen years.[108] The People's Procuratorate was retrieved from Cultural Revolution oblivion at the First Session of the Fifth National People's Congress, and at the Second Session Peng Zhen's Legal Commission introduced the first codification of law in the history of the People's Republic.

Other reforms designed to facilitate vertical mobility have also been inaugurated. The Central Advisory Committee in the Party and the position of State Councillor in the government were introduced in order to facilitate the phased retirement of senior cadres from leadership positions; although it has not been entirely successful in this endeavor at the central level, the institutions are in place there and will be set up at the provincial and local levels as well, where they may be somewhat more efficacious.[109] There has also been a concerted effort since 1982 to encourage the accelerated promotion of outstanding younger officials, visible for example in the new membership of the Party Secretariat elected by the Twelfth Congress. Many of the governors or vice-governors at the provincial level are now young functional specialists: the mayor of Shanghai, for example, is a prestigious industrial specialist within the Party; Yao Jun, as of April 1983 (non-Party) vice-mayor of Tianjin, was once associate general engineer and vice-manager of the municipal chemical industry corporation; a former vice-director of the bureau of provincial mechanical industry with a Master's degree in mechanical engineering from the United States is now vice-governor in charge of mechanical industry in Zhejiang.[110] On the government side, a further step designed to stimulate the circulation of elites and forestall fossilization has been the introduction of fixed terms of office for most leadership positions: the premier, the president, the Standing Committee chairman, and other top governmental officials (excepting only the chairman of the

108. In addition, from October 11 to 23, 1979, China's eight democratic parties, and the All-China Federation of Industry and Commerce (a group of "national bourgeoisie" analogous to a chamber of commerce) simultaneously held their respective national congresses in Beijing, meeting for the first time in some twenty years. Zhen Ming, "An Appraisal of the Destiny of Mainland China's Democratic Parties," *DX*, no. 14 (November 16, 1979): 7–8.

109. Mu Fu, "Communist China Moves to Cut Its Deadwood," *Qishi Niandai*, no. 4 (1982): 20–23. Between December 1982 and May 1983, nearly a third of the Party provincial first secretaries and all but three of the provincial governors were replaced. Altogether nearly two-thirds of the country's top fourteen hundred provincial officials either resigned or "retired to the second line" as advisers. Christopher Clarke, "The Shakeup Moves Down," *China Business Review*, September–October 1983.

110. *Ming Bao*, March 30, 1983; *RR*, August 20, 1983; *RR*, January 4, 13, 1984. Between late 1982 and mid-1983, the average age of provincial governors and vice-governors dropped by nearly eight years, and the percentage in those posts with college education increased by 26.6 percent. The percentage of cadres at the prefectural, county, municipal, and town levels with college education rose by 14 percent. Christopher Clarke, "China's Third Generation," *China Business Review*, March–April 1984, pp. 36–38.

Central Military Commission) are to be limited to two five-year terms. Although the Party Constitution incorporated neither limited tenure nor restrictions on the number of positions concurrently occupied by one leader at its Twelfth Congress, these two principles were affirmed as guiding principles for future reforms.

To control elite corruption, a number of devices have been introduced in place of direct mass monitoring. Since elimination of the "four big" in 1981, there has been an emphasis on institutional mediation (letters to the editor, legal channels)—far less disruptive to the offending agency, but also more risky to the protester (who must relinquish anonymity). The chief weapon against elite privilege and corruption is organizational, consisting of a combination of external control hierarchies (primarily the Central Discipline Inspection Committee and its subordinate organs), along with such internal disciplinary techniques as criticism and self-criticism. A good example of the mode of implementation of such techniques is provided by the Party rectification campaign launched at the Second Plenum of the Twelfth Party Congress (October 11–12, 1983): its launching was preceded by more than a year's preparation, including pilot implementation in selected units, and the Party has proceeded from the top down and from the center outward, on a staggered schedule, with relatively little publicity. It is impossible to measure the efficacy of such monitoring agencies and techniques relative to the iconoclastic populism they have replaced, but the limited evidence so far available suggests a mixed verdict.[111]

The Rule of Law

Perhaps the most conceptually ambitious reform of structure involves the introduction of the "rule of law," inasmuch as this would potentially impose a structure of rules on social behavior of such abstract universalizability that many of the existing institutional constraints on lateral mobility might eventually be dispensed with or at least placed on a more voluntary basis. The regime has at this writing done little more than make a beginning, however, and it is not clear whether Party leaders understand the full implications of the steps they have taken. This beginning consists of the introduction of seven basic laws at the Second Session of the Fifth NPC (June 1979) as the first stage in what promises to be a more general codification of law, plus the attempt through constitutional revision to place political organization and legislative procedure on a more secure legal footing.

Legal codification has proceeded at a deliberate pace, led by work in international law designed to provide a favorable climate for foreign

111. See Lawrence R. Sullivan, "The Role of the Control Organs in the Chinese Communist Party, 1977–83," *AS* 24, no. 6 (June 1984): 597–618.

investment and trade. So long as the "Open Door Policy" remains in effect, it may be expected to stimulate continued progress within the realm of international law and perhaps to have some spillover effects, as the analogous precedents of Japan and Taiwan suggest.

Constitutional guarantees of democratic legislative procedure and certain civil rights of citizenship are not unique to the post-Mao era but are nonetheless important, going further than such formulations have in the past and for the first time making some reasonably realistic provision for enforcement. None of the previous Constitutions set forth such clear and definite provisions on the question of limiting the Party's activities to the sphere allowed by the Constitution and the laws, for example.[112] Unprecedented sanctity has been attributed to law, some reform advocates even viewing law as the legal expression of "scientific laws." The enactment and enforcement of law have been touted to replace the mass movements as a means of implementing policies.[113] As Marxists, the reformers rationalize the current salience of legality in terms of an inexorable developmental process:

> The socialist system has already solidified into a firm rule, and the former classes of landlords, rich peasants and capitalists do not exist anymore. The target of our dictatorship has shrunk, while the circle of "people" has widened, and as a consequence the most important thing in the strengthening of the socialist legal system, in a certain sense, is the adjustment of the various kinds of social relations that have arisen among the people.[114]

In 1954, the previous high-water mark of socialist legality, the PRC adopted only the constitutional terminology and forms from the West, rejecting in principle the spirit of the Western "rule of law" or *Rechtsstaat*. And whenever the constitution proved inconvenient, the Party did not hesitate to abandon it, invoking ideology to justify its acts. The 1982 Constitution, in contrast, introduces certain constitutional guarantees. Whereas all previous Constitutions had been drafted by the Party CC and presented to the NPC for ratification, in 1982 the Constitution was prepared by an NPC drafting committee. For the first time, an organ has been specified for the enforcement of the Constitution and the laws; namely, the Standing Committee of the NPC, which has been provided with a permanent staff and several specialized committees, and meets

112. Staff commentator, "The Party Must Operate within the Scope of the Constitution and the Law," *Minzhu yu Fazhi* (Shanghai), no. 9 (September 25, 1982): 2–3. The 1982 Party Constitution stipulates that the "Party shall act within the limits of the [state] Constitution and the laws"; it also stipulates that Party members must obey the laws of the state. The provision that "the Communist Party of China is the leading core of the people of the whole country," found in both previous versions, has been deleted.

113. According to Tang Tsou, in "Reflections," pp. 142–43.

114. Zhang Youyu, "Revolution and the Legal System—Written in Commemoration of the Sixtieth Anniversary of the Founding of the CCP," *Minzhu yu Fazhi*, no. 7 (July 25, 1981): 5–9.

more frequently than in the past. When the Standing Committee is in session it may put forward bills of inquiry to the State Council, the Supreme People's Court, or the Supreme People's Procuratorate, which are in turn under obligation to answer. The NPC itself has the power to amend the Constitution (for example, two amendments were drafted to the 1978 Constitution at the Second and Third Sessions of the Fifth NPC), to make and amend basic laws, and to formulate edicts (i.e., resolutions apart from the law); amendments require a two-thirds majority vote, laws a simple majority. Delegates are immune from arrest and trial without permission of the NPC or its Standing Committee; they cannot be prosecuted for speeches or votes at any session of the NPC.[115]

However, notwithstanding the precedent-shattering declaration that the Party will abide within legal limits, there are no external restraints on the Party, making this provision entirely dependent upon the self-restrictive capacity of the Party's leadership and the value it places on the constitutional rules of the game. The Constitution has neither legal guarantees for its implementation nor legal procedures to enable the people to invoke it on behalf of their constitutional rights and freedoms. It is also important to bear in mind that although the "rule of law" has been invoked by its legal proponents in the scholarly (and even the popular) press,[116] the leadership at this point endorses only the "Chinese socialist rule of law," reserving the option to differentiate that concept from "bourgeois" legality should that become politically expedient.[117]

However tenuous its foundation, so long as the emphasis on socialist legality persists, this implies a concomitant revitalization of legislative activity. This revitalization is already visible in the increasing focus on democratic parliamentary procedure, including elections by secret ballot and the right of assembly delegates to pose questions to responsible authorities. In the Party, secret ballots for Party committees at each level and for delegates for higher levels have been introduced; in these ballots a certain range of discretion has been permitted for competition (no recommended ratio is stipulated, only that there should be more candidates than positions).[118] At the Twelfth CPC Congress in September 1982, for

115. Wang Shuwen and Zhou Yanrui, "New Developments of the People's Congress System," *Faxue Yanjiu* (Beijing), no. 3 (1982): 9–14; Chen Yunsheng, "Immunity of Representatives in the Draft Constitution," *Faxue* (Shanghai), no. 7 (July 1982): 16.

116. See for example Xu Chongde, "Ten Proposals for Revising the Constitution," *Minzhu yu Fazhi*, no. 3 (March 20, 1981): 7–10.

117. Lu Yonghong, "Is the Age of Deng Xiaoping the Chinese Communist Party's Constitutional Age?" *Mingbao Yuekan*, vol. 18, no. 6 (June 1983): 19–25.

118. For example, during the election of the Secretariat at the Fifth Plenum of the Eleventh CC, Geng Biao and Chen Muhua were originally on the list of nominees. But during the discussion period questions were raised, and in the end they were not elected; instead Song Renqiong and Yang Dezhi were elected. Luo Bing, "Inside Information on the Election of the Secretariat," *ZM*, no. 30 (April 1980): 3–8.

example, a preliminary election was held on September 8 to draw up a name list of candidates for Central Committee membership; following this preliminary election, the Presidium of the Party Congress drew up a formal list, after which a final election was held in which those receiving the most votes on the list were elected (vacancies appearing subsequently in the CC would be filled by alternates in order of the number of votes by which they were elected, so vote totals apparently played some role in establishing a pecking order).[119] People's congresses were empowered to elect, by a similar procedure, the county head, county standing committee, and other leading county officials as well as delegates to the higher-level people's congress. Delegates to the congresses may raise questions about government programs, pass resolutions, and make "delegates' motions" (proposals for government action that require a second of three delegates, are passed on to the relevant government authorities, and require an official response.)[120] Delegate participation in the National People's Congress was particularly salient at the Third Session of the Fifth Congress, where delegates held serious debate and grilled officials about various controversial issues, even casting a few negative votes.[121] Subsequent developments suggest that this trend will continue, albeit with zigs and zags.[122]

As in any case in which elites introduce more democratic measures from the top down (e.g., Meiji Japan, Wilhelminian Germany), legislative reform is inherently ambiguous. Elites would like power distributed more broadly in order to protect themselves from charismatic autocracy,

119. Hu Sisheng and Chen Min, "Elections—Eye-catching Moment," *RR*, September 11, 1982, p. 4; Gan Wei, "Many Special Features in List of Alternate CC Members," *Da Gong Bao* (Hong Kong), September 15, 1982, p. 2.

120. The Fifth session of the CPPCC (held immediately following the First session of the Fifth NPC in February 1978) was also said to be more open than previous sessions. It included communication among groups as well as within them, more oral discussion and less written material, and some sharp criticisms. Ren Gu, "San wen zhengxie weiyuan" [Three questions to a member of the CPPCC], *ZM*, no. 6 (April 1978): 17–20.

121. Delegates asked for an explanation of the "Bohai No. 2" incident, and demanded an investigation into the criminal responsibility of Song Zhenming, former minister of the petroleum industry, and Chen Yonggui, former vice-premier. Tang Ke, minister of the metallurgical industry, was questioned about problems of investment and industrial pollution at the Baoshan Iron and Steel Works; Zhou Huamin, vice minister of foreign trade, was questioned about waste of foreign exchange in building the Beijing Foreign Trade Center. Yao Yilin's report came under fire for placing too much emphasis on industry and too little on agriculture, or too much on heavy industry and too little on light. The Hong Kong–Macao delegate criticized the foreign exchange certificates. Delegates also aired their views on bureaucratization, the system of economic management, the "four freedoms," and on problems in education and the publishing industry. Commentator, "Preliminary Observations on the 3rd Plenary Session of the 5th NPC," *Dong Xi Fang*, no. 21 (September 10, 1980): 12–13.

122. Cf. Xi Xing, "Issues Raised by the 4th Session of the 5th NPC," *ZM*, no. 1 (January 1, 1982): 18–20.

and yet they are reluctant to divest themselves of power or to run any risk that their own interests might be jeopardized. Withal, the prospect of intramural democracy (within the NPC, the CC, the Party branch or the work unit) seems more likely now than the prospect that the elite will open itself to meaningful mass input on issues of national importance.

REVOLUTION DISCONTINUED?

In the "Resolution on CPC History" adopted by the Sixth Plenum, the Party has come closer to announcing an official termination of the Chinese revolution than ever before. Although the resolution states that "the triumph of the Chinese revolution is the most important political event since World War II and has exerted a profound and far-reaching impact on the international situation and the development of the people's struggle throughout the world,"[123] that revolution is conceived in chronologically discrete terms. None of the identifiably Maoist attempts to prolong or revive the revolution in the post-Liberation era, from the acceleration of agricultural cooperativization in 1955 to the campaign to criticize Deng in 1976, receive favorable notice. The theory of continued revolution under the dictatorship of the proletariat, said to have provided the theoretical rationale for the Cultural Revolution, is repudiated for being "obviously inconsistent with the system of Mao Zedong Thought." Thus, one concurrent article notes that although Marx said explicitly (in *The Class Struggle in France, 1848–1850*) that "this kind of socialism is to declare an uninterrupted revolution," he and Engels later modified their position: "we can now say that uninterrupted revolution is only a tactic under special historical circumstances."[124] Another article carefully distinguishes between revolution and reform, salvaging the latter from the Marxist terminological trashpile as the preferred mode of political change for postrevolutionary systems:

> Before the overthrow of the exploiting system, they [viz., reformism and revolution] were absolutely incompatible; revolution precluded reformism. However, after the overthrow of the exploiting system, the relations between them are completely different. Not only are they tolerant of each other, but the means of reform must be used to complete the new revolutionary tasks.... To promote a political revolution whereby one class overthrows another after the proletariat has seized political power will inevitably create nationwide chaos.[125]

123. *Resolution*, p. 10.
124. Guang Chuizhan, "Marx and the Idea of Uninterrupted Revolution," *Shangyao Shizhuan Xuebao*, no. 1, 1981, as quoted in *Xinhua Yuebao*, August 1981.
125. Xue Hanwei and Pan Guohua, "On Revolutionary Reformism," *Xuexi yu Tansuo* [Study and exploration] (Harbin), no. 6 (1981): 4–9; this article is approvingly cited in Liu Hefu, "On Revolutionary Reformism," *GM*, January 12, 1982, p. 3.

All the same, in the concluding section of the resolution, the need to "carry on revolutionary struggles with determination" is resoundingly reaffirmed:

Socialism aims not just at eliminating all systems of exploitation and all exploiting classes but also at greatly expanding the productive forces, improving and developing the socialist relations of production and the superstructure and, on this basis, gradually eliminating all class differences and all major social distinctions and inequalities which are chiefly due to the inadequate development of the productive forces until communism is finally realized. This is a great revolution, unprecedented in human history.[126]

To be sure, the type of revolution to be "carried on" is implicitly redefined: "this revolution is carried out not through fierce class confrontation and conflict, but through the strength of the socialist system itself, under leadership, step by step and in an orderly way." The revolution has entered a "period of peaceful development" that will "not only take a very long historical period to accomplish but also demand many generations of unswerving and disciplined hard work and heroic sacrifice."[127] It is consistent with this redefinition that many historical transformations previously denigrated as "reformist" are now conceived to have revolutionary aspects (e.g., the Xinhai Revolution of 1911).[128] As Zhao Ziyang puts it in his report on the work of the government, neatly conflating the two apparent alternatives, "This reform is a revolution, but of course it is not a fundamental change in the social system and must

126. *Resolution*, p. 84.
127. Ibid., pp. 84–85. It is worth noting that "revolution" as now conceived more closely resembles that revolution described by Marx in the *Communist Manifesto*:

The bourgeoisie, wherever it has got the upper hand, has put an end to all feudal, patriarchal, idyllic relations.... The bourgeoisie cannot exist without constantly revolutionizing the instruments of production, and thereby the relations of production, and with them the whole relations of society.... The bourgeoisie, by the rapid improvement of all instruments of production, by the immensely facilitated means of communication, draws all, even the most barbarian, nations into civilization. The cheap prices of its commodities are the heavy artillery with which it batters down all Chinese walls.... (Marx, *Manifesto of the Communist Party*, in Robert C. Tucker, ed., *The Marx-Engels Reader* [New York: W. W. Norton, 1978 ed.], pp. 475–77.)

The theoretical implication of a "bourgeois democratic revolution" under the auspices of a firmly entrenched Communist Party leadership would be a return to a New Democratic regime (wherein bourgeois democratic and socialist revolutions could be "telescoped"). Although it is now often conceded that the departure from this earlier "stage" was forced and premature, there is at this point still a theoretical aversion against turning back the historical clock.
128. See also He Fangchuan, "Reform Movements in the Upper Levels of Eastern Countries in the Middle of the 19th Century," *Lishi Yanjiu*, no. 4 (August 15, 1981): 88–101; and Ma Hongliang, "The 1898 Reform Movement," *RR*, September 15, 1981, p. 5.

not rock or depart from the socialist system. Rather it represents self-improvement and self-perfection on the basis of socialism itself."[129]

The ambiguity of this somewhat forced synthesis[130] left it open to further revision, and in retrospect the Sixth Plenum might be viewed not only as the high-water mark in the repudiation of the concept of continuing revolution but as the beginning of a regrouping of the forces most reluctant to relinquish it. No sooner had the leadership of the "Maoist" factional network been decapitated, it seems, than its ideological initiatives began to find official favor.[131] Contrariwise, the boldest advocates of reform fell upon political hard times, particularly after the Twelfth Congress.[132] The fact that Deng's faction prospered organizationally rather than suffering in the course of this shift suggests that Deng agreed with it or at least wished to give its advocates their lead.

Why the turn to the left, after eliminating the leading leftists? Partly, perhaps, in order to co-opt their political base. After all, unless the propaganda organs were to be altogether disbanded, they had to be given something to do; "practice as the sole criterion" rendered them superfluous, and morale was apparently sagging.[133] Among the population

129. Tang Wensheng and Jia Chenfeng, "Reform is Self-perfection of the Socialist System," *HQ*, no. 13 (July 1, 1983): 32–36.

130. Outside observers have sometimes welcomed the reconstrual of revolution in terms of modernization (see for example Donald Zagoria, "China's Quiet Revolution," *Foreign Affairs* [Spring 1984]: 880). But in the context of China's revolutionary experience, before and after Liberation, any such analogy appears superficial and unconvincing. The changes now under way fundamentally repudiate charismatic leadership, mass mobilization, a "breakthrough" mentality—all the earmarks of revolution as it has been practiced for the last thirty years. Although the political structure is not unaffected, it is no longer the mainspring or focus of change.

131. Since the fall of the "small gang of four," the residual "whatever faction" has reportedly taken great interest in "political and ideological work," in the name of "resisting the erosion of bourgeois ideology." Their initiatives in this area have included a major attempt to reorient art and literature toward the praise of socialist virtue. Bi Dingtang, "Beijing Coup and Beijing Reform," *Dong Xi Fang*, no. 19 (July 10, 1980): 72–76.

132. Though not purged, many of the most prominent reformers were demoted, including Feng Wenbin, Hu Jiwei, Wang Ruoshui, and Liao Gailong. In the elections to the Twelfth Congress, neither Hu Jiwei (former *RR* editor-in-chief, "kicked upstairs" to the post of director in May 1982) nor Deputy Editor-in-Chief Wang Ruoshui were listed among CC members, though the new editor-in-chief, Qin Chuan, became a full member. Feng Wenbin, already replaced by Hu Qili as director of the CC General Office, was relegated to the CAC. Liao Gailong was transferred from the CC's Policy Research Office to the Party History Research Center; his name was not to be found on any of the committees at the Twelfth Congress. *HQ* editor-in-chief Xiong Fu also failed to be elected to the CC, although his deputy (Wang Renzhi) became an alternate member. Qi Xin, "Personnel Changes of the CCP Twelfth Congress," *QN*, no. 10 (October 1982): 16–19.

133. This morale problem was apparent in efforts to clad ideological work in the more prestigious raiments of "science" (previously, the transfer of status had been in the opposite direction!); see for example Zhang Weiping, "Why Is Ideological and Political Work a

at large, de-Maoization seemed to have given rise to a "crisis of faith," in which doubt was fairly openly expressed about the legitimacy of the Communist Party and Marxist-Leninist ideology.[134] The leadership associated this ideological secularization with a juvenile crime wave, black marketeering, corruption, and other problems stemming from a more materialist worldview, betimes deeming all to be manifestations of renascent "class struggle."[135] It was both morally distasteful and economically infeasible to displace ideological crusades with pragmatic materialism at one fell swoop, the leadership seems to have concluded,[136] so an induced mass consensus upon certain ideological verities was still useful—even as reform continued. This revival entailed the suppression of "erroneous" notions as well as an educational effort designed to generate a popular consensus around "correct" tenets. Toward this end, the leadership has returned to a number of time-tested techniques, including the institutions of "study" and "criticism and self-criticism," which had apparently been permitted to lapse in many places.[137]

Science?" *Xin Shiqi* [New era] (Beijing), no. 11 (November 1981): 2–4; also Chao Yang, "Is Publicizing Communist Ideology Contradictory to the Principle of Social Existence Determining Social Consciousness?" *HQ*, no. 4 (February 16, 1983): 48 Still, the press noted that "many cadres do not care for the study of theory," considering this "useless," because "theories are changing all the time." *Fujian Ribao*, June 19, 1982.

134. Two secret polls taken among students at Fudan University in Shanghai in 1979 and September 1980 by the Federation of Students and then briefly posted on the university's bulletin boards suggest that this crisis of faith is fairly widespread. Asked what they thought of current leaders' ability to achieve the Four Modernizations, 78 percent took a "wait and see" attitude; when asked whether people like the Gang of Four might return to power within the next ten years, only 5.4 percent responded with a firm "no," while half thought it was "possible" and 39 percent considered it "difficult to avoid." With regard to what the students believed in, only a third said "Communism," nearly a quarter said "fate," and 25 percent said "nothing at all." *Time* 116, no. 19 (November 10, 1980): 57.

135. There is also a tendency to attribute such degenerative tendencies to Western influence—and indeed there is some evidence to support such a thesis, at least in some areas. See Deng Ziben, "Guangzhou qing shaonian wenti" [Problems of youth in Guangzhou], *Guang Jiao Jing*, no. 98 (November 16, 1980): 8–12, which documents the change of value patterns in Guangzhou through statistics, implying that these may be traced to Western influence emanating from Hong Kong. See also Lin Nan, "Zhongguo de zhengzhi daigou" [The political generation gap in China], *ZM*, no. 32 (June 1980): 36–39; and Luo Bing, "Wu zhong quan hui he qiangren zhengzhi" [The Fifth Plenum and strongman politics], *ZM*, no. 29 (March 1980): 5–9.

136. "We cannot subscribe to the view that once the economy improves the ideology of people in various sectors will automatically become better," warns Hu Yaobang. "On the contrary, there is actually this kind of condition even in countries with very flourishing economies. The people (naturally not all the people) lack ideals and convictions and suffer from a spiritual void." Quoted from Hu's speech at a forum on ideological problems convened by the CC Propaganda Department on August 8, 1981, in *HQ*, no. 23, pp. 2–22.

137. "Owing to the damage caused by Lin Biao and the Gang of Four, the Party's tradition of attaching importance to theoretical study was suspended for a fairly long time," concedes

But the restoration of institutions of routine political resocialization alone was apparently deemed inadequate. Conceding that the CC renounced political campaigns at its Third Plenum and had subsequently reaffirmed this decision "many times," one writer justified its tacit reversal in terms of "the need for everyone to concentrate more on opposing a certain tendency, or solving a certain problem":

> Not carrying out political campaigns naturally does not mean that no campaigns whatever should be carried out. To resolve certain problems, the adoption of the form of the mass movement is necessary. For example, in promoting sanitation, we must persevere and make it a habit. However, mobilizing everyone to do a crash job sometimes creates enthusiasm which often leads to better results.... There remain certain problems which, like all the relatively widespread unhealthy tendencies, will be difficult to resolve if we do not build strong public opinion pressure and have a definite momentum.[138]

Thus the period from the spring of 1981 to the fall of 1983 witnessed the mobilization of three consecutive "noncampaigns," one positive, two negative: the criticism of "bourgeois liberalization," the promotion of "socialist spiritual civilization," and the drive to clear up "spiritual pollution."

The first ideological initiative was launched preemptively by the PLA just prior to the Sixth Plenum, by publishing (apparently unilaterally) a series of articles criticizing a screenplay (never actually produced) entitled "Unrequited Love" (*Kulian*), by a military writer named Bai Hua. The campaign won CC endorsement at the Sixth Plenum in June, and criticisms were then somewhat grudgingly taken up by *People's Daily* and the other pace-making media.[139] The campaign continued through

---

HQ, "The problem in which some cadres look down on and even detest and reject theoretical studies has not been completely solved." Zhao Shouyi, "The Key to Building the Two Civilizations," *HQ*, no. 1 (January 1, 1982): 13–14; see also Li Biyan, "Put an End to the Practice of Allowing Theoretical Study to Take Its Natural Course," *HQ*, no. 1 (January 1, 1982): 18.

138. Shen Baoxiang, "Do Not Exaggerate the Concept of 'Political Campaign,'" *Jiefang Ribao*, November 12, 1981, p. 4. This argument was however controversial, particularly among intellectuals. At a forum held at the Chinese Academy of Social Sciences under the auspices of *Guangming Ribao*, Li Shu, editor of *Lishi Yanjiu*, opined; "Just as we have announced that we will no longer launch political movements in the future, I think we should explicitly proclaim that we will not launch academic criticism movements again." He complained that "articles that are in conflict with current policies are not permitted to be published." NCNA Beijing, September 15, 1979, reported in *GM* on the same date; translated in *JPRS* no. 74296 (October 3, 1979): 1–8.

139. On July 17, 1981, Deng reportedly summoned a meeting in Zhongnanhai whose participants included Wang Renzhong, Zhou Yang, Hu Jiwei, Zeng Tao, and Zhu Muzhi, in which he attacked the Party leadership of literature and art for its "slackness" (*huansan*

the summer, broadening into a critique of "bourgeois liberalization" (*zichan jieji ziyouhua*), and the possibility of "peaceful evolution," raising the old specter of a "capitalist road." [140]

The "socialist spiritual civilization" drive was intended to "foster socialist ethics and educate the young people to have ideals, pay attention to morality and discipline, be polite and work hard," according to Deng Xiaoping. "Everyone should be patriotic and have a sense of national dignity. All these are closely connected with our efforts to modernize the country." [141] In language redolent of the Kuomintang's "New Life" movement of the 1930s, mass organizations were urged to pay attention to the "five stresses, four beauties, and three loves," [142] or the "four haves, three attentions, and two fear-nots." The concept of "socialist spiritual civilization," nowhere to be found in Marx, Engels, or Lenin, is based on the Maoist premise that the ideological superstructure is to some degree autonomous from the economic base, thereby justifying continuing Party leadership in moral and ideological socialization efforts—crime or immorality are not to be blamed on the material environment (even on class background), but on disobedience to the Party. [143]

The flip side of "spiritual civilization" is "spiritual pollution," which came under attack following the Second Plenum of the Twelfth CC in mid-October 1983, with Deng's strong endorsement. In its initial phase this movement focused on the polluting influence of Western ideology, as manifested for example in the concepts of "alienation" and "humanism" (ironically both Marxist terms, deriving from Marx's earlier writings). But before long it gave rise to interference in economic reforms by resentful local cadres. Beginning in November 1983, agricultural and industrial issues were thus exempted, restricting the field of investigation

---

ruanruo), calling for criticism of Bai Hua, Ye Wenfu, et al. At a meeting of the CC Propaganda Department in early August, Hu Yaobang relayed this message to the Party leadership of the cultural sector. Immediately after this meeting, the Party issued CD no. 30, containing the speeches of Deng and Hu as well as other materials. Luo Bing, "Deng Xiaoping fadong da pipan neiqing" [The inside story of the mass criticism launched by Deng Xiaoping], *ZM*, no. 48 (October 1981): 7–17.

140. See for example Li Jiansheng, "The Threat of 'Peaceful Evolution' Is Far from Being Eliminated," *Dazhong Ribao* (Jinan), April 1, 1982, p. 3.

141. "Deng on China's Open Policy," *BR*, vol. 25, no. 10 (March 8, 1982), p. 9.

142. The "five stresses" are on decorum, courtesy, hygiene, discipline, and morals; the "four beauties" are of mind, language, behavior, and environment; the "three loves" (appended in early 1983) are of the motherland, socialism, and the Party.

143. See Zhang Qihua's two articles, "On Spiritual Civilization and Marxism," *HQ*, no. 10 (May 16, 1982): 39–43; and "Is There Class Character in Spiritual Civilization?" *HQ*, no. 23 (December 1, 1982): 38–39; also An Tung, "Why Is It Necessary to Carry Out Communist Ideological Education at the Socialist Stage?" *HQ*, no. 22 (November 16, 1982): 41–43; and Commentator, "Socialist Spiritual Civilization," *BR*, no. 45 (November 8, 1982): 13–17, 30.

to the ideological and literary fronts;[144] under these constraints, the drive soon lost momentum.

Do such countercyclical developments signal a revival of "continuing revolution"—or even simply the arrest of reform (the two are not equivalent)? In answer to this question, a final review of the three functional requisites of continuing revolution is in order: charismatic leadership, mass mobilization, and an antistructural animus.

1. Charismatic leadership on the whole played a functional role in the achievement of the revolutionary objectives of the 1950s, declining significantly at the end of the first decade as a result of having accomplished the basic revolutionary agenda on the one hand and having overreached itself in going beyond it on the other. Having to a considerable degree personified itself in the charismatic leader as a way of enhancing its mass appeal, the regime had an interest in preserving Mao's charisma and increasingly resorted to artificial techniques to shore it up, in the process losing control of the source of its own legitimacy. All of this redounded disastrously during the Cultural Revolution, when the charismatic leader and the bureaucracy became pitted against one another. Despite charisma's triumphant revival in 1966–68, the economically austere and culturally bleak prospects of continuing the revolution adversely prejudiced the mass verdict even before Mao's demise. Charisma degenerated into despotism, as the emancipatory slogans of cultural revolution became transformed into a socially enforced form of totalitarianism. Even so, it took several years thereafter for the renunciation of charismatic ideology to be publicly worked through.

Chinese politics still responds to personal power bases that are more independent of the institutional structure in which they are embedded than in most political systems, and a regeneration of charismatic leadership under critical circumstances cannot be precluded.[145] Yet the public commitment to collective leadership (led by Deng himself, who rose to power on a critique of the cult of personality) is firmer than ever before, and it has become rooted in institutional arrangements that seem to be functioning effectively. As a whole, Chinese bureaucrats must see considerable risk to their security interests in any reconcentration of power under monocratic leadership. Barring a crisis of comparable magnitude

144. See Deng Liqun, in *RR*, December 10, 1983, p. 3; also Bo Yibo's statement in *RR*, January 6, 1984, p. 1.
145. Although he has repudiated the "personality cult" and the concept of "continuing revolution," Deng has occasionally manifested monocratic propensities, as in his support of Democracy Wall activists in the fall of 1978 (for which he subsequently made a self-criticism), or his outspoken public refutation of an apparent NPC commitment not to post PLA troops in Hong Kong (in May 1984). *NYT*, May 26, 1984; *FEER*, 124:23 (June 7, 1984): 13–14.

to that which hit Weimar Germany in the 1920s, China's newly established institutional arrangements and commitment to orderly growth have foreclosed radical policy breakthroughs emanating unpredictably from the charismatic imagination of an heroic leader. More likely than authentic charisma, perhaps, is the advent of the "charismatic illusion" characteristic of systems (such as the United States or the Soviet Union) with well-institutionalized political structures. Here the popular yearning for charisma arises not from the disarray of institutions but from their firmly entrenched positions in defense of the status quo, in which the rhetoric of a magnetic personality appears to offer the only hope for dramatic change. Upon the leader's winning office this prospect however vanishes like a mirage, as the leader for pragmatic reasons shifts from an anti-establishment posture to a more compromising and cooperative role. (As should be clear from the foregoing chapters, the problems of over-institutionalization should still be considered remote ones for China.)

2. Mass mobilization was motivated by a combination of remunerative and normative incentives during the first post-Liberation decade, and principally by normative incentives thereafter. Experience since that time has demonstrated that normative incentives may be motivationally effective only if the regime allows significant latitude for mass initiative—which in turn reduces the steering capability of the elite, permitting the movement to factionalize uncontrollably. In the post-Mao era, after initially renouncing mobilizational approaches to the generation of mass support, the regime seems to have reconsidered. But having detached mass mobilization from the fragile economic sector that once supplied material incentives, and having sharply circumscribed the ambit for mass initiative (à la democracy movement), the regime seems to have approximately the same chances of really "moving" the masses as Mao had of persuading incumbent cadres to participate actively in the Cultural Revolution.

Though apparently a case of *plus ça change*, closer scrutiny reveals important differences in the "noncampaigns" launched after 1981.[146] First, they are not as all-encompassing as previous such efforts, coinciding indeed with continuing reform efforts in the economic and political sectors (e.g., the 1982 constitutional reforms). Second, such human targets as Bai Hua and Ye Wenfu (another young military writer, who had written a poem, "General, You Cannot Do This," about a rehabilitated Cultural Revolution victim who converts an orphanage into his private villa) were publicly criticized but not "struggled" against, and were apparently able to continue to work and live normally; the campaign was

146. See Tang Tsou, "Political Change and Reform: The Middle Course," in Tang Tsou, *The Cultural Revolution and Post-Mao Reforms: A Historical Perspective* (Chicago: University of Chicago Press, 1986), pp. 219–59.

not permitted to spread beyond a few initial targets.[147] Third, there was less pressure upon members of the intellectual community to conform with the public opinion wave being orchestrated from above; although no one dared publish a "countercriticism" disputing the attacks made on the leading liberals, it was apparently possible to remain silent, and many leading intellectuals in fact did so.[148]

3. In its first decade, the regime succeeded in smashing the frames of the residual political and social structure. When it then turned its attentions to the aversive structures that had emerged in the course of constructing a modern socialist system, it became much more difficult to generate a politically decisive consensus, due to the vested interests that had arisen in defense of the new status quo. Mao eventually succeeded in generating sufficient support to smash emergent structures (in part by tapping cumulative popular resentment of earlier radical fiascoes, ironically enough), only to find that his vision of what lay beyond those structures was either incoherent or politically impractical. Though the repudiation of "continuing revolution" signifies above all a reconciliation to the existence of structures, popular attitudes toward them are likely to remain ambivalent and even perhaps somewhat volatile as long as structures inhibit the movement of people, commodities, or ideas. A satisfactory synthesis of structure and movement remains the task of structural reform.

BEYOND REVOLUTION

Postrevolutionary political development has always suffered from relative theoretical neglect, yielding pride of place to the more dramatic dynamics of revolution itself. This neglect hinders attempts to speculate

147. Yan Yue, "Tou xiang tequan de zhadan—Ye Wenfu de shizuo yanjiang ji aipi jingguo" [A bomb dropped on the privileged class—Ye Wenfu's poems, speeches, and how he is being criticized], ZM, no. 52 (February 1982): 20–24; Gong Qigong, "Ye wenfu shou pi" [Ye Wenfu is criticized], ZM, no. 51 (January 1982): 30–32. Ye was criticized not for the poem cited above, but for a more recent poem, "Jiangjun, haohao xiyixi" [General, have a nice bath], which tells of how a general has a sapper company work on his house, building a bathtub that alone costs 10,000 yuan.

148. Shanghai's Wenyi Bao, for example, received numerous letters in support of Bai Hua (Bai himself reportedly received more than a thousand letters from well-wishers), but there were so few writers willing to write critical articles that the journal was hard put to find enough critical articles for its special issue criticizing Bai Hua. Editorial, "Qing shao 'pipan' zhe" [Please stop the 'criticism'], ZM, no. 48 (October 1981): 1. Zhou Yang supported "the necessary freedom and democracy of literary and artistic workers" in his speeches on December 15–16, 1981, and he is rumored to have submitted his resignation (which was not accepted) rather than join in the criticism. Luo Bing, "Inside Story"; see also Ying Zi, "Fan 'Ziyouhua' fengshi ruole" [The "anti-bourgeois liberalization" wind abates], ZM, no. 49 (November 1981): 11–12.

on a firm comparative evidential basis about the future of Chinese politics. The concepts of "Thermidor" and the "routinization of charisma" have hitherto dominated thinking about the process of postrevolutionary adjustment, and in fact both of these notions concur in certain respects.[149] The postrevolutionary political system will revert to a situation in which the leadership stabilizes, a new equilibrium is established among various classes and groups, mass participation declines in scope and intensity, political authority demands (and receives) respect and obedience, and millenarian expectations give way to mundane concerns. All of which is to say little more than that the political system returns to "normalcy," while ignoring the range of possibilities this term encompasses.

The following schematization of the prospects for future Chinese political development attempts to subdivide "postrevolutionary normalization" into two broad alternatives, and to endow each alternative with specific mass and elite constituencies, political objectives, material and ideal interests, and functional *raisons d'être*. At the outset of its postrevolutionary era, the Chinese system stands poised, once again, between "two roads": one leading toward *institutionalized revisionism*, the other toward the *ritualization of charisma*.

"Institutionalized revisionism" is a particular variant of state socialism that has emerged in a variety of contexts in response to the functional imperatives of modernization.[150] The intellectual forebears of institutionalized revisionism include Bernstein, Bukharin, Khrushchev (with qualification—Khrushchev also had radical impulses), Liu Shaoqi, and Dubček (before August 1968, of course). The social base of the revisionists is that of the intelligentsia and the "new middle class," or salariat (not all intellectuals are revisionists, but most revisionists happen to be intellectuals). The priority commitment to rapid economic development makes expertise a functional requisite, entailing universal education and the proliferation of meritocratic criteria for recruitment and promotion, eventually giving rise to a fairly large, strategically located coalition of professional groups of broadly similar collective consciousness. The intellectual background of revisionists predisposes them to adopt liberal and relatively cosmopolitan cultural and educational policies, to entrust the economy to academically trained economists, to favor the functional

149. See Crane Brinton, *The Anatomy of Revolution* (New York: Vintage Books, 1960); and Max Weber, ed. by Guenther Roth and Claus Wittich, *Economy and Society: An Outline of Interpretive Sociology* (Berkeley: University of California Press, 1978), vol. 2: 1111–58.
150. Ludz coined the term to refer to those revisionists having a firm institutional base and political constituency, as opposed to such intellectual deviants as Schaff and Kolakowski in Poland, Kosik in Czechoslovakia, Havemann in East Germany, or Lukacs in Hungary. See Peter C. Ludz, *The Changing Party Elite in East Germany* (Cambridge, Mass.: The M.I.T. Press, 1972).

division of labor in most walks of life, and to prefer complex hierarchical or market-oriented institutions to a more direct, populist approach to the masses. The distinctive ideological innovation shared by revisionists is a de facto abandonment of the dialectic, entailing an attenuation of support for class struggle, for violent revolution as a necessary prerequisite for socialism, and for the dictatorship of the proletariat. In place of class struggle and normative incentives, revisionists prefer easily calculable material incentives to motivate the work force; in place of the proletarian dictatorship they opt for socialist legality and a (highly formalized) representative democracy; in place of violent revolution they prefer "peaceful coexistence" and economic competition under political détente as a way of gradually realigning the international power balance.[151]

The attempt to "ritualize" charisma [152] leads to a Marxist form of neo-traditionalism similar to that which has characterized Soviet politics since the purge of Khrushchev.[153] Socialist neo-traditionalism consists of an attempt to revive revolutionary forms in the absence of any obviously revolutionary task to perform, enemy to destroy, "frame" to "smash." The violent revolutionary crusade thus becomes a legitimating ritual. Its most conspicuous departure from revolutionary "engineering" consists of a disenchantment with mass mobilization (thus it was Deng who mobilized the "masses" in 1978–79, not the "Maoists"). Hua Guofeng has been perhaps the most prominent spokesman of this course of development in the post-Mao era, and, although his own lack of a political base finally obliged him to succumb, there is evidence that this "line" still has considerable underlying support among veteran military and Party cadres. Still harkening to a charismatic conception of leadership in the admitted absence of appropriate tasks (or candidates) therefor, legitimation consists of memorialized heroism deriving from historical "contributions" (gonglao). Thus charismatic legitimacy transmutes into seniority, as personified by Ye Jianying—yet time goes by, and this is a dying breed. With the closing of the gates of charismatic revelation, ideology petrifies into a sort of holy writ, the attitude toward which partakes of traditional feelings of filial piety. Neo-traditionalism harbors a certain affinity for cultural essentialism and xenophobia, though the

151. See Dittmer, "Chinese Communist Revisionism in Comparative Perspective," *Studies in Comparative Communism* 13, no. 1 (Spring 1980): 3–41.

152. Cf. Robert Middlekauff, "The Ritualization of the American Revolution," in Stanley Coben and Lorman Ratner, eds., *The Development of an American Culture* (Englewood Cliffs, N.J.: Prentice-Hall, Inc., 1970), pp. 31–44.

153. Ken Jowitt has accounted for the resurgence of neo-traditionalism by the assumption that "A Leninist Party's charismatic features normally coincide with and unintentionally reinforce many cultural predispositions present in a traditional or status society." See Jowitt, "Soviet Neotraditionalism: The Political Corruption of a Leninist Regime," *Soviet Studies* 35, no. 3 (July 1983): 275–97; also see Weber, *Economy*, vol. 2: 1122.

recent disgrace of Maoism handicaps the quest for effective icons. For the nonce the neo-traditional grouping must be assumed still to have considerable power, based on well-articulated networks of personal connections and a "lingering fear" of breaking ideological taboos; they may perhaps also count on mass support from the military, the propaganda network, less successful enclaves among the peasantry, and unionized labor (depending on the economic conjuncture).

The inherent attractiveness of each of these "lines" to a given functionally specialized bureaucratic constituency, occupational sector, or "faction" may be expected to vary according to how well it "fits" the ideal interests of that group or quasi-group. But this "closeness of fit" can never be calculated with great precision, due to the incompleteness of the functional division of labor and the ideologically based refusal to concede the existence of diverging interests. Thus, empirically, the recruitment of adherents to these alternative tendencies will rely on a mixture of appeals to functional interests, ideological preferences, and informal personal connections. Considerable overlap and cross-cutting cleavage may be anticipated.

Though defined as programmatic alternatives of some internal ideological coherence, these alternative lines may each be considered functionally complementary to the system as a whole rather than mutually exclusive. The ritualization of charisma is sensitive to system needs for ideological legitimation, whereas institutionalized revisionism responds more flexibly to the shifting requirements of economic growth and productivity. This informal functional division of labor was not strictly adhered to in the initial post-Mao period (i.e., the "neo-traditionals" first seized control of the economic apparatus, whereas the "revisionists" made their play in the ideological arena), due to the allocation of power in the original postsuccession "deal," but there appears to be a tendency to gravitate to such an alignment in the wake of the resolution of that cleavage.[154]

In the immediate post-Mao caesura the tendency was to assume that the diametrically opposite course to anything so widely loathed as the Cultural Revolution must be "correct," and to move toward an increasingly pure form of institutionalized revisionism. But time has shown that neither alternative is a panacea and has reinforced the sense of interdependence between the two "lines." The neo-traditional approach to economic development, an uneasy amalgam of the Great Leap Forward with massive import-led capital investment in technologically advanced

154. See Xiao Cheng, "Some Signs of Intensification of the Restrictive Policy," *ZM*, no. 47 (September 1, 1981): 12–13, who points to an emergent coexistence between relaxation and continued experimentation in the economic realm (controlled by the pragmatists) with increasing restrictiveness in politics and culture.

heavy industry, came a cropper, appearing to bear out revisionist critiques of Maoist development strategy. The revisionist alternative, leading toward the ultimate destination of some form of market socialism, has achieved noteworthy successes in some sectors, particularly agriculture and light industry. It has in its turn, however, also precipitated unanticipated consequences (particularly bouts of unemployment and inflation) and bears partial responsibility for the problems of trade imbalance and deficit financing, and it still seems puzzled by the problems of industrialization and price reform. The revisionist "right" nevertheless retains the initiative for the time being, while the neo-traditional "left" retreats to a passive position to await targets of opportunity presented by revisionist setbacks. If the left is handicapped by its lack of a coherent alternative developmental strategy, the right has been discountenanced by the lacuna at the core of its eclectic, pragmatic approach to ideology, having been obliged to contain this void with the "four fundamental principles"—its own version of "whateverism."

The oscillatory pattern that has long characterized Chinese policymaking processes has thus not abruptly ceased, though the end of the revolution has modified its character. The left and right alternatives are no longer so far apart: united by their common commitment to modernization, they appear to differ only with regard to tactics and pace, and their differences are modulated by an agreement on the procedural rules of the game. Leadership disputes and elite factionalism continue to exist (ideological proximity does not altogether preclude political cleavage). However, the left no longer publicly accuses the right of attempting to restore capitalism, and the right no longer publicly accuses the left of threatening to overthrow all political authority and foment chaos. The last factional disputes to be resolved in purge and ideological recrimination stemmed from the cleavages of the Cultural Revolution; those ideological or policy differences between groups to have been detected since then (involving, say, the "petroleum faction," or the rivalry between "reformers" and "adjusters") have been resolved short of purge. There seems to be growing awareness that, notwithstanding the intellectual attractions of an internally congruent idea system, neither the left nor the right can at this time proffer realistically expedient alternatives fully compatible with the shifting and sometimes contradictory requirements of a modernizing socialist system. In the light of this recognition there is a tendency to grope for an ideologically incoherent but politically practical position somewhere between these two logical alternatives.[155]

155. See Tsou, "Political Change and Reform."

Interview Protocol

1. Name, telephone number, address
2. Sex
3. Marital status, children
4. Date of birth, place of birth
5. Home (*jiguan*)
6. Occupation, educational level of parents
7. Have you or any of your siblings had difficulties with the authorities?
8. When did you come to Hong Kong? Legally or illegally? Why did you leave China?
9. What have you been doing for a living since you left school?
10. Educational level
11. Family background (*jiating chushen*), individual class status (*geren chengfen*)
12. Party member? Red Guard? Cadre? What rank? Other political organizations?
13. Basic unit situation: (a) What was the conduct of the Party members? What was the proportion of good members to bad ones? (b) What was the conduct (*biaoxian*) of Communist Youth League (CYL) members, and what was the proportion of good ones to bad ones? (c) Activists? (d) The "four category elements" (*si lei fenzi*: renegades, spies, capitalist-roaders, purged cadres)?
14. What in your view is the "mass line"? (a) Do the masses really play a role in the mass line? More or less of a role after the Cultural Revolution than before? (b) Did the existing units more or less understand the mass line? When it was not understood did this often create contradictions? Give examples.
15. What was your view of the unit leadership? What was your attitude (*taidu*)? (a) Did the basic unit leadership behave differently before and after the Cultural Revolution, and if so, how? (b) Were the masses clear about the powers and sphere of competence of the leaders? Were there occasions when the leader exceeded his/her powers? Would this create friction with the masses? (c) Did the leaders play different roles before and after the Cultural Revolution? (d) What was the difference in the masses' attitudes toward the leaders before and after the Cultural Revolution? (e) Did your own attitude toward the central leaders change during the Cultural Revolution? Why? (f) If you were a central leader, would you do things differently? How?

16. Mao Zedong said that the purpose of the Cultural Revolution was not merely to purge the revisionists, but to transform people's thinking. Do you think that Mao Zedong had a way of changing people's thinking? (a) What thoughts did he want to change, and why? (b) Do you think his method of changing people's thinking was effective? Why or why not?

17. Did you participate in the Cultural Revolution? In what capacity? (a) Did the Cultural Revolution succeed? If so, why, and if not, why not? (b) Did you once have hopes for the Cultural Revolution? If so, what did you hope for? (c) Were you ever disappointed (shiwang) in the Cultural Revolution? If so, when? What caused you to lose hope?

18. What was the difference between political study (zhengzhi xuexi) before and after the Cultural Revolution? (a) Was there more or less political study before and after the Cultural Revolution? Was the time period stipulated? (b) What was the attitude of the masses toward political study before and after the Cultural Revolution (i.e., how did it change)? Why? (c) What was the general procedure for political study? Were specific materials assigned for each study meeting? Which materials? Did the procedure change during campaigns, and if so, how? How about "Living Study and Living Use of Mao Zedong's Thought" meetings? (d) Did the unit leadership more heavily emphasize the transformation of people's thinking after than before the Cultural Revolution? If so, how?

19. What was the general procedure in criticism and struggle meetings (pipan douzheng dahui)? (a) What was the procedure and overall atmosphere in small unit criticism and struggle meetings? (b) What about large unit (e.g., brigade, commune) criticism and struggle meetings? Please give examples, specifying time, place, persons, and situation. (c) Who spoke in criticism and struggle meetings? Were there spontaneous speakers, or were the speakers previously selected (zhidingde)? What proportion? What was the background of the speakers—masses? activists? cadres? other?

20. What were the consequences for those within the unit who made mistakes? (a) Who decided whether a person had made a mistake? Was there ever any controversy or discussion before deciding that a person had made a mistake? Any difference between the pre- and post-Cultural Revolution situation in that regard? (b) After deciding that a person had made a mistake, what types of meetings were held? (c) In the meeting at which the person's mistake was discussed, was the mistake accurately characterized? Was it distorted or exaggerated? (d) After the person making a mistake had made a self-criticism, how was it decided whether his self-criticism was acceptable? Who decided?

21. Were you personally ever criticized? Were the criticisms just? (a) Aside from your mistake, were there other reasons why you were criticized? For example, because your class background was not good, or because of different ideological views? If not, what was the reason for your being targeted? (b) Were you unfairly treated otherwise? If so, for what reason? How did you react? Did you speak out (fayan), and if so, with what results? (c) To whom did you usually express your complaints? Beyond complaining, did you and the people who agreed with you use any other means of expressing your feelings? Did you take any action? If so, with what results?

22. What sort of people were activists in your unit? (a) What was their class background and character (*xingge*)? What role did the activists play in work? in study? What was their relation with the masses? (b) Do you think the masses were truly an advance guard (*xianjin fenzi*)? How could you tell? (c) What was the difference between activists before and after the Cultural Revolution (if any)? How do you account for it?

23. What is the difference between class struggle and line struggle? What about factional struggle? (a) Why does Mao Zedong encourage people to struggle? Do you think struggle can transform people's thoughts? (b) Does it transform the thoughts of those who are criticized or struggled against? Sincerely? (c) Does it transform the thoughts of those who participate in mass criticism or struggle? (d) Did it transform your thoughts? Did it change your attitude toward struggle? (e) Did class struggle in your unit function to promote production? How did production proceed before struggle, and how did this change in the course of struggle? Cite examples. (f) Did struggle become more frequent and intense in the course of the Cultural Revolution decade, and if so, why? (g) What would be the result if there were no struggle?

24. How was the reconciliation of struggle (*tuanjie*) conducted after the Cultural Revolution? How did this compare with the pre-Cultural Revolution modus operandi? (a) How was reconciliation conducted between units, between cadres, between cadres and masses, among the masses, among Party members, between Party members and masses? How did this compare with before the Cultural Revolution? (b) After the target of struggle had corrected his/her mistakes, did the unit masses and leadership still have a bad impression, or was this improved?

25. Was there factional struggle in your unit? How many factions? Did you participate in any faction? What proportion of the unit participated? (a) Generally speaking, did the factions have an internal structure or leadership? What kind of people participated in factions? Why? (b) Have factions always been present? At what times did factions generally arise? Why? (c) After the conflict had been resolved, did factionalism persist, or dissipate? When did personal interest override factional commitment? When did organizational discipline override factional commitment?

26. Do you think equalitarianism is a necessary component of socialism? (a) Do you think equalitarianism became more pronounced because of the Cultural Revolution? If so, why? (b) Did equalitarianism become yet more pronounced in the 1968–76 period?

27. Why do you think Mao Zedong emphasized "politics takes command"? (a) Did you discuss politics more after the Cultural Revolution than before? With whom did you talk? Why did you talk with those persons rather than someone else? (b) When discussing political questions, did you often get into debates over ideological issues? What were the results of these debates? (c) When discussing politics did you discuss central politics or unit affairs more? (d) After the Cultural Revolution did you come to a better understanding of the political situation outside your unit?

28. Do you remember when the first big-character poster appeared in your unit? How did you feel—happy? puzzled? opposed? Why? Did you help write it?

Why not? Did you later post any big-character posters? Why? (a) In your opinion, what did Liu Shaoqi represent? During and after the Cultural Revolution, did your feelings about Liu Shaoqi change? (b) What do you now think of Lin Biao? Do you believe the "September 13" (1971) incident was real? Did the Lin Biao affair affect your belief in socialist ideals? (c) Do you think Lin Biao had any relation to Confucius? Is there any relation between Zhou Enlai and Confucius? Do you personally have any feelings for Confucius? Did the movement to criticize Lin Biao and Confucius affect your opinion of Confucius? (d) Why was Song Jiang, of *Water Margin*, targeted for criticism? What did Song Jiang represent? (e) What do you think is the meaning of "going against the current"? Is there any difference between "going against the current" (*fan chaoliu*) and "reactionary" (*fandong*)? What? Do you think going against the current is a good thing? Were there more who dared go against the current after the Cultural Revolution than before? Were you acquainted with anyone who went against the current? What was the result? (f) When did you learn of the Zhang Tiesheng matter? What were your feelings at the time? Now? If you had been in Zhang's position in 1973 what would you have done? (g) What are "bourgeois rights"? What do you think of them? What sort of people have bourgeois rights? How does one get the power to have such rights? Do you think it is fair for some people to have privileges? Why or why not? When is it right for those who have privileges to utilize bourgeois rights? If people abuse bourgeois rights, how should the masses react?

29. Did you participate in any of the following campaigns: the Criticism of Lin Biao and Confucius, the Anti–Bourgeois Rights, the Criticism of *Water Margin* and Song Jiang, Going against the Current, or the Oppose the Rightist Reversal of Just Verdicts campaigns? (a) What did these campaigns have in common with the Cultural Revolution (1966–68), and how did they differ? (b) Did a work team come to your unit to help mobilize the masses? Who sent them? What was the main task they performed? (c) Did these campaigns have any impact on your relations with the masses, or with the leadership? (d) Was anyone in your unit made a criticism target in any of these campaigns? How and when were targets selected for mass criticism or struggle? Who decided? What were the main errors for which they were criticized? (e) Were these movements more or less effective than the Cultural Revolution in transforming people's thinking? Why?

30. Do you have any personal experience with "taking the back door"? (a) Did most people know who practiced taking the back door? What was the general attitude toward them? What was your attitude? (b) What sort of people most often took the back door? (c) Why do you think that sort of phenomenon (viz., taking the back door) occurred? (d) Did any of the campaigns mentioned above reduce the incidence of taking the back door? (e) Do you know of anyone who used the back door to get into college, a factory job, or into a bureaucratic position, was then criticized on that account and sent back to the original unit? What do you think would have to be done to finally eliminate the phenomenon of taking the back door?

31. Are you an educated youth who participated in "up to the mountains and

down to the countryside"? What is your opinion of the latter? (a) If you participated, did the experience change your attitude about work or about working people? If so, why did you leave the place to which you were sent? (b) Upon returning to the city (*daoliu*), how did one earn a living? What was your experience? (c) What impact did those flowing back to the city have on the sent-down youth remaining in the countryside?

32. How was the rehabilitation of cadres handled after the Cultural Revolution? (a) How did "liberated" cadres prove that they had rectified their mistakes? (b) How was one able to determine the authenticity (*zhenshixing*) of cadre rectification? (c) Did you personally resolutely hate "four category elements"? What was your attitude once they had been liberated?

33. Did you ever participate in a May 7 Cadre School? (a) Did cadres in such schools frequently participate in manual labor? (b) After the Cultural Revolution, did your branch implement "open door rectification" (*kaimen zhengfeng*)? With what results? (c) Did having gone to a May 7 Cadre School or experienced rectification transform your attitude toward the masses or toward manual labor? If so, how; if not, why not?

34. Did you ever participate in a strike? How did such a phenomenon come about? Did the leadership participate? Why? (a) Did you have any experience with slow-down strikes (*daigong*)? Why did the slow-down occur? What was the context? (b) Did you participate in labor unrest (*saodong*) or riots? In what context? (c) Is there any relationship between strikes, slow-down strikes, or unrest and mass movements?

35. What do you think of the purge of the "Gang of Four"? (a) Do you think the Gang wanted to transform people's thinking? Were they successful or ineffective in doing so? Why? (b) Do you think Hua Guofeng tried to use another method to change people's thinking? Why? With what results? (c) Mao Zedong once said that every seven or eight years there will be a Cultural Revolution. Do you think so? If so, under what circumstances do you think another Cultural Revolution is likely to occur?

36. Did you often feel uneasy after the Cultural Revolution? Why? Because of politics? Because you were personally criticized or struggled against? Because you were unable to adapt to the post-Cultural Revolution environment? Or for other reasons?

Glossary

anding tuanjie	安定团结
Anhui	安徽
Anhui Wenyi	安徽文艺
ba er qi	八二七
ba pi-Lin pi-Kong de douzheng jinxing dao di	把批林批孔的斗争进行到底
bagong	罢工
Bai Hua	白桦
Bai Rubing	白如冰
Banyue Tan	半月谈
banzhang	班长
Banzhuren	班主任
Baoding	保定
Baoji	宝鸡
Baoshan	宝山
Baotou	包头
Beida	北大
Beidaihe	北戴河
Beijing	北京
Beijing zhi Chun	北京之春
Bengbu	蚌埠
benxing	本性
bi	笔
biaoxian	表现
Bo Yibo	薄一波
Bohai	渤海
buyu	哺育
Cankao Xiaoxi	参考消息
Cankao Ziliao	参考资料
cha e xuanju zhi	差额选举制

Chang'an Street	长安街
Changjiang	昌江
Changsha	长沙
changzhang	厂长
Chao Gai	晁盖
Chaoyang	朝阳
Chen Boda	陈伯达
Chen Jun	陈浚
Chen Xilian	陈锡联
Chen Yi	陈毅
Chen Yonggui	陈永贵
Chen Yun	陈云
Chen Zaidao	陈再道
Chen Zhengren	陈正人
Cheng Zihua	程子华
Chengdu	成都
Chi Heng	池恒
Chi Qun	迟群
Chiang Kai-shek	蒋介石
Chongqing	重庆
Chu Lan	初澜
chuanda huiyi	传达会议
chuangjiang	闯将
Chuangye	创业
chuanlian	串连
chuxiao liangpiao	除消粮票
Conghua	从化
da bendan, da caobao	大笨蛋大草包
da gong wu si	大公无私
da luo shui gou	打落水狗
da pipan	大批判
da shengren	大圣人
Dagang	大港
daibiao dahui	代表大会
daigong	呆工
dang shi lingdao yiqie de	党是领导一切的
dang'an	档案
dangquan de tongzhi jituan	当权的统治集团
dangquan pai	当权派
danwei	单位
danwei suoyouzhi	单位所有制
daoliu	倒流

Daqing	大庆
Dazhai	大寨
Dazhong Dian Bao	大众电报
Deng Liqun	邓力群
Deng Tuo	邓拓
Deng Xiaoping	邓小平
Deng Yingchao	邓颖超
Deng Zihui	邓子恢
"Diaodong"	调动
diaozi gao de ren neng shangqu	调子高的人能上去
Di Fucai	狄福才
Ding Sheng	丁盛
Dong Biwu	董必武
Dong Zhongshu	董仲舒
duanlian	锻炼
Dushu	读书
fan chaoliu	反潮流
fandong	反动
Fang Hai	方海
Fanghualian	防化连
fangpi	放屁
fanji youqing fan'an feng	反击右倾翻案风
fayan	发言
Feng Wenbin	冯文彬
Feng Youlan	冯友兰
fengshui	风水
fenjia	分家
Fu Yuehua	傅月华
Fudan University	复旦大学
Fujian	福建
Fuzhou	福州
fuzhu gongzi	辅助工资
gan	敢
gan nu bu gan yan	敢怒不敢言
Gansu	甘肃
gao gan lou	高干楼
Gao Gang	高岗
gaoji ganbu	高级干部
Geng Biao	耿飙
Gengshen	庚申
geren chengfen	个人成分

geren mixin	个人迷信
gong dai hui	工代会
Gongchanzhuyi shi tiantang/ Renmin gongshe shi qiaoliang	共产主义是天堂；人民公社是桥梁
gonglao	功劳
gongzuo fenpei	工作分配
Guangdong	广东
Guangming Ribao (Guangming Daily)	光明日报
Guangxi	广西
Guangzhou	广州
guanliaozhuyi	官僚主义
Guiyang	贵阳
Guizhou	贵州
Guo Linxiang	郭林祥
Guo Moruo	郭沫若
guojia ganbu	国家干部
Guojia jihua weiyuanhui	国家计划委员会
Guojia tongji ju	国家统计局
Haidian	海淀
Hailang Hua	海浪花
Hainan Island	海南
Haixia	海霞
Han Xianchu	韩先楚
Hangzhou	杭州
Hao Liang	浩亮
Harbin	哈尔滨
He Changgong	何长工
He Long	贺龙
He Qiu	何求
He Zhengwen	何正文
Hebei	河北
hei bang	黑帮
hei dian	黑店
hei hua	黑话
hei qi	黑旗
hei shu	黑书
hei wu lei	黑五类
hei xian	黑线
Heilongjiang	黑龙江
Henan	河南
hong deng	红灯
hong haiyang	红海洋

hong hua	红花
hong taiyang	红太阳
hong wu lei	红五类
hong xiao bing	红小兵
hong xin	红心
Hong Yuan	洪原
houtai laoban	后台老板
Hu Feng	胡风
Hu Jiwei	胡绩伟
Hu Qiaomu	胡乔木
Hu Qili	胡启立
Hu Sheng	胡绳
Hu Yaobang	胡耀邦
Hua Guofeng	华国锋
Huai-Hai	淮海
Huang Kecheng	黄克诚
Huang Yanpei	黄炎培
Huang Yongsheng	黄永胜
huansan ruanruo	缓散软弱
huaqing jiexian	画清界限
Hubei	湖北
hui	会
Hunan	湖南
huopo	活泼
huoxue huoyong Mao Zedong sixiang jiji fenzi daibiao hui	活学活用毛泽东思想积极分子代表会
Ji Dengkui	纪登奎
Jia Qiyun	贾启允
Jiang Qing	江青
Jiang Tian	江天
Jiang Weiqing	江渭清
jiangjun haohao xiyixi	将军好好洗一洗
Jiangsu	江苏
Jiangxi	江西
jianjue chedi ganjing quanbu de	坚决彻底干净全部的
jiaodaiguo	交代过
jiating chushen	家庭出身
jiceng danwei	基层单位
jide liyi jituan	积得利益集团
Jiefang Ribao	解放日报
jieji touxiang	阶级投降
jiguan	机关

Jiji	集集
jiji fenzi	积极分子
Jilin	吉林
Ji'nan	济南
jing er yuan zhi	敬而远之
Jinggangshan	井冈山
Jinggangshan	井冈山
Jinhua	金华
jinzhang	紧张
jiu yao liu	九一六
jiu yao qi	九一七
jiu yi san shijian	九一三事件
jizao maojin	急躁冒进
kaimen zhengfeng	开门整风
Kang Sheng	康生
Kexue Huabao	科学画报
ku	苦
kuangkuang	框框
kuanggong	旷工
Kulian	苦恋
Kunming	昆明
Lanzhou	兰州
lao hao ren	老好人
Li Da	李达
Li Dazhao	李大钊
Li Desheng	李德生
Li Fuchun	李富春
Li Lisan	李立三
Li Ruishan	李瑞山
Li Shu	黎澍
Li Xiannian	李先念
Li Yizhe	李一哲
Li Zuopeng	李作鹏
liang bao yi kan	两报一刊
Liang Shuming	梁漱溟
Liang Xiao	梁效
Lianhuan Huabao	连环画报
Lianjiang documents	连江文件
Liao Gailong	廖盖隆
Liao Zhigao	廖志高
Liaoning	辽宁

lijiao	礼教
Lin Biao	林彪
Lin Jie	林杰
Lin Liguo	林立果
Lishi Yanjiu	历史研究
Liu Bing	刘冰
Liu Bocheng	刘伯承
Liu Jianxun	刘建勋
Liu Qingtang	刘庆棠
Liu Shaoqi	刘少奇
Liu Xianquan	刘贤权
Liu Xinwu	刘心武
Liu Zihou	刘子厚
liumang	流氓
Lu Xinhua	卢新华
Lu Xun	鲁迅
Lu Ying	鲁瑛
Lü, Empress	吕后
luan	乱
Luo Ruiqing	罗瑞卿
Luo Siding	罗思鼎
Lushan	庐山
Ma Ning	马宁
mamuhua	麻木化
Mao Yuanxin	毛远新
Mao Zedong	毛泽东
Mei di Su xiu	美帝苏修
mei fa bi de	没法比的
Meixian	梅县
minkan	民刊
mou yi zhong sixiang	某一仲思想
mu	亩
Mu Xin	穆欣
Nanchang	南昌
Nanhai	南海
Nanjing	南京
Nanning	南宁
nei	内
nei sheng wai wang	内圣外王
nei wai you bie	内外有别
neibu	内部

Ni Zhifu	伲志福
Nie Rongzhen	聂荣臻
niugui sheshen	牛鬼蛇神
niulang zhinü	牛郎织女
pa	怕
Peng Chong	彭冲
Peng Dehuai	彭德怀
Peng Zhen	彭真
pin xiazhong nong daibiao huiyi	贫下中农代表会议
pi-Deng	批邓
pi-Kong	批孔
pi-Lin	批林
pi-Lin pi-Kong	批林批孔
pipan	批判
pipan douzheng dahui	批判斗争大会
pixiu zhengfeng	批修整风
Qi Benyu	戚本禹
qian gong jiao renyuan	前公教人员
qiao weiba	翘尾巴
Qin	秦
Qin Chuan	秦川
Qin Shihuang	秦始皇
Qingdao	青岛
Qinghai	青海
Qinghua University	清华大学
Qingming	清明
Qingnian Wengao	青年文稿
Qiu Huizuo	邱会作
quanwei	权威
Rao Shushi	饶漱石
rencai liudong	人才流动
Renmin wuzhuang bu	人民武装部
Renmin yiyuan	人民医院
ruan, lan, san	软, 懒, 散
san dai hui	三代会
san zhong ren	三种人
sanba zuofeng	三八作风
saodong	骚动
Shaanxi	陕西

Shandong	山东
shang	上
Shanghai	上海
shangpin zhidu	商品制度
shangshan xiaxiang	上山下乡
Shanxi	山西
Shaoguan	韶关
shehui shufu	社会束缚
Sheng Shicai	盛世才
shengchan jianshe bingtuan	生产建设兵团
Shengli oil fields	胜利油田
Shenyang	沈阳
shiwang	失望
shiyuan	师员
shuang zhui	双追
shui	税
Shuihu	水浒
shuo jiahua de ren neng shangqu	说假话的人能上去
si lei fenzi	四类分子
si xiang jiben yuanze	四项基本原则
Sichuan	四川
sige di yi	四个第一
Siwu Luntan	四五论坛
Sixiang Zhanxian	思想战线
Song Jiang	宋江
Song Peizhang	宋佩章
Song Renqiong	宋任穷
Song Zhenming	宋振明
Su Zhenhua	苏振华
Sufan	肃反
Sun Feng	孙丰
Sun Yat-sen	孙逸仙(孙中山)
suowei	所谓
suqing ancang fangeming	肃清暗藏反革命
taidu	态度
Taishan	台山
Tan Qilong	潭启龙
tanbai congkuan, kangju congyan	坦白从宽抗拒从严
Tang Ke	唐克
Tang Xiaowen	唐晓文
Tangshan	唐山
Tansuo	探索

Taoyuan	桃源
tashangqu gun	踏上去滚
tequan	特权
Tiananmen	天安门
tiancai	天才
tiancailun	天才论
Tianjin	天津
tigao bianbie zhenjia Makesizhuyi de nengli	提高辨别真假马克思主义的能力
ting bu qingchu	听不清楚
tingzhi fanxing	停职反省
Tongji University	同济大学
toulan	偷懒
tuanjie	团结
Tuanjiebao	团结报
tuigong	退工
tuihua bianzhi fenzi	蜕化变质分子
wai	外
Wang Dongxing	汪东兴
Wang Hongwen	王洪文
Wang Jian	王谦
Wang Li	王力
Wang Mantian	王曼恬
Wang Renzhong	王任重
Wang Ruoshui	王若水
Wang Xizhe	王希哲
Wang Zhichang	王知常
Wangfujing	王府井
Wei Guoqing	韦国清
Wei Jingsheng	魏京生
wenge pai	文革派
wenhua zu	文化组
Wenyi Bao	文艺报
Wenzhou	温州
Wu, Empress	武后
wu bu pa	五不怕
Wu De	吴德
Wu Faxian	吴法宪
Wu Guixian	吴桂贤
Wu Han	吴含
Wu Lengxi	吴冷西
wu yao liu	五一六
Wuhan	武汉

xia	下
xia xiang	下乡
xiafang	下放
xian	县
xiang	乡
xianjin fenzi	先进分子
Xiao Hua	肖华
Xiao Luan	小峦
Xiao pinglun	小评论
Xiao Qiu	小丘
xiaobao	小报
xiaojiang	小将
Xiaojinzhuang	小靳庄
Xiaoshuo Yuebao	小说月报
xiaozu	小组
Xidan	西单
Xie Fuzhi	谢富治
Xie Jingyi	谢静宜
xiezuo zu	写作组
xiguan quanli	习惯权力
xinchang	心肠
xingge	性格
Xinhai Revolution	辛亥革命
Xinhui	新会
Xinjiang	新疆
Xiong Fu	熊复
xitong	系统
Xu Dixin	许涤新
Xu Shiyou	许世友
Xu Xiangqian	徐向前
xuebao	学报
xuexi	学习
Xuexi yu Pipan	学习与批判
xuezhe	学者
Xushui	徐水
Xuzhou	徐州
Yan'an	延安
Yang Chengwu	杨成武
Yang Dezhi	杨得志
Yang Yong	杨勇
Yang Zirong	杨子荣
yangbanxi	样板戏
Yangcheng Evening News	羊城晚报

yansu	严肃
yanzhong de cuowu	严重的错误
Yao Dengshan	姚登山
Yao Wenyuan	姚文元
Yao Yilin	姚依林
Ye Jianying	叶剑英
Ye Qun	叶群
Ye Wenfu	叶文福
yi da san fan	一打三反
yi dao qie	一刀切
yi ku fan	忆苦饭
yingxiong shiguan	英雄史观
yiyuanhua	一元化
You Taizhong	尤太忠
Yunnan	云南
Yutian xian	玉田县
Zeng Siyu	曾思玉
Zeng Tao	曾涛
Zhanbao	战报
zhandui	战队
Zhang Bojun	章伯钧
Zhang Chunqiao	张春桥
Zhang Liguo	张立国
Zhang Pinghua	张平化
Zhang Tianmin	张天民
Zhang Tiesheng	张铁生
Zhao Xinchu	赵辛初
Zhao Ziyang	赵紫阳
zhaoji	召集
Zhejiang	浙江
Zhengfan	整反
zhengfeng	整风
zhengzhi jichu	政治基础
zhengzhi xuexi	政治学习
Zhengzhou	郑州
zhenli de biaozhun	真理的标准
zhenshixing	真实性
zhidingde	指定的
zhiheng	治衡
zhishi	知识
Zhong Yueqiu	钟粤秋
zhongfa	中发

Zhongguo Qingnian	中国青年
Zhongnanhai	中南海
Zhongshan	中山
zhongyang wenjian	中央文件
Zhou, Duke of	周公
Zhou Enlai	周恩来
Zhou Huamin	周化民
Zhou Yang	周杨
Zhu De	朱德
Zhu Kejia	朱克家
Zhu Muzhi	朱穆之
Zhu Yongjia	朱永嘉
Zhuang Zedong	庄则栋
zhuanjia	专家
zhuchi	主持
zichan jieji ziyouhua	资产阶级自由化
zige	资格
zong fudaoyuan	总辅导员
zou houmen	走后门

Selected Bibliography

FREQUENTLY CITED PERIODICALS

Periodicals in English

Beijing Review (Peking Review). Beijing.
China Aktuell. Hamburg: Institut für Asienkunde.
China News Analysis. Hong Kong.
Current Background. Hong Kong: U.S. Consulate General.
Far Eastern Economic Review. Hong Kong.
Issues and Studies. Taipei: Institute of International Relations.
Survey of China Mainland Press. Hong Kong: U.S. Consulate General.
Survey of People's Republic of China Press. Hong Kong: U.S. Consulate General.
U.S. Joint Publications Research Service. Arlington, Va.

Periodicals in Chinese

Periodicals from the People's Republic of China

Faxue 法学 [Law]. Shanghai.
Faxue Yanjiu 法学研究 [Studies on law].
Guangming Ribao 光明日报 [Illumination daily].
Hongqi 红旗 [Red flag].
Hongweibing 红卫兵 [Red guard].
Jiefangjun Bao 解放军报 [Liberation army daily].
Minzhu yu Fazhi 民主与法制 [Democracy and legal institutions]. Shanghai.
Renmin Ribao 人民日报 [People's daily].
Wenhui Bao 文汇报 [Wenhui daily].
Xin Shiqi 新时期 [New era].

Periodicals from Hong Kong

Dangdai 当代 [Contemporary monthly].
Dong Xi Fang 东西方 [East and west].
Dongxiang 动向 [Trends].
Guang Jiao Jing 广角镜 [Wide angle lens].
Mingbao Yuekan 明报月刊 [Ming Bao monthly].
Qishi Niandai 七十年代 [The seventies].
Zhanwang 展望 [Prospect].
Zhengming 争鸣 [Contend].

Periodicals from Taiwan

Feiqing Yuebao 匪情月报 [Communist information monthly].
Zhonggong Yanjiu 中共研究 [Chinese communist studies].

BOOKS AND MONOGRAPHS

Ahn, Byung-joon. *Chinese Politics and the Cultural Revolution: Dynamics of Policy Processes*. Seattle: University of Washington Press, 1976.

Arendt, Hannah. *The Origins of Totalitarianism*. New York: Harcourt Brace Jovanovich, 1973 edition.

Avakian, Bob. *The Loss in China and the Revolutionary Legacy of Mao Tse-tung*. Chicago: RCP Pub., 1978.

Baker, Hugh D. R. *Chinese Family and Kinship*. New York: Columbia University Press, 1979.

Barnett, A. Doak. *Communist China: The Early Years, 1949–55*. New York: Frederick A. Praeger, 1964.

Baum, Richard. *Prelude to Revolution: Mao, the Party, and the Peasant Question, 1962–66*. New York: Columbia University Press, 1975.

Baum, Richard, and Frederick Teiwes. *Ssu-ch'ing: The Socialist Education Movement of 1962–66*. Center for Chinese Studies, Research Monograph no. 2. Berkeley, 1968.

Bennett, Gordon, and Ronald Montaperto. *Red Guard: The Political Biography of Dai Hsiao-ai*. Garden City, N.Y.: Doubleday & Co., 1971.

Bernstein, Richard. *From the Center of the Earth: The Search for the Truth about China*. Boston: Little, Brown, 1982.

Bernstein, Thomas P. *Up to the Mountains and Down to the Villages: The Transfer of Youth from Urban to Rural China*. New Haven, Conn.: Yale University Press, 1977.

Bettelheim, Charles, and Neil Burton. *China since Mao*. New York: Monthly Review Press, 1978.

Brinton, Crane. *The Anatomy of Revolution*. New York: Vintage Books, 1960.

Broyelle, Claudie, et al. *China: A Second Look*. Trans. Sarah Matthews. Atlantic Highlands, N.J.: Humanities Press, 1980.

Brugger, Bill. *China: Liberation and Transformation, 1942–1962*. London: Croom Helm, 1981.

———. *China: Radicalism to Revisionism, 1962–1979*. London: Croom Helm, 1981.

Bunce, Valerie. *Do New Leaders Make a Difference? Executive Succession and Public Policy under Capitalism and Socialism*. Princeton: Princeton University Press, 1981.

Butterfield, Fox. *China: Alive in the Bitter Sea*. New York: Times Books, Quadrangle Publications, 1982.

CCP Documents of the Great Proletarian Cultural Revolution. Hong Kong: Union Research Institute, 1969.

Cell, Charles. *Revolution at Work: Mobilization Campaigns in China*. New York: Academic Press, 1979.

Chan, Anita. *Children of Mao: Personality Development and Political Activism in the Red Guard Generation.* New York: Macmillan, 1985.

Chan, Anita, Richard Madsen, and Jonathan Unger. *Chen Village: The Recent History of a Peasant Community in Mao's China.* Berkeley: University of California Press, 1984.

Chang, Parris H. *Power and Policy in China.* University Park: Pennsylvania State University Press, 1978. Second enlarged edition.

Chang, Y. C. *Factional and Coalition Politics in China: The Cultural Revolution and Its Aftermath.* New York: Praeger, 1976.

Chen, C. S., ed. *Rural People's Communes in Lien-chiang.* Trans. Charles Price Ridley. Stanford: Hoover Institution Press, 1969.

Ch'en, Jerome, ed. *Mao Papers.* London: Oxford University Press, 1970.

Chuang, H. C. *The Great Proletarian Cultural Revolution: A Terminological Study.* Berkeley: University of California, Center for Chinese Studies, August 1967.

———. *The Little Red Book and Current Chinese Language.* Berkeley: University of California, Center for Chinese Studies, 1968.

Croll, Elisabeth. *The Politics of Marriage in Contemporary China.* Cambridge: Cambridge University Press, 1981.

Crook, Isabel, and David Crook. *The First Years of the Yangyi Commune.* London: Routledge & Kegan Paul, 1966

Ding Wang 丁望. *Wang Hongwen Zhang Chunqiao Pingzhuan* 王洪文张春桥评传 [Biography of Wang Hongwen and Zhang Chunqiao]. Hong Kong: Ming Bao, 1977.

Ding Wang, ed. *Mao Zedong Xuanji Buyi* 毛泽东选集补遗 [Supplement to the selected works of Mao Zedong], vol. 3. Hong Kong: Ming Bao Monthly Pub., 1971.

Domes, Jürgen. *China after the Cultural Revolution: Politics between Two Party Congresses.* Trans. Annette Berg and David Goodman. Berkeley: University of California Press, 1975.

Fraser, John. *The Chinese: Portrait of a People.* New York: Summit Books, 1980.

Friedrich, Carl J., and Zbigniew K. Brzezinski. *Totalitarian Dictatorship and Autocracy.* Cambridge, Mass.: Harvard University Press, 1965.

Frolic, B. Michael. *Mao's China: Sixteen Portraits of Life in Revolutionary China.* Cambridge, Mass.: Harvard University Press, 1980.

Funabashi, Yuichi. *Neibu: One Report on China.* Tokyo: Asahi Shimbun, Pub., 1982.

Gardner, John. *Chinese Politics and the Succession to Mao.* New York: Holmes & Meier, 1982.

Glaubitz, Joachim. *Opposition Gegen Mao: Abendspräche am Yanshan und andere politische Dokumente.* Olten: Walter Verlag, 1969.

Goodstadt, Leo. *China's Watergate: Political and Economic Conflicts, 1969–1977.* New Delhi: Vikas Pub., 1979.

Gottlieb, Thomas M. *Chinese Foreign Policy Factionalism and the Origins of the Strategic Triangle.* Santa Monica, Calif.: RAND Corp., R-1902-NA, November 1977.

Grey, Anthony. *Hostage in Peking*. London: Michael Joseph, 1970.

Guillermaz, Jacques. *The Chinese Communist Party in Power, 1949–1975*. Boulder, Colo.: Westview Press, 1976.

Habermas, Jürgen. *Strukturwandlung der Öffentlichkeit: Untersuchungen zu einer Kategorie der bürgerlichen Gesellschaft*. Neuwied: Hermann Luchterhand Verlag, 1962.

Han Suyin. *My House Has Two Doors*. New York: G. P. Putnam's Sons, 1980.

Hao Ran 浩然. *Jin Guang Da Dao* 金光大道 [The bright golden road]. Beijing: People's Literature Publishing Co., 1972. 2 vols.

Harding, Harry. *Organizing China: The Problem of Bureaucracy, 1949–1976*. Stanford: Stanford University Press, 1981.

Hinton, Harold C. *The Bear at the Gate: Chinese Policymaking under Soviet Pressure*. Stanford: Hoover Institution Press, 1971.

Hoffman, Rainer. *Kampf zweier Linien: Zur politischen Geschichte der chinesischen Volksrepublik, 1949–1977*. Stuttgart: Ernst Klett Verlag, 1978.

Hoffmann, Charles. *The Chinese Worker*. Albany: State University of New York Press, 1974.

Howe, Christopher. *China's Economy: A Basic Guide*. New York: Basic Books, 1978.

Howkins, John. *Mass Communication in China*. New York: Longman, 1982.

Hsia, Adrian. *Die Chinesische Kulturrevolution*. Neuwied: Hermann Luchterhand, 1971.

Hughes, T. J., and D. E. T. Luard. *The Economic Development of Communist China, 1949–1958*. London: Oxford University Press, 1959.

Hunter, Neale. *Shanghai Journal: An Eyewitness Account of the Cultural Revolution*. New York: Praeger, 1969.

Jain, J. P. *After Mao What? Army, Party and Group Rivalries in China*. New Delhi: Radiant Pub., 1975.

Johnson, Chalmers. *Peasant Nationalism and Communist Revolution*. Stanford: Stanford University Press, 1962.

———. *Revolutionary Change*. Stanford: Stanford University Press, 1982. Revised edition.

Johnson, Kay Ann. *Women, the Family, and Peasant Revolution in China*. Chicago: University of Chicago Press, 1983.

Jowitt, Kenneth. *Revolutionary Breakthroughs and National Development*. Berkeley: University of California Press, 1971.

Kau, Ying-mao, ed. *The Lin Piao Affair*. White Plains, N.Y.: International Arts & Sciences Press, 1975.

Kornhauser, William. *The Politics of Mass Society*. New York: The Free Press, 1959.

Kraus, Richard C. *Class Conflict in Chinese Socialism*. New York: Columbia University Press, 1981.

Kuhn. Thomas. *The Structure of Scientific Revolutions*. Chicago: University of Chicago Press, 1962.

Lai Ying. *The Thirty-sixth Way: A Personal Account of Imprisonment and Escape from Red China*. Trans. Edward Bahr and Sidney Liu. New York: Doubleday, 1969.

Lardy, Nicholas R. *China's Economic Readjustment: Recovery or Paralysis?* New York: China Council of the Asia Society, March 1980.

Lee, Hong Yung. *The Politics of the Chinese Cultural Revolution: A Case Study.* Berkeley: University of California Press, 1978.

Legge, James, trans. *The Chinese Classics, II: The Works of Mencius.* Reprint of 1895 ed. Hong Kong: Hong Kong University Press, 1960.

Levenson, Joseph. *Confucian China and Its Modern Fate: A Trilogy.* Berkeley: University of California Press, 1968 ed.

Lévi-Strauss, Claude. *The Savage Mind.* Chicago: University of Chicago Press, 1966.

—————. *Structural Anthropology.* New York: Basic Books, 1963.

Liang Heng and Judith Shapiro. *Son of the Revolution.* New York: Alfred A. Knopf, 1983.

Liao Luyan 廖鲁言. *Yijiuwuwu nian Nongcun Gongzuo Wenti* 一九五五年农村工作问题 [Rural work in 1955]. Beijing: People's Press, 1955.

Lieberthal, Kenneth G. *Sino-Soviet Conflict in the 1970s: Its Evolution and Implications for the Strategic Triangle.* Santa Monica: RAND Corp., R-2342-NA, July 1978.

Lieberthal, Kenneth, ed. *Central Documents and Politburo Politics in China.* Ann Arbor: University of Michigan, Center for Chinese Studies Monograph no. 33, 1978.

Lifton, Robert Jay. *Thought Reform and the Psychology of Totalism: A Study of "Brainwashing" in China.* New York: W. W. Norton, 1963.

Ling, Ken. *The Revenge of Heaven: Journal of a Young Chinese.* New York: G. P. Putnam's Sons, 1972.

Lipset, Seymour Martin. *Political Man.* Baltimore, Md.: The Johns Hopkins University Press, 1981. Expanded edition.

Liu, Alan P. L. *Political Culture and Group Conflict in Communist China.* Santa Barbara, Calif.: Clio Press, 1976.

Louie, Kam. *Critiques of Confucius in Contemporary China.* Hong Kong: Chinese University of Hong Kong Press, 1980.

Lu Xinhua et al. *The Wounded: New Stories of the Cultural Revolution, 1977–78.* Trans. Geremie Barme and Bennett Lee. Hong Kong: Joint Pub., 1979.

Ludz, Peter C. *The Changing Party Elite in East Germany.* Cambridge, Mass.: The M.I.T. Press, 1972.

MacFarquhar, Roderick. *Origins of the Cultural Revolution: I. Contradictions among the People, 1956–1957.* London: Oxford University Press, 1974.

Madsen, Richard P. *Morality and Power in a Chinese Village.* Berkeley: University of California Press, 1984.

Malraux, André. *Anti-Memoirs.* Trans. Terence Kilmartin. New York: Holt, Rinehart & Winston, 1968.

Mao Zedong. *A Critique of Soviet Economics.* New York: Monthly Review Press, 1977.

Mao Zedong Ji 毛泽东集 [Collected works of Mao Zedong]. Vol. 1. Hong Kong: Yishan, 1976.

Mao Zedong Sixiang Wan Sui. 毛泽东思想万岁 [Long live Mao Zedong Thought]. Three volumes. Hong Kong: n.p., 1967, 1969.

Martin, Helmut. *Cult and Canon: The Origins and Development of State Maoism.* Armonk, N.Y.: M. E. Sharpe, 1982.

Martin, Helmut, and Wolfgang Bartke. *Die Massenorganisation der Volksrepublik China.* Hamburg: Institut für Asienkunde, Mitteilung no. 62, 1975.

Martin, Roberta. *Party Recruitment in China: Patterns and Prospects.* New York: Columbia University, East Asian Institute Occasional Papers, 1981.

Mathews, Jay, and Linda Mathews. *One Billion: A China Chronicle.* New York: Random House, 1983.

Meijer, M. J. *Marriage Law and Policy in the Chinese People's Republic.* Hong Kong: Hong Kong University Press, 1971.

Meisner, Maurice. *Marxism, Maoism and Utopianism.* Madison: University of Wisconsin Press, 1982.

Moore, Barrington. *Injustice: The Social Bases of Obedience and Revolt.* White Plains, N.Y.: M. E. Sharpe, 1978.

———. *Soviet Politics: The Dilemma of Power.* New York: Harper & Row, 1965.

Mosher, Steven. *Broken Earth: The Rural Chinese.* New York: The Free Press, 1983.

Munro, Donald J. *The Concept of Man in Contemporary China.* Ann Arbor: University of Michigan Press, 1977.

Nyomarkay, Joseph. *Charisma and Factionalism in the Nazi Party.* Minneapolis: University of Minnesota Press, 1967.

Opletal, Helmut. *Die Informationspolitik der Volksrepublik China: Von der "Kulturrevolution" bis zum Sturz der "Viererbande" (1965 bis 1976).* Bochum: Studienverlag Brockmeyer, 1981.

Planning Division of the Agricultural Department of the Central Government, ed. *Liangnian lai de Zhongguo Nongcun Jingji Diaocha Huibian* 两年来的中国农村经济调查汇编 [A collection of investigations of China's rural economy over the past two years]. Beijing: Zhonghua Book Co., 1952.

Resolution on CPC History (1949–1981). Beijing: Foreign Languages Press, 1981.

Robinson, Thomas. *A Political-Military Biography of Lin Piao, Part II. 1950–1971.* Santa Monica: RAND Corp., 1971.

Rosen, Stanley. *Red Guard Factionalism and the Cultural Revolution in Guangzhou (Canton).* Boulder, Colo.: Westview Press, 1982.

Rue, John E. *Mao Tse-tung in Opposition, 1927–1935.* Stanford: Stanford University Press, 1966.

Rush, Myron. *How Communist States Change Their Rulers.* Ithaca, N.Y.: Cornell University Press, 1974.

———. *Political Succession in the USSR.* New York: Columbia University Press, 1965.

Scheff, T. J. *Catharsis in Healing, Ritual and Drama.* Berkeley: University of California Press, 1979.

Schweitzer, Arthur. *The Age of Charisma.* Chicago: Nelson Hall, 1984.

Shils, Edward. *Center and Periphery: Essays in Macrosociology.* Chicago: University of Chicago Press, 1975.

Shue, Vivienne. *Peasant China in Transition: The Dynamics of Development toward Socialism, 1949–1956.* Berkeley: University of California Press, 1980.

Siu, Helen F., and Zelda Stern, eds. *Mao's Harvest: Voices from China's New Generation*. New York: Oxford University Press, 1983.

Snow, Edgar. *The Long Revolution*. New York: Vintage Books, 1973.

———. *Red Star over China*. New York: Grove Press, 1968. Rev. and enlarged edition.

Socialist Transformation of the National Economy in China. Beijing: Foreign Languages Press, 1960.

Solinger, Dorothy. *Chinese Business under Socialism: The Politics of Domestic Commerce, 1949–1980*. Berkeley: University of California Press, 1984.

Spengler, Tilman. *Der Sturz von Lin Piao: Paradigm fuer milittaerisch-zivile Konflicte in der Volksrepublic China?* Hamburg: Institut fuer Asienkunde, Mitteilung no. 76, 1976.

Stacey, Judith. *Patriarchy and Socialist Revolution in China*. Berkeley: University of California Press, 1983.

Starr, John Bryan. *Continuing the Revolution: The Political Thought of Mao*. Princeton: Princeton University Press, 1979.

Teiwes, Frederick C. *Leadership, Legitimacy, and Conflict in China: From a Charismatic Mao to the Politics of Succession*. Armonk, N.Y.: M. E. Sharpe, 1984.

———. *Politics and Purges in China: Rectification and the Decline of Party Norms, 1950–1965*. White Plains, N.Y.: M. E. Sharpe, 1979.

Turner, Victor. *Dramas, Fields and Metaphors: Symbolic Action in Human Society*. Ithaca, N.Y.: Cornell University Press, 1974.

———. *The Forest of Symbols: Aspects of Ndembu Ritual*. Ithaca, N.Y.: Cornell University Press, 1967.

Union Research Institute. *Communist China, 1949–1959*. Hong Kong: Union Research Press, 1960.

Urban, George, ed. *The "Miracles" of Chairman Mao*. Los Angeles: Nash, 1971.

Walker, Kenneth R. *Food Grain Procurement and Consumption in China*. Cambridge: Cambridge University Press, 1984.

Weber, Max. *Economy and Society: An Outline of Interpretive Sociology*. Ed. Guenther Roth and Claus Wittich. Vol. 2. Berkeley: University of California Press, 1978.

———. *On Charisma and Institution Building*. Ed. S. N. Eisenstadt. Chicago: University of Chicago Press, 1968.

Whyte, Martin King. *Small Groups and Political Rituals in China*. Berkeley: University of California Press, 1974.

Whyte, Martin King, and William L. Parish. *Urban Life in Contemporary China*. Chicago: University of Chicago Press, 1984.

Willner, Ann Ruth. *The Spellbinders: Charismatic Political Leadership*. New Haven: Yale University Press, 1984.

Wu, Tien-wei. *Lin Biao and the Gang of Four: Counter-Confucianism in Historical and Intellectual Perspective*. Carbondale: Southern Illinois University Press, 1983.

Wylie, Ray. *The Emergence of Maoism: Mao Tse-tung, Ch'en Po-ta, and the Search for Chinese Theory, 1935–1945*. Stanford: Stanford University Press, 1980.

Xue Muqiao 薛暮桥 et al. *Zhongguo Guominjingji de Shehuizhuyi Gaizao* 中国国民经济的社会主义改造 [The socialist transformation of China's national economy]. Beijing: People's Press, 1959.

Yan Jingwen 严静文. *Zhou Enlai Pingzhuan* 周恩来评传 [Critical biography of Zhou Enlai]. Hong Kong: Bowen Shudian, 1974.

Yang Jiang. *A Cadre School Life: Six Chapters.* Trans. Geremie Barme. Hong Kong: Joint Publishing Co., 1982.

Yao Mingle. *The Conspiracy and Death of Lin Biao.* New York: Knopf, 1983.

Ye Jianying. *Speech at the Meeting in Celebration of the 30th Anniversary of the Founding of the People's Republic of China.* Beijing: Foreign Languages Press, 1979.

Yue Daiyun and Carolyn Wakeman. *To the Storm: The Odyssey of a Revolutionary Chinese Woman.* Berkeley: University of California Press, 1985.

ARTICLES

Ahn, Byung-joon. "Adjustments in the Great Leap Forward and Their Ideological Legacy, 1959–1962." In Chalmers Johnson, ed., *Ideology and Politics in Contemporary China*, pp. 257–301. Seattle: University of Washington Press, 1973.

Bannister, Judith. "Population Policy and Trends in China, 1978–83." *China Quarterly*, no. 100 (December 1984): 717–42.

Bartke, Wolfgang. "Die politische Profilierung von Chiang Ching." *China Aktuell* (Hamburg, Institut für Asienkunde), February 1975, pp. 44–46.

Bastid, Marianne, and Jean-Luc Domenach. "De la Revolution culturelle à la critique de Confucius: L'évolution de la politique interieure chinoise, 1969–1974," pp. 126–72. In Claude Aubert et al., eds., *Regards froids sur la Chine.* Paris: Seuil, 1976.

Bensman, Joseph, and Michael Givant. "Charisma and Modernity: The Use and Abuse of a Concept." *Social Research* 42, no. 4 (Winter 1975): 570–615.

Bernstein, Thomas P. "Communication and Value Change in the Chinese Program of Sending Urban Youths to the Countryside." In Godwin Chu and Francis L. K. Hsu, eds., *Moving a Mountain: Cultural Change in China*, pp. 341–63. Honolulu: University Press of Hawaii, 1979.

———. "Leadership and Mass Mobilization in the Soviet and Chinese Collectivization Campaigns of 1929–30 and 1935–56: A Comparison." *China Quarterly*, July–September 1967.

———. "Stalinism, Famine, and Chinese Peasants: Grain Procurements during the Great Leap Forward." *Theory and Society* 13, no. 3 (May 1984), pp. 339–77.

Bord, Richard J. "Toward a Social-Psychological Theory of Charismatic Social Influence Processes." *Social Forces* 53, no. 3 (March 1975): 485–97.

Bradsher, Henry S. "China: The Radical Offensive." *Asian Survey* 13, no. 11 (November 1973): 989–1001.

Brugger, Bill. "Rural Policy." In Bill Brugger, ed., *China since the "Gang of Four*," pp. 135–73. London: Croom Helm, 1980.

Chen Chi 陈驰. "'Hongqi' zazhi qiguai de chenmo" 《红旗》杂志奇怪的沉默

[The strange silence of *Red Flag*]. *Zhengming*, no. 13 (November 1978): 16–17.

Chen Fenghua 陈风华. "Wei Antonioni fan'an" 为安东尼奥尼翻案 [Reverse the verdict on Antonioni]. *Zhengming*, no. 11 (September (1978): 14–16.

Chen Zhihui 陈芝荠. "Mao Zedong de jiating beiju" 毛泽东的家庭悲剧 [Mao Zedong's family tragedy]. *Zhengming*, no 18 (April 1979): 44–47.

Cheng Huang. "China: Purloined Letter." *Far Eastern Economic Review* 78, no. 49 (December 2, 1972): 10–11.

"China." In *Far Eastern Economic Review Yearbook 1974*, pp. 117–39. Hong Kong.

Clarke, C[hristopher]. "China's Third Generation." *China Business Review*, March–April 1984, pp. 36–38.

———. "The Shakeup Moves Down." *China Business Review*, September–October 1983.

Copper, John F. "The Rise and Fall of Teng Hsiao-p'ing." *Asian Affairs* 4, no. 3 (January/February 1977): 184–96.

Dai Dan 待旦. " 'Da pipan' he 'yi da san fan' " 「大批判」和「一打三反」["Great criticism" and "one hit, three anti"]. *Zhanwang*, no. 209 (October 16, 1970): 8.

Deng Xiaoping. "Concluding Speech." In *The Eleventh National Congress of the Communist Party of China* (Documents), pp. 192–93. Beijing: Foreign Languages Press, 1977.

———. "Speech to the National Conference on Science and Technology." *Peking Review* 21, no. 12 (March 24, 1978): 11.

———. "The 'Two Whatever' Policy Does Not Accord with Marxism" (May 24, 1977). *Beijing Review*, no. 33 (August 15, 1983): 14–15.

Deng Ziben 邓自本. "Guangzhou qing shaonian wenti" 广州青少年问题 [Problems of youth in Guangzhou]. *Guang Jiao Jing*, no. 98 (November 16, 1980): 8–12.

Ding Wang 丁望. "Beijing 'da shen pan' de falü genju boruo" 北京"大审判"的法律根据薄弱 [The legal basis of the Beijing 'Great Trial' is weak]. *Dangdai*, no. 3 (November 15, 1980): 28–30.

Dittmer, Lowell. "Bases of Power in Chinese Politics: A Theory and an Analysis of the Fall of the 'Gang of Four.' " *World Politics* 31, no. 1 (October 1978): 26–61.

———. "Chinese Communist Revisionism in Comparative Perspective." *Studies in Comparative Communism* 13, no. 1 (Spring 1980): 3–41.

———. "Death and Transfiguration: Liu Shaoqi's Rehabilitation and Contemporary Chinese Politics." *Journal of Asian Studies* 40, no. 3 (May 1981): 455–80.

———. "The Formal Structure of Central Chinese Political Institutions." In Sidney Greenblatt et al., eds., *Organizational Behavior in Chinese Society*, pp. 47–76. New York: Praeger, 1981.

Editorial Board. "Shenqie huainian Deng Zihui tongzhi" 深切怀念邓子恢同志 [Deeply cherish comrade Deng Zihui's memory]. *Nongcun Gongzuo Tongxun* 农村工作通迅 [Report on rural work], no. 5 (May 5, 1981): 7–9.

Emerson, John Philip. "Employment in Mainland China." In Robert

300 ★ SELECTED BIBLIOGRAPHY

Dernberger, ed., *An Economic Profile of Mainland China: Studies Prepared for the Joint Economic Committee of Congress*, vol. 2 (February 1967): 458–59.

Falkenheim, Victor C. "The Cultural Revolution in Kwangsi, Yunnan and Fukien." *Asian Survey* 9 (August 1969): 580–97.

Fallaci, Oriana. "Deng: Cleaning Up Mao's 'Feudal Mistakes.'" *Washington Post*, part 1, August 31, 1980, pp. D1 ff; part 2, September 1, 1980, pp. A1 ff.

Fenichel, Otto. "The Counterphobic Attitude." In Otto Fenichel, *Collected Papers*, pp. 163–74. London: Routledge & Kegan Paul, 1955.

Fletcher, M. D. "Industrial Relations in China: The New Line." *Pacific Affairs* 52, no. 1 (Spring 1979): 78–95.

Gittings, John "Inside China." *Ramparts* 10, no. 2 (August 1971): 10–20.

Gong Qigong 龚其工. "Ye Wenfu shou pi" 叶文福受批 [Ye Wenfu is criticized]. *Zhengming*, no. 51 (January 1982): 30–32.

Goodman, David S. G. "The 6th Plenum of the 11th CC of the CCP: Look Back in Anger?" *China Quarterly*, no. 87 (September 1981): 518–28.

Goodstadt, Leo. "China: Calendar of the Conspiracy." *Far Eastern Economic Review* 74, no. 48 (November 27, 1971): 20–25.

———. "Purifying Profit." *Far Eastern Economic Review* 73, no. 38 (September 18, 1971): 7–8.

Government Administrative Council of the Central People's Government. "Guanyu shixing liangshi de jihua shougou he jihua gongying de mingling" 关于实行粮食的计划售购和计划供应的命令 [Decree on planned procurement and planned supply of food grain]. In *Nongye Shehuizhuyi Gaizao Wenji* 农业社会主义改造文集 [Essays on the socialist transformation of agriculture], vol. 1: 190–93. Beijing: Finance & Economy Pub., 1955.

Gupta, Krishna Prakash. "Mao after Mao: A Marxist Debate in China." In V. P. Dutt, ed., *China: The Post-Mao View*, pp. 162–81. New Delhi: Allied Pub., 1981.

Harding, Harry. "Maoist Theories of Policy-Making and Organization." In Thomas W. Robinson, ed., *The Cultural Revolution in China*, pp. 113–65. Berkeley: University of California Press, 1971.

He Wenxing 何文星. "Beijing, kexi, keyou" 北京 · 可喜 · 可忧 [Happiness and worry about Beijing]. *Zhenming*, no. 49 (November 1981): 13–15.

Hinton, William. "Hundred Day War." *Monthly Review* 24 (July–August 1972).

Hofheinz, Roy, Jr. "The Ecology of Chinese Communist Success: Rural Influence Patterns, 1923–1945." In A. Doak Barnett, ed., *Chinese Communist Politics in Action*, pp. 3–78. Seattle: University of Washington Press, 1969.

Houn, Franklin. "The Eighth Central Committee of the Chinese Communist Party." *American Political Science Review*, June 1957, pp. 392–404.

———. "Rejection of Blind Obedience as a Traditional Chinese and Maoist Concept." *Asian Thought and Society* 7, no. 19 (1982): 18–31; and 7, no. 21: 264–79.

Hua Guofeng. "Continue the Revolution under the Dictatorship of the Proletariat to the End." *Peking Review*, no. 19 (May 6, 1977): 15–27.

———. "Political Report to the Eleventh National Congress of the Communist Party of China" (August 26, 1977). *Peking Review*, September 2, 1977, pp. 16–23.

———. "Report on the Work of the Government." *Beijing Review*, no. 38 (September 22, 1980): 21.

———. "Unite and Strive to Build a Modern Powerful Socialist Country: Report to the Fifth National People's Congress" (February 26, 1978). *Peking Review*, no. 10 (March 10, 1978): 39.

Hua Yang 华羊. "Wenge moqi Zhonggong de xiezuo banzi" 文革末期中共的写作班子 [The Chinese Communist writing groups at the end period of the Cultural Revolution]. *Zhonggong Yanjiu*, January 1981, pp. 138–50.

Huai Bing 怀冰. "Ping 'Zai shehui de dang'an li'" 评《在社会的档案里》 [Criticism of "In the files of society"]. *Zhengming*, no. 28 (February 1980): 78–79.

Huo Huisheng 霍辉生. "Chen Boda kuatai yu Mao pai mingyun" 陈伯达垮台与毛派命运 [Chen Boda's fall and the fate of the Mao faction]. *Zhanwang*, no. 233 (October 16, 1971): 15–19.

Jian Yan 简焰. "Tiananmen shijian de an fandingle!" 天安门事件的案翻定了! [Reversal of the case of the Tiananmen Incident]. *Dongxiang*, no. 1 (October 1978): 30–33.

Jiang Xinli 姜新立. "Cong Huang Kecheng zhuanwen kan Zhonggong pi-Mao yundong" 从黄克诚专文看中共批毛运动 [Looking at the criticize Mao movement from the perspective of Huang Kecheng's speech]. *Feiqing Yuebao* 23, no. 11 (May 1982).

Jiang Youbei 江游北. "Xiang tequan tiaozhan de Zhonggong wenyi" 向特权挑战的中共文艺 [Chinese Communist literature that challenges special privileges]. *Zhengming*, no. 26 (December 1979): 27–29.

Jin Fang 金方. "Zhonggong huaju mianshang de fengfeng leilei" 中共话剧面上的风风雷雷 [Storm in Chinese drama]. *Zhengming*, no. 28 (February 1980): 32–33, 66.

Jowitt, Kenneth. "Soviet Neotraditionalism: The Political Corruption of a Leninist Regime." *Soviet Studies* 35, no. 3 (July 1983): 275–97.

Kau, Ying-mao. "The Urban Bureaucratic Elite in Communist China: A Case Study of Wuhan, 1949–65." In A. Doak Barnett, ed., *Chinese Communist Politics in Action*, pp. 216–71. Seattle: University of Washington Press, 1969.

Kojima Reiitsu. "Accumulation, Technology, and China's Economic Development." In Mark Selden and Victor Lippit, eds., *The Transition to Socialism in China*, pp. 238–66. Armonk, N.Y.: M. E. Sharpe, 1982.

Kraus, Richard. "Class Conflict and the Vocabulary of Social Analysis in China." *China Quarterly*, no. 69 (March 1977): 54–74.

LaBarre, Weston. "Some Observations on Character Structure in the Orient. II. The Chinese, Part 1." *Psychiatry* 9, no. 3 (August 1946): 215–39.

Lee, Hong Yung. "The Political Behavior of the Radical Students and Their Social Characteristics in the Cultural Revolution." *China Quarterly* 63 (September 1975).

Lee Ngok. "Lin Piao's Military Tactics as Seen in the 115th Division." University of Hong Kong: Centre of Asian Studies Working Paper, April 22, 1970.

Li Mingfa 李明法. "Zhonggong gaoceng dui panjue Jiang Qing de zhengyi" 中共高层对判决江青的争议 [The dispute among high-ranking Chinese Communist officials concerning the sentence of Jiang Qing]. *Zhengming*, no. 40 (February 1981): 22–24.

Li Yizhe 李一哲. "Guanyu shehuizhuyi de minzhu yu fazhi" 关于社会主义的民主与法制 [Concerning socialist democracy and law]. *Ming Bao Yuekan*, November 27, 1975, pp. 11–20.

Liao, Gailong. "Historical Experiences and Our Road of Development: A Report on the History of the CCP." (Report delivered October 25, 1980, at the National Party School, transcribed from taped record without the speaker's verification.) Translated in *Issues and Studies*, part 1, October 1981, pp. 68–71; part 2, November 1981, pp. 81–110.

Lieberthal, Kenneth. "Strategies of Conflict in China during 1975–1976." *Contemporary China* 1, no. 2 (November 1976): 7–14.

Lin Biao. "Informal Address at Politburo Meeting" (May 18, 1966). Trans. in Martin Ebon, ed., *Lin Biao: The Life and Writings of China's New Ruler*, pp. 253–67. New York: Stein & Day, 1970.

Lin Nan 林楠. "Zhongguo de zhengzhi daigou" 中国的政治代沟 [The political generation gap in China]. *Zhengming*, no. 32 (June 1980): 36–39.

Liu Qing. "Prison Memoirs." Ed. by Stanley Rosen and James D. Seymour. *Chinese Sociology and Anthropology* 15, nos. 1–2 (Fall–Winter 1982/3).

Liu Shaoqi 刘少奇. "Lun gongchandangyuan de xiuyang" 论共产党员的修养 (On the self-cultivation of Chinese Communist Party members). (Yan'an, July 8, 1939.) Translated as "How to Be a Good Communist," in *Collected Works of Liu Shao-ch'i*, vol. 1: 151–219. Hong Kong: Union Research Institute, 1969.

———. "Report on Problems Concerning Agrarian Reform." Presented to the Second Session of the National Committee of the CPPCC. In *People's China*, July 16, 1950, pp. 28–29.

———. "Zai Huabei zhigong daibiao huiyi shang guanyu gonghui gongzuo wenti de baogao" 在华北职工代表会议上关于工会工作问题的报告 [A report delivered before the North China Workers' Representative Conference on Problems Concerning Labor Union Work] (May 1949). In *Liu Shaoqi Wenti Ziliao Zhuanji* 刘少奇问题资料专辑 [A special collection of materials on Liu Shaoqi], pp. 200–220. Taipei: Chinese Communist Research Center, 1970.

Liu Ying 柳莹. "Tingqian muhou de Jiang Qing" 庭前幕后的江青 [Jiang Qing at court and behind the scenes]. *Zhengming*, no. 40 (February 1981): pp. 18–21.

Loewenthal, Richard. "Development vs. Utopia in Communist Policy." In Chalmers Johnson, ed., *Change in Communist Systems*, pp. 33–117. Stanford: Stanford University Press, 1970.

———. "The Post-Revolutionary Phase in China and Russia." *Studies in Comparative Communism* 16, no. 3 (Autumn 1983): 191–203.

Lu Shi 鲁实. "'Mao xuan' wu juan yingdang chong shen chong bian" 《毛选》五卷应当重审重编 [The fifth volume of 'Mao's Selected Works' should be reexamined and reedited]. *Zhengming*, no. 24 (October 1979): 16–17.

Luo Bing 罗冰. "Beijing da shenxun zhongzhong" 北京大审讯种种 [About Beijing's great trial]. *Zhengming*, no. 37 (November 1980): 8–10.

———. "Da shenxun taiqian muhou" 大审讯台前幕后 [On the stage and behind the scenes of the great trial]. *Zhengming*, no. 38 (December 1980): 7–11.

———. "Deng Xiaoping fadong 'da pipan' neiqing" 邓小平发动「大批判」内情

[The inside story of the mass criticism launched by Deng Xiaoping]. *Zhengming*, no. 48 (October 1981): 7–17.

———. "Hua Guofeng cizhi muhou" 华国锋辞职幕后 [Behind the scenes of Hua Guofeng's resignation]. *Zhengming*, no. 39 (January 1980): 7–10.

———. "Renda de muhou xinwen" 人大的幕后新闻 [The inside story of the People's Congress]. *Zhengming*, no. 51 (January 1982): 8–13.

———. "Shei yao qudai Hua Guofeng diwei" 谁要取代华国锋地位 [Who will replace Hua Guofeng?]. *Zhengming*, no. 39 (January 1981): 12–13.

———. "Wu zhong quan hui he qiangren zhengzhi" 五中全会和强人政治 [The Fifth Plenum and strongman politics]. *Zhengming*, no. 29 (March 1980): 5–9.

MacDougall, Colina. "Another Backyard Boom." *Far Eastern Economic Review* 67, no. 12 (March 19, 1970): 27–28.

———. "Walking the Rustic Tightrope." *Far Eastern Economic Review* 67, no. 10 (March 5, 1970): 46–49.

Machetzki, Ruediger. "The People's Republic of China: The Condition of Its Economy and the Limits of Reform." *Vierteljahresberichte* (Bonn: Forschungs-institut der Friedrich-Ebert-Stiftung) 92 (June 1983): 123–35.

Maloney, Joan M. "Problems in China's Party Rebuilding." *Current Scene* 15, no. 3 (March 1977).

Mao Zedong [Mao Tse-tung] 毛泽东. "Beat Back the Attacks of the Bourgeois Rightists" (July 9, 1957). In *Selected Works of Mao Tse-tung*, vol. 5: 459. Beijing: Foreign Languages Press, 1977.

———. "Dui Chen Zhengren tongzhi dundian baogao de pishi" 对陈政人同志蹲点报告的批示 [Comments on comrade Chen Zhengren's report on his stay on a spot] (January 29, 1965). In *Mao Zedong Sixiang Wan Sui* 毛泽东思想万岁 [Long live Mao Zedong Thought], vol. 3: 31. Hong Kong: n.p., 1967.

———. "Get Rid of the Baggage and Start the Machinery" (April 12, 1944). In *Selected Readings from the Works of Mao Tse-tung*, p. 306. Beijing: Foreign Languages Press, 1971.

———. "Liu Shao-ch'i and Yang Shang-k'un Criticized for Breach of Discipline in Issuing Documents in the Name of the Central Committee without Authorization" (May 19, 1953). In *Selected Works of Mao Tse-tung*, vol. 5: 92. Beijing: Foreign Languages Press, 1977.

———. "On the Cooperative Transformation of Agriculture" (July 31, 1955). In *Selected Works of Mao Tse-tung*, vol. 5: 184. Beijing: Foreign Languages Press, 1977.

———. "On the Correct Handling of Contradictions among the People." In *Selected Works of Mao Tse-tung*, vol. 5: 409. Beijing: Foreign Languages Press, 1977.

———. "On Policy" (December 25, 1940). In *Selected Works of Mao Tse-tung*, vol. 2: 442–43. Beijing: Foreign Languages Press, 1964.

———. "Rectify the Party's Style of Work" (February 1, 1942). In *Selected Works of Mao Tse-tung*, vol. 3: 50. Beijing: Foreign Languages Press, 1965.

———. "Report on an Investigation of the Peasant Movement in Hunan" (March 1927). In *Selected Works of Mao Tse-tung*, vol. 1: 23–28. Beijing: Foreign Languages Press, 1964.

———. "Speech at the CCP's National Conference on Propaganda Work"

(March 19, 1957). In *Selected Readings from the Works of Mao Tse-tung*, pp. 493–94. Beijing: Foreign Languages Press, 1971.

———. "Speech at the Tenth Plenary Session of the Eighth Central Committee." Translated in *Chinese Law and Government* 1, no. 4 (Winter 1968–69): 91.

———. "A Study of Physical Education" (April 1917). In Stuart Schram, *The Political Thought of Mao Tse-tung*, pp. 94–102. New York: Praeger, 1963.

———. "Talk at an Enlarged Central Work Conference" (January 30, 1962). Trans. in Stuart Schram, ed., *Chairman Mao Talks to the People*, p. 168. New York: Macmillan, 1975.

———. "Talk to Leaders of the Center" (July 21, 1966). Trans. in Stuart Schram, ed., *Chairman Mao Talks to the People*, pp. 253–56.

———. "Talks at the Chengdu Conference" (March 10, 1958). Trans. in Stuart Schram, ed., *Chairman Mao Talks to the People*, pp. 99–100.

———. "Talks at a Conference of Secretaries of Provincial, Municipal, and Autonomous Region Party Committees" (January 1957). In *Selected Works*, vol. 5: 369–74. Beijing: Foreign Languages Press, 1977.

———. "Talks at the Yenan Forum on Literature and Art" (May 2, 1942). In *Selected Works of Mao Tse-tung*, vol. 3: 73. Beijing: Foreign Languages Press, 1965.

———. "Toward a New Golden Age" (July 1919). In Stuart Schram, *The Political Thought of Mao Tse-tung*, pp. 105–6. New York: Praeger, 1963.

———. "Where Do Correct Ideas Come From?" In *Selected Readings from the Works of Mao Tse-tung*, pp. 502–4. Beijing: Foreign Languages Press, 1971.

———. "Zai zui gao guowuhuiyi shang de jieshu hua" 在最高国务会议上的结束话 [Concluding remarks at a supreme state conference] (March 1, 1957). In *Mao Zedong Sixiang Wan Sui*, pp. 90–100. Hong Kong: n.p., 1969.

"Mao Tse-tung: Speeches at the Zhengzhou Conference" (February and March 1959). *Chinese Law and Government* 9 (Winter 1976–77): 18.

Martin, Helmut. "Sprachpolitik." In Brunhild Staiger, ed., *China*. Tübingen: Horst Erdmann, 1980.

Marx, Karl. "Manifesto of the Communist Party." In Robert C. Tucker, ed., *The Marx-Engels Reader*, pp. 475–77. New York: W. W. Norton, 1978 edition.

Mohanty, Manoranjan. "Party, State and Modernization in Post-Mao China." In V. P. Dutt, ed., *China: The Post-Mao View*, pp. 45–67. New Delhi: Allied Pub., 1981.

Nethercut, Richard. "Lin Piao and the Cultural Revolution." University of Hong Kong, Centre of Asian Studies Working Paper, May 1970.

Oksenberg, Michel. "Local Leaders in Rural China, 1962–65: Individual Attributes, Bureaucratic Positions, and Political Recruitment." In A. Doak Barnett, ed., *Chinese Communist Politics in Action*, pp. 155–216. Seattle: University of Washington Press, 1969.

———. "Methods of Communicating within the Chinese Bureaucracy." *China Quarterly*, no. 57 (January–March 1974): 1–39.

Opletal, Helmut. "Four Observations on Chinese Mass Media." *The Asian Messenger* 2, no. 3/3, no. 1 (Autumn/Winter 1977): 38–40.

Orleans, Leo. "Communist China's Education: Politics, Problems, and Prospects." In Robert Dernberger, ed., *An Economic Profile of Mainland China: Studies Prepared for the Joint Economic Committee of Congress*, vol. 2 (February 1967): 515.

Parish, William L. "Socialism and the Peasant Family." *Journal of Asian Studies* 34: 3 (May 1975): 613–31.

Piepe, Anthony. "Charisma and the Sacred: A Reevaluation." *Pacific Sociological Review* 14, no. 2 (April 1971): 147–63.

Powell, Ralph L. "The Party, the Government and the Gun." *Asian Survey* 10, no. 6 (June 1970): 441–72.

Qi Xing 齐辛. "'Shirenbang' da shen de you guan wenti" 十人帮大审的有关问题 [Issues concerning the trial of the 'Gang of 10'"]. *Qishi Niandai*, December 1980, pp. 8–14.

Qiang Yuangan 强远淦 and Lin Bangguang 林邦光. "Wo guo nongye jitihua de zhuoyue zuzhizhe Deng Zihui" 我国农业集体化的卓越组织者邓子恢 [Our country's outstanding organizer of agricultural collectivization, Deng Zihui]. *Xinhua Wenzhai* 新华文摘 [New China digest], no. 7 (1981): 187–90.

Ren Gu 任古. "San wen zhengxie weiyuan" 三问政协委员 [Three questions to a member of the CPPCC]. *Zhengming*, no. 6 (April 1978): 17–20.

Robinson, Thomas W. "The Sino-Soviet Border Dispute: Background, Development, and the March 1969 Clashes." *American Political Science Review* 66, no. 4 (December 1972): 1175–1202.

Schram, Stuart. "Classes, Old and New, in Mao Zedong's Thought, 1949–1976." In James L. Watson, ed., *Class and Social Stratification in Post-Revolutionary China*, pp. 29–56. Cambridge: Cambridge University Press, 1984.

———. "Mao Tse-tung and the Theory of Permanent Revolution." *China Quarterly*, no. 46 (April–June 1971): 221–45.

Selden, Mark, and Victor Lippit. "The Transition to Socialism in China." In Mark Selden and Victor Lippit, eds., *The Transition to Socialism in China*. Armonk, N.Y.: M. E. Sharpe, 1982.

Sharp, Ilsa. "The Saplings." *Far Eastern Economic Review* 69, no. 28 (July 2, 1970): 17.

Skinner, G. William, and Edwin O. Winckler. "Compliance Succession in Rural Communist China: A Cyclical Theory." In Amitai Etzioni, ed., *A Sociological Reader on Complex Organizations*, pp. 410–38. New York: Holt, Rinehart & Winston, 1969. Second edition.

Solomon, Richard. "Mao's Effort to Reintegrate the Chinese Polity: Problems of Authority and Conflict in the Chinese Social Process." In A. Doak Barnett, ed., *Chinese Communist Politics in Action*, pp. 271–365. Seattle: University of Washington Press, 1969.

———. "One Party and 'One Hundred Schools': Leadership, Lethargy, or Luan?" *Current Scene* 7, nos. 19–20 (October 1, 1969): 25–26.

Spencer, Martin E. "What Is Charisma?" *British Journal of Sociology* 24, no. 3 (September 1973): 341–55.

Starr, John Bryan. "Conceptual Foundations of Mao Tse-tung's Theory of Continuous Revolution." *Asian Survey* 11, no. 6 (June 1971): 610–28.

Suleski, Ronald. "Changing the Guard in Shanghai." *Asian Survey* 17, no. 9 (September 1977): 886–98.

Sullivan, Lawrence R. "The Role of the Control Organs in the Chinese Communist Party, 1977–83." *Asian Survey* 24, no. 6 (June 1984): 597–618.

Sun Shangqing 孙尚清 et al. "Zai lun shehuizhuyi jingji de jihua yu shichang-xing xiangjiehe de jige lilun wenti" 在论社会主义经济的计划与市场性相结合的几个理论问题 [Further discussion of some theoretical issues concerning the combination of planning and market mechanisms in socialist economy]. In *Shehuizhuyi Jingji zhong Jihua yu Shichang de Guanxi* 社会主义经济中计划与市场的关系 [Relations between planning and market mechanisms in socialist economies], vol. 1: 98–99. Beijing: Chinese Social Science Press, 1980.

Terrill, Ross. "The 800,000,000, Part II: China and the World." *The Atlantic* 229 (January 1972): 39–63.

Tong, T. K. "Red Guard Newspapers." *Columbia Forum* 12, no. 1 (Spring 1969): 38–41.

Tsou, Tang, and Morton H. Halperin. "Mao Tse-tung's Revolutionary Strategy and Peking's International Behavior." *American Political Science Review* 59, no. 1 (March 1965): 80–99.

Turner, Victor. "Symbols in Ndembu Ritual." In Dorothy Emmet, ed., *Sociological Theory and Philosophical Analysis.* New York: Macmillan, 1970.

Unger, Jonathan. "The Class System in Rural China: A Case Study." In James L. Watson, ed., *Class and Social Stratification in Post-Revolutionary China,* pp. 121–42. Cambridge: Cambridge University Press, 1984.

Van Ness, Peter. "Black, White and Grey in China Research." *Far Eastern Economic Review* 123, no. 6 (February 9, 1984): 30–31.

Vogel, Ezra F. "From Revolutionary to Semi-Bureaucrat: The 'Regularization' of Cadres." *China Quarterly,* no. 29 (January–March 1967): 36–60.

Walder, Andrew G. "Some Ironies of the Maoist Legacy in Industry." *The Australian Journal of Chinese Affairs,* no. 5 (1981): 21–39.

Walker, Kenneth. "Collectivization in Retrospect: The 'Socialist High Tide' of Autumn 1955–Spring 1956." *China Quarterly,* no. 26 (April–June 1966): 1–43.

Wang En 王恩. "Dazibao shengji shuoming le shemma?" 大字报升级说明了什么? [What does the promotion of big-character posters indicate?]. *Zhan-wang,* no. 299 (July 16, 1974): 9–11.

———. "Yijiuqisi nian zhonggong zhengju yanbian tedian" 一九七四年中共政局演变特点 [Characteristics of Chinese Communist political developments in 1974]. *Zhanwang,* no. 311 (January 16, 1975): 9–11.

Watson, Andrew J. "A Revolution to Touch Men's Souls: The Family, Interpersonal Relations and Daily Life." In Stuart Schram, ed., *Authority, Participation and Cultural Change in China,* pp. 291–331. Cambridge: Cambridge University Press, 1973.

Weakland, John. "Chinese Film Images of Invasion and Resistance." *China Quarterly,* no. 47 (July–September 1971): 438–71.

Weggel, Oskar. "Ideologie im nachmaoistischen China: Versuch einer Systematisierung." *China Aktuell,* January 1983, pp. 19–40.

Wei Ming 巍明. "Zhongguo xin yi dai de zhengzhijia" 中国新一代的政治家 [China's new generation of politicians]. *Qishi Niandai*, no. 2 (February 1981): 15–20.

White, Gordon. "The Post-revolutionary Chinese State." In Victor Nee and David Mozingo, eds., *State and Society in Contemporary China*, pp. 30–31. Ithaca, N.Y.: Cornell University Press, 1983.

———. "Urban Employment and Labor Allocation Policies." In G. White et al., eds., *Revolutionary Socialist Development in the Third World*, pp. 257–87. Sussex, England: Harvester Press, 1983.

Whitehead, R. L. "Liturgical Developments in China's Revolutionary Religion." *China Notes* (East Asian Department, National Council of Churches, New York) 7, no. 3 (Summer 1969).

Whyte, Martin King. "Bureaucracy and Modernization in China: The Maoist Critique." *American Sociological Review*, no. 38 (1973): 149–63.

Winckler, E. O. "Policy Oscillation in the People's Republic of China: A Reply." *China Quarterly*, no. 68 (December 1976): 734–51.

Womack, Brantly. "Chinese Political Economy: Reversing the Polarity." *Pacific Affairs* 54, no. 1 (Spring 1981): 57–82.

———. "Modernization and Democratic Reform in China." *Journal of Asian Studies* 43, no. 3 (May 1984): 417–41.

———. "The 1980 County-level Elections in China: Experiment in Democratic Modernization." *Asian Survey* 22, no. 3 (March 1982): 261–77.

Wong, Christine. "Material Allocation and Decentralization: Impact of the Local Sector on Industrial Reform." In Elizabeth J. Perry and Christine Wong, eds., *The Political Economy of Reform in Post-Mao China*. Cambridge: Harvard University Press, 1985.

Wu Shengzhi 武绳之. "Zhonggong dui Mao Zedong sixiang pingjia de xin fazhan" 中国对毛泽东思想评价的新发展 [New developments in the evaluation of Mao Zedong thought]. *Dongxiang*, no. 1 (October 1978).

Xiao Ying 小鹰. "Bei hang jian wen suo ji" 北行见闻琐记 [Miscellaneous information from my trip north]. *Zhengming*, no. 28 (February 1980): 29–30.

Xu Dixin 许涤新. "Lun wo guo guominjingji de biange yu fazhan" 论我国国民经济的变革与发展 [An essay on the transformation and development of our national economy]. In Editors of *Jingji Yanjiu* 经济研究 [Economic research], eds., *Shehuizhuyi Zhengzhi Jingjixue Ruogan Jiben Lilun Wenti* 社会主义政治经济学若干基本理论问题 [Some basic theoretical issues of socialist political economy]. Shandong: People's Press, 1980.

Yan Jingwen 严静文. "Beijing quanli douzheng jinru xin gaochao" 北京权力斗争进入新高潮 [Beijing's power struggle advances to a new high tide]. *Zhanwang*, no. 283 (November 16, 1973): 6–9.

Yan Ling. "The Necessity, Possibility and Realization of Socialist Transformation of China's Agriculture." *Social Sciences in China* (Beijing) 3, no. 1 (March 1982): 94–123.

Yan Yue 颜悦. "Tou xiang jiquan de zhadan—Ye Wenfu de shizuo yanjiang ji aipi jingguo" 投向极权的炸弹—叶文福的诗作,演讲及挨批经过 [A bomb dropped on the privileged class—Ye Wenfu's poems, speeches, and how he is being criticized]. *Zhengming*, no. 52 (February 1982): 20–24.

Ying Zi 莹子. "Fan 'Ziyouhua' fengshi ruole" 反「自由化」风式弱了 [The "anti-bourgeois liberalization" wind abates]. *Zhengming*, no. 49 (November 1981): 11–12.

Young, Graham, and Dennis Woodward. "From Contradictions among the People to Class Struggle: The Theories of Uninterrupted Revolution and Continuous Revolution." *Asian Survey* 18: 9 (September 1978): 912–34.

Zhou Enlai. "Report to the Tenth National Congress of the CPC" (August 24, 1973). In *The Tenth National Congress of the CPC*, p. 8. Beijing: Foreign Languages Press, 1973.

Zong Lei 宗雷. "Hunan xuesheng zheng minzhu fan guanliao de xingdong" 湖南学生争民主反官僚的行动 [Hunan student movement for democracy against bureaucratism]. *Qishi Niandai*, December 12, 1980, pp. 19–20.

UNPUBLISHED SOURCES

Bachman, David. "To Leap Forward: Chinese Policy-Making, 1956–1958." Ph.D. dissertation, Stanford University, 1983.

Bernstein, Thomas. "Reforming China's Agriculture." Unpublished paper presented to the conference "To Reform the Chinese Political Order." Harwichport, Mass., June 18–23, 1984.

Cheng Yang. "Socialism and the Quest for Modernization: The Political Economy of China's Development Strategy." Ph.D. dissertation, University of California, Berkeley, 1985.

Dittmer, L. "Charismatic Leadership and the Crisis of Succession: Changing Conceptions of Legitimacy in the PRC." Unpublished paper presented at the Association for Asian Studies, Los Angeles, Calif., February 1979.

———. "The Chinese Marriage Law of 1950: A Study of Elite Control and Social Change." M. A. thesis, University of Chicago, 1967.

Fenwick, Ann. "The Gang of Four and the Politics of Opposition: China, 1971–1976." Ph.D. dissertation, Stanford University, 1983.

Henderson, Gail. "Danwei: The Chinese Work Unit." Ph.D. dissertation, University of Michigan, 1982.

Lee, Hong Yung. "Changing Patterns of Political Participation in China: A Historical Perspective." Unpublished paper presented at Workshop on Studies in Policy Implementation in the Post-Mao Era, Columbus, Ohio, June 20–24, 1983.

———. "The Political Mobilization of the Red Guards and Revolutionary Rebels in the Cultural Revolution." Ph.D. dissertation, University of Chicago, 1973.

Meany, Constance Squires. "Political Conflict in China: 'Reversal of Verdicts' and the Campaign to Suppress the 'Gang of Four's Bourgeois Factional Setup,' 1977–1978." Berkeley, Center for Chinese Studies, 1980.

Munro, Robin. "The Chinese Democracy Movement, 1978–1982." Unpublished paper, 1983.

Naughton, Barry. "The Decline of Central Control over Investment in Post-Mao China." Unpublished paper, December 20, 1983.

Tong, James. "The Radical Elite and Anti-Americanism and Xenophobia in the

PRC, 1974–1976." Unpublished paper, Political Science Department, University of Michigan, 1978.

Tsou, Tang. "The Middle Course in Changing the State-Society Relationship and Reforming the Political Structure." Unpublished paper, Political Science Department, University of Chicago, 1982.

———. "Reflections on the Formation and Foundation of the Communist Party-State in China." Unpublished paper, University of Chicago, 1983.

Wagemann, Mildred L. E. "The Changing Image of Mao Tse-tung: Leadership Image and Social Structure." Ph.D. dissertation, Cornell University, 1974.

Zweig, David. "A View from Beida." Seminar paper, University of Michigan, 1978.

———. "Agrarian Radicalism in China, 1968–1978: The Search for a Social Base." Ph.D. dissertation, University of Michigan, 1983.

Index

Designer: Barbara Llewellyn
Compositor: Asco Trade Typesetting Ltd.
Text: 10/12 Plantin Medium
Display: Plantin Medium
Printer: Thomson-Shore, Inc.
Binder: John H. Dekker & Sons